LORDSHIP AND LIBERATION IN PALESTINE-ISRAEL

LORDSHIP AND LIBERATION IN PALESTINE-ISRAEL

THE PROMISE OF DECOLONIAL SOVEREIGNTIES

MUHANNAD AYYASH

Columbia University Press   *New York*

Columbia University Press
Publishers Since 1893
New York   Chichester, West Sussex
cup.columbia.edu

Copyright © 2025 Columbia University Press
All rights reserved

Library of Congress Cataloging-in-Publication Data

Names: Ayyash, Mark Muhannad author
Title: Lordship and liberation in Palestine-Israel : the promise of decolonial sovereignties / Muhannad Ayyash.
Description: New York : Columbia University Press, 2025. | Includes bibliographical references and index.
Identifiers: LCCN 2025008620 (print) | LCCN 2025008621 (ebook) | ISBN 9780231220804 hardback | ISBN 9780231220811 trade paperback | ISBN 9780231563390 ebook
Subjects: LCSH: Israeli-Palestinian conflict—1993– | Palestine question (1948–) | Settler colonialism—Palestine | Land tenure—Political aspects—Palestine
Classification: LCC DS119.76 .A964 2025 (print) | LCC DS119.76 (ebook) | DDC 956.9405—dc23/eng/20250505
LC record available at https://lccn.loc.gov/2025008620
LC ebook record available at https://lccn.loc.gov/2025008621

Printed and bound by CPI Group (UK) Ltd, Croydon, CR0 4YY

Cover design: Noah Arlow
Cover image: Haitham Imad/Shutterstock

GPSR Authorized Representative: Easy Access System Europe, Mustamäe tee 50, 10621 Tallinn, Estonia, gpsr.requests@easproject.com

In loving memory of my grandmother,
الحاجة نفيسه عبد الله عثمان ناصر
ام عياش

Palestine was the horizon of her world. A horizon so vast, beyond which one cannot fathom another world, especially when, if like her, one made the effort to know everyone's life stories on this land.

CONTENTS

Acknowledgments ix

Prelude 1

Introduction 3

1 Settler Colonial Sovereignty 39

2 Lordship as Violence in the Settler Colony 73

3 The Indigenous-Settler Distinction and the Interlocking of Enemy-Siblings 115

4 The Four-Dimensional Operation of Violence: Fragmentation, Isolation, Dehumanization, and Lordship 149

5 A Literary Critique: Toward Decolonial Sovereignties 191

6 Decolonial Sovereignties 219

Conclusion 263

Postscript 269

Notes 273
Bibliography 323
Index 343

ACKNOWLEDGMENTS

This book was largely written during the first two years of the COVID-19 pandemic. Prior to the pandemic, I spent part of my sabbatical at the Department of Politics, The New School for Social Research, during the fall term of 2019, and at the Department of Arabic Language and Cultures, University of Sydney, during the spring of 2020. Conversations with faculty and students at the New School as well as Columbia University in New York, and at the University of Sydney in Australia greatly enhanced my thinking about the topic of this book. I am particularly grateful for my conversations and exchanges with Hamid Dabashi, Mahmood Mamdani, Lana Tatour, Gil Anidjar, Heike Schotten, Leila Farsakh, Benoit Challand, Lucia Sorbera, and Dirk Moses. This sabbatical as well as the indexing of this book was supported by the Internal Research Grants Fund and a Faculty of Arts grant at Mount Royal University.

The pandemic presented many challenges, but also opportunities. With the normalization of virtual meetings, I was able to connect with scholars more easily. I am particularly grateful for my conversations with Khaled Furani, Rana Barakat, Juman Abujbara, Radhika Mongia, members of the *Palestinian-Canadian Academics and Artists Network*, particularly Nahla Abdo, Yasmeen Abu-Laban, Rehab Nazzal, and Ardi Imseis, as well as members of *Al-Shabaka, The*

Palestinian Policy Network, particularly Yara Hawari, Tareq Baconi, Tariq Da'na, Fathi Nimer, and Haidar Eid.

It was my honor to virtually present a paper on settler colonial sovereignty at the *Institute for Palestine Studies Annual Conference* in partnership with *Muwatin* at Birzeit University in the fall of 2020. I learned so much from all the speakers at this conference, especially on Palestinian resistance. Thanks also to Pheroze Unwalla for inviting me to give a keynote lecture on decolonial sovereignties at UBC's *Middle East and Islamic Consortium of British Columbia Annual Conference* in the winter of 2023. In addition, I presented parts of this book at the *Annual Palestine Forum*, which was hosted by the Arab Center for Research and Policy Studies & the Institute for Palestine Studies in Doha in 2023 and 2024. I learned a lot from the conversations at these conferences. I was fortunate enough to present other parts of the book at the *Humanities in Session Series*, hosted by the Centre for Humanities Research in partnership with the Consortium for Humanities Centers and Institutes' Humanities Administration Network at the University of Western Cape in 2024. My two-and-a-half month visiting position at the Centre for Humanities Research during the beginning of 2024 generated so many fruitful ideas for me, and I am so grateful to Heidi Grunebaum, Premesh Lalu, Valmont Layne, Lee Walters, and others for their incredible hospitality and deep intellectual engagements.

I also want to thank the two anonymous reviewers for their close reading of the manuscript, and their rich and insightful questions, suggestions, and comments. It was my great pleasure also to work with Columbia University Press, particularly Wendy K. Lochner, for her outstanding professionalism and dedication to seeing this book published. A special thanks also to Alyssa M. Napier and Kathryn Jorge for their diligent and efficient work in producing the book, Lis Pearson for her excellent copyediting, and Paula Durbin-Westby for producing such a wonderful index.

And that brings me to my greatest teacher, one that always guides me in my work: the first intifada. I was eight years old when it began in 1987. The intifada was difficult and beautiful, painful and inspiring, agonizing and hopeful, and it was also for me an early awakening into politics and resistance. When you experience the gathering of massive numbers of people, mobilizing everything that they have no matter how little, directing all their energies toward the one shared goal of collective liberation—this sight and memory lives forever. It becomes a moral, intellectual, and emotional compass against which one judges politics, justice, peace, and liberation.

This book attempts to live up to the lofty standards of those ideals of liberation that the Palestinian collective chased in those years and continues to chase today.

To my friends, comrades, and companions in the struggle for decolonial liberation, in Palestine, on Turtle Island, and beyond: you are too numerous to list, but this book was inspired by you and written for you.

To my parents, Said and Samia, my brothers, Mahmoud and Mutaz, to my partner in life, Sarah, I hope that putting up with my laser focus on Palestinian liberation is worth it, and that this book, which is not mine but ours, will make you proud. Your love and support mean everything to me and keep me going.

LORDSHIP AND LIBERATION IN PALESTINE-ISRAEL

PRELUDE

They say the stench of death forever changes one's sense of smell. It reconfigures the nostrils.

Once it enters the nose, the nostrils can only distinguish between the smell of death and a smell that is not of death.

"The nostrils offer a pathway to touching the untouchable," I learned from a *fellah* [peasant] in Jericho when I was a young child.

He tilled the soil. He was intimate with the soil. He learned some of its many secrets. Why it was at times stubbornly opposed to fertility and why it was at most times amiable to rewarding his toil. But he never claimed to know the depth of the soil and the marvelous life which spawns from its depth.

He carried the stench of the soil on his body. It was his armor.

Wars come and go, he taught me, and all that remains is the stench of the soil. Not the stench of soil that is drenched with human blood. But the soil that is drenched with human sweat.

> At the height of the first intifada,
> fear and settler colonial violence saturated the atmosphere,
> with the stench of death.
> The sounds of the curfew ordered,
> the end of sound.

Everyone relieved themselves,
of their daily toil,
and turned their homes into prisons.

But this one *fellah* remained on his soil. "We've been circulating stories about their weapons faster than the stench of death can saturate our atmosphere," he said. "I heard every which way their bullets will brutally kill us. Let them come. It will be a battle for the ages. The stench of their weapons against the stench of the soil. I have no doubt about the outcome of *this* battle. This is *my* kind of battle, on *my* grounds, in accordance with *my* rules, the battle of the stenches. My ancestors withstood the Zionist invasion by remaining close to their soil. Being one with the soil. The stench of the Zionist military machines will run away upon the first whiff of the outer dimensions of my breeze alone. Believe me, I cannot lose!"

I recall from my home as prison,
His life on the soil, of the soil, with the soil, fighting
against the stench of death,
which on that day, never even dared come forth,
to the battle of the stenches

INTRODUCTION

> *These lands are not worth the disasters we have brought on ourselves . . . but in the end a man owns only the earth in which he lies; five cubits of ground are all we inherit, linen covers us, and we lie in the grave.*
>
> —Abolqasem Ferdowsi, *Shahnameh*

This book was written and completed a month before the ongoing Israeli genocidal operation in the Gaza Strip that began in October 2023. Apart from adding this brief note to the introduction and a brief "postscript," I did not make any changes to the materials in the book.

According to the United Nations Office for the Coordination of Humanitarian Affairs, as of this writing on October 9, 2024, at least 41,689 Palestinians have been killed and 96,625 injured, at least 1.9 million of the 2.3 million Palestinians living in the Strip have been displaced at least once, many five times or more, and virtually across the entire Strip, hospitals, clinics, schools, universities, residential neighborhoods, marketplaces, agricultural fields, and critical infrastructure, have been destroyed beyond recognition. In the West Bank, at least 695 Palestinians have been killed since October 7, more than 7,000 imprisoned with at least fifty-six Palestinians dying inside Israeli prisons as a result of neglect or torture, 1,200 Palestinians from twenty-five rural communities across the West Bank have been expelled and their lands colonized by Israeli settlers, hundreds of Palestinian-owned structures, from homes to businesses, have been demolished.

The sheer magnitude of death, destruction, pain, and suffering is beyond the ability of words to capture. It will take many years to take into account the horrors that Palestinians, especially in Gaza, are currently experiencing. It will take many more before healing can even begin. Can you even heal from something like this? Is there such a thing as "forgiveness" in a context this saturated with suffering and pain? All these questions will be asked and debated for a long time. But the saddest and also most terrifying part of reality in this moment is that this genocidal operation was entirely predictable, which is why I did not need to change the materials in the book, and the end of the genocide is nowhere in sight. The genocide of the Palestinian people did not start in 2023, nor will it end in 2024 or anytime in the near future, unless impactful action and policies which place economic and political pressure on the Israeli state are adopted by institutions and states the world over. The root causes of all of this violence and destruction, which also includes approximately 1,200 Israelis killed and 5,432 injured, can only be illuminated and explained by examining the Israeli settler colonial project, and settler colonial sovereignty specifically.

As this book argues before these events took place, serious scholarly analysis cannot explain such horrors by following Israeli state discourse which seeks to paint itself as always acting in self-defense. The armed operation that took place on October 7, 2023, was a pretext for, not the cause of this genocidal operation. Only by moving the discussion to root causes are scholars, activists, policymakers, public intellectuals, media and cultural figures and institutions, and civil society able to properly understand violence and take appropriate actions to, if not eliminate it completely, then at the very least limit violence. As a community of people who are seeking justice, freedom, liberation, and real peace, we have to take on this task and not just explain the root causes of violence but offer an alternative pathway.

The path that we are currently on can only produce genocide and war. If we fail to remove our collective selves from this path, we will continue to suffer its deadly and brutal consequences, which the Palestinian people are currently bearing, all on their own, deserted and left to die by an uncaring and brutal world. Before these events took place, this book made clear that we can only expect more settler colonial genocidal violence should we remain on the path of settler colonial sovereignty and colonial modernity more broadly. Nothing is more urgent than outlining an alternative path forward. Although a book cannot turn an alternative path into reality, it can clearly outline and illuminate it. This is what this book does.

The relationship between land and people as well as the related relationship among and in between people is at the core of this book's inquiry into settler colonialism, decolonization, violence, and sovereignty, and more broadly the question of the social-political relationship. Generally speaking, I understand the "social" as the sphere in which the collectivity of individuals is formed, sustained, and continuously reinvigorated, and the "political" as the sphere which specializes in fulfilling certain necessary functions in order for a collectivity to nourish and grow (i.e., mobilization and distribution of resources, community safety, health and well-being, etc.). But more than their general definitions, this book is more interested in the *relationship* between the two spheres, particularly the manner of the opposition between the social and the political as either decisive (in the sense of forceful and separative) or complementary (in the sense of balancing and harmonizing). Specifically, there are two types of this social-political relationship that will be the focus of my study: a settler colonial decisive type that is marked by "lordship" where people are lords of the land and lordship is exercised over people; and a decolonial complementary type that is marked by "land as life" where people and land exist in a reciprocal relationship of inhabiting one another, and people come to inhabit one self as co-constitutive of another.

Lordship is about private ownership, possession of the land, the molding of heterogeneity into homogeneity, and most of all, the violence of settler colonial expulsion. Land as life is about communal ownership, belonging to the land, a disposition of heterogeneity, and crucially the critique of the violence of expulsion. These two general types have been in opposition across different contexts, historically and into the present, and they are at the core of the Palestinian-Israeli struggle where Israeli settler colonialism operates on what I will call a "posture of lordship," and Palestinian decolonial resistance operates on the philosophy and practice of land as life.

This is not to say that all Palestinian resistance falls within this decolonial category. There are some Palestinian forms of resistance that replicate, even if not intentionally, settler colonial logics and systems. It is also the case that Israelis can and do belong to anti-Zionist decolonial resistance. But it is misleading to conclude from these caveats that we cannot generalize an Israeli position and a Palestinian position as settler colonial and decolonial, respectively. The overwhelming trend, as will become clear in this book, is that Israeli settler colonial violences have become so dominant in this struggle that it will be difficult to see at the end of this book how transformation is even at all possible. Israel, as a settler colony, has deeply cemented this colonial path—a path of colonial modernity—to such an extent that it has become difficult to see the future as becoming something other than an Israeli settler colonial project in perpetuity.

This book holds that trends and patterns, no matter how entrenched and dominant, can and do transform. In fact, transformation is not only possible, but also always already occurring. The violence of settler colonial expulsion is itself transforming Israelis into a direction that yields more settler colonial violence, and not the promised establishment and securing of a sovereign Jewish self. As I argued in my first book, *A Hermeneutics of Violence*, although violence can achieve instrumental ends and does in some respects make possible a sovereign Jewish self, it also necessarily makes it impossible to achieve that sovereign self as violence forges enemies into enemy-siblings, interlocking them as enemy-siblings.[1] The term "enemy-siblings" can conjure varied meanings for different readers (biblical, heteronormative, selfsameness, harmony, etc.), but this book adopts it to specifically mean that Israelis cannot become sovereign Israeli Jews through violence but are rather constituted through their violence as a subjectivity that necessitates the use of violence in a never-ending effort to expel the Palestinian, thus becoming interlocked with the Palestinian who can never be fully or definitively eliminated and expelled. Much like it is difficult, on the whole and generally speaking, to unlock oneself from a sibling even if one tries, I use the term "enemy-siblings" to ascribe that same kind of difficulty to the effort to unlock the "self" from an enemy "other," even when there is a concerted attempt to separate. Indeed, as I will argue in this book, the more violence is used to separate the "sovereign Jewish self" from what it posits as the "evil object," that is the Palestinian "other," the deeper the interlocking becomes.

It is on the basis of this always already ongoing transformation which interlocks enemy-siblings, that activists, scholars, artists, political leaders, and communities can work to change the direction of the transformation and move against the violence of settler colonial expulsion. There are no guarantees on this path, but the alternative, as this book will show, is simply more of the same and the continuation and propagation of settler colonial violence. Although the decolonial path offers no guarantees, we can find guidance as we travel on it from the rich tapestry of Palestinian decolonial resistance.

This resistance is not our guide because it is *Palestinian* per se but because it manifests from the positionality of those who suffer the violence of settler colonial expulsion. The positionality of decoloniality and indeed indigeneity is thus shaped, not by nationality, religion, culture, ethnicity, or race, but rather by virtue of its oppression by systems and logics of settler colonial domination.[2] This means that only resistance that directly critiques the violence of settler colonial expulsion can serve as our guide in this decolonial endeavor. There are numerous forms of Palestinian resistance that fit this criterion, and I will focus on one specific form—the popular committees of the first intifada—to delineate this decolonial path that promises to transform the settler colonial project and usher an alternative epoch in social and political modes of organization. This decolonial path is not to be traveled only by Palestinians. It is of course necessary that Israelis join this path, because only when the enemy-siblings work together in a true decolonial effort that the interlocking of enemy-siblings, a ground that we cannot wish away but can only work from, can be transformed and moved into a different direction.

If I may borrow from Ferdowsi in the epigraph and reformulate for our contemporary context, these lands are not worth the disasters brought forth by colonial modernity, which is the development and constitution of modern social and political life (the nation-state, private property, individualism, capitalist division of labor, etc.) in and through the European colonial project from the fifteenth century onward. But these lands are worth the decolonial struggle that promises an alternative world—for a different relationship between the people and the land and among people to take hold and become our dominant guide, philosophy, and practice. That is this book's message in its simplest form.

Of course, we cannot arrive at this simple insight with confidence and direction unless we travel through the complexity of social and political systems and logics that mark settler colonialism and decolonization. In taking this journey, *Lordship and Liberation in Palestine-Israel* tackles the interconnected questions of sovereignty, violence, and the social-political relationship through the prism of settler colonialism vs. decolonization. In probing these topics, this book engages in a critical hermeneutic (re)interpretation of academic texts from philosophy, sociology, and political science, as well as materials from the Palestinian-Israeli struggle, both through secondary analysis of academic texts on the struggle as well as primary textual analysis of certain features of it (for example, the construction of the colonial/apartheid Wall, the siege of Gaza, the popular committees, etc.).

As I did in my first book, I adopt here a dialogical approach to the study of violence, which continuously chases after the subject matter of violence in its elusiveness without a desire to reach the final word on violence since no one can definitively or absolutely define, describe, or represent violence in its totality.[3] In *A Hermeneutics of Violence*, I called this elusiveness the "(un)knowability of violence" and offered a philosophical analysis of it, largely through a (re)interpretive reading of the Derrida-Gadamer encounter and the concept of critical hermeneutics. I do not want to repeat or summarize that dense discussion here. What I will point out is that my earlier philosophical analysis of this (un)knowability indeed reveals the (un)knowability of violence in a much more concrete way that is more relevant to this study: that the pileup of violence constituted in and by settler colonial violence, which we can know and document in numbers of people killed and maimed, in destruction of vital infrastructure, in the razing of villages, towns, and cities, etc., is simultaneously unknowable because it is unbearable and impossible to understand the full scope and meaning of death and destruction. Methodologically speaking, it is critical that we document violence at the same time that we remain committed to the idea that violence can never be captured in its full totality or essence. Not only is this approach, in its refusal to rest on fixed and essentialized grounds, necessary for the study of violence, but it is also important in the effort to counter a settler colonial sovereignty that rests on a dictatorial sovereign voice that claims to be the first to know and announce the origin of things.

ORIGINS, FIRSTS, AND THE DICTATORIAL SOVEREIGN VOICE

One could say that the question of "origins" and "firsts" is obsessively pursued in academe. This obsession is perhaps most salient in modern Eurocentric discourses against postcolonial and decolonial theorizations of colonial encounters. One of the most prevalent features is the Eurocentric claim that European paradigms do not center the "West" within a complex of colonial knowledge/power as postcolonial theory charges; rather, they are simply stating the "fact" that Europe was the "origin" of this or that invention, the "first" to accomplish this or that feat or build this or that institution, and so on. Gurminder K. Bhambra illustrates in her work that this Eurocentric critique of postcolonial theory is very much active and alive in both modernist and postmodernist scholarship and will likely remain so for some time to come.[4]

Less prevalent but still operative, we find that some postcolonial or decolonial studies are, under a different register, concerned with the question of which decolonial or postcolonial theorist presented the "first" conceptual analytic for understanding coloniality/colonialism and advanced decoloniality/decolonization. Catherine E. Walsh is critical of this tendency, and as she puts it, scholars who are interested in understanding the workings of coloniality and the advancement of decoloniality should not be concerned with debates over the "ownership of terms or words," or engaged in competitions "about who named and/or referred to first the ongoing colonial regime, matrix, or system of economic, racial, gender, and patriarchal power, or who best represents . . . decolonial theory and practice."[5] It is of course necessary to properly reference the sources from which certain ideas were learned, especially when it comes to referencing the oppressed, colonized, and marginalized, whose knowledge has long been appropriated and concealed by the colonial matrix of knowledge/power. But the point remains that encasement of ideas within the framework of "origins" and "firsts" is a different matter altogether because such encasement gives the statement and the author a colonial type of sovereign authority.

Therefore, I have no interest in joining this fray over "origins" between different versions of addressing colonialism/coloniality. While there are disciplinary, geographical, and temporal differences between the "Latin American" coloniality/decoloniality school (Aníbal Quijano, María Lugones, Walter D. Mignolo, and others) and the "Eastern" postcolonial school (Edward Said, Gayatri Spivak, and others), both schools are connected, among other things, in "their radical potential in unsettling and reconstituting standard processes of knowledge production."[6] They share an emphasis on the complex of knowledge/power and how the colonial world is situated and operates, not only in the material socioeconomic and political structures and institutions of our world, but in how we conceive being, doing, and thinking.[7] In short, they elucidate how colonial power is not restricted to the stage of direct colonialism but traverses across time and space in various forms. Moreover, in both, a decolonial alternative does not constitute an immanent critique of colonialism but a break with colonialism and the radical transformation of colonial modernity.

The fact that ideas germinate and emerge from different parts of the post/neo/settler colonized world is all the better. That scholars are learning and producing similar theoretical ideas from their own set of teachers and contexts is all the more reason to believe that those ideas have hit their mark in describing and analyzing colonialism/coloniality and present us with a potentiality toward decolonization/decoloniality. This must always be foregrounded as opposed to entering a debate about who said what "first," who was "first" to establish a before/after type of conceptual contribution, and so on. In this book, then, I draw insights from across the divides between decolonial theorizations of the "Old" and the "New" worlds. This does not mean that I wish to eliminate the differences between Indigenous theory, "Eastern" postcolonial theory, and "Latin American" decoloniality, but in this book, I move freely across them to draw from their different yet complementary lessons and teachings about settler colonialism and decolonization.

I stress this emphasis on the "first" in this introduction because it has much to do with settler colonial sovereignty. The connection between sovereignty and academic claims of being the "first" and "original" voice is lucidly observed in Jacques Derrida's critique of Giorgio Agamben's work. Derrida points out numerous places in *Homo Sacer* where Agamben makes the claim of not just being "the first" to claim something (namely, that the distinction between *bios* and *zoē* is the founding event of modern politics), but of making the first claim that various thinkers (e.g., Michel Foucault) were the first to claim X and Y.[8] This is not simply a matter of ego or the state of academic writing in its obsessive chase after "originality." Rather, as Derrida points out, this has everything to do with sovereignty:

> He who posits himself as sovereign or intends to take power as sovereign always says or implies: even if I am not the first to do or say so, I am the first or only one to know and recognize who *will have been* the first. And I would add: the sovereign, if there is such a thing, is the one who manages to get people to believe, at least for a while,

that he is the first to know who came first, when there is every chance that it is almost always false, even if, in certain cases, no one ever suspects so.⁹

The obsession with "firsts" and "origins," then, is part of the problematic of sovereignty, and I would add that what Derrida is speaking to is specifically a colonial type of sovereignty—i.e., a type of sovereignty that would not have emerged in the form it did without Euro-American colonialism.

The claim of being the "first" carries with it the attribute of a settler colonial sovereign claim—a claim that inaugurates and constitutes the sovereignty of the sovereign over and above all other claims, thus concealing, eliminating, and replacing multiple Indigenous claims of sovereignty. This is a claim, and I will develop this idea in chapter 1, that attempts to secure, through a dictatorial voice, the sovereign self as a totalized, absolute, and indivisible sovereign over and above an edifice of hybridity, heterogeneity, and difference. What is at stake in this debate over "origins" and "firsts" is not just critiquing the facticity of such claims (although that remains an important task), but also the possibility of a critique of settler colonial sovereignty that does not itself rest on the structure of a colonial sovereign claim that gives itself the ground of foundational knowledge—a claim that gives the enunciator the right to dictate because they are the first to discover and announce (and therefore are closest or most intimate with) the origin and the pure, thus erasing all other voices, histories, experiences, and claims of belonging, knowing, and doing. The dictatorial voice, in short, is a sovereign claim that posits itself as the first and absolute voice on what came first and is therefore pure, uncorrupted, natural, and pre-political—it becomes the only voice that can properly inaugurate social and political orders. Whether it is itself the first or it is that which best knows the first, this is a colonial sovereign claim that summons the authority of a singularity, and no critique of settler colonial sovereignty will be possible from such a ground.[10]

So, what does this mean for the theoretical and methodological approach of this book? Specifically, how do I approach Europe and so-called European ideas and theoretical paradigms that encase themselves in the language of "firsts" and "origins" in a work that professes to follow a decolonial path that refuses the authority of a singularity? I follow Hamid Dabashi's and Mahmood Mamdani's analysis of this question. For Dabashi, the mythology of a universalized Europe, along with the colonial and postcolonial destruction this has reaped across the world, has run its course as an episteme: "The condition of coloniality that had given intellectual birth to us—from Césaire through Fanon to Said—has run its course. That episteme is no longer producing any meaningful knowledge."[11] In the new emerging world, European philosophers and thinkers are not dismissed by virtue of their "Europeanness"—for Dabashi, this is a shallow and superficial kind of critique that more or less repeats some of the logics of imperial Europe. Rather, when they are dismissed, ignored, or brushed aside, it is because they refuse to step away from that imagined mantle of the "objective" arbiter of reality; that is, of being the sovereign dictatorial voice on what counts as reality, justice, freedom, humanity, etc. It is only when European thinkers are willing to acknowledge the knowledge/power complex from which they speak, and work *together with* philosophers, intellectuals, poets, and academics from across the world who are heard in accordance with their own voice (i.e., not assimilated within a European worldview), that new potentialities open up, and together we can begin in earnest the critical and timely work of dismantling the settler colonial, neocolonial, and postcolonial world that we all inhabit.[12]

Admittedly, I'm not certain if every European thinker this book draws on would willingly and wholeheartedly join such a project of dismantling. This is most notably the case with Derrida given his deeply flawed position on the question of Palestine.[13] Therefore, I adopt an approach where I put the ideas of such thinkers to work for a decolonial project. I read their ideas back to their positions, against the grain of their readings of Palestine-Israel and settler colonialism, in order to transgress those positions for the sake of dismantling settler colonial sovereignty (much like how Judith Butler approaches the ideas of Emanuel Levinas who was, even more than Derrida, eliminatory of the Palestinian cause as liberatory and decolonial).[14]

To dismantle settler colonial sovereignty, we of course have to first understand it, and this begs the question: What is the role of European theoretical paradigms in explaining the oppressive colonial and settler colonial systems themselves? Here I find Mamdani's work useful as a guide. For Mamdani, postcolonial theory must drop "abstract universalism" (e.g., modernization theory) and "intimate particularism" (e.g., ethnographic studies lifted out of their context) that, in different ways, only "see in the specificity of experience nothing but its idiosyncrasy," and instead "establish the historical legitimacy" of the colonized "as a unit of analysis."[15] Mamdani's masterful study of colonial and postcolonial Africa reveals how universalist modernization studies are shallow and erroneous when they apply Western constructed concepts to the social and political life of the colonized under the assumption that not even the slightest modification of concepts and formulas is necessary (e.g., assuming that the "peasantry" means and signifies the same thing in South Africa or Nigeria as it does in England or France). At the same time, Mamdani's study traces the social, political, economic, and cultural transformations that were/are being experienced in the lands of the (post)colonized as European colonialism forcibly constituted and instituted systems and mechanisms of power/knowledge in the (post)colony. This reveals how dynamics of a similar order (e.g., the emergence and development of an urban-rural distinction) can be observed as they unfold in entirely different ways across Europe and Africa.

The main problem, as Mamdani sees it, is that we are often unable to conceptualize and examine cultural and political transformations as multidirectional and riddled with tensions. For instance, scholars often use terms such as the "Romanization" or "Arabization" of different cultures when explaining transformations brought forth by empire. But by naming just a single party, centralizing and prioritizing it, the majority of scholarship tends to paint cultural and political transformations as a pure imposition of one supposedly whole, fixed, bounded system upon another.[16] Instead, we need to pay attention to how these cases involve a complex movement back and forth between systems of theorizing, knowing, doing, and living while still, of course, being attentive to the asymmetrical power differential at play between an overpowering empire and an overpowered, invaded society. The emphasis on interchange is important since it sheds a different light on the cultures in contact, and "because the final product partakes of both, no matter how unequally, and does not quite resemble either, the process is also identity-transforming for both sides."[17] This is especially critical for this book since I already argued in *A Hermeneutics of Violence* that these processes of identity transformation are not only linked with whether or not the empire was open and inclusive (as was the Roman Empire for example according to Mamdani and other historians), but it is identity transforming because of the use of violence. Thus, to Romanization and Arabization, which for Mamdani differed from British and other European empires on the basis that they were more open and inclusive of colonized and ruled cultures (as opposed to modern European empires that seek to transform the subjectivity of the colonized masses), I would also add Europeanization and Americanization (or, Euro-Americanization). This is because the mechanism that transforms the identity of the "self" is what I called in my previous book four-dimensional violence, and not whether or not the "self" was open, predisposed to transformation, and so on.

Four-dimensional violence interlocks enemies as enemy-siblings, transforming the identities of the sides in the process. Thus, against the conventional Euro-American theoretical paradigms that keep intact a masterful, independent, and unalloyed Euro-American self, a Western civilization self, etc., this book works and advances in the space of the interlocking of selves that occurs in and through violence. Because it focuses on interlocking, it will neither dismiss nor centralize Euro-American ideas and theories but rather dismiss Euro-American paradigms that necessarily centralize Euro-American experiences, systems, ideas, and institutions (e.g., centralizing the Westphalian nation-state). Instead, this book examines certain ideas about sovereignty and violence from Euro-American thinkers and places these ideas in a more properly interlocking framework—or as Edward Said might put it, a contrapuntal framework—that refuses the dictatorial sovereign voice of purity, origins, and firsts. This will be especially the case for the idea of "lordship," which brings me to the question of violence and origins.

ORIGINS OF VIOLENCE VS. FOUR-DIMENSIONAL OPERATION OF VIOLENCE

This book combines theorizations of settler colonial sovereignty with the four-dimensional conception of violence. The four dimensions which are always interlinked and operate simultaneously are: instrumental, linguistic, mimetic, and transcendental.[18] I will not reconstruct the philosophical elaboration of these concepts in this book. Instead, I will only present, briefly and in as clear and narrow terms as possible, how the concepts I philosophically developed in my first book are being used in this book. Readers who are interested in further theoretical elaborations can find those in *A Hermeneutics of*

Violence, and for readers who are more interested in the application of these concepts, the brief descriptions in this book should suffice and stand alone. So, very briefly to start, the instrumental dimension concerns violence as an instrument that serves political, economic, social, and/or cultural ends. But violence always exceeds its instrumental purposes, and it moves into the second dimension, which concerns the ways in which violence shapes subjectivities long after the "end" of a violent "event." These transformations in subjectivity are often hidden from the protagonists, and this is where we find the third dimension, which concerns the interlocking of enemies as enemy-siblings who come to form the possibility and impossibility of one another. The main reason that these transformations are hidden is because the fourth dimension, which cannot be directly observed, concerns the (un)knowability of violence, where postures of incommensurability are forged producing incommensurable positions that ensure the continuation of violence. In this book, I specify the elements that belong to each dimension in Palestine-Israel (although this is not an exhaustive list of all the elements that *could* belong to the different dimensions).

Critically, I make the case that lordship (as a particular kind of relationship between people and land and among people) constitutes a posture of incommensurability that is operative in the fourth transcendental dimension of violence. I call this a "posture of lordship" because the posture, although it cannot be directly observed, continuously animates, shapes, and constitutes a specific configuration of the world that follows the logics and features of lordship. This posture of lordship is of colonial modernity and theoretically has thus been forged in and through violence for centuries. Although as a fourth dimension of violence it is not directly observable, this posture has manifested in varied forms, types, structures, and architectures of violence that have long been connected in anticolonial historiographies: since at least the Crusades to the Spanish

Inquisition to the settler colonization of the "New World" to the rise of European empires to the creation of colonial and postcolonial modern nation-states and most pertinently for my purposes to the settler colonization of historic Palestine.

I previously theorized that postures of incommensurability in the fourth dimension continuously produce incommensurable positions on the surface from deep *shared* dispositions. Because the posture of lordship is long in the making as I am proposing here, it is shared, not necessarily between Israelis and Palestinians, but across the various colonial and settler colonial projects of colonial modernity which continuously produce incommensurable positions between a colonizer and a colonized (a distinction which Frantz Fanon named as the core of colonial modernity).[19] In the case of Palestine-Israel, this posture of lordship manifests in the violent structure of settler colonial expulsion. Marked by a purist and absolutist racialized binary between settler (colonizer) and Indigenous (colonized), this structure of expulsion contains three interconnected features of violence: the fragmentation, isolation, and dehumanization of the colonized Palestinian.[20] These three features can be observed, respectively, in the instrumental, linguistic, and mimetic dimensions of Israeli settler colonial violence. These observable dimensions can help us understand how they (re)produce and are themselves (re)produced by the posture of lordship in the fourth dimension. It is important to clarify here that in the enactment of settler colonial violence, all four dimensions operate simultaneously. In addition, I do not mean to suggest that the feature of isolation is only linguistic, or fragmentation is only instrumental, and so on. For conceptual clarity, I focus on each feature as it illuminates each of the dimensions, but it is important to keep in mind that the three features along with the posture of lordship are interconnected, operate simultaneously, and therefore elements of isolation are visible in the instrumental dimension, elements of dehumanization are visible in the linguistic dimension, elements of lordship operate in all of the dimensions, and so on.

One of the significant insights generated in the analysis is the formation of enemy-siblings at the foundation of the settler colonial state. Far from securing the desired goal of a sovereign self, settler colonial violence interlocks the enemies as enemy-siblings. This constitutes what I previously called the possibility-impossibility of enemy-siblings.[21] The interlocking makes possible and enables the violence of expulsion in the sense of rendering as "real" or "potentially real" the sovereign self. Let me make clear here that when I place "real" or "reality" in scare quotes, it is because I want to underscore that the violence of expulsion always necessarily obfuscates the reality of violence with what it constitutes as "real": i.e., the violence of expulsion will appear for those who use and justify it as a righteous violence that has successfully secured the freedom, liberation, and sovereignty of Israeli Jews, and this conceals its reality as settler colonial expulsion. At the same time, the interlocking makes clear the impossibility of such a sovereign self by virtue of the transformation of the self, where violence, and specifically the posture of lordship, comes to produce a *subjectivity of lordship* that necessitates the continued expulsion of the Indigenous. I understand subjectivity here as "the felt interior experience of the person that includes his or her positions in a field of relational power."[22] Instead of focusing on how victims and survivors (re)make their subjectivity and direct it toward healing, my analysis is instead focused on how violence shapes the subjectivity of perpetrators of settler colonial violences.[23] The subjectivity of lordship is about the felt interior experience of being a lord, which is not always explicitly articulated as such by the subject in the field of settler colonial power relations. I argue in this book that the settler, far from securing the self as sovereign, unalloyed, and independent of the Indigenous, becomes none other than a self always on the road of expelling the Indigenous.

The violence of expulsion produces not a specific sovereign identity (along national, ethnic, cultural, or racial lines), but rather lords who must continuously and in perpetuity use violence to secure their positionality as lords.

I want to underscore here that this book's emphasis on the posture of lordship is not done so as to assign a point of "origin" in Europe, but rather to point the analysis toward an interpretive path that is transfixed on the effort to elucidate the four-dimensional operation of settler colonial violence. I approach the fusion of land and people as lordship in terms of how it took hold and developed in Palestine-Israel *as settler colonial violence*. This is not done for the sake of clarifying the European feudal version of lordship, nor for outlining its genealogy as a sociolegal doctrine; but for the sake of outlining a critical posture of incommensurability in the fourth dimension of Israeli settler colonial violence. I do not make the claim that my analysis of the posture of lordship in the case of Palestine-Israel is universally valid, or that a European version of the posture of lordship is universally valid because it appears outside of Europe in Palestine. Rather, like other European versions of constructs, ideas, dynamics, institutions, logics, it is "transmitted through the structural violence of colonialism into the rest of the non-European . . . worlds—and because it comes from a position of power and hegemony, it becomes universally valid."[24] In Dabashi, this universal validity is not based in "natural" or "objective" criteria of scientific validity, but rather becomes valid because it is forcefully imposed and asserted as valid. And moreover, in this case, I am studying the very mechanism of transmission: that is, the violence of settler colonial expulsion.

This book hence argues that instead of searching for an "original" violence within Europe and then tracing its application and development, scholars ought to focus on delineating precisely how a posture of lordship manifests in specific contexts within specific historical periods in order to understand and radically move beyond it. Put differently, the posture of lordship, as one dimension of settler colonial violence, cannot be described in its universal essence as such and/or in accordance with a specific point of origin. But scholars can piece together the operation of this posture in its specific manifestations, and these specific and particular understandings are all that is needed to properly deconstruct this posture of lordship and delineate a path that moves beyond it. Perhaps it is impossible to completely destroy such a long-standing posture, but I hold that it is possible to weaken, marginalize, and eventually replace it. What we can say by the end of this book's analysis is that the posture of lordship is a critical component of understanding what differentiates decolonial sovereignties from settler colonial sovereignty, and without an elucidation and critique of the posture of lordship, decolonial alternatives run the risk of reproducing as opposed to transforming settler colonial sovereignty.

The last statement should make it clear that this book unapologetically stands on the side of decolonial liberation and affirms decolonial sovereignties against settler colonial sovereignty. In other words, the analysis of sovereignty, violence, and the social-political relationship occurs within a long-established decolonial approach that searches for and promotes decolonial alternatives to, and liberation from, settler colonialism. Within this rich tradition, especially throughout the twentieth century, we have seen an emphasis on the nation-state and how it may play a role in decolonial liberation projects. Therefore, some preliminary discussion on the nation-state and the project of decolonial liberation is necessary at the outset of this inquiry. This discussion is important because it shows why I situate the opposition between settler colonial sovereignty vs. decolonial sovereignties, not within the debate over the nation-state necessarily, but within the larger and more abstract question of the social-political relationship.

DECOLONIAL LIBERATION AND THE SOCIAL-POLITICAL RELATIONSHIP

In differentiating between decolonization and decoloniality, Walter D. Mignolo writes, "decoloniality has changed the terrain from aiming at forming sovereign nation-states (decolonization) out of the ruins of the colonies to aiming at decolonial horizons of liberation (decoloniality) beyond state designs, and corporate and financial desires."[25] Mignolo here is restating a distinction that was prominent in the writings of thinkers associated with the decolonization struggles of the post–WWII era. Perhaps decoloniality is shifting the contemporary political and grammatical terrain, but it is doing so by rejuvenating what was always at the core of decolonization struggles (and continues to be in recent struggles such as the Arab uprisings of the early 2010s). These struggles emphasized that the true goal of decolonialization is liberation, freedom, equality, and the creation of the "new human" who will destroy the colonial and postcolonial world (along with its institutions, logics, and grammar) and set upon the task of creating a decolonized life and world.[26] In this task, the end is not the establishment of sovereign nation-states per se, but rather these states are seen as a means toward the true goal of decolonial liberation.[27]

Academically speaking, this is notably seen in the writings of Frantz Fanon and Edward Said, among others. The hard part has been answering how exactly this radical transformation toward decolonial liberation is to be accomplished. For Fanon, a strong leadership is necessary in directing the fighting masses toward the goal of national liberation and the introduction of a "new human" who would destroy the colonial world, logics, institutions, and create a new epoch in human history.[28] For Edward Said, the creation of a decolonial resistance culture is necessary to set the groundwork for a true decolonial liberatory movement across the world, creating the "new human" who traverses the interconnected and infinitely plural crossing and mixing of cultures, histories, worldviews, beliefs, and identities.[29] For Mignolo, the paths of decoloniality, in their plurality, must all deal with changing the terms of the conversation, and not simply reorganizing them or modifying the contents of the terms.[30] There are of course many more authors I can cite here, but the point I want to emphasize is that despite their different emphases and accentuations, they all called upon a decolonial liberation that goes beyond Eurocentric colonial and postcolonial modalities of freedom, justice, liberty, and humanity. Crucially, their positions on the nation-state are largely ambivalent insofar as the nation-state is never an end in itself.

When we examine the question of what states are meant to accomplish in the (post)colony and settler colony, we must center the social, cultural, economic, and political lives of people. States ought to exist in order to serve people, regardless of race, ethnicity, religion, gender, sexuality, or class, and not the other way around as has been the trend in Palestine-Israel and beyond.[31] A useful path in conceptualizing this shift of emphasis toward the lived experiences of people is in situating this discussion not within the nation-state per se, but rather within the larger question of the social-political relationship. To elaborate on this point, I explore a constructive tension between Mamdani's book on the settler and native distinction and Dabashi's book on the inevitable demise of the nation-state.

Dabashi argues that the postcolonial state is a relic that is left over from the European colonial project which sought to destroy and subdue the majority of the world's societies and cultures under European white supremacy—all for the sake of producing great wealth for the European powers. The state, as a mode of social and political organization, was always designed to rule over people, and it remains that way in its postcolonial form. Thus, the state holds no legitimacy or organic connection with the people, the nations, for whom the state has brought mass death, suffering, and destruction.[32] In opposing the violences of the state, Dabashi suggests "a complete decoupling of the nation and the state."[33] The nation in his work is indeed similar to my understanding of the social sphere in this book. Building his insights from what the Palestinian nation teaches, Dabashi argues that the nation is the collectivity of the people who have a shared and layered (as opposed to a univocal and bounded) historical archive, set of lived experiences, interests, identities, struggles, and sense of belonging in the world.[34] With each revolution in the postcolonial world, the nation further reveals the sheer brutality of the state and its complete lack of legitimacy with the nations over which it mercilessly rules, just as colonial power had done before it.[35] The state has responded with even more brutality in its efforts to combat the revelation of its true nature and operation, leaving us with "total states" that are "predicated on pure violence" and "with no claim to public sovereignty and/or political legitimacy."[36] Examples of such states are Iran, Saudi Arabia, Egypt, and Israel. For Dabashi, these total or more properly in the case of Israel, settler colonial "garrison states," leave people as nations who are in effect (Egyptians, Iranians, etc.) or in official status (Palestinians), stateless: "States become organized monopiles of violence, of will to power, while nations become a collective will to resist power."[37]

Dabashi makes the case that Palestinians and the Palestinian struggle for decolonial liberation is exemplary of postcolonial "political lives," as nations struggling to free themselves from the overpowering and illegitimate power of states.[38] The rootedness of Palestinians in their land and national home—their national consciousness—is a core feature of the century-old Palestinian resistance to the Zionist settler colonization of their lands. This resistance simultaneously conjures the pre- and post-state memories and aspirations of other nations suffering under postcolonial states.[39] The Palestinian struggle therefore stands for more than just a struggle that exists for Palestinians; it also offers a glimpse into a shared colonial and postcolonial experience. Dabashi's disposition and relationship to Palestine is therefore one where the "truth" of Palestine acts as an "allegory" "of all other nations, ruled by ruthless, illegitimate states . . . the postcolonial state coming home to a settler colony to see itself in a mirror."[40] Palestine both illuminates the settler colonial and postcolonial experience, and in doing so pushes the political imagination toward a new and decolonized path.

National liberation and national consciousness (but not the state-building project of nationalism) are crucial to this struggle, as Fanon also argued.[41] In Dabashi, the nation is neither held nor secured by the state (as is conventionally asserted), but is rather suppressed, oppressed, and eliminated by the state. In this struggle, nations are striving to achieve "their own stateless sovereignty": a national sovereignty that both precedes and exceeds the state.[42] The nation, then, is a domain that is sovereign from the state precisely because the state can never fully control/eradicate it, or saturate its possibilities and forever thwart its resistance and revolutionary potential. Dabashi's critical insight is that Palestinian resistance, as well as decolonial resistance writ large, is predicated on liberating the nation from the colonial and postcolonial states, where nations "begin to recognize and assert themselves against the backdrop of their national (not state-sponsored) anticolonial struggles before the false promises of a postcolonial state laid any bogus claims on them."[43] This is the retrieval or rejuvenation of the core of decolonization struggles that I alluded to earlier, before decolonization moved into a direction that Mignolo rightly critiques and opposes with the concept and practice of decoloniality.

Before leaving the state behind and rendering it incapable of leading us toward a more just and liberated future though, it is important to consider another approach to the problem of (post)colonialism and settler colonialism. Like Dabashi, Mamdani calls for a decoupling of the nation and the state, but in Mamdani, it is the state that needs to be rescued from the nation. For Mamdani the birth of the modern nation-state can be traced to 1492, when the Castilian monarchy employed ethnic cleansing of the Moors and Jews in order to create a homogenous nation of Christian Spaniards, and embarked on the centuries-long project of genocide in the Americas.[44] These events set the stage for the development and expansion of colonial modernity, which proceeded through violence and force to create nation-states across the world. Without delving into the details of colonial indirect rule and its various types, the outcome was basically the formation of states that created permanent national majorities and national minorities.[45] Through colonial mechanisms and systems of rule, and for the purpose of entrenching and expanding the exploitative power of the colonial masters, these political national identities became institutionalized and associated with state rewards and punishments. Whether a person is a full and free citizen, shares in the resources, enjoys the protections of the state, and more, all of it becomes dependent not on whether a person resides within that state, but whether that person belongs to the majoritarian nationality of that state. This institutionalization outlasted the colonial orders themselves. Decolonization brought about the overthrow of the colonial masters, but not the logics, grammars, and systems of power that they created, with devastating consequences (as we have seen in Rwanda and Sudan for example).[46]

Thus, we end up with postcolonial and settler colonial states that have come to simply accept the naturalness of national identities, instead of critically examining them as historically and politically produced identities that we ought to decouple from state institutions. Full, free, and equal citizenship rights and protections ought to cut across national identities and be provided to everyone and anyone who resides within the boundaries of a state. The problem, then, is not the state structure itself—as a structure, akin to my understanding of the political sphere, which (re)distributes resources, provides safety and protection, builds a social welfare system, produces and enacts laws, etc.—but the hijacking of this state structure by a majoritarian national identity that then oppresses, exploits, and brutalizes minority nationalities (from interpersonal violence to ethnic cleansing to genocide).

Mamdani is of course not calling for a leveling of cultural diversity or ignoring demands for autonomy and sovereignty that arise in states, especially in settler colonies like the United States and Israel.[47] His point, rather, is to promote a state structure where cultural diversity and even multiple sovereignties may flourish because national identity would no longer be politicized in a fierce battle over state resources and control over state institutions. In the case of Israel, for example, he argues that Israel is not a democracy since the majority is not politically formed but based purely on a national identity.[48] This means that even for the second-class Palestinian citizens of Israel, democracy does not exist because they are a national minority: "the permanent minority may have voting rights, but it is ever unable to exercise sovereignty."[49]

To radically oppose and transform the nation-state, therefore, Mamdani calls for decolonizing the political where: (a) citizenship is granted "on the basis of residence rather than identity"; (b) we "denationalize states" wherein overarching nonnational federal state structures can enable local autonomy, sovereignty, and help flourish diversity; and (c) we reeducate the public imagination toward a critical reflexivity that accentuates how our identities can be politically remade, "bolstering democracy in place of neoliberal human rights remedies."[50] The challenge of decolonizing the political is to "[strip] away the nation, or the tribe as nation, as a locus of political identification and commitment."[51] A new decolonial understanding of the political community beyond the grammar of the nation is therefore required in order to overcome the legacies of the colonial era.

When we juxtapose Dabashi and Mamdani, we arrive at the agreed insight that the nation and the state ought to be decoupled, but which needs to be rescued from the other is not so clear. Dabashi and Mamdani are not very different in what they desire: a decolonized world that frees itself from the grammar, logic, and systems of colonial modernity. But the paths taken are significant in their differences in terms of historiography. Dabashi's historiography centralizes the critique of the monopolization of violence that is a key feature of the modern state, whereas Mamdani's historiography centralizes the critique of the nation as a hierarchical institutionalization of politically produced identities. Posing these critiques to each other leads to the following theoretical oppositions: Dabashi's nation is incapable of properly revolutionizing the (post)colonial and settler colonial state precisely because it owes its existence to that state structure, as it simultaneously drives that state structure into more extreme political violence as nationalities vie for more powerful positions within the state. At the same time, Mamdani's state is incapable of producing the equitable and just decolonial world and indeed decolonized political identities precisely because the very foundation and marquee feature of the state is the monopolization of violence and ethnic cleansing and genocide (i.e., the state can only be multicultural because a master ethnos is unchallenged in their supremacy).

Each thinker of course can and does respond to both critiques: Dabashi would argue that there is that element of excess within the nation that the state can never fully capture. This is the sovereign element of the nation: the deep well of shared lived experiences and collective histories from which the nation draws in its efforts to counter the state and revolutionize modes of social and political organization. As it is embedded in the social lives of people, this element is very much the power of the social that opposes and can potentially transform the political. Mamdani would argue that even though the state is founded and maintained through a monopoly of violence, and although this monopoly has served the project of ethnic cleansing and genocide and has rendered "effective nonviolent political action impossible in many cases," this is largely due to the problem of the nation-state and not the state per se.[52] Thus, a properly diverse and free body politic that is critically reflexive on the question of political identities can direct this state monopoly toward a revolutionary project. It can help decolonize the political. For Mamdani, focusing on issues of social justice, on the social, in absence of this more foundational political revolution is bound to fail. Social justice can only be achieved after the political has been decolonized.[53] In a sense, for Mamdani, the political sphere is more critical for decolonization than is the social sphere.

It is important to pause here and ask: Is not a decolonization of the social as foundational and necessary as a decolonization of the political? If we understand the social as the space where the social collectivity forms and takes shape—that social bond of the collective "we," that `asabiyyah that Ibn Khaldûn illuminated—if we understand the social as this space, where colonized people marked for erasure and elimination set themselves on the path of opposing their fragmentation, of asserting and reasserting their humanity, of articulating and rearticulating their collectivity, of reinvigorating their ability to mobilize and wield the power of the "we," cannot and should not that social space serve as equally foundational to the project of decolonization?[54] Is that not necessary for a properly decolonial political space? Or, more properly, is not that activity also always already political, belonging to the realm of the political, although not necessarily belonging to institutions that we commonly mark as political? Mamdani seems to reduce the social sphere to social justice projects, but is not the social more than social justice? Social justice is a concept that is useful in describing specific projects for equity, equality, redistribution of resources, and so on. But social justice as a cluster of specific and contextual projects is not to be conflated with the social as such. Could the social be the space where decolonization may indeed gain its vitality, formative structure, and direction?

Conversely, is there not always a need for a political space that is distinct from the social sphere? A political sphere that specializes in and is dedicated to the functions of sovereignty (the securing and distribution of food, housing, community safety, health care, education, and so on)? How does that social resistance to the power of the political sphere in Dabashi translate into its own political sphere that is distinct yet not absolutely and decisively separated from the social sphere?

Instead of taking a firm position on whether the nation or the state, the social or the political, can guide us toward a decolonized future making an either/or decision, I maintain that keeping them apart in a continuous complementary form of opposition may be the best path forward.[55] In our decolonial efforts, I think both Mamdani and Dabashi will agree that we need to radically rethink the forms of state and society and the very nature of their relationship. Thus, I propose that we conceptualize the social-political relationship as a Mouffeian style agonism, as a constant tension between the social and the political that does not produce a winner, where one side overpowers the other.

I argue that decolonial scholars must oppose the coupling of the nation-state as a *decisive* oppositional relationship between the social and the political. To judge whether decolonial sovereignties reproduce or oppose settler colonial sovereignty, we therefore need to situate the analysis within the larger question of the social-political relationship. Settler colonial sovereignty can only operate on the decisive separation of the social-political as two distinct spheres that are then reconfigured into a relationship whereby the sphere of the political comes to dominate the sphere of the social (i.e., the separation of the rulers *as lords* who rule over their subjects). Decolonial sovereignties must oppose this kind of either/or opposition between the social and the political and imagine and practice their relationship in a *complementary* fashion.

As I will argue later in this book, this kind of complementary relationship between the social and the political already takes place in certain forms of Palestinian decolonial resistance. Crucially, these decolonial alternatives offer a critique of the interlocking of enemy-siblings and are in direct opposition to the structure of settler colonial expulsion. I argue that a critique of the violence of expulsion and the posture of lordship is a necessary criterion for determining whether or not a form of resistance is decolonial, and that the critique of colonial modernity's social-political relationship is a necessary feature of an alternative form of sovereignty that can replace settler colonial sovereignty. This book shows that these two critiques, and not a strict focus on the nation-state per se, are intimately connected and necessary for the project of decolonial liberation. Thus, the social-political relationship constitutes the larger universe, as it were, in which the four-dimensional operation of settler colonial violence takes place (see figure 0.1).

Admittedly my position is tied to a much more specific geographical focus—Palestine-Israel—than is found in either Dabashi's or Mamdani's comparative works. Although both study and analyze Palestine-Israel, and convincingly place it among other cases and contexts, I remain fixated on just this case. This is not because this case is unique or radically different. I believe that it is neither of those things, and it certainly falls within the larger context of colonial modernity. The reason I remain focused within that context is that perhaps more than any other context, it combines so many diverse elements of colonial modernity and consequently presents one of the greater challenges in the contemporary period in countering colonial modernity. My claims on the social-political relationship and sovereignty are therefore limited to that context (as were my claims on political violence in my previous book), and although I believe that they are applicable to other contexts, I leave that work for a future project.

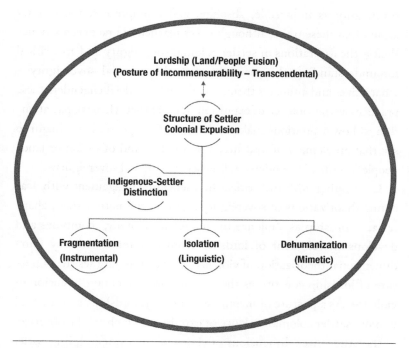

FIGURE 0.1 Four-dimensional operation of settler colonial violence. This structure of violence constitutes settler colonial sovereignty, which operates within the larger framework of colonial modernity's construct of the social-political relationship as a decisive opposition.

BOOK OVERVIEW

The book is divided into six chapters. Although the following main concepts will appear (implicitly and explicitly) and be analyzed throughout the book, broadly speaking, chapters 1 and 2 deal with settler colonial sovereignty, chapters 3 and 4 with four-dimensional violence, and chapters 5 and 6 with decolonial sovereignties.

The first chapter, "Settler Colonial Sovereignty," engages with academic theorizations of sovereignty in order to argue that settler colonial sovereignty is to be understood and studied both in its aspirations and practices. Instead of dismissing understandings of sovereignty as indivisible, absolute, and omnipresent, the chapter argues that these traits, although never reached in practice, are nonetheless the aspirations of settler colonial sovereignty and are critical for understanding the practices of settler colonial sovereignty—what drives and animates them, but also what indeed engenders these practices as the violence of expulsion. I argue that when we pay attention to how aspirations make certain practices possible, we begin to see that an element of lordship, a particular kind of fusion of land/people, is critical to understanding settler colonial sovereignty.

Continuing with my critical hermeneutic engagement with academic theorizations of sovereignty and also the nation-state, chapter 2, "Lordship as Violence in the Settler Colony," combines and develops the element of lordship from chapter 1 with my four-dimensional theorization of violence. The chapter argues that a posture of lordship constitutes the fourth transcendental dimension of violence. As a posture of incommensurability, lordship can only lead to more settler colonial violence of expulsion, which can be observed in the other three dimensions of violence: instrumental, linguistic, and mimetic. I argue that each of these dimensions can be observed in many different types and forms of Israeli violence. My focus in this study will be on the violences of fragmentation (instrumental), isolation (linguistic), and dehumanization (mimetic). Although neatly separated for analytical clarity, these dimensions and types of Israeli violence operate simultaneously in the Israeli settler colonial project. To capture this simultaneity, I identify a prominent feature of the violence of expulsion which can be seen across the four-dimensional operation of violence: the racialized Indigenous-settler distinction.

Chapter 3, "The Indigenous-Settler Distinction and the Interlocking of Enemy-Siblings," explores how scholars can theorize and study the Indigenous-settler distinction in Palestine-Israel. Although it shares certain elements and features with postcolonial Africa and Asia, the case of Palestine-Israel is foundationally settler colonial. The chapter argues that we must affirm the Palestinian Indigenous vs. Israeli settler distinction as the ground from which we then work to transform that distinction. We cannot wish away the distinction, dissolve it to serve settler colonial power, or imagine it as fixed and never-changing in its separation of Indigenous and settler, but rather understand how violence interlocks the Indigenous-settler as enemy-siblings that can no longer be separated despite the settler colonial effort to eliminate and expel the "enemy-other." In order to critique, counter, and transform the binary distinction, we must first study and illuminate the four-dimensional operation of violence.

Chapter 4, "The Four-Dimensional Operation of Violence: Fragmentation, Isolation, Dehumanization, and Lordship," explores and examines how the violence of expulsion operates and ensures the propagation of Israeli settler colonial violence. Although the four dimensions operate in each type or form of Israeli violence, I highlight for simplicity's sake, a different type of violence for each of the three observable dimensions of violence. For the instrumental dimension, I examine the violences of fragmentation as can be observed in the construction of the Separation/Annexation Wall; for the linguistic dimension, I interrogate the violences of isolation as can be seen in the settlements and the settlement movement as well as the discourse around it; and finally for the mimetic dimension, I investigate the violences of dehumanization which can be studied in the siege and military onslaughts on the Gaza Strip. Enabled by the fourth dimension of violence, the posture of lordship, the chapter examines how settler colonial violence produces a subjectivity of lordship that continuously leads to more violence, producing not Israeli Jewish selves that have answered once and for all the Jewish Question of anti-Semitic Europe, but rather produces lords of the land. As we come to an understanding of how settler colonial violence propagates itself, we reach the limit of what settler colonial sovereignty produces and can only produce: a never-ending violence of expulsion. This moves the book into the last two chapters where a decolonial alternative is explored.

It is necessary to tackle the unbearable violence of interlocking in order to transform the world of settler colonial sovereignty. Chapter 5, "A Literary Critique: Toward Decolonial Sovereignties," begins the movement into decolonial sovereignties. In a critical reading of the literary writings of Elias Khoury and Mahmoud Darwish, the chapter attempts to think of decolonial sovereignties on alternative grounds, which might help us avoid the replication of settler colonial grammar and logics. Specifically, the chapter explores a different kind of writing "I" that would oppose and present an alternative to the dictatorial sovereign voice. Instead of the pure, superior, absolute, and indivisible "I" that constitutes the primal scene of settler colonial sovereignty, we find a multiplying "I" that exhibits the intimate connection between self-annihilation and self-liberation, showing us how we may think of the liberation of the self as another. I argue that this decolonial grammar, which among other things emphasizes the plurality of sovereign*ties*, can help us better theorize decolonial sovereignties and their potentiality.

Chapter 6, "Decolonial Sovereignties," focuses on the criterion that marks decolonial sovereignties as decolonial, and identifies three features of decolonial sovereignties that, in exhibiting a complementary opposition between the social and the political, distinguish them from settler colonial sovereignty. Engaging with Indigenous and decolonial theory, I argue that the main criterion for decoloniality is a critique of the settler colonial violence of expulsion. For decolonial formations to avoid the replication of settler colonialism they must engender a constant critique of such violence and the subjectivity of lordship, although it is not necessary that they critique *all* forms and types of violence—which, although admirable, is probably an impossibility in the context of colonial modernity. When this criterion is met, we can observe certain social and political formations that can be called decolonial sovereignties. The long history of Palestinian resistance contains a few manifestations of these decolonial sovereignties, most notably, the popular committees of the first intifada. In my analysis of these committees through primary and secondary analysis, I argue that these sovereignties, *in both* aspiration and practice, were layered, shared, and multiplying. Although these particular committees were ultimately defeated by settler colonial power, they offer a window into how we can imagine and practice decolonial sovereignties.

Lordship and Liberation in Palestine-Israel concludes with some reflections on the two main paths that this book delineates and studies. The option before us is not one between one state vs. two state, peace vs. conflict, violence vs. nonviolence, West vs. East, civilized vs. terrorist, a free Palestine that would mean the destruction of Israelis, or whatever else the Israeli violence of expulsion has come to constitute as "real." The option before us is one between the continuation of the Israeli settler colonial project in particular and the project of colonial modernity in general, or the commencement of a decolonial age in Palestine-Israel and indeed beyond. A better world is not only possible, it is waiting.

A NOTE ON TERMINOLOGY

There is one important phrasing that I must explain at the outset of the book so as to avoid misinterpretation. This concerns my use of Palestine-Israel with a dash as opposed to the more common slash or the separation of the two terms with an "and." As I argued in my first book, violence forges enemies into enemy-siblings, creating a dash between the "sides" that makes it virtually impossible to think of one without the other—a dash that makes each of the "sides" both possible and impossible. Crucially, I argued that this interlocking transforms the "sides" making it possible and impossible to speak of two unchanging sides that are locked into a "conflict" with one another. It is on this basis that I use the dash in this book: to speak to the interlocking of enemy-siblings as enemy-siblings.

Some critical and decolonial scholars and activists might argue that this dash makes it impossible to speak of Palestine, the Palestinian people, history, aspirations, modes of social and political life, and so on, independently of Zionist settler colonialism, thus erasing Palestine. Certainly, the idea that you cannot think of Palestine without Israel and Zionism has been used to serve Zionist discourse and ensure the erasure of Palestine and Palestinians from public discourse in North America and Europe.[56] But my point here is that the intertwinement goes much deeper than the strategic uses Israel and Zionists have made of it. Furthermore, I do not believe that the writing of the dash is what accomplishes such an erasure of Palestine.

What propagates the erasure of Palestine is the violence of expulsion. Using the dash in fact highlights this structure of expulsion and what it seeks to erase, not conceal it. There is much to learn from Palestinian modes of social and political life, which I highlight explicitly in the last two chapters of this book, but which are indeed guiding this analysis throughout. In short, the dash in this book opposes the erasure of Palestine and makes clear that there can never be an Israel that has definitively and conclusively erased Palestine. A new understanding of the dash, or perhaps eventually no dash at all, where Palestine and Palestinian social and political life is foregrounded, learned from, flourishes, and thrives is precisely the conversation that this book advances and invites. It is only when the expulsion of Palestine and Palestinians not only ceases but is reversed and undone as a structure of violence, that we can begin to say that we have commenced on a path of decoloniality.

1

SETTLER COLONIAL SOVEREIGNTY

The sovereign is one who has his end in himself or is the end of everything.
— Jacques Derrida, *The Beast and the Sovereign, Volume I*

This chapter critically (re)interprets theorizations of sovereignty in order to make the case that these theorizations do not properly illuminate or name a core feature of settler colonial sovereignty, which is lordship. The first section foregrounds the critical question of space and sovereignty in our theorization of sovereignty. In conventional political and social theory, much debate is centered on the problematic of *territory* and sovereignty and the vexing question of which takes precedence or comes first. I argue that theorizing the intractable relationship between sovereignty and *space* is a more useful path for opening up the concept of sovereignty beyond its dominant Eurocentric theorization. When we move beyond Eurocentric theorizations and historiographies, we can see that territory/territorialization belongs to the larger question of space/spatialization, which can take on varied forms that inform the problematic of sovereignty across temporal periods and geographical regions. Adopting the lens of space/spatialization allows scholars to interpret the concept of sovereignty as a foundational claim of belonging—or, as a claim on the relationship between land and people.

The second section explores the element of the indivisibility of sovereignty, which has drawn much attention as a key marker of sovereignty. Instead of accepting indivisibility as a universal marker of sovereignty, I engage with this element as a core feature of settler colonial sovereignty and refer to it as lordship. Lordship in my book is a particular kind of claim on the relationship between land and people where lords are lords by virtue of their aspiration for indivisible, absolute, and omnipresent power. This is a claim that is, first and foremost, created, grounded, built, developed, and propagated in and through violence. This leads me to theorize that lordship constitutes the fourth dimension of violence, and this, not sovereignty as understood through the prism of the Westphalian nation-state, ought to be our analytical focus.

Scholarship working within the Westphalian paradigm foregrounds the statist and nationalist forms of sovereignty, reifying in the process the nation-state as the basic unit of analysis. From this ground, scholars then attempt to advance a more equitable, democratic, and peaceful social and political life, beyond the violent founding of the nation-state. This debate usually unfolds in the distinction between civic and ethnic nationalism. The third section opposes the argument that civic nationalism can counter the force and violence that marks the emergence of the modern nation-state. Following decolonial critiques, I argue that the distinction between civic and ethnic nationalism conceals more than it reveals the structure of violence in the settler colony. I instead focus on the violent founding, maintaining, and expansion of the territorially bounded settler colonial state: it is not territoriality or the nation-state but violence that is centered in my critique. This sets the stage for chapter 2 where I argue that the fusion of land and people as lordship, *as the posture of settler colonial violence*, is the most significant core feature of settler colonial sovereignty, animating its operations and varied structures, forms, and shapes.

SPACE AND SOVEREIGNTY

In this section, I engage with approaches to the study of sovereignty from international political theory, political sociology, and postcolonial theory. To begin, this book agrees with Jens Bartelson's argument that the concept of sovereignty does not possess a timeless essence.[1] Bartelson illustrates how different European philosophical traditions as well as modern approaches in international political theory and macrosociology essentially fail to present definitive answers to three key questions about sovereignty: "the *source* of sovereignty," "the *locus* attributed to sovereignty," and "the *scope* of sovereignty."[2] Together these three questions have haunted (because they cannot yield definitive answers) philosophical and political discussions of sovereignty within the European tradition. His deconstructive critique of sovereignty seeks to reopen the concept toward more fruitful engagements in the contemporary world, particularly rethinking the distinction between international and domestic politics.

I need not delve into all of his deconstructions here. Instead, I want to focus in this section on one crucial area of analysis that is revealing of how the three questions remain inconclusive in political and social theory. An important debate surrounding the concept of sovereignty across its different iterations, definitions, and political usages concerns the question of space and territory. In much of international political theory, "sovereignty is taken to be a political or legal fact *within* an already given and demarcated territory, simultaneously signifying sovereignty *over* the same territory, and everything that happens to be inside this portion of space."[3] This co-conceptualization of space and sovereignty never definitively answers the question of what comes first, sovereignty or territory, and thus international political theory tends to take two different routes: "a bounded territory can either be interpreted as a necessary condition of sovereignty, or conversely, sovereignty can be interpreted as a necessary condition of a bounded territory."[4] The route taken will determine much of our understandings of empirical cases of war and conflict, where scholars either assert the supremacy of sovereignty rendering territory as derivative and malleable, or they elevate the status of territory to irrefutability rendering sovereignty as dependent on an unaltered territory.

In macrosociology, the problem is formulated differently as it is transported from the conceptual to the empirical level. Bartelson argues that the interplay between the politicization of space (material power relations in lands owned, revenue generated from the land, etc.) and the spatialization of politics (the production of a bounded territory) "leads to the rise of the state as a territorially organized unit."[5] The state as a foundational unit of analysis becomes integral to the conceptualization of sovereignty in macrosociology (i.e., sociology's focus on the bounded society), upon which rests the discipline's attempt to circumvent the question of what comes first, territory or sovereignty. Certainly, the discipline of sociology has changed much since the middle of the 1990s and has addressed (with varying degrees of success) the transnationality of the social. Regardless of disciplinary differences (and the current state of disciplines in regard to the transnational), the point here is that this chicken-and-egg scenario cannot be resolved once and for all as it is ultimately inconclusive;[6] rather, our answers to such quandaries will often guide (and are *guided by* I would add) our political praxis, models, and explanations.

This book adopts the assertion that the chicken-and-egg scenario between sovereignty and territory is a futile line of inquiry. Indeed, the very framing of the territory-sovereignty debate in macrosociology and international political theory is always already situated within a particular form of Euro-American sovereignty with its roots in colonial modernity, not in the universal essence of what sovereignty is, must be, and/or should be. It is important not to present a universalist solution to the questions of sovereignty posed by Bartelson and others. But that does not mean that we discard the concept of sovereignty altogether since it remains critical for scholarly understanding of political and social reality. We can begin the analysis of sovereignty from the understanding that it is and will remain indefinable in the sense of being composed of timeless specific elements. But we can attribute to sovereignty abstract and general elements that are themselves malleable and can take on varied forms. The reason this is necessary is that the concept clearly speaks to dynamics, objects, processes, and structures of the social/political world in ways that cannot be accomplished through other concepts (namely, autonomy or power).[7]

To avoid Orientalist and colonialist approaches that contribute and (re)produce the knowledge/power matrix of (neo)colonialism,[8] and informed by debates surrounding sovereignty and space/spatialization, I begin with a highly generalized understanding of sovereignty: the concept is drawn upon to speak to a claim of belonging, a claim that establishes the nature of the relationship between people and land, and which also necessarily involves the relationship between and among people. I intentionally leave out of this foundational understanding the most pressing questions that have been wedded to sovereignty: that is, questions about legitimacy, authority, rule/governance, law, and justice. I do so for a simple reason: all such questions are contextual, and how they take shape in Indigenous communities on Turtle Island, Western Africa, the Middle East, or in Western Europe will be different. Eurocentric approaches render universal what are in fact provincialized forms of authority, governance, legitimacy, and so on and then proceed to judge the ability of the "rest" to live up to European "ideals," which ignores how diverse communities have developed complex political, social, legal, economic, and cultural structures that are geared toward justice, cooperation, specific notions of the public or common good, and so on.[9]

Within the context of colonial modernity, sovereignty takes on a specific form: here we find an *indivisible claim* on land and people. As Khaled Furani puts it, this element of indivisibility is the "central sustaining principle" of the "foundational conceptual structure of the sovereignty paradigm" in Euro-American thought and practice and certainly in Israeli settler colonialism.[10] Although emergent as a Euro-American form of settler colonial sovereignty, this is not going to be a simple matter of delineating a purely European form of sovereignty that is then transplanted elsewhere—we must never forget that settler colonial sovereignty was forged in the colonies. As will become evident shortly, I am making the concept of sovereignty much more malleable than is found in conventional approaches that reify the concept of sovereignty (often by making the Westphalian nation-state the "singular path to sovereignty").[11] Most crucially, the kind of indivisibility that I am theorizing here did not simply emerge in Europe, ready for application elsewhere, but was rather formed in the violent intertwinement that is colonialism and settler colonialism.

So, to avoid confusion, I do not use the term "indivisible" in the classic sense advanced by Jean Bodin (nor for that matter, the replication of that sense in thinkers like Thomas Hobbes, Jean-Jacques Rousseau, and many others). I am not following Bodin's claim that sovereignty cannot be divided among different agencies, sectors, or departments of government, nor will I follow Bodin's "marks of sovereignty," such as the declaration of war and peace, the appointing of magistrates and assigning of official duties, and the ordaining and repealing of laws.[12] Bodin's notion of indivisibility—indeed his accounting of the main traits of sovereignty as the power that underlies government actions, wherein "such power had to be supreme, absolute, indivisible and perpetual"—this notion and his ideas are not the essential clarifications of the concept of sovereignty that Bodin believed them to be.[13] Rather, these ideas are tied to his particular sociopolitical context (monarchist France) and the ancient Greek and Roman texts he was primarily engaging with (i.e., Bodin's rejection of the ancients' argument for a mixed commonwealth—e.g., Aristotle's *politeia*—informed his indivisible conception of sovereignty). I will have more to say on these traits (absolute and infinite power) through Jacques Derrida shortly, but for now, I simply want to emphasize that for the purposes of addressing the settler colony in Palestine-Israel, I understand as indivisible the very force that underpins the claim to land/people. Settler colonial sovereignty is indivisible in the sense that the entity that proclaims itself sovereign is making a claim of indivisibility: that is, it is making a claim of the foundational and sole ability to capture, determine, own, represent, and manage a specified land/people.

This does not mean that indivisible control and authority exists in the practices of the sovereign. The idea that the state can in fact act as an indivisible sovereign within or beyond its territory has long been rightly questioned and critiqued. Historically and into the present, there are numerous examples of how the "actual practice of state sovereignty" never matches the "mythic ideal" of how scholars theorize state sovereignty as indivisible.[14] Scholars should heed Robbie Shilliam's argument that if the academic "debate seeks to understand sovereignty as (now) multi-dimensional and extra-territorial, it usually does so via an understanding of historical transformation that is uni-linear in character."[15] Instead of studying sovereignty as if it endogenously emerged within and for Europe, and then focusing on the European Union as the exemplary transformation of sovereignty in our age, Shilliam's decolonial critique illustrates through an analysis of Pan-Africanism and Black Jacobinism how there is an "ongoing multi-linear transformation of sovereignty in the modern epoch."[16] Sovereignty (in its political articulations, usages, conceptualizations) never has been, and it is not now, univocal, unilinear, or universal. Sovereignty has always been formed and transformed in complex ways by the varied political subjects it has constituted and who have constituted it. Across its complexity, sovereignty is always ensconced (in one way or another) with some structure or another of space/spatialization, only one of which takes the form of territory/territorialization that we have become accustomed to seeing, theorizing, living, and understanding in the form of the modern nation-state.[17] When we move beyond Eurocentric articulations, we can see that territory/territorialization belongs to the larger question of space/spatialization. One of the critical forms of space/spatialization for this book concerns a complementary type of opposition between the social and the political, in contradistinction to the decisive separation and opposition of the two spheres in the Westphalian nation-state of colonial modernity.

An illustrative and insightful example of the latter point is Amy Niang's analysis of the precolonial, colonial, and postcolonial state in the Voltaic region of Western Africa. Niang shows how precolonial polities in this region operated on a complex tension between stateness and statelessness, both of which contained and operated upon different forms of political authority and legitimacy—i.e., it is not only in the unitary and centralized "state" that we find politics, order, legitimacy, but these can be found in non-state and decentralized forms of sociopolitical organizations. She specifically examines how social (*Tenga*—"the sphere of rituals," the "nonpolitical") and political (*Naam*—"the sphere of power," the "political") principles of authority intermingled in the formation of precolonial centralized states.[18]

Generally speaking, different forms of governance, politics, legitimacy, authority, subjectivity, order, and meaning operated in each sphere, but without the intermingling of the two spheres of the social and the political (as resistance, accommodation, hospitality, confrontation, and so on), the formation of centralized states in this region, transient as they were, would have been unthinkable and perhaps impossible.[19] The key point here is that conceptions of state sovereignty established to explain Western European contexts are highly inadequate for capturing and explaining this complementary tension between the social and the political spheres. Indeed, the two sets of principles operated on a different conception of space and therefore sovereignty. While the *Naam* and the political authority operated on the integration of various social/political bodies into bounded territories (even if transient and shifting), the *Tenga* and the social authority was boundless and rejected rigid hierarchies and hierarchization, instead operating on notions of "moral stability."[20]

Here we have a kind of social sovereignty that transcends the territorial bounding of space and has relatively nothing to do with centralized structures in general and a political sovereignty that rests on politicizing space as territorial.[21] So even though closer to the European territorial state, we must keep in mind that the centralized state in precolonial Western Africa was very different insofar as it did not impose its order upon the "nonpolitical" spheres, but to various degrees, merged with them—its authority ultimately rested on the continued transference of sovereignty from the "nonpolitical" to the "political."[22] There is a tension here, then, between the unboundedness of space and the bounded territory, to which we must pay attention when examining this form of sovereignty.[23]

In settler colonial sovereignty, this tension is violently and forcefully suppressed, marginalized, brought almost to the point of eradication (but never total eradication due to the resistance of the colonized), and we largely find the victory and dominance of a bounded territory (although the specific boundaries themselves are expansive) that today suffers little to no tension and threat from the unboundedness of space. But the violent imposition of this new bounded territorial order remains in a sense artificial, never developing roots in communities that operate in accordance to different and often competing registers of the political, politics, order, the social, justice, and so on—and in such cases, the outcome can only be states that attempt to rule *over* and *against* societies, with devastating consequences for the majority of people who are ruled. Settler colonial sovereignty is always an imposition and always destructive not just of the lives of the colonized, but also of complex systems, processes, and structures of social and political life, and this for the purpose of replacing the destroyed social and political worlds with systems of power and structures of rule that are of and for the settler colonists.

Hence, territorialization is not the universal form of sovereignty, but rather is part of the larger issue of space/spatialization which is fundamental, in its territorial form, to settler colonial sovereignty. When we adopt the lens of space/spatialization, we begin to observe that only certain forms of sovereignty are territorially bounded where the political sphere rules over and overpowers a separated social sphere. This kind of sovereignty is especially prevalent in the settler colony, which seeks to eradicate all alternative modes of social and political organization. We will later visit in this book how Palestinian decolonial sovereignties operate on a complementary form of opposition between the social and the political, much in the same way as Niang shows is the case in her analysis of the Voltaic region. For now, it is important to explore and theorize the kind of indivisible *claim* that operates in settler colonial sovereignty which forges the people and the land within a bounded territory.

It is not solely the practice of sovereignty that guides this study, but also the aspirations of sovereignty which are most clearly captured in the *claim to sovereignty*—and of course, the claim is constantly being supported and enacted (and also resisted and modified, even transfigured) in various projects, practices, and policies. I am not using the claim to sovereignty in the sense of its effectiveness in gaining acceptance for the claimant from internal (the body politic) and external audiences (whether in international law, the international system, or international society).[24] Analyses of the normative frameworks that are used for assessing the claim, the ways in which the claim is constructed, the sociopolitical context in which the claim arises (often when sovereignty is insecure, uncertain, and malleable) are all important. In a limited sense, these questions appear in this book's analysis, but they will not frame my analysis of the claim to sovereignty. Rather, I want to reach behind these questions and go to the force that gives the very claim its direction, purpose, and shape. Force in this book is not seen in the conventional way of being one element of sovereignty that is separate from the legitimation processes of sovereignty,[25] but rather force is what gives the sovereign the very validity and legitimacy of the sovereign's rule: force is, in short, brute violence.

This brute violence can be seen when we look at a specific target of the claim: the colonized, who cannot afford to not take the claim of indivisibility seriously, since it directly attacks and robs the colonized of their claim to sovereignty. That is, regardless of the gap between what sovereignty effectively does and what it claims—a gap that is most often the direct result of the resistance of the colonized and the oppressed—the very claim of indivisibility in settler colonialism is itself the primary objective as that claim is the suppression and/or the eradication of the sovereign claim of the colonized. Because of Indigenous resistance, this eradication is not straightforward, smooth, immediate, quick, or definitive—this story is complex, and it is of course necessary to study this complexity that we can find between the aspirations and practices of settler colonial sovereignty. But equally if not more important is the study of the aspiration itself—of settler colonial sovereignty as a claim of indivisibility that eradicates all Indigenous claims to sovereignty.[26]

For my purposes, then, I am not concerned with answering the questions of source, locus, scope, and it must be added enactment of sovereignty for "our time" or "our phase of modernity" or "our political reality in the contemporary era." Rather, I am pursuing the question of sovereignty in the specific case of Palestine-Israel and focusing on this force that gives the claim to sovereignty the very attribute of claiming, or the very ability to proclaim an indivisible claim on land and people. I argue that the claim of indivisibility summons the promise of absolute power and potency, which we can understand through what Derrida in a series of lectures (in 2001–2003) refers to as the analogy between the beast and the sovereign.

INDIVISIBILITY OF SOVEREIGNTY

I need not delve into all of Derrida's complex deconstructions of the analogy between the beast and the sovereign (in the works of Hobbes, Schmitt, Rousseau, Aristotle, Agamben, Heidegger, among others), or delve into how he follows specific lines of interpretation and thinking from one lecture to the next. For my purposes, I want to emphasize four elements from Derrida's lectures (mainly drawing on Volume I) that characterize this analogy: (1) the resemblance between, or the coupling of, the two figures of the beast and the sovereign; (2) the self-identity of the sovereign, or the assertion of a sovereign self; (3) the relation between indivisibility and the figure of God; and (4) the positionality of the two figures above the law. I leave aside the fourth point for chapter 2 when I engage with Agamben's work on the paradox of sovereignty. The first three points are crucial in building toward a fresh, comprehensive understanding of the claim of indivisibility.

First, while seemingly at opposite ends of a spectrum of civilization, the two figures for Derrida, present us with a "resemblance" that forces us to look for and find "the face of the beast under the features of the sovereign; or conversely . . . it is as though, through the maw of the untameable beast, a figure of the sovereign were to appear."[27] In their coupling, "the beast becomes the sovereign who becomes the beast."[28] While certain theorizations of the sovereign (especially in Hobbes) seek to exclude the beast in "the contract at the origin of sovereignty," the two figures are always already inside one another.[29] In theorizations of political sovereignty, we find assertions of a human reason that constructs sovereignty as above animals and animality, beasts and bestiality, while simultaneously positing political sovereignty "as the manifestation of bestiality or human animality."[30] For example, the United States may designate other states as "rogue" and other leaders as "beasts" (e.g., Iraq and Saddam Hussein), but they ultimately themselves behave as rogues and beasts in the international arena, continuously violating human rights and international law, asserting the sovereign will of the powerful against the weak under the guise of law but really through the old adage of "might makes right."[31] Thus, despite efforts to separate and decouple the beast and the sovereign, they resemble each other on a few different levels for Derrida, two of which I think are most interesting and useful for my study: both figures are above the law (which I come back to in chapter 2), and both are marked by fear and terror.

Derrida's deconstruction of Hobbes—of "political theories that have made fear or panic (and so terror or terrorism as knowing how to make fear reign) an essential and structural mainspring of subjectivity, of subjection, of being-subject, of submission or political subjection"—plays with notions of fear and terror in order to show that "there we should find, as close as can be to sovereignty—which is, as it were, its correlate—fear: fear as it is defined by the Leviathan, for example."[32] What I garner from Derrida's analysis of Hobbes and Agamben is that fear and terror correlate with the sovereign in three general and interconnected senses: fear and terror (a) drive the sovereign into being—the sovereign's promise to protect and guard subjects from fear and terror gives rise to the sovereign as sovereign (this is the Hobbesian premise); (b) in being enacted by the sovereign (in the state of exception—in the uninhibited use of violence), fear and terror constitute the sovereign as sovereign (this is the Agambean premise); (c) enable the sovereign to continue to guard the social and political order that it constituted (this is the premise of most social and political theory in regard to sovereignty), whether in the Hobbesian tradition where the sovereign demands subjection as the price of protection, or I would add in the Lockean tradition of a sovereign power that is held accountable for its actions (i.e., subjects are protected from, as they are protected by, the sovereign).[33] Together, these three senses point us toward the resemblance between the beast and the sovereign insofar as the sovereign is that which protects us from the beast (fear and terror) precisely because the sovereign acts the most beastly of all beasts: "Sovereignty causes fear, and fear makes the sovereign" and "terror is equally opposed to the state as a challenge as it is exerted by the state as the essential manifestation of its sovereignty."[34] Thus, when this book refers to settler colonial sovereignty, the specter of bestiality is never far removed. What I essentially mean by that is that fear and terror are never far removed—that violence, in its four-dimensional operation, is never far removed. While I do not pursue the Derridean terminology of beasts and bestiality throughout this book, this particular sense of fear and terror is crucial for my own discussion on settler colonial sovereignty and four-dimensional violence.

Henceforth, my critique of settler colonial sovereignty concerns an analysis that remains focused and fixated on violence, not ideology, as the foundation *and engine* of settler colonial sovereignty. I want to take a brief tangent here and acknowledge that this is certainly not the only path of critique. C. Heike Schotten, for an insightful example, has shown that the ideological apparatus of settler colonial sovereignty should be critiqued through its own meanings, logics, and values for the sake of, not redeeming some element or another of the apparatus, or attempting to take hold of the powerful or more desirable positions within it (i.e., joining it, becoming part of it), but for the sake of destroying it. In her analysis, Schotten holds that "just as the meaning, coherence, and legitimacy of modern settler sovereignty is established *materially* through violence, these are established *ideologically* through the futurist temporalization of desire."[35] Her work shows how the futurist temporalization of desire concerns a moralization of "life" and "death," not as biological determinates, but rather as that which produces what/who counts as a desired "civilized life" that is valuable, worthy of history, democracy, human rights, protection, and so on, and what/who counts as a "savage" or "terrorist" that only desires and symbolizes death, destruction, backwardness, barbarity, unworthiness, a threat to civilized life, and so on.

Settler sovereignty, for Schotten, operates simultaneously on a biopolitics of "life" and necropolitics of "death" that render settler sovereignty as only possible when it eradicates and eliminates any peoples, groups, political forces (e.g., Indigenous peoples, Muslim "terrorists," Black liberation) that oppose its material violences. Thus settler sovereignty is what drives and constitutes the biopolitical and necropolitical operations of the settler colonial state.[36] There is, of course, scholarly and political value in the kind of work undertaken by Schotten, and there is a great deal of affinity between that work and this book's analysis. This book, however, accentuates more the question of violence. The ideological apparatus is powerful in its effects and in the ability of systems of power to maintain themselves; I do not deny this long-held axiom of critical theory (going back to at least Gramsci). Moreover, I acknowledge that violence and ideology are always interconnected, and the analysis of brute violence always implicates and augments the analysis of ideology and vice versa. But I also maintain that without the violences that found and maintain, then ideologies are not nearly as effectual as we may believe. In this work, I will not acknowledge violence as foundational and then focus on ideology; I will instead acknowledge ideology and then focus on violence as that which helps us properly situate and understand ideology. The importance of this slight shift will become clearer later in the analysis of Zionist ideology.

Back to Derrida—the second element I want to highlight from Derrida is the assertion of a sovereign self across political, social, and individual sovereignty. While Derrida does not systematically develop what he initially calls the "different and terribly problematical dimensions" of sovereignty, we can gather from his discussion that political sovereignty concerns the well-trotted questions around the state (legitimacy, political subjectivities, political subjection, and so on).[37] Much less clear and left undeveloped in the lectures is what Derrida means by social sovereignty, but I take it to mean the sovereignty of the people or the nation. Individual sovereignty can refer to the person of the monarch, but it more importantly has two other senses. The first sense concerns the notion of a person's protection of, or claim for, one's autonomy and liberty, which is often claimed in opposition to what is deemed as an overreach of the political sovereignty of the state that violates the sovereignty of the "personal subject" (or "the sovereignty of man").[38]

The second sense (which is more significant in Derrida and for my study) concerns the solitary individual, the person that is isolated from beast, animal, God, and indeed other selves, and thus rules absolutely and decides sovereignly in the world.[39] In his deconstruction of *Robinson Crusoe*, Rousseau, and Heidegger, Derrida reveals that this figure underpins political sovereignty, and this can be seen in how this figure is preoccupied with reinvention.[40] Particularly in his deconstruction of *Robinson Crusoe*, Derrida highlights how there is an emphasis on reinvention in the novel's fictional island, whether of machines, tools, knowledge, or sovereignty itself.[41] Derrida sees this reinvention as "an act of sovereignty and a question of life or death when a living being invents all alone, by himself, a technique, a machine designed to ensure his survival, to decide as to his life and his death."[42]

This trope or conceptual strategy is key in creating the distinction between human and beast. Adding to this analysis his deconstruction of Heidegger, Derrida concludes that the "absolute difference between beast and man, of a transcendence or of an emergence of the power of man (speech, technics, knowledge of beings as such, etc.)" is complicated "when it comes to interpreting this power as *sovereignty*."[43] In other words, we are not simply observing here the old idea that the human is distinct from the animal by virtue of the human's control and manipulation of the natural world; rather, when this kind of power is viewed as sovereignty, then we begin to see that the sovereignty of the individual is that which not only underpins political sovereignty, it is also that which exceeds it: sovereignty becomes here the excess—"that of a sovereignty so sovereign that it overruns any historical configuration of an onto-theological and therefore also theologico-political type."[44] While Derrida acknowledges the seeming absurdity of assigning excess (a sovereignty so sovereign that it is virtually godlike insofar as it is creation itself) to an already excessive concept like sovereignty (the idea of an indivisible and absolute power), I read him as suggesting that excess and the absurdity of the excess (of sovereignty as excess and of the excess of sovereignty), is indeed part and parcel of the conceptualization of sovereignty. That is, sovereignty, regardless of its actual operations in all of their limitations, is conceptualized and thought of as that which exceeds and must always exceed (i.e., promises a pure, unalloyed, absolute, and indivisible power that is not subject to any specific political or social order) in order to exist, and this goes both before and beyond the state. This will be critical for understanding settler colonial sovereignty where the state is by no means the most relevant actor.

Keeping in view these differences in modality, this notion of excess suggests that across all three (political, social, individual, especially the second sense of the individual) there is a shared feature, which Derrida even calls an "essence" of sovereignty: the power to dictate ("that dictatorial agency"), to posit the sovereign as *the (self-)same, oneself*," and this can come in the form of the monarch, the individual, the state, and the people.[45] This is a Eurocentric way of positing the so-called essence of sovereignty, as other forms do not at all operate on a dictatorial agency and are indeed much more malleable and driven toward cooperation and *interdependence* as for example Niang argues is the case in some of the decentralized societies she examines, and as Indigenous studies has highlighted in different forms of Indigenous sovereignties.[46] I come back to these forms of sovereignty later in this book, but my interest is in settler colonial sovereignty at this stage, and that kind of sovereignty does operate, I agree with Derrida, on a dictatorial agency.

As I read Derrida, this concerns the dictation, the nonreciprocal assertion, of a sovereign self that speaks on behalf of, while simultaneously speaking as, a complete self, oneself that is unalloyed to other selves—"the thought of sovereignty and its majesty in the figure of present and self-present ipseity . . . the 'I.'"[47] As can be read in Derrida's quote in the epigraph, the sovereign self is where there is no end beyond the end of the claim to self: the *telos* of the self is not outside the self, but *telos* is the very realization of the self as selfsame. This particular positionality of the sovereign as "the Head, the Dictator" who sees all from a height up above marks the "sovereignty of the sovereign."[48] The higher the view, the more powerful the sovereign is; which does not necessarily have to do with the size and scale of the sovereign since this kind of height can be as much claimed on the most miniscule of levels (e.g., the individual) as it can be on the grandest (e.g., an international superpower).[49] For me, this association of sovereign power—"a potency, an 'I can,' is the maximum of potency, the greatest potency, an absolute power"—this kind of potency and height signifies the association of dictatorial assertion with an abstract view of the whole, upon which the sovereign looks down, asserts that the array of lives, actions, beliefs, identities, individual and group trajectories, the entire edifice of alterity and hybridity, as capturable by the sovereign.[50] This project of "*homogenizing heterogeneity*," which is integral to the construction of Euro-American modern states,[51] is an attempt to capture the milieu of heterogeneity and mold it into one selfsame substance in the name of the sovereign, as sovereign. Without this kind of power, and this occurs across the individual, social, and political levels, settler colonial sovereignty would lose any and all of the meanings that the word is *meant* to (not does) capture.

Third, and the first two points were building toward this, is the question of indivisibility. As Derrida teaches, this question is intimately connected with another figure that is excluded in the contract at the origin of sovereignty: God. While Bodin and Hobbes (and many theoretical traditions thereafter) "want to untie so-called modern state sovereignty, as established by convention or institution, from divine sovereignty," such efforts are not so simply realized and accomplished.[52] Without delving into Derrida's specific deconstructive maneuvers of certain passages in Bodin's and Hobbes's texts, Derrida argues that both thinkers attempt to exclude divine sovereignty, "a convention with God," from all human institutions of sovereignty and conventions.[53] What is interesting for Derrida is that God constitutes "the model of sovereignty," or, what is being excluded "is beyond the sovereign but as the sovereign's sovereign."[54] What Derrida's deconstruction shows (not just in this case but in many of his deconstructions) is that which is excluded is not simply cast out and left behind in the emergent theoretical structure, but is indeed the condition of possibility for the theoretical structure that excluded it.[55] That is precisely what takes place in both Hobbes and Bodin. For Derrida, neither thinker manages, despite their explicit efforts, to emancipate sovereignty from the divine, but instead their efforts at "anthropologization, modernization, this secularization . . . remains essentially attached by the skein of a double umbilical cord" to the divine.[56]

So now we are left with three figures: the sovereign, the beast, and God. Both the beast and God are excluded from the human convention but for two different reasons, both of which revolve around language: "The beast does not understand our language, and God cannot respond to us, that is, cannot *make known* to us" God's acceptance of/participation in the contract.[57] In neither case are we able to share speech and ensure that either beast or God will or will not accept our convention. There cannot be an exchange through language with either figure, and also there cannot be agreement, negotiation, compromise, response to the convention, responsibility to the convention, and so on. Derrida is critical of the assignation to these figures the inability to respond and the attribute of nonresponsibility, but more critical for my purposes is in Derrida's argument that indeed such attributes and abilities—the nonresponsiveness and nonresponsibilty—*are part and parcel of so-called secular and modern sovereignty*. It is worth quoting Derrida at length here:

> The sovereign does not respond, he is the one who does not have to. . . . He is above the law . . . and has the right . . . to suspend the law. . . . Like God, the sovereign is above the law and above humanity, above everything, and . . . he looks like the beast, and even like the death he carries within him. . . . If sovereignty were (but I don't believe it) proper to man, it would be so much *like* this expropriating ecstasy of irresponsibility, like this place of nonresponse that is commonly and dogmatically called bestiality, divinity, or death.[58]

The indivisibility of sovereignty may seem "mythic" to modern secular scholars perhaps because of its association with divinity and the beast, or with death (and Derrida does not believe it "proper to man" in the quote above). But the solution to this insight cannot be the attempt to complete the exclusion of the beast and God from the sovereign since this seems impossible. It is impossible because such contrasts (either between human and God, or between human and beast) are not real distinctions in the sense of establishing an abyss between two self-contained and isolated entities; but rather are mechanisms of exclusion that remain blind to the ways in which that which is excluded indeed becomes the condition of possibility of that which excludes. Hence, instead of an attempt to exclude the beast or the divine from scholarly theorizations of the sovereign, I follow the Derridean path of exploring the play between either/or binary oppositions.[59] If settler colonial sovereignty is posited as indivisible and absolute, immortal and transcendental, it is precisely because sovereignty is divisible and nonabsolute, mortal and historical (i.e., finite).[60] Derrida is here explicitly referencing the work of Hobbes, but I think this applies to entire theoretical traditions that seek to secularize the concept of sovereignty. The point, of course, is not that I oppose such secularization because I belong to the opposite side, that is, to the divination or theologizing of the political, but rather because the secular-theological distinction does not withstand deconstructive scrutiny. Much of Derrida's deconstructions seem to largely point out how the secular fails to transplant the theological, but it is equally important to recognize that the theological (in the sense of the Abrahamic) itself never transplanted the secularization of the political that preceded it.[61] In other words, I am not engaging here with the question of what came first, which is impossible to answer (once we expand the theological, as we should, beyond and before the Abrahamic).[62] I simply want to push aside having to take sides in this so-called opposition, and instead play with the possibilities that present themselves when we open up the analysis of settler colonial sovereignty to the divisible and indivisible, the mortal and the immortal (and so on) and move freely across these terms.

Important to emphasize, then, is that not against but *through* this claim of indivisibility is the divisible operation of sovereignty: that operation does not constitute the real sovereignty against the imagined indivisibility of sovereignty; it also does not constitute the historical sovereignty that we can observe and judge against an original, truer, and more revolutionary indivisible sovereignty.[63] Rather, the operation of a divisible sovereignty is only possible because of the claim of indivisibility (i.e., the aspirations of settler colonial sovereignty). The divisibility of the sovereign is the continuous effort to reach the aspirations and ideals of indivisibility, which it will never reach, *but without which all of its operations would be without potency*. Although humans cannot attain the status of God, the indivisible, absolute, and omnipresent power (e.g., the nonresponsiveness and nonresponsibility) attributed to God become the condition of possibility of the secular sovereign's claim in the modern territorial state.

In some respects, this Derridean understanding brings together both the Agambean (following Carl Schmitt) understanding of the sovereign as the one who declares the state of exception, and the more classic Hobbesian understanding of the sovereign as the one who constitutes life as such.[64] It draws from both in a way that makes it different from each. This understanding does not necessarily concern the production of *homo sacer*, nor the establishment of a secure and protected individual who can then pursue civilized activities in peace and security, which then constitute others outside of this so-called civilized life as unworthy, backward, and so on. It rather highlights the violent founding and maintenance of a unified and sovereign self, constituted as the proprietor of, not "civilized life" (which of course is also produced and does play an ideological role, the contents of which are ever-changing), but foundationally of land and people, at the foundation of the state. The sovereign self I am speaking about here does not gain its foundational structure from the ideological constructs which emerge one on top of the other as markers of the civilized self (i.e., the sedimented ideological architecture of the state), but rather the sovereign self is the very violent foundation upon which various ideologies of the racialized civilized self in opposition to the "savage" or "terrorist" then come to be built. It is this foundational structure that I want to zoom into, because without it, without the brute violence that builds and maintains it, its ideological contents would hold no power over life, death, and everything in between. In short, in the force of sovereignty, that is, in brute violence, we can observe the formation of the primal scene of settler colonial sovereignty, which is a structure where a racialized pure, superior, and absolute sovereign self (re)creates social, political, and legal orders and institutions. When I emphasize the force of the claim of indivisibility, and this brings together the Derridean elements, I am referring to *the manner in which the sovereign claim presupposes and seeks to constitute a sovereign self, unalloyed to any other, mustering fear and terror into the very constitution of the unalloyed self, constructing and maintaining the sovereign self at the foundation of the sovereign state (i.e., the sovereign "self" underpins and exceeds the state) in and through force.*

Needless to say, when I speak of the sovereign self at the foundation the state (as that which underpins and exceeds), I am not referring to the person of the monarch, but rather in the Derridean sense, of that to which the architecture of sovereignty has been transferred: the nation (and not only on the large scale of the entire nation, but on the level of the individual, communities, and so on). Theorizing this transfer of sovereignty, Derrida argues that sovereignty was not revolutionized but rather transferred in the French Revolution:

> The structure of this setup of knowing-power, power-to-know, knowing-how-to-see, and sovereign being-able-to-see is not, fundamentally, revolutionized by the French Revolution. It is not interrupted, and at the death of the king one can still say: "The King is dead, long live the King!" One has simply changed sovereigns. The sovereignty

of the people or of the nation merely inaugurates a new form of the same fundamental structure. The walls are destroyed, but the architectural model is not deconstructed—and will . . . continue to serve as a model and even as an international model.[65]

There is no doubt that important sociopolitical changes occurred in the movement from monarchist to popular sovereignty, which Derrida acknowledges when he labels these changes as constituting a "new form."[66] But I believe that one can make this point at the same time asserting that, on a fundamental level, the architecture of monarchical sovereignty remained untouched.[67] What we have here is basically a "transfer of sovereignty"—the "transfer, translation, transition, tradition, inheritance, economic distribution" of sovereignty that are undertaken within "a relation of force between drives to power that are essentially divisible."[68] In other words, within the territorially bounded nation-state, competing forces vie for the power and potency of being the sovereign who aspires toward indivisible, absolute, and omnipresent power.

One of the main reasons I draw on Derrida in this book is that the competition for this power of the sovereign, the position of the sovereign as maximum potency, is somewhat obscured as a transfer of the foundational architecture of sovereignty in international political theory as well as political and macrosociology. Working from the reified concept of the nation-state, these conventional conceptual paradigms have directed the analytical gaze to the distinction between "national" and "statist" sovereignty. Both types highlight territoriality and the legitimacy of the governing authority, but whereas state sovereignty "stresses the link between sovereign authority and a defined territory," national sovereignty "emphasizes a link between sovereign authority and a defined population."[69] Having said that, there is "a continuum from statist to national legitimation of sovereignty, and nation-states always show some characteristics of both."[70]

Without delving into how these two types engender different justifications and explanations of the international system of states (briefly, legitimation stems either from a nationalist "community of sentiment" or from a statist legal claim of ownership and possession),[71] the main point for my purposes is that territorially bounded sovereignty is always entangled with the management, control, and claim of and over *both* land and people. When these theories shift the terrain of the debate to the type of sovereign claim being made as one that *either* accentuates the land (statist) or the people (national), the underlying claim of indivisibility that forges land and people in a particular way (in and through lordship) is obscured. Instead of following such conventional paradigms, this book remains fixated on the forging of land and people as the mark of the settler colonial sovereign. Or, the settler colonial sovereign is sovereign precisely because the sovereign produces (or aspires to produce) out of the heterogeneity of life a selfsame substance.

It is important to explain here why I do not extensively engage with the literature on the nation-state in general: within a settler colonial context, the state is not as crucial as it may seem at first sight. In the words of Patrick Wolfe:

> Settler colonialism is an inclusive, land-centred project that coordinates a comprehensive range of agencies, from the metropolitan centre to the frontier encampment, with a view to eliminating Indigenous societies. Its operations are not dependent on the presence or absence of formal state institutions or functionaries. Accordingly . . . the occasions on or the extent to which settler colonialism conduces to genocide are not a matter of the presence or absence of the formal apparatus of the state.[72]

Wolfe explains that it is often the "lawless" actions of settlers on the frontiers that end up creating the bounded territories of the emergent settler colonial state; in other words, everywhere that the settlers expel, replace, and settle, the settler colonial state expands—and the settler colonial project is in many cases a "historical force that ultimately derives from the primal drive to expansion."[73] There is therefore a dynamic process that is operative between settlement and the state: at times, people who forcefully settle lands come to be seen as those who carry the mark of the settler sovereign, while at others "sovereign subjecthood" is granted to people so that they can come to "own rather than merely occupy" settled land.[74] Settlement operates both before and beyond the state, at the same time that the state enables and secures settlement.[75]

Nevertheless, it is important to engage with some discussion on the formation of the territorial state in order to deal with the debates that obscure the core of settler colonial sovereignty, which is lordship. Foremost among those is the suggestion, which builds on the distinction between statist and national sovereignty, that the problem of the settler colony is ethnic nationalism, correctable by a turn to civic nationalism. If we remain within this Eurocentric distinction, we cannot properly conceptualize and study the structure of expulsion that underpins settler colonial sovereignty. The emergence of the territorial state as an enclosed, bounded, homogenous space that is cartographically demarcated is not a universal form of rule or mode of political and social organization.[76] Rather, the territorial state emerged in its modern form within a complex of knowledge/power that spanned the fifteenth to the twentieth centuries not just in Western Europe as is conventionally posited, but indeed was coproduced across the metropole and the colony.[77] The modern sovereign territorial nation-state, in other words, is best traced through what Radhika Mongia calls "a colonial genealogy" as opposed to a diffusionist or mimetic framework that posits the emergence of the modern state in Western Europe and then examines the dispersal of that formation to other parts of the globe.[78] In the next section, I turn to decolonial theory to underline certain aspects of this emergence, allowing us to see the relationship between the nation-state and sovereignty without, to go back to Bartelson, macrosociology's adoption of the state as a foundational and reified unit of analysis.

SOVEREIGNTY AND THE MODERN NATION-STATE

Gurminder K. Bhambra argues that a postcolonial critique of modernity must, to put it simply, account for the experiences of the colonized. Modernity was not endogenously produced in Europe and then disseminated around the globe; rather, modernity was always (and continues to be) constituted across various connected histories and colonizing/colonized spaces—in short, "Modernity . . . has to be understood as formed in and through the colonial relationship."[79] To decenter Europe from social and political theory, Bhambra argues that scholars must pay attention to the manner in which all of the ideas and institutions that we associate with modernity (e.g., enlightenment, bureaucracy, modern nation-state) are a result of complex connected histories, and not the endogenous products of a hermetically sealed and autonomous civilization called the "West." Of central importance for my purposes is Bhambra's discussion on the emergence of the nation-state in this regard.

Conventional and still dominant historiography locates the creation, the "original" moment, of the modern nation-state in the French Revolution.[80] With the transfer of power and authority from the absolute monarch to the public, a major shift occurred that rendered the "public" an object that is knowable and actionable.[81] As the "public" arose in prominence legally and politically, so did the concept of nationalism in social and political theory, which attempted to account for this emergent popular sovereign—"The identification of the person of the sovereign with the state gave way to the state being identified with the people, who were then considered a nation."[82]

During the nineteenth century, we saw the emergence of two kinds of nationalisms that still guide our understanding of the nation-state today (from political sociology to international political theory to legal studies): a civic nationalism (where everyone under the authority of any given state administration can have full rights and duties), and an ethnic nationalism (where only a particular ethnos can enjoy full rights and duties). In civic nationalism's transcendence of parochial social categories of hierarchization, and its promise to deliver widespread autonomy and liberty, was placed great progressive hope for many social and political theorists during the Enlightenment. The French Revolution's emphasis on civic nationalism, the elimination of feudal laws, and the overthrow of absolutism thus made it a model for social and political theory. As Bhambra summarizes, "The shift from royal absolutism to popular sovereignty, together with the doctrine of national self-determination" made the French Revolution the "original" model of the modern nation-state, which social and political theory attested is to be (and ought to be) followed and replicated everywhere in order to advance the universal cause of equality, freedom, and autonomy.[83]

One of the major shortcomings of this Eurocentric approach can be seen in the theorization of civic vs. ethnic nationalisms. The conventional story goes something like this: Western Europe created the notion of a civic nationalism which provided freedom and autonomy to all regardless of religious and ethnic backgrounds; but when nationalism was exported outside of Western Europe, illiberal regimes and peoples (beginning with Eastern Europe and then the colonized world) introduced ethnic nationalism which severely restricted or rejected outright the rights of minorities. What this story misses, however, is the fact that multiple strands of anti-colonial struggles did indeed engage with questions around minority rights, majoritarianism, democracy, and popular sovereignty in complex ways (even if some of the more radical voices were marginalized in the postcolonial state);[84] but also and more directly for my purposes, as Bhambra points out, this ignores the ways in which the colonized and enslaved peoples were violently ejected from the civic nationalism of Western Europe. Indeed, it is only when we contextualize the rise of civic nationalism against the violent exclusion of racialized bodies in the colonies that we can properly understand how it was that something like civic nationalism emerged in these colonizing European countries.[85] The limits of civic nationalism in modern nation-states like Canada, for example, which often touts its multiculturalism policies as a model to be followed elsewhere, are especially evident when we view it from postcolonial, decolonial, and Indigenous perspectives.

In her important colonial genealogy of the modern nation-state, Mongia argues that scholars should historicize the emergence of state sovereignty vis-à-vis colonial and racialized migrations, as opposed to naturalizing its modern features, such as control over borders and migrations, as essential attributes of state sovereignty.[86] Her work shows how when the movement of Indian migrants to the plantation colonies introduced dilemmas and problems to be resolved, the empire-state's sovereignty was expanded through the construction of a massive bureaucracy, as an exceptional measure, in order to facilitate such movement. When nonindentured Indian migrants began to move to white settler colonies, we begin to observe the emergence of a nation-state that justified the state's monopoly over migration in order to limit the numbers of Indians in these polities. Since it was difficult to enforce such limitations in the explicit name of race (since Indians were "British subjects" and this afforded them universal rights, in theory), these restrictive regulations on Indian migration and Indian life in the settler colonies were carried out it in the name of "nation" and "nationality."[87]

What this shows is that the so-called liberal conception of the people did not only emerge with a dark side in its underbelly, which we can then suppress and prevent from reaching the level of murderous ethnic cleansing.[88] Rather, the very notion of nation is constituted, not just *through* the exclusion of racialized bodies, but also *because* of racialized bodies and the challenge they presented to polities that, on the one hand, proclaimed to hold universal and grandiose ideals such as equality, liberty, and freedom of and for all human beings, and on the other hand, did not actually welcome or want racialized bodies that were constituted as inferior and backward. Multiculturalism cannot then be relied upon to oppose and counter an ethnic nationalism especially in the settler colony because the two are joined at the hip; or more properly, because nationalism in the settler colony is ultimately a *settler colonial nationalism*. In the effort to curtail, restrict, and control the migration of racialized bodies, the modern nation-state developed as a formation that has a monopoly on the movement of people across territories through the very construct of "nationality," which "comes to signify a privileged relation between people and literal territory."[89] Viewed from this lens, we can begin to trace and examine how "'white-settler-colonies' become such, in part, through their concerted efforts to regulate (predominantly Asian) migration and to become white."[90] This process is not simply ongoing despite multicultural efforts to combat it; rather, it continues unabated, and insofar as multiculturalism also assumes the primacy of the master white ethnos, is not a framework or policy that is capable of combating ethnic nationalism. The "citizen/migrant distinction" continues to operate as the "primary distinction of . . . differentiation" in all modern nation-states, ensuring that the colonial dimension of the nation-state remains active at the very foundation of these social and political formations.[91]

The serious shortcomings of multiculturalism are further seen from an Indigenous perspective, where we can observe how the "politics of recognition" in Canada have simply continued the dispossession of Indigenous peoples.[92] Multiculturalism has and continues to operate in settler colonies in ways that conceal and therefore continue the genocidal violences of the state's emergence.[93] Liberal thought in the United States for example, whether of the Right (e.g., Michael Walzer) or the Left (e.g., Seymour Martin Lipset), emphasizes multiculturalism in a way that imagines American society as an "immigrant society" (i.e., open to social mobility, equality across race, religion, etc.) as opposed to its reality as a settler society (i.e., as fundamentally eliminatory of the natives).[94] In its ideas and practices, multiculturalism (among other things) seeks to pacify and co-opt Indigenous peoples, reducing them to often closed and narrow definitions of "culture" while continuing to deny Indigenous peoples substantive and substantial freedom, liberty, and indeed sovereignty.[95]

Importantly, Indigenous scholarship has shown that the civic/democratic/liberal conception of the "people" was built in the settler colony through the positing of an "alien" and "pure" Indigenous other. Only when the Indigenous was constituted through ideas of racial "purity"—of having "pure blood"—which completely ignored and attempted to erase the complex, diverse, and inclusive ways in which Indigenous peoples understood belonging, sovereignty, and nationhood; only then, did the settler claim a civic conception of the "people."[96] In other words, the very condition of possibility of a liberal civic nationalism "inside" the democratic state is the constitution of an "outside" in the political being of the Indigenous "other" as ethnic nationalism—in violently excluding the Indigenous "other," the "inside" of the democratic state postulates the "outside" of the state as a stand-in for barbarism, savagery, and backwardness.

Contra Eurocentric theories which outrightly separate and protect the inside (the metropole) from the outside (the colony) where the latter is seen as without relation to the former, where "empire . . . is not deemed to be significant for understanding the history or contemporary society of the nation state," postcolonial, decolonial, and Indigenous theory show that without the outside (the colony), the inside (the metropole) could not have attained and built the *nomos* surrounding civic nationalism.[97] Instead of separating civic from ethnic nationalism, and then assigning the enlightened former to the "West" and the backward latter to the "East," these theories challenge the distinction itself as an absolute or real distinction, instead highlighting how Europe could only become "liberal," "tolerant," "free," by projecting its own colonial violences onto the racialized other who became "violent," "despotic," "intolerant," and the rest.[98]

Following decolonial theory, this book does not follow the conventional story told and accepted in social and political theory, which insists that any discussion of the state and sovereignty must begin with (or at the very least, foundationally engage with) a sealed European "origin" (Westphalia, French Revolution, etc.). The story is neither purely European, nor is it the province of only European thinkers.[99] Moreover, this book does not accept the rather simple separation between civic and ethnic nationalisms as two sperate species of nationalism. As I will argue specifically in the case of Palestine-Israel in chapter 3, the problem of settler colonial sovereignty is not simply a problem of ethnonationalism, correctable by a turn toward civic nationalism as is often argued in liberal and even some critical scholarship and politics. Rather, the two kinds of nationalism are interconnected *across a continuum of violence.* The separation of civic and ethnic nationalisms cannot serve as an explanatory paradigm for violence because it is indeed a part of a continuum that is grounded in the violence of settler colonial sovereignty. To understand settler colonial sovereignty, we must remain fixated on the force of the claim of indivisibility, the structure of violence that renders it possible, and without which it can never become "real."

CONCLUSION

To understand lordship—the fusion of land and people as the self-same substance—we must examine its operation as a posture of violence in the space of interlocking that is settler colonialism. As Bhambra's analytic of connected histories or sociologies convincingly argues, the traversal across the spaces of colonizer and colonized does not ignore or brush aside the European.[100] It does not supplant them and places them on the bottom of a new hierarchical order; it simply decenters, deprioritizes, and de-universalizes Europe where it no longer serves as the standard model or ideal against which all other cultures, peoples, histories, epistemologies, and ontologies are then judged, incorporated, and/or subsumed. Following in the footsteps of Edward Said's contrapuntal approach, she is "arguing for recognition of intertwined histories and overlapping territories as a more adequate basis for the development of our conceptual categories than purified national histories."[101] In a decolonial critique, it is integral to *not concede* certain concepts and conceptualizations, ideas and material conditions, institutions and practices to a European "origin." Here, we must drop the idea that the oppressed must never use the "master's tools." Certainly, this type of critique is still valid and necessary against approaches that posit the substance of the law, for example, as neutral, designed and structured to primarily check and balance status quo power structures. This critique of such naïve approaches notwithstanding, I think that we must drop this critique not only because decolonial thought can engage with/utilize these tools and transcend the master's house in building their own new and decolonial houses (i.e., not simply become a part of the colonial house), but because these tools were never the master's "own" to begin with.[102] To argue, for example, that the colonized utilize "European" terms and concepts such as "civic nationalism" or the "state" or "sovereignty" in order to battle/resist European (neo)colonial power is itself a Eurocentric statement since it assumes that all such conceptions and ideas are originally and endogenously "European" in the "first" place.[103] In far too many cases, the "European" is allotted capabilities and powers that are ahistorical and factually incorrect.

For my purposes, then, it is important to recognize that the story of Palestine-Israel has European dimensions and thus an engagement with ideas, concepts, theories, institutions, which have taken shape in specific ways (not originated) in that part of the world cannot and should not be avoided. But in order to avoid the centralization of Europe, I do not draw on established schools of thought regarding the nation-state (e.g., from political sociology, international political theory) where there is an entrenchment of the dominant historiographical tradition of centralizing and sealing Europe from the "rest."[104] I do not draw on reified concepts of the territorial state and Westphalian state sovereignty in the next chapter. Instead, I examine the work of a particular European thinker—Norbert Elias—who I think reveals significant dynamics regarding the nation-state and sovereignty, allowing the discussion to delve into the substantive dynamics of the state and sovereignty without (despite Elias's own line of thinking) ossifying those dynamics within sealed Eurocentric concepts and conceptual frameworks that obfuscate settler colonial sovereignty.

2

LORDSHIP AS VIOLENCE IN THE SETTLER COLONY

The often-quoted dictum: "No land without a lord," is not only a basic legal principle. It is also a social watchword of the warrior class.
—Norbert Elias, *The Civilizing Process*

This chapter zeroes in on the structure of expulsion that is the key marker of settler colonial sovereignty. The first section elucidates the fusion of land and people as lordship. By critically (re)interpreting Norbert Elias's work, I show how lordship can be theorized, not as a specific legal doctrine or political institution or socioeconomic system, but primarily as an underlying posture of violence that engenders various systems and institutions in the era of colonial modernity. Specifically in the settler colony, lordship becomes about a never-ending structure of expulsion that aims to produce an unalloyed sovereign self that rests on the continuous distinction from and elimination of Indigenous peoples and Indigenous modes of sovereignty.

The second section conceptualizes the posture of lordship in the four-dimensional operation of violence in the settler colony. In the first subsection, I follow Indigenous theory and decolonial theory in the idea that the backbone of the settler colony is not capitalist political economy, but rather a structure of expulsion that is situated on an Indigenous-settler distinction. As decolonial and Indigenous theory teach, this structure of expulsion means that Eurocentric paradigms that prioritize the rise and spread of capitalism in our understanding of settler colonialism are inadequate to theorizing the settler colony. Building on that work, I explain in the second subsection a logic of sovereign abandonment that animates and orients this structure of expulsion wherein settler colonial violence aims to eliminate and replace the Indigenous.

The third section specifies that this can be observed in the three observable dimensions of the violence of expulsion: instrumental (fragmentation), linguistic (isolation), and mimetic (dehumanization). Concluding this chapter, I bring together all of the book's arguments thus far to clarify the conceptual order (see figure 0.1 in the introduction) through which an analysis of settler colonial violence can commence.

THE FUSION OF LAND AND PEOPLE AS LORDSHIP

Some of the discussion in this section appears in the works of many prominent sociologists who have added to Elias's work and focused more than he did on the emergence of the nation-state as their object of study.[1] The main reason I draw on Elias's classic work, *The Civilizing Process*, is that it offers a historical sociology framework that unlike many other canonical works emphasizes underlying dynamics of the state as opposed to a reliance on reified concepts of the "state" (whether framed as national, nonnational, and/or territorial), "private property," "capitalism," "feudalism," and so on. Thus, an analysis of his work is more useful in delineating the underlying structure of settler colonial sovereignty, which is often lost when we center a reified concept of the modern nation-state. Instead of the common referral to John Locke, Hugo Grotius, and other political and legal theorists of the modern colonial era as foundational to the project of settler colonialism, an exploration of Elias through a decolonial lens opens the door for an analytical emphasis on mechanisms and dynamics that supersede specific thinkers, legal doctrines, and separated historical "Ages." Much of the material from Elias will be too familiar to historical and political sociologists and unfamiliar to others, so I will try to be both brief and thorough enough to elucidate the structure that I am after. I will start with his discussion on the Crusades.

Elias explains the colonial project of the Crusades through political-economic pressures that revolved around land ownership. The pressures concerning land that were heightening within Western European regions (particularly the western Frankish regions) in the eleventh century served as the "sociogenesis" of the Crusades.[2] Land was the primary means of wealth, production, and social standing during the Middle Ages. Without land, a person could not become a lord, and as the dictum in the epigraph expresses, without a lord, a piece of land is deemed unproductive, barren, and wild. This meant that land was deforested, cultivated, and made productive to a great extent during the eleventh and twelfth centuries. As the "internal colonization" of new land reached a point of saturation, the "external conquest of new territory" began to expand.[3]

This expansion was not preplanned—"At the outset we have the population pressure and the blocked opportunities at home, the emigration of individuals whose success attracts others; at the end we have an empire."[4] The Church, for Elias, played an important role to be sure, but that role was one of directing "this pre-existing force" that placed an immense social pressure on individuals to acquire distant lands.[5] The individuals affected came from all strata of society as many peasants, serfs, and bondsmen partook in the colonization projects, but for Elias, the "main impulse came from the knights' shortage of land" which would be "conquered by the sword."[6] The upper classes drove the appropriation and acquisition of new lands, as the "younger sons" of the upper classes sought to maintain their standard of living by acquiring their own land, and as rich and powerful landowners sought to expand their wealth and power (driven by a fear of decline) by acquiring and appropriating more lands.[7] Elias maintains that the drive toward the accumulation of more property (the "acquisitive urge") is not peculiar to capitalism, but as is shown in the case of the feudal Middle Ages, this urge was very much present in the expansion of *land* ownership (as opposed to accumulation and ownership of *capital* that underpins capitalism)—what Jane Burbank and Frederick Cooper refer to as a "politics of lordship" which by the time of Charlemagne and into the Carolingian Empire "had become entrenched in the nearly four hundred years since the coming apart of the Roman empire."[8]

This economic urge for more land—this politics of lordship—was interconnected with the question of sovereignty: "Military action and political and economic striving were largely identical, and the urge to increase wealth in the form of land came to the same thing as extending territorial sovereignty and increasing military power."[9] Drawing on examples from the Norman conquest of England, Elias argues that if a lord remained content with the land they owned and claimed sovereignty over, then that lord faced the serious risk of being swallowed up by the ever-expanding territorial rulers. The more land owned, the greater the military and political power of the territorial ruler, the greater the risk it is for the smaller territorial rulers, thus the greater is the drive for them to obtain more lands, and so on.[10]

In Elias's model of development, this dynamic of land acquisition and ownership laid the groundwork for the emergent feudal system. As the prospects of land acquisition began to close and the system began to gain a certain rigidity, there emerged a particular form of social organization that divided the landowner from those who dwelled on the land: this was a mode of organization that created a stark separation between the ruler and the ruled (which I argue is also a marquee feature of colonial and postcolonial power as seen in the separation of the political (ruler) and the social (ruled)).[11] The landowner was vested with title over the land and thus possessed all of the military and political powers that came along with it. But the lords of these vast lands required others to service the lands in order to make them productive. This gives rise to a group of people who effectively controlled the land, which they did not own. This can be seen in Elias's discussion of the alliance between the "liege lords" (who possessed large areas of land) and their "vassals" (weaker partners who possessed smaller pieces of land). The vassals performed services for the liege lords as they themselves would receive services from those below them in the social hierarchy.[12] In the process of feudalization, the vassals slowly gained the upper hand over the liege lords since they were the ones who really controlled the land, especially as they needed the protection of liege lords less and less. This leads Elias to assert (and this is a perfect example of how he highlights specific dynamics and processes over and above reified concepts): "The disintegration of property, the passing of land from the control of the king to the various gradations of the warrior society as a whole . . . this and nothing else is 'feudalization.'"[13] This process of disintegration contained also within it a countermovement of centralization. For Elias, centralization and centrifugal forces were always in contention with one another. This particular countermovement—what historians call the "Age of Absolutism"—carried with it the sociogenesis of the state, centered on, from at least the Middle Ages, the acquisition and territorial sovereignty over land—in short, lordship over land.[14]

Without delving into the specific details of how the sociogenesis of the state occurred in France, England, and Germany, the general mechanism of centralization boils down for Elias to monopolization of land, violence, and taxation.[15] As smaller territorial rulers fought to gain more land in order to ensure their survival, a mechanism of monopolization of land took hold: "elimination contests" took place through many battles that reduced the field of contestation to fewer and fewer lords until one absolute territorial ruler emerged as the victor.[16] This was not a straightforward process, and it contained many detours pulling toward decentralization at certain points, and centralization at others, but the point for my purposes here is that the move toward a centralized absolute monopoly does eventually emerge and with it the formation of modern states.[17] As the victor emerges and monopolizes violence (forbidding opponents from the violent means to challenge and overthrow the victor), the pacification, "suppression and control of violence over large areas" takes place.[18] A "state" is formed, not from the intentions of particular individuals and meticulously formulated plans, but from this mechanism of monopolization.

Monopoly rule was centered on taxation and the use of physical violence, but this particular move toward centralization was unlike any seen before because it was taking place within increasingly differentiated societies in which complex divisions of labor and functions were emerging (among other things, Elias is referring to the emergence of the money economy and the rise of the bourgeoisie). Elias captures the transformation into the modern state as such:

> The land-owning king distributing land or tithes had become a money-owning king distributing salaries: this gave centralization a power and solidity unattained hitherto. The strength of the centrifugal forces had been finally broken. . . . But even if at this stage the king's personal control of the monopolized opportunities were great, it was anything but unlimited. In the structure of this relatively private monopoly there were already unmistakable elements which would finally lead from personal control of the monopolies to public control by ever-broader sections of society.[19]

The rise of the bourgeoisie and their ability to defeat the nobility and other elements within society would introduce that public takeover of these monopolies, end the "Age of Absolutism," and give rise to the modern state.[20] What kept the absolute monarch in power, for Elias, was the inability of the groups beneath the monarch (namely, the nobility and the bourgeoisie) to either reach a compromise with one another or for one of the groups to emerge as victorious over the other; in short, the constant antagonism between the different groups that did not yield a victor (a sort of Arendtian or Mouffeian "agonism") ensured the monarch's power and control over the centralized system of power and rule.[21] Through a series of complex dynamics, structures, events, and actions, the bourgeoisie began to overcome the nobility and to slowly chip away at the monarch's hold over power until it finally seized the "central function" (monopoly over taxation and violence) in the name of the public.[22] In this transition, these monopolies remained intact and the struggle moved from destroying one monopoly to create another (i.e., one house destroying the ruling house to create a new monopoly over land, taxation, and violence) to a struggle over the existing centralized monopolies where greater numbers of people (associations of different groups) strive to shape and mold the "distribution of their [i.e., the monopolies of taxation and violence] burdens and benefits."[23] As they become an indispensable function that are fought over through nonviolent means (i.e., the emergence of "democratic regimes" which determine how the central authority will distribute burdens and benefits), theses monopolies define the modern state: "It is only with the emergence of this continuing monopoly of the central authority and this specialized apparatus for ruling that dominions take on the character of 'states.'"[24] Without these two monopolies, without a lord that is absolute and supreme in their violence and hold on resources much like we saw in the politics of lordship, there is no order that we call the "state."

From this discussion on Elias and some of the ideas I highlight below which are also found in other analyses of lordship such as the classic work of Otto Brunner,[25] I want to emphasize the following two points: (1) lordship is not simply a legal doctrine that belongs to the "feudal age," antecedent to modernity and simply confined to a premodern era; rather, it is a posture of violence that runs through different "ages," shifting and reshaping but always transforming around a constant core in which land and people are welded together in such a way where land can only be deemed of value, worth, and as *an object of belonging* (as something that people can lay a claim of belonging and attachment) when it is under a supreme (even if in practice transient) lordship; (2) lordship *over* land is necessarily a lordship over the people who dwell on the land, where the posture of lordship necessarily engenders the violence of holding the people who dwell on the land under the suzerainty of the lord (as protection, imposition, punishment, and so on). The lord thus can only become a lord when the lord claims supreme sovereignty over land/people. Moreover, I want to ask: What happens when we reconsider these dynamics through the co-constitutive role of the colony and when we do not analytically delimit violence as decreasing through the "civilizing process," as does Elias? Both of these interventions, I believe, will add an important reorientation to the study of settler colonial sovereignty.

For Elias, the question of land is relegated to the notion of dominion as the money economy develops, beginning with the transformation of the "land-owning king" into a "money-owning king." What this does not take properly into account is the colonial acquisition of land that allowed the king to own the vast amounts of money in the first place; or put differently, the ways in which the colonial and especially settler colonial forceful and brutal acquisition of Indigenous lands enabled and facilitated the transition to agrarian and market capitalism as well as land reforms in the metropole.[26] In other words, far from *relegating* lordship into historical antecedents to the monopoly of taxation and violence, the modern state *displaces* the same dictum of lordship onto distant lands (albeit in varied and complex legal ways), generating the wealth required—in addition to the wealth generated in the slave trade and slavery—for the emergence of the modern capitalist economy, and therefore all of the massive transformations that Elias outlines under the heading of the "civilizing process."[27] This relationship between the colonial generation of wealth and the "civilizing process" is indeed clear to Elias himself when he attests, without "a relatively high standard of living and a fairly high degree of security" the civilizing process would be impossible: "classes living permanently in danger of starving to death or of being killed can hardly develop or maintain those stable restraints characteristic of the more civilized types of conduct."[28]

The interpretive path I want to highlight here is that without this enormous wealth that was distributed (albeit unevenly and inequitably) across the social groups in European societies as well as the displacement of the social and political tensions from colonizing to colonized territories and peoples, the state and its central function would not have held.[29] Both the rise of industrial capitalism, land reforms and regimes of property ownership, and the rise of the nation-state in European colonizing countries, simply put, cannot be understood without properly and equally accounting for what occurred in the colonies in terms of the back-and-forth traveling of ideas, cultures, peoples, and modes of knowing, being, doing, thinking; in terms of dynamic translocal processes that shaped and molded changes and transformations across vast geographical regions; and in terms of the transfer of great wealth from the colonies to the colonial empires.

As Eqbal Ahmad succinctly puts it from a postcolonial perspective:

> As colonizing entities, these [colonial] European states were the instruments of corporate expansion abroad—a process which served the

double purpose not only of exploiting the colonized but also of exporting to the colonies the social and political tensions produced by the shift from feudalism to capitalism. The ability to export the tensions associated with social change made possible the growth of liberal democracies involving a subtle and complex balance between institutions of coercion and consensus.[30]

For Ahmad, the emergence of a national bourgeoisie independent of the "state sector" (or the class of the state bourgeoisie) is necessary for the development of democratic regimes and systems of power. Furthermore, the colonial states were able to accomplish the balance of coercion-consensus necessary for democracy precisely because they could release their social tensions onto the colony—a dynamic of export that Elias points out as well in his framing of the Crusades as an endeavor that was driven by internal social conflicts. Ahmad was of course interested in how the modern state in the postcolonized world continues to operate on the basic foundations of the colonial state where institutions of coercion overpowered (and continue to overpower) shaky and under/de-developed institutions of consensus and participation.[31]

I need not enter the complex and highly contested terrain of comparative work on the question of coercion-consensus (although this debate is connected to my arguments regarding the social-political relationship which will be further explored later in this book). Instead, I want to further develop another point: that in those distant places that were colonized, whether the Americas, Africa, the Caribbean, Asia, or the Middle East, the fusion of land and people as lordship took hold—not as a simple replication of the European feudal system, but as the underpinning mechanism of colonialism and settler colonialism, where this fusion developed its own unique character.

In settler colonies especially, the expulsion of peoples from their lands is the crucial feature (and we should add "possession" of oceans and seas as well).[32] As Patrick Wolfe states, "The primary motive for elimination [of the native] is not race (or religion, ethnicity, grade of civilization, etc.) but access to territory. Territoriality is settler colonialism's specific, irreducible element."[33] The drive toward endless market expansion, the internal conflicts and labor contradictions within European societies, and the seismic shifts and movements of populations with the emergence of the European nation-state (among other factors) drove large numbers of people toward the colonial settlement of distant lands, all at the expense of Indigenous peoples.[34] Regardless of whether Indigenous peoples were in fact nomadic, settled, or a mixture of both, and regardless of the different forms of Indigenous land ownership that were operative in those societies, racial settler colonial ideology represented all of them and their lands as uncivilized, rootless, undeveloped, and unproductive. For all intents and purposes the land was for the settler colonists, "*terra nullius*," which, as Carole Pateman argues, designated two senses: "first, they claimed that the lands were uncultivated wilderness . . . second, they argued that the inhabitants had no recognizable form of sovereign government."[35] Only in the first sense is this settler colonial view of the land similar to the "internal colonization" of land that took place within Europe as discussed earlier through Elias. The second sense is where there is a vast difference between the experiences of the Indigenous peoples of the "New World" and the peasantry of the "Old World"—so vast a difference that it renders the term "internal colonialism," as Wolfe puts it, "a pious oxymoron" since colonizers always "come from elsewhere" to replace Indigenous inhabitants; otherwise we risk diluting and obscuring the uniqueness of Indigenous dispossession and the invasion of Indigenous lands.[36] It is important to note here that although it is also the case, such as

Palestine-Israel, where some Indigenous people—Palestinian Jews—are interpolated into the settler colonial project and turned into settlers,[37] the very impetus of the project—what turns a minority of the Indigenous people into settlers—comes from elsewhere (Ashkenazi European Jews).

Significantly, the doctrine of *terra nullius* provided the legal justification and political legitimation for the settlers to uproot and dispossess Indigenous peoples across the globe.[38] Because Indigenous peoples displayed and *maintained a particular kind of sovereign claim on the land*, they had to be removed regardless of their potential productivity or contribution to the political economy of the settler colonial or the colonial state.[39] In other words, the question of sovereignty reigns supreme in the settler colony and any challenge to the sovereignty of the settler colonists by claims to and of Indigenous sovereignty is not permissible.[40] The enactment of settler sovereignty always occurs with the destruction of an Indigenous sovereignty in the settler colonial context—settler colonial sovereignty is always inherently a "replacement."[41] If the rights of Indigenous peoples are acknowledged at all, then they are to be framed within the unalterable sovereignty of the settler colonial state: "Inside the territory of a modern state there can be only one sovereign power."[42] The idea of an Indigenous sovereignty questions the very legitimacy and foundation of the settler colonial state and hence cannot be tolerated. Settler colonial sovereignty therefore attacks "with a death drive to eliminate, contain, hide and in other ways 'disappear' what fundamentally challenges its legitimacy: Indigenous political orders."[43]

Without a continuous emphasis on "territoriality, the fusion of people and land," without at the same time reducing the entire project of settler colonialism to the nation-state and the philosophico-political doctrine of private property, then settler colonial sovereignty will evade the scholarly purview.[44] Certainly, the nation-state, private property, and settler colonialism are all connected, but my point is that settler colonial sovereignty cannot be reduced to these concepts. This is why I engage with Elias and conceptualize territoriality and the state in the specific direction of the land/people fusion as lordship: I argue that the posture of lordship, not private property, capitalism, or the modern state, underlies settler colonial sovereignty.

In its "feudal" form in Western Europe, this fusion is marked by the economic and political pressures on lords to own more land and claim their supreme and absolute sovereignty over as much land as possible in order to survive: this is a form of lordship, in the sense of absolute and supreme authority, that we later see in the "Age of Absolutism" and the "modern state"—what Jacques Derrida calls a transference of absolutist indivisible sovereignty. Beyond and beneath socioeconomic and sociopolitical specificities, I want to highlight a dynamic whereby lordship over land becomes synonymous with the survival of the lord *as* lord. As these pressures engendered the ebb and flow of centralization and decentralization, we saw the emergence of the state in the move toward centralization, where the emergence of the state was centered on this posture of lordship on a grand scale. Just like the politics of lordship preceding it, this expansion was a matter of survival: without the lordship over as much land as possible, the state could not survive *as* a state. The state, in other words, is perhaps merely one configuration of the posture of lordship—a case of transference of lordship from one form to another. I cannot make this claim conclusively since it is beyond the scope of this book. I believe that different scholars will have to study this posture of lordship in other contexts and test its suitability and veracity as a conceptual tool. But this should not hamper this particular study. Instead of a genealogical tracing of lordship as a knowable legal doctrine, political-economic, sociopolitical, and socioeconomic system, across its transferences, I focus in this book on lordship as violence, and follow a theoretical-interpretive path of lordship as a posture of incommensurability in the fourth dimension of violence, which is unknowable in the sense of a fixed entity with essential and identifiable elements and attributes, all in an effort to understand specifically settler colonial sovereignty in Palestine-Israel.

In its settler colonial form, the land/people fusion as lordship is marked by a structure of expulsion that seeks to destroy, definitively and absolutely, alternative configurations of a people/land relationship, and institute a lordship configuration of people/land. This deconstruction/construction is construed as a matter of survival: only in the acquisition of land in the manner of lordship, can the settler colonial state exist *as* a state. Lordship over land becomes, not just a matter of owning an object (which can then be sold, exchanged, kept, and so on), but more importantly the very sign of the existence of the lord as lord, the settler state as state; in short, of the sovereign as sovereign, as possessing no equal or even a challenger.

This is what Audra Simpson refers to as settler colonial sovereignty's death drive: the sovereign cannot tolerate the idea or even the prospect of an alternative mode of sovereignty. This is a force that is deeper than the positing of land as property: *it is the force* that gives certain actors the very claim and ability to own a specific land as property in the first place. I agree with Wolfe that "the settler/Native confrontation . . . is not between claims to ownership but between frameworks for allocating ownerships. It is between sovereignties, which are primordially external to one another."[45] My contribution to what Wolfe has argued is that I am theorizing the force, the brute violence, behind the sovereign claim itself in its four-dimensional operation, and not this force just as the violences (physical eliminations, assimilation policies, etc.) of one sovereignty against another.[46] Wolfe argues that this force is the "simple relationships of inequality" and power that operate beneath complex (and supposedly, in certain cases, more "effective" at elimination) political, legal, and socioeconomic structures (guided by the logics of racialization).[47] In contrast, I argue that this force, this brute violence, is itself quite complex when we begin to consider its four-dimensional operation. In short, settler colonial sovereignty does not claim: "subjects can purchase, own, keep, exchange, sell properties in accordance to our laws because we fundamentally *own* the land"; it rather claims: "subjects can purchase, own, keep, exchange, sell properties in accordance to our laws because we fundamentally *have established lordship* over the land." This is close to what Wolfe also argues, but my interest is specifically in the very force that allows for such a claim to establish and render as "real" (constituted and enforceable) a specific kind of order in the first place. This is the shift in analytical emphasis that I am seeking to explore.

Henceforth, the posture of lordship speaks, not to a particular legal doctrine, political order, or socioeconomic system whose genealogy we may trace in order to understand the legal machinations through which Indigenous peoples are dispossessed; rather, it reveals the violent machinations through which Indigenous peoples are robbed of their sovereign claim. Instead of a genealogy of law, politics, and society, it shifts our attention to the brute violences that establish and maintain settler colonial sovereignty and directs our analytical gaze toward the raw force which gives legal and political machinations, regardless of their specificities, the power of knowing and doing. Lordship over land is a particular way of conceptualizing land as an object which can only attain significance and meaning when it is lorded over; and it is only in lording over land—constituting a specific area of land as an object under lordship—that a lord can gain meaning and significance. Without the fusion of people/land as lordship, neither lord nor land/people can attain (within the world of settler colonial sovereignty) substance in their meaning, neither enters history. This is what this posture's fundamental conceptions of the human, space, and time asserts and attempts to constitute as "real," and upon which massive social, political, cultural, and economic structures have been constructed. Furthermore, as indicated in the epigraph, the posture of lordship is also intimately connected with a warrior class. I am less interested in this group as a specific historical class and more concerned with the idea that lordship is the purview of those for whom war and warfare is an integral part of their being.[48] The fusion is wedded to warriors, to war, to the forceful taking of land, making land one's exclusive domain through force, maintaining the domination and lordship of and over the land by force, ensuring the submission of people by force, protecting the people with force, and so on.[49] Succinctly put, we cannot theorize the fusion without understanding the violence that establishes, secures, sustains, and expands it as a fusion—not in the Eliasian sense of how violence became monopolized or in Brunner's sense of delineating the complex medieval legal, social, and political structures of governance within which violence appears, but in the sense that violence forges the elements of land and people as a particular kind of fusion. Such forging unfolds in the four-dimensional operation of violence that (contra Elias, Brunner, and others) moves far beyond the instrumental logics of the state as well as non-state actors who continuously fight to seize the monopoly of violence. In the next section, then, I will explain how scholars can conceptualize the posture of lordship in the complex four-dimensional operation of violence in the settler colony.

THE STRUCTURE OF EXPULSION IN THE SETTLER COLONY

Settler Colonial Domination as Expulsion

Going back to the earlier discussion on the colonial acquisition of land—it is tempting for many scholars, especially in the tradition of Marxist political economy, to assert that the structure of expulsion in the settler colony is similar to the one experienced by the

European peasantry as Europe transitioned from feudalism to capitalism—a process that Karl Marx refers to as "primitive accumulation." This argument suggests that what people outside of Europe experienced through settler colonialism is essentially the transition to capitalism, and therefore their experiences should be understood mainly through the framework of Marxist political economy. Postcolonial theory and studies have, since at least the work of Gayatri Spivak and Subaltern Studies in the 1980s, long critiqued and deconstructed this analytical viewpoint.[50] In more recent scholarship in Indigenous theory, Glen Coulthard has convincingly established the uniqueness of settler colonialism in regard to the question of Marxist political economy. Coulthard defines the settler colonial relationship as "one characterized by a particular form of *domination*; . . . where power . . . has been structured into a relatively secure or sedimented set of hierarchical social relations that continue to facilitate the *dispossession* of Indigenous peoples of their lands and self-determining authority."[51] Coulthard finds Marx's concept of "primitive accumulation" both useful and limited in shedding light on the settler colonial relationship, particularly in terms of how noncapitalist forms of life were eliminated and replaced with capitalist structures.

There are two main elements in Marx's concept: dispossession and proletarianization—capitalism "forcefully opened up what were once collectively held territories and resources to privatization . . . which, over time, came to produce a 'class' of workers compelled to enter the exploitative realm of the labor market for their survival."[52] While in the European context, proletarianization takes precedence over dispossession in the transition to capitalism, in the settler colonial context, it is dispossession that takes precedence over proletarianization— this was also true in Palestine.[53] This shift of emphasis is crucial as it reveals four insights that would be otherwise missed if we simply applied Marxist political economy and the European model of capitalist relations to the settler colony.

First, this shift does not normalize the colonial dispossession through "evolutionary" development models, which claim that such transitions, while violent and painful, are necessary in the advancement of human civilization and progress. A critical shortcoming of such models is that they conceal the alternative modes of social organization and social/political life that the colonized have to offer.[54] Second, Coulthard illustrates how "the history and experience of *dispossession*, not proletarianization, has been the dominant background structure shaping the character of the historical relationship between Indigenous peoples and the Canadian state."[55] Dispossession in this case is not an event that occurred at the origin of capitalist expansion, and is now replaced by other forms of labor exploitation; rather, it is an ongoing process and structure and much of the anti-colonial resistance is engaged, in one way or another, with the question of land and dispossession.[56] The third and fourth insights deal with the broadening of our critical perspective where we avoid an instrumental understanding of nature, and where we steer clear from economic reductionism.[57]

It is critical to underscore that much like the state, capitalist relations are not simply developed endogenously within Europe and then exported to the settler colony or the colony, but rather they are formed in and through colonial, settler colonial, and imperial relations.[58] Capital-labor relations are not the foundational dynamics that are then exported through colonialism and settler colonialism, but are indeed themselves the product of interconnected histories and are rooted in the dispossession of Indigenous peoples and the extraction of their resources, as well as the commodification of those lands, resources, and indeed of people. Thus, there is a dynamic that deserves our more immediate attention since it forms the backbone of the settler colony: a structure of expulsion that is situated on an Indigenous-settler distinction.[59] As is made clear in Coulthard's work, this structure of expulsion not only means that Eurocentric understandings of the transition to capitalism are inadequate to theorizing the settler colony, but also it differentiates settler colonialism from colonialism.

Although there are some important similarities and overlapping features between them, settler colonialism operates on a structure of expulsion that is different from exploitative structures that are operative in colonialism. Settlers move to a land with the intent of remaining there creating an entity that is separate and independent from the colonizing metropole, whereas colonialism remains tied to the metropole to which "colonial sojourners—administrators, missionaries, military personnel, entrepreneurs, and adventurers—return."[60] Settler colonialism does not seek to exploit the labor of Indigenous peoples as do colonial projects, but to dispossess and replace them through varied means and modes of transfer.[61] Such transfers constitute the very structure of settler colonialism and they are always ongoing barring a complete genocide or removal of Indigenous populations. As Wolfe has shown, the logic of elimination (the European invasion of Indigenous societies) is a structure and not an event in the settler colony, what he later calls "structural genocide."[62]

Underpinning this structure of seizing the land that is (to be) emptied of Indigenous peoples is a mode of settler colonial sovereignty. Drawing on varied examples from different settler colonies (namely, the United States, Canada, Israel, and Australia), Lorenzo Veracini summarizes the latter as such:

> The sovereignty claimed by settler collectives does not focus on the state and insists on the law-making corporate capacity of the local community, on its self-constituting ability, on its competence to control the local population economy, and on a subordination to the colonizing metropole that is premised on a conditional type of loyalty.[63]

For Veracini, "settlers see themselves as founders of political orders," who possess "an inherent sovereign claim that travels with them" from the metropole, but which is "ultimately, if not immediately, autonomous from the colonizing metropole."[64] Veracini asserts that "settler sovereignty" is not primarily concerned with the establishment of state institutions, but rather concerns, foundationally speaking, the establishment of "self-government and suzerainty."[65] Akin to Derrida's discussion on individual sovereignty and the isolated person in particular, settlers tend to view their ability to reinvent their sovereignty wherever they move as a matter of life and death, and thus their sovereign acts are always engulfed in a politics of life and death, are always engulfed in violence—in ruling violently, in coming to existence and living through violence, even as violence.[66]

There is often an element of excess in the actions, beliefs, practices, and projects of the settler sovereigns—they carry sovereignty with them, but not as carriers of another sovereignty that represents them or that they are representative of (e.g., of the settler state), or as carriers of the sovereignty of another (e.g., the monarch), but as themselves constituting the sovereignty of the settler state in a direct expression of its will. They reinvent the state, most often against the interests of the imperial state (the metropole), but also not always in full congruence (although foundationally in agreement as we will see later) with the settler state from which they come and which they expand. They position themselves as the expression of the true purpose of the settler state, as their constitution of settler sovereignty in their expansive settlements draws its will and force from the founding violence of the settler state.

Corporate enterprises form at the foundation of settler communities, wherein these communities formulate their own settler identity beyond the identity of the metropole and are driven by interests/forces that go beyond the imperial and colonial capitalist accumulation of wealth.[67] Insofar as settler sovereignty constitutes a distinct sense of peoplehood that excludes both the metropole (through movement into spaces beyond the reach of the metropole, wars of independence, trade policies, etc.) and the Indigenous populations (through extermination, genocide, transfer), and insofar as this settler sovereignty insists on the self-governing and self-regenerating capacities of local settler communities, they present in many ways a challenge to colonial and imperial sovereignties.[68] Although the two exist in a dialectical relationship, they remain distinct in their features (relation to the Indigenous population) and modes of operation (how they expand into "open" territories).[69] Indeed, it is in their expansive territorialization that settler sovereignties are most unique in that the sovereignty is always moving and can always move to wherever the settlers move.[70] In short, the settlers carry their sovereignty with them, transferring whatever populations they come across, suppressing and eradicating (or attempting to eradicate) Indigenous claims to sovereignty. As was made clear through insights from the works of Simpson, Wolfe, Pateman, Coulthard, and many others, any Indigenous claim of sovereignty brings to the fore what settler colonial sovereignty cannot bear: the idea that its sovereignty does not manage the population economy, and that other claims of sovereignty are not fully suppressed or eradicated within its expansive confines.

For Veracini, at the core of settler colonial sovereignty and the state and non-state institutions that enact it is the logic of transfer, or the logic of elimination as Wolfe calls it. In this book, I prefer to use the structure of expulsion to describe what is at the core of settler colonial sovereignty. Whereas transfer better speaks to the laws/policies that enact the removal of populations, expulsion better speaks to the *force* of such law/policies. While elimination and expulsion can be interchangeable, I opt for expulsion for two reasons. First, elimination gives the misleading impression to readers that Indigenous peoples, modes of organization, philosophies, etc., have indeed been eliminated; whereas expulsion clearly indicates that although they have been dispossessed, killed, removed, etc., they remain as Indigenous peoples and that the alternative to colonial modernity is still embodied in their presence, in their being, doing, and thinking. Second, as I previously argued, I want to acknowledge ideology and then focus on violence. In Wolfe, the *logic* of elimination speaks to the ideological (super)structure that continues the "crude massacres" of the initial invasion (i.e., ideologies of assimilation that continue the structure of genocide).[71] In this book, the *structure* of expulsion speaks to the killings and elimination of Indigenous Palestinians from large areas of their homelands, where my focus remains on the varied violent acts of expulsion. Certainly, all of these acts constitute genocide or a structure of genocide, but the aim of this book is to highlight *the force that gives rise to actions/policies/laws that the legal concept of genocide is meant to capture*, which is why I am opting for the term expulsion to refer to this core structure of settler colonial sovereignty. In other words, the structure of expulsion that is theorized in this book is greater in analytical scope than the specific crime of genocide, since it theorizes the very force that allows for an indivisible settler colonial claim to establish and render as "real" the settler colony through genocidal acts/policies/laws.

In the dialogical analytic to the study of violence, violent acts, including genocidal acts, are not just the brute and crude violences that need not much explanation because they are self-evidently horrific, destructive, and clear in their motivations, intentions, and consequences; conversely, ideological (super)structures (i.e., assimilation policies) do not constitute the more subtle, complex, and difficult-to-see-for-what-they-are mechanisms that continue the elimination that was set in motion in the crude moments of violence. Rather, the dialogical analytic follows the subtle, complex, and difficult-to-see-for-what-they-are paths through which violence travels and transforms what are in most cases indeed clear motivations and intentions, but whose *consequences* are highly complex and not always directly visible.[72] Conversely, the ideological (super)structures are indeed a continuation of these violences, but again, in more complex ways than imagined insofar as they continue a violent dialogue that remains hidden from view for the participants (and I do of course acknowledge that the ideological mechanisms and sociolegal structures are indeed complex in their often-Kafkaesque operations).

Therefore, the structure of expulsion cannot be divided into crude violences on the one hand and complex ideological and legal superstructure on the other. Rather, the structure of expulsion is best conceptualized, studied, and analyzed as a structure of violence, which includes physical acts of violence as well as the violence of ideologies, laws, policies, and so on. The structure of expulsion unfolds in a myriad of ways (not all of which will appear in the traditional sense of physical violence) and across a long continuum of violence. It is impossible to cover all the possible definitions and types of violence in one book. Future research can fill the gaps of this book, but the critical conceptual intervention of this book is to show how analyses of four-dimensional violence can proceed in those future projects.

Before outlining the four main elements of the structure of expulsion, I want to analyze the orientation of the structure of expulsion. Basically, I want to answer the question of what it is that this structure is oriented toward achieving. In the next section, I focus on the logic of sovereign abandonment as the answer to this question. Deeply rooted in Zionist settler colonial practices, ideas, and policies is a tendency to not just expel the Palestinian from the land that is to become Israeli territory, but to abandon the expelled Palestinian within a space of continuous political estrangement. In their abandonment, the expelled Palestinian is rendered toxic, contagious, and untouchable within the parlance of the international political system. The Palestinian is attacked on multiple levels, which attempt to not just secure the success and finality of the expulsion from the land of historic Palestine, but to secure an estrangement of the Palestinian from the realm of politics, even from the political as such. Through racial logics and structures that distinguish between settler and

Indigenous, the racialized Palestinian subject is cast outside history, civilization, and humanity.[73] Therefore, abandonment as the estrangement of the Palestinian from politics and the political is nothing other than an attempt to expel the physical, symbolic, and political existence of the Palestinians as an entity of human history and life.

The Logic of Abandonment

The logic of abandonment I am referring to is partly theorized in Giorgio Agamben's work and how he understands abandonment in relation to the sovereign ban. Here we come to a feature of theorizing sovereignty that has vexed social and political theorists for centuries: the inside/outside of sovereignty.[74] Rather than explore this feature across historical and theoretical iterations of sovereignty, I focus on it exclusively in Agamben's work, since his work illuminates the inside/outside of sovereignty, not as an either/or binary, but rather as relational in the state of exception. His theorization of the state of exception has been useful for many critical scholars, including decolonial scholars studying Israeli violence, who want to better understand how the violence of the state includes that which it excludes and expels, although some modifications to Agamben's theory are necessary.[75]

In a previous work, I critique Agamben's Eurocentric approach to understanding and theorizing the state of exception, where he overlooks the (post)colony, which I argue is precisely the site where the state of exception ought to be theorized and resistance to it examined.[76] In this subsection, I want to draw out Agamben's theorization of the sovereign ban and then pursue a different line of interpretation from it. For Agamben, "the paradox of sovereignty consists in the fact the sovereign is, at the same time, outside and inside the juridical order."[77] In declaring a state of exception, the sovereign suspends the juridical order (stands outside it, is not held accountable to it) but this is accomplished by virtue of the juridical order (which gives the sovereign the legal ability to suspend the laws). The exception, for Agamben, establishes a relation to what is excluded; that is, the law in being excluded in the exception is not without relation to the exception. Indeed, the law comes to gain its validity precisely in being excluded in the exception.[78] This included exclusion becomes the mark of the juridical order and the modern state:

> The "sovereign" structure of the law, its peculiar and original "force," has the form of a state of exception in which fact and law are indistinguishable. . . . Law is made of nothing but what it manages to capture inside itself through the inclusive exclusion of the *exceptio*: it nourishes itself on this exception and is a dead letter without it. . . . The sovereign decision traces and from time to time renews this threshold of indistinction between outside and inside, exclusion and inclusion, *nomos* and *pyhsis*, in which life is originally excepted in law. Its decision is the position of an undecidable.[79]

Much like Derrida's discussion on the sovereign's molding of alterity and hybridity into the selfsame substance, the sovereign decision is also that which molds the so-called chaos of an uninhibited violence into the foundation of law: as the foundation of law that turns it from a dead letter to that which is enforced and enforceable. Indeed, these two senses of molding are interconnected insofar as the molding of uninhibited violence into the validity of the law is also simultaneously the molding of the difference and hybridity of life into a selfsame substance. Put differently, a sovereign is the entity that creates selfsameness by rendering all life (potentially) as *homo sacer*. The uninhibited killing within the state of exception ("the production of bare life" which "is the originary activity of sovereignty"), where the state as quoted above "renews the threshold of indistinction," provides the juridical order with its very validity as law.[80] This is not the scene of total chaos from which we can only emerge with the creation of a Leviathan; this is rather the scene of total and uninhibited violence (which holds no consequences for the state's production and killing of *homo sacer*) from which the state can renew itself and the state order. Moreover, Agamben writes:

> If the exception is the structure of sovereignty, then sovereignty is not an exclusively political concept, an exclusively juridical category, a power external to law (Schmitt), or the supreme rule of the juridical order (Hans Kelsen): it is the originary structure in which law refers to life and includes it in itself by suspending it.[81]

Sovereignty, then, consists in the (re)molding of uninhibited violence into a validation of a legal, social, political, economic, and cultural state order that is of the selfsame substance. This is accomplished through the ban, through abandonment: *"The originary relation of law to life is not application but Abandonment."*[82] When the state of exception abandons bare life, then bare life is not cast out into the wilderness as it were, free from the rules and regulations of the sovereign power that excluded it, but rather remains within the grasp of that sovereign power as an included exclusion.

The paradox of sovereignty or the sovereign ban is marked then by abandonment, where life is abandoned in an included exclusion: "human life is politicized only through an abandonment to an unconditional power of death."[83] The sovereign is sovereign precisely because it may produce life as *homo sacer*, and *homo sacer* may then be killed without consequence or limitation: whoever or whatever creates and kills *homo sacer* is sovereign. Agamben's discussion on how this abandonment has been missed by ancient, classic, and modern theorists and his proscription to basically turn our back against the law to challenge the sovereign ban, however, are not useful or sound in an analysis of the sovereign ban.

To explain why I take this position, let us at this stage come back to the fourth element from Derrida's lectures that I left behind in chapter 1: the positionality of the two figures, the beast and the sovereign, above the law. The figures are positioned above the law in a related general sense but are situated differently:

> It is as though both of them were situated by definition at a distance from or above the laws, in nonrespect for the absolute law, the absolute law that they make or that they are but that they do not have to respect. Being-outside-the-law can, no doubt, on the one hand (and this is the figure of sovereignty), take the form of being-above-the-laws, and therefore take the form of the Law itself, of the origin of laws, the guarantor of laws, as though the Law, . . . the condition of the law, were before, above, and therefore outside the law, external or even heterogenous to the law; but being-outside-the-law can also, on the other hand (and this is the figure of what is most often understood by animality or bestiality), . . . situate the place where the law does not appear, or is not respected, or gets violated.[84]

Derrida insists that the difference does not take away from the resemblance between the two (and indeed between them and the criminal); each situation contains the other. In the sovereign suspension of the law for the purposes of founding Law is also the disappearance of the laws, in nonrespect toward the laws, in violating them without consequence, and vice versa.

In making this point, Derrida is critical of Agamben's reading of Aristotle, particularly in the idea that in Aristotle's thought there exists a "clear and secure" distinction between *bios* (natural life) and *zoē* (qualified life). Derrida points out that Aristotle's *Metaphysics* designates God with a qualified but not natural life. If the distinction or differentiation is not as stark as Agamben presents it in ancient Greek thought, then Agamben's claim about "a modern entry . . . into a zone of irreducible indifferentiation" is "difficult to sustain."[85] And this limitation becomes especially critical for Agamben's claim to have pointed out the so-called founding event of modernity and modern politics: the inclusion of "bare life" as an exclusion. Derrida does not, of course, assert that there is nothing "new" or "novel" about modern politics, but he does challenge the Agambean conceptual maneuver that makes the ancient distinction between *bios* and *zoē* the secure basis of such claims on novelty. To be sure, Agamben does not argue that biopolitics is entirely new, which is evident when he acknowledges that in ancient Greek thought the stark distinction does not operate as a stark distinction: even in ancient Greek thought, *zoē* is included in *bios* as an included exclusion. But for Derrida this is more reason to question the idea of a so-called founding event of modernity: Derrida argues that Agamben "clearly recognizes . . . that biopolitics is an arch-ancient thing (even if today it has new means and new structures). It is an arch-ancient thing and bound up with the very idea of sovereignty."[86] This realization for Derrida should shift our conceptual thinking away from the newness of biopolitics as such, and toward asking the question of what is new about biopolitics today.

I agree with this critique, and I do not follow Agamben's prescriptions or even the concept of *homo sacer*. Since I do not follow through with his theory, I need not give much attention to the potential pitfalls of an Agambean theory such as the positing of the victims of sovereign violence—*homo sacer*—as helpless, lacking agency, and unable to resist.[87] I want to instead emphasize from Agamben how the excluded, banished, abandoned object remains within the grasp of that which abandoned it as an included exclusion.

What I draw from Agamben is indeed also present in Derrida's formulation of the two figures being above the law. And each thinker provides my theorization of the logic of abandonment with a unique element: from Agamben the idea of including what is excluded in the sense of (re)molding the uninhibited release of violence as the formation of law, as the force that gives laws their very validity, not just once in one event but continually as a structure; and from Derrida the sense, not of a "diachronic succession" nor a "synchronic simultaneity" that explain the movement, development, and changes of the sovereign ban from the ancients to the moderns, but an emphasis on how violence enables the (re)molding of hybridity and difference into the selfsame substance.[88]

In my previous book, I drew on Derrida's work in order to theorize the fourth transcendental dimension of violence. I argued that scholars must deconstruct the distinction between a founding vs. a continuing moment of violence and instead examine postures of incommensurability that form in the transcendental dimension. Instead of conceptualizing the founding violence as originary, fixed, brute, and crude (although it is of course brutal), scholars ought to follow how a posture of incommensurability continuously animates, shapes, and constitutes as "real" a specific configuration of the world that follows the logics and features of this posture. An analytical focus on this posture of lordship in this case allows us to examine how it validates settler law, state, and society, propagating the perpetual unleashing of settler colonial expulsion.

Critical to this unleashing is the Indigenous-settler distinction, which I will discuss in more detail in chapter 3. But it is important to note here that this distinction is always tied to the logic of sovereign abandonment. In animating and orienting the structure of expulsion to the elimination of Indigenous peoples and sovereignties, the logic of abandonment can help us see how the Indigenous-settler distinction is always wedded to the validation of settler colonial law, politics, culture, and society in and through violence (across its founding and maintaining continuum). Succinctly put, abandonment helps us make sense of how this Indigenous-settler distinction marks the operation of four-dimensional violence and is especially useful in helping scholars conceptualize how the dimensions link up in and through the transcendental dimension of violence.

As I argued in *A Hermeneutics of Violence*, the transcendental dimension is a murky and fluid space, and it cannot be directly observed, but the posture of lordship can and should be observed in its effects. To explain how this is the case, it is now appropriate to examine how four-dimensional violence can be added to the discussion on settler colonial sovereignty and present a cohesive explanation of figure 0.1 (see figure 0.1 in the introduction).

The Four-Dimensional Violence of Expulsion

I will not repeat all the details of my argument regarding four-dimensional violence here. For my purposes in this book, I want to briefly highlight how four-dimensional violence fits with this discussion on settler colonial sovereignty. In *A Hermeneutics of Violence*, I made the case that the fourth dimension of transcendental violence, which cannot be directly observed, makes possible and impossible our understandings of violence in the three other observable dimensions of violence: instrumental, linguistic, and mimetic. I posited in the fourth dimension a concept of violence the "thing itself," not as a fixed independent thing that exists behind or beyond language, but in order to highlight how the knowability and unknowability of violence (the (un)knowability of violence) come together within that dimension, preventing us from ever reaching a final, total, or absolute definition of violence as *it is*. Before outlining the specific operation of four-dimensional violence in the case of Palestine-Israel, I want to first revisit and clarify my position on the question of the (un)knowability of violence and the problem of power in the analysis of violence.

The focus on the (un)knowability of violence has important implications for how scholars can study what social agents know and do not know about their violent actions. I argued that in order to give violence direct analytical attention, scholars must follow not just the agents' misrecognition of their own violent actions (I was engaging with Pierre Bourdieu on this point), but that which evades them because it cannot be captured, neither by agents nor by the analyst—that is, violence the "thing itself." This claim stems from Hans-Georg Gadamer's philosophical hermeneutics. The hermeneutic principle that asserts the failure of the agents to fully comprehend "all of what they know when they know" is certainly underscoring a kind of misrecognition on the part of the agents. But in Gadamer's philosophical hermeneutics, the misrecognition is not primarily viewed in terms of power relationships that prohibit the agents from full comprehension. Rather, the subject matter itself always prohibits full comprehension by virtue of its elusive character, and this, as I have argued, is very much the case with violence.

So instead of misrecognition, it is critical to emphasize what always evades recognition, which is the evasiveness of the subject matter. This does not mean that we ignore how power practices/structures/relations limit what we see, know, understand, and believe; rather, it means that in addition to focusing on limitations imposed in/through/of power, we must also emphasize the limitations of our very ability to understand violence: what I am emphasizing in this book as the unbearability of the horrors of violence.

The dialogical approach, which is very much shaped by critical hermeneutics, avoids absolutizing and totalizing the conception of power wherein all of our beliefs, values, and actions are explained by power structures and our strategic maneuvers within them, at the same time that it probes into the very constitutive force of power in which both critic and agent are encompassed: critical hermeneutics seeks to "uncover constitutive power effects precisely where we were previously accustomed to seeing nothing but 'reality.'"[89] This hermeneutic effort, in delineating the constitutive power relations that otherwise remain unarticulated and taken for granted as simply "reality," becomes most fruitful in offering "a space for reflection and action over against established interpretations and structures of domination."[90] The constraining and limiting role of power in self-determination and self-construction (especially of the marginalized and oppressed) are thus named, articulated, and laid bare for a critical reflection that challenges, opposes, and potentially overturns them.

Crucially, this hermeneutic effort does not posit the critic as the objective observer of the truth and reality of power structures, relations, and practices but as dialogically engaged with social agents in a collective effort to illuminate and articulate the constraints and limitations of power: neither the critic nor the agent has access to an objective viewpoint of reality and truth but in their dialogical encounter, they can reach a more incisive interpretation of the power that constrains them both (albeit differently).[91] In this encounter, social agents basically play the role of co-analysts where critic and social agent can bring different elements to the analysis: "while the theorist helps the agent to get a clearer understanding of how power works, the agent helps the theorist to recognize which structural constraints should count as power."[92]

It is perhaps especially the case in the analysis of violent acts that theorists and critics are tempted to explain violence purely or primarily as an expression of power (utilizing violence to establish, secure, and expand power), and/or as an effort to overturn and resist status quo power relations (utilizing violence to resist oppression, elimination, expulsion, etc.). The dialogical analytic for the study of violence recognizes that violence can play both roles, and that we ought to analytically approach each type of violence differently—but the questions remain: To what degree do we incorporate power into the analytical framework of violence? How do we account for power relations without subordinating violence to a great concept—power—that explains it? In *A Hermeneutics of Violence*, I argued that it is necessary to avoid such a subordination if we are to understand the complexity of violence.

It is obvious that violence takes place across a spectrum of scenarios from one of symmetrical warring belligerents, to a one-directional kind of violence of the powerful targeting an oppressed group, to a revolutionary decolonial war of liberation, and so on. These different scenarios and forms of violence are very much shaped by power relations. But instead of beginning and ending with power relations, the dialogical analytic takes these power dynamics as part of the materials from which to launch the study of violence. This means that how we approach the concerned social agents will be different under different power dynamics. For example, in the case of symmetrical warring belligerents, it would be most fruitful and illuminating to follow how social agents from all sides fail to comprehend their own violence. I have indeed previously used this approach in the study of violence in Palestine-Israel.[93] However, there is a deficiency in this approach when we are studying a context where one side is significantly overpowering another. Although I attempted to account for this asymmetry in those previous analyses, and to some degree managed to do so, I now believe that it is necessary to account for the asymmetry in the very framing of the analysis, not within it, *and at the same time* avoid the subordination of the concept of violence to the concept of power.

Therefore, I will focus in this book on how the Israeli state fails to capture the full scope of their own violence and its effects as well as, not anti-colonial Palestinian violence, but the Palestinians' inability to *fully* capture the settler colonial violence to which they are constantly subjected. When we follow each of those paths where violence escapes the ability of the agent to fully comprehend it, we can come to a much better understanding of the form of violence that saturates this context from its foundations upward and sideways: the settler colonial violence of expulsion.

The Israeli state believes that it is in full control of its settler colonial violence, as an instrument that achieves its goals and ends. But the dialogical analytic teaches that no matter how powerful the entity that wields violence, it does not have the ability to fully control violence. Violence, in its flux, moves beyond the instrumental dimension and produces other effects that are often ignored, unnoticed, and unarticulated by the social agents who enact and proclaim violence. This book traces the fluid movement of violence beyond instrumentalism to a dynamic that is born of violent acts, what I call violent dialogue. The very enactment of settler colonial violence, I argue, ensures the failure of containing the effects of violence as it comes to produce subjectivities that are not about the creation of sovereign Israeli Jewish selves but rather a subjectivity of lordship that must continuously expel the Indigenous Palestinian.

On the other hand, we have the inability of Palestinians to *fully* know and comprehend Israeli settler colonial violence. To be clear, Palestinians understand much about Israeli settler colonial violence, and indeed I would argue that all of the knowledge scholars have produced and are producing about Israeli settler colonial violence (and that includes this book), even when it comes from non-Palestinians, is always based on what Palestinians and their experiences reveal about this violence. At the same time, it is impossible for anyone to fully capture and represent violence—this is the unbearability of the horrors of violence, and it gives us an opening through which we can better illuminate the operation of violence and how we might oppose it. In other words, the (un)knowability of violence in the case of the colonized provides the opening that the dialogical analytic seeks to probe, explore, and articulate in a continuous critical (re)interpretation that may illuminate a path that would effectively address power relations and show or clarify a path toward a more just and peaceful social/political life. This follows Hans-Herbert Kögler's idea that the critic's role is to, on the basis of what oppressed social agents reveal as power, help oppressed social agents "get a clearer understanding of how power works" and also how violence works in/through/and beyond the power structures that it is meant to only serve.

Succinctly put, the social agents' views and actions, always short of capturing the subject matter, can and should be followed to launch us into a dialogue over the subject matter of violence, allowing the analyst to chase the elusiveness of violence the "thing itself" in the fourth dimension where it cannot be directly seen but is observable through its effects. These effects can be gleaned in the very inability of the agents who proclaim and use violence to (a) fully capture violence, give a definitive or totalizing account of violence, and (b) understand their very transformation by the subject matter of violence through the dynamic of violent dialogue. Ultimately, the dialogical analytic is an effort that is made possible by the revelations of reality by the colonized (this is why I argued in *A Hermeneutics of Violence* that the voices of the dead are so important to opening us up toward the movement of violence across dimensions), and is thus aimed toward the replacement of our conceptions of what violence, in any given context, has come to constitute as "reality."

In *A Hermeneutics of Violence*, I argued that the formation of certain deep postures, and not the cyclical exchange of violence between the sides, is what ensures the propagation of violence. Violence the "thing itself" is impossible to observe, because in the enactment of violence, words falter and dissipate, and we become speechless. But it is precisely in this dimension that deep postures are formed, and while they cannot be represented in the sense of a definitive and fixed essence that we can observe in a particular institution, legal doctrine, mechanism of violence, political ideology, and so on (this is again why I do not pursue a genealogy of lordship as a knowable doctrine)—that is, while they constitute the uncertain nonpresence that cannot represent itself (in the Derridean sense formulated in "Force of Law")—they can be observed in that which substitutes for the incommunicable and the unrepresentable.[94] There are two main substitutions here. One is the substitution of violent dialogue for postures of incommensurability, and the other is the substitution of "peaceful dialogue" (the language of the "peace process," "respectful coexistence," etc.) for violent dialogue (and vice versa).

The substitutions are not to be confused with separations of violence across subspecies. The substitutions, following Derrida's philosophy, are always inherently incomplete and constitute a movement—hence the continuous propagation of substitutions as the different dimensions persistently link up with one another. So, what passes as peaceful dialogue carries with it elements of violence (e.g., Israel's idea of peace is the elimination of the Palestinian right of return, which is an attempt to secure the 1948 settler colonial conquest of Palestine; the Oslo agreements cemented and expanded Israel's settler colonial hold on the occupied West Bank and Jerusalem, etc.); violent dialogue carries with it elements of peaceful dialogue (e.g., Israel presents its violence as needed for the separation of the two communities in order to create peace; Israeli claims that the Palestinian rejection of Israeli "peace proposals" forces Israel to commit unilateral acts of violence, etc.); and crucially, violent dialogue substitutes for postures of incommensurability in the form of the Indigenous-settler distinction. That is, the logic of abandonment points us toward how a racialized Indigenous-settler distinction springs from the posture of lordship as the substitution of the incommunicability and irrepresentability of violence the "thing itself." This is not a kind of distinction that separates, but particularly one that necessarily abandons, that is, includes what it excludes as an included exclusion—an abandonment that must be repeated to validate the sovereign as lord and the land/people as the selfsame substance.

When the dialogical analytic chases the fourth dimension of violence, it is for the sake of discovering not the impossible identity of violence itself, but the very thing that makes violence knowable. The formation of postures, which takes place in this fourth dimension, cannot be proven by direct observation. The operation of such postures, however, can be observed by following the substitutions, and social scientists can begin to piece these postures together through a direct observation of their effects (and it is precisely in this sense that my approach borrows from Bourdieu's theory of dispositions)—effects such as the formation of enemy-siblings.[95] In short, instead of locating an "original" violence, the dialogical analytic seeks to bring to the forefront the element of (un)knowability, shifting the emphasis from a view of violence as a fixed and sealed occurrence that determines in its aftermath various social and political relations/institutions/formations, and instead examining how the (un)knowability of violence reveals and makes possible a dynamic of violent dialogue.

Violent dialogue basically concerns the formation of enemy-siblings. As opposed to conceiving enemies as distinct and separate from each other (as whole selves who meet violently in their difference, maintaining their difference in and through violence), we must examine how it is that the sides in violence become interlocked as enemy-siblings. This interlocking cannot be wished away as it has been forged in and through violence for decades. We can, however, transform the interlocking from enemy-siblings into what I will later analyze as the multiple co-constitution of the self—of the self as another. In order to enable this transformation, we need to better understand the interlocking of enemy-siblings as enemy-siblings and how we may transform it by working from that interlocked basis.

In moving from the philosophical analysis in *A Hermeneutics of Violence* into a theoretical and textual analysis, *Lordship and Liberation in Palestine-Israel* asserts that a posture of lordship makes up the fourth dimension of violence in the case of the Zionist Israeli settler colonial conquest of Palestine. This posture of lordship is not directly observable in acts, systems, institutions of violence in the settler colony. Rather, this underlying posture is concealed in the horror and the unspeakability of violence in its enactment. This posture of lordship will not appear explicitly, cohesively, or clearly in the violences of the military, legal, political, social, economic, and cultural spheres of the settler colony. But scholars can glean the contours of the posture of lordship in the three observable dimensions of violence, which in this case are, the violences of fragmentation (instrumental dimension), isolation (linguistic dimension), and dehumanization (mimetic dimension).

Generally speaking, fragmentation concerns the commencement and establishment of expulsion; isolation concerns the securing and expansion of the expulsion; and dehumanization concerns the proclamation and cementation of a sovereign self that has nothing to do with the expelled enemy-other (it seeks to annihilate the dehumanized other that is destined for only elimination and expulsion). Put together, the structure of settler colonial expulsion serves the purpose of establishing, securing, and expanding settler sovereignty (fragmentation and isolation) and eliminating Indigenous sovereignty (dehumanization).

The three dimensions make up the observable structure of expulsion, and we can think of that structure as a manifestation of the posture of lordship. This does not mean that the structure is reducible to just that posture, or that the posture can only produce or engender this particular structure. Rather, this is a structure that arises as one of many potential manifestations of the posture of lordship, but one that also cannot operate as it does in the three observable dimensions without the posture of lordship. In other words, the posture of lordship both enables and is enabled by this structure of expulsion in the settler colony.

As I argued in *A Hermeneutics of Violence*, the four dimensions operate simultaneously and should not be conceptualized in an ascending or descending order. This means, for example, that the posture of lordship is as much present in the discussion of fragmentation as is isolation and dehumanization in that discussion, and so on. The four dimensions are always present and are always already inseparable. Even though I will highlight and prioritize isolation in the violences of settlement, for example, this does not mean that the other three dimensions could not be prioritized in that analysis; they indeed can be. But since examining each type of violence across the four dimensions is neither necessary nor practical in this book, I will present the three observable dimensions in a way where I prioritize each for a different type of Israeli violence. For fragmentation, I focus on the violences of the apartheid/colonial Wall; for isolation, the violences of settlement; and for dehumanization, the siege and full military onslaughts on the Gaza Strip. I believe that this will make a stronger presentation of how four-dimensional violence operates as a structure of expulsion across a broad spectrum of Israeli violences.

But I also want to make sure that the simultaneity of the operation of the four dimensions is not lost in the analysis. I do not want to sacrifice an illumination of that simultaneity only for the sake of conceptual clarity. Therefore, I have identified a critical feature of the structure of settler colonial expulsion, the Indigenous-settler distinction, which captures the simultaneity of the four-dimensional operation of violence. The Indigenous-settler distinction constitutes certain elements that we can find in all the dimensions of violence, and referring back to it will help illuminate the simultaneity of four-dimensional violence. Since this distinction is connected closely in this book, not with legal doctrines and specific political and social institutions, but rather with the logic of sovereign abandonment—with the force that gives validity to settler law, state, and society and molds heterogeneity into the selfsame substance—it allows the analysis to remain fixated on the force of a settler sovereign claim. As opposed to a focus on the ideological superstructure that is built on top of crude violences concealing them and continuing them through other means (law, cultural norms, political ideologies, social and political institutions, etc.), a focus on the Indigenous-settler distinction as always connected with abandonment allows us to remain fixated on the violence and force that gives the superstructure its very validity. As such, this feature will allow the analysis of violence to link back to the question of settler colonial sovereignty as it in turn links up with the even larger question of the social-political relationship.

In the analysis of four-dimensional violence, this book shows how violent acts produce effects that betray the goal of creating a sovereign self, even as they render it possible and "real." The more the effort to establish the sovereign self comes up short, the more the posture of lordship is activated and pushes the settler sovereign toward even more violence, evermore absolute, indivisible, and omnipresent in its aspirations. Violent dialogue in this case becomes the interaction between the different violent acts of the settler, where the posture of lordship persistently propagates violence.

CONCLUSION

When we add four-dimensional violence to our theorization of settler colonial sovereignty, what starts to emerge is the idea that the violence of expulsion, far from achieving instrumental ends only, instead forges an interlocking of enemy-siblings. In this interlocking, the expelled always lingers behind, leaves a trace, carries a trace of the expulsion, always becomes that which co-constitutes the expeller. When the foundation of the settler colonial state is settler colonial sovereignty, is the violence of expulsion, what that means is indeed that at the foundation of the settler colonial state is an interlocking of enemy-siblings, not the establishment of a sovereign self.

When we follow this line of theorization, then we begin to see that the consequences for the claim of indivisibility are indeed enormous. The claim of indivisibility summons "that dictatorial agency," which attempts to mold the edifice of alterity and hybridity into a selfsame substance, to posit the sovereign as "the (self-)same, oneself," and claim lordship over land and people. This is invariably connected to the remolding of uninhibited violence into the validity of law, state, and society. The two can never be separated as violence is inevitable on this path that is of and for lordship. The violence that is called upon to forge the land/people fusion as lordship, to establish the sovereign self as that which underpins and exceeds the state, ensures both the possibility and impossibility of this sovereign self. In addition to forging the fusion of land/people (the possibility of the sovereign self), violence also forges enemy-siblings as enemy-siblings at the foundation of the state (the impossibility of the sovereign self). While the former underpins and exceeds the state, the latter is hidden beyond the purview of the state.

In order to examine properly how this takes place in the operation of four-dimensional violence, it is important to capture the simultaneous nature of that operation where the four dimensions consistently link up. The Indigenous-settler distinction, as the marquee feature of the violence of expulsion will be key in showing that simultaneity: it can act, conceptually and analytically, as the common thread through which we can observe simultaneity. In order to accomplish this, it is important to first clarify in the beginning of the next chapter the specificity of the Indigenous-settler distinction in Palestine-Israel.

3

THE INDIGENOUS-SETTLER DISTINCTION AND THE INTERLOCKING OF ENEMY-SIBLINGS

Israel would not be simply the state of its citizens . . . but the state of the whole Jewish people, having a kind of sovereignty over land and peoples that no other state possessed or possesses.
    —Edward Said, *Zionism from the Standpoint of Its Victims* (emphases added)

The native point of view . . . is not an ethnographic fact only . . .; it is in large measure a continuing, protracted, and sustained adversarial resistance.
    —Edward Said, *Representing the Colonized: Anthropology's Interlocutors*

As I argued in chapter 2, the Indigenous-settler distinction in settler colonial ideology and practice necessarily abandons the colonized, includes the colonized as an included exclusion, in order to validate the settler sovereign as lord, and this happens regardless of whether the colonizer posits themselves as either "settler" or "Indigenous." In both cases, the colonizer, because they operate on a posture of lordship, must constitute the "self" as a selfsame substance through a never-ending expulsion of the colonized.

This chapter explains the specific manifestation of the Indigenous-settler distinction in Palestine-Israel through a critical hermeneutic reading of academic texts that have grappled, implicitly and explicitly, with this subject matter. It is important to emphasize that this critical hermeneutic reading is not merely a literature review, but rather a critical (re)interpretation of existing literature that places our understanding of a subject matter within a new conceptual order.[1] Specifically, this chapter situates the Indigenous-settler distinction within the conceptual order of the interlocking of enemy-siblings, and in the process elucidates both the specific case of Palestine-Israel and the concept of interlocking. This is critical in setting up the analysis of violence in chapter 4.

The first section explores why and how scholars must combine various features of the Indigenous-settler distinction, which appears in different ways depending on whether we are observing it in the context of the postcolony or the settler colony. Mahmood Mamdani's work prescribes a dissolution of the distinction across both of these contexts, but this approach, although of great merit and value in decolonizing the postcolony, does not properly address some of the unique difficulties in decolonizing the settler colony. Instead of a universal prescription, I argue alongside Indigenous and decolonial scholars that we must be attentive to how the dissolution of the distinction can indeed serve the liberal and neoliberal settler colonial state and diminish Indigenous resistance and alternatives to settler colonialism. Having said that, I argue that holding onto the binary distinction between Indigenous and settler *can also serve* the settler colonial state. Therefore, I make the case that the project of decolonization must aim for challenging and eventually dissolving the Indigenous-settler distinction, but paradoxically this has to take place by first cementing this distinction, in its decolonial form, as the ground from which we build and advance decolonial sovereignties. Cementing this distinction in its decolonial form means an unequivocal rejection of Zionist settler colonial ideology.

The second section shows how Zionist settler colonial nationalism makes it impossible for even a reformed Zionism to be part of the decolonial project. Through a critical analysis of historiographies that attempt to redeem Zionism, I argue that Zionism is hopelessly settler colonial, root and stem. Against the trend, even in critical historiography, to distinguish between the national (as the redeemable side of "who Zionists are") and the colonial (as the destructive side of "what Zionists do to others") parts of Zionism, I show how Zionism follows the path of colonial modernity in creating and operating upon a racialized distinction between settler and Indigenous. The racialized casing of the distinction (regardless of whether Israeli Jews are posited as "settlers" or "Indigenous" in Zionist ideology) is always geared toward creating an absolute distinction where the enemies never touch.

This of course does not mean that Jewish life on the land is hopelessly settler colonial, but rather that Jewish Israeli presence on the land has to be reimagined, reenvisioned, and rematerialized within a new framework of decolonial sovereignties. The rich tapestry of Jewish life, history, philosophy, and emancipatory aspirations provides a large archive that escapes the Zionist attempt to mold that diverse and heterogenous richness into the selfsame substance. Thus, it is the non-Zionist excess, what Zionism tries but fails to capture, that can and should be reignited in its non-Zionist form to join the path of decolonial sovereignties with Indigenous Palestinians.

To counter the settler colonial violence of expulsion that is fundamental to Zionism, we must have a better understanding of the dynamic of the interlocking of enemy-siblings. This interlocking is the opposite effect of what settler violence is intended to achieve, which is the establishment of pure, absolute, sovereign selves. Section three of this chapter examines the consequences of this interlocking on our conceptualization of the Indigenous-settler distinction.

Beginning with my engagement with critical scholarship on the mirroring between Palestinian and Jewish experiences of great violences that are of colonial modernity, and ending with the critical work of Joseph A. Massad on the intertwinement of the Palestinian and Jewish Questions, I argue that the clearest and most fruitful analytical path that can be taken to challenge the Indigenous-settler distinction is to examine a shared fundamental question that cuts across the political identities of Indigenous and settler. I make the case that the Palestinian Question and the Jewish Question spring from the same well: the posture of lordship—a kind of sovereign claim that, in and through great violence, posits a sovereign as the absolute authority on the "origin," the "first," which eradicates all other claims of belonging, nationhood (in the Hamid Dabashi sense), and social/political life by, among other things, the racialization of Indigenous bodies as inferior and as not of, and not good for, the land.

The very violence that seeks to secure the separation of the "self" from the "other," though, becomes the locus of the intertwinement between the Palestinian and Jewish Questions, thus showing how the interlocking of enemy-siblings cannot be avoided, and is always indeed being cemented. This will set the stage for the analysis of four-dimensional violence in chapter 4.

THE INDIGENOUS-SETTLER DISTINCTION IN PALESTINE-ISRAEL

The Postcolony and the Settler Colony

Since it serves as the standard against which different analytical categories are measured, the Indigenous-settler distinction is critical to our understanding of the Palestinian-Israeli struggle.[2] By analytical categories, I refer to everything from general categories such as gender, sexuality, labor, class, race, nationality, and ethnicity to more specific categories such as Mizrahi, Druze, Ashkenazi, Palestinian, Arab, Jew, to the categorization of things like the Green Line, checkpoints, the Wall, settlements, the Old City of Jerusalem, etc. Insofar as it serves as the background that makes intelligible what we study, and insofar as it marks the simultaneity of the four-dimensional operation of violence as I argued in chapter 3, the Indigenous-settler distinction deserves special attention.

Of course, this distinction is not unique to Palestine-Israel, and it has garnered scholarly attention in other regions of the world. Most famously, Mamdani challenges scholars to disentangle the relationship between a fixed ethnic identity and the nation-state, particularly in the context of postcolonial Africa. In order to properly counter and critique (post)colonial power, he asserts that scholars must challenge the Indigenous-settler distinction and the identification of either the "settler" or the "Indigenous" (as exclusive of one another) with the legal/political structures of the nation-state. A decolonial alternative to colonialism would break apart from the legacy, grammar, and institutions of colonialism by dissolving the distinction altogether.[3]

Crucially for Mamdani, in the case of Rwanda for example, the idea of "authentic" and "original" inhabitants of the land came to be associated with a specific ethnicity (the Hutu), which had dire and tragic consequences for other inhabitants (the Tutsi) who were rendered as foreign settlers even though they have been there for many generations, and certainly were never foreign settler colonists in the mold or typology of modern Euro-American settler colonialism.[4] Mamdani is correct to conclude from his study of cases like Rwanda that scholars, the intelligentsia, and the political class should advance a strident critique of the Indigenous-settler distinction in the postcolony. A decolonial alternative must, first and foremost, unsettle and eradicate that distinction from the legal apparatus and political grammar of the postcolonial state. Failing the destruction of the

Indigenous and the settler "as political identities," we will continue to witness the persistence of the violence and destruction that was implanted by colonial systems of power.[5]

Mamdani's *Neither Settler nor Native* moves beyond postcolonial Africa and asserts that this dynamic of separating Indigenous-settler identities operates in both postcolonial and settler colonial spaces, from Rwanda to Sudan to the United States to Canada to Palestine-Israel. I am not entirely convinced, though, that the problem appears in the same way in each of those cases. While Mamdani recognizes that differences exist across the cases, he does suggest that eradicating the Indigenous-settler distinction is necessary in all of them. He indeed suggests that the difference between a postcolonial and settler colonial context is not as relevant as the similarity they share, which is the Indigenous-settler distinction as the generator of the modern nation-state. This is why he can place his analysis of Sudan (where there is no settler group coming from elsewhere in the Euro-American mold of settler colonialism) alongside cases like the United States and Palestine-Israel. But the fact that "settlers" in Sudan are produced purely through racist, invalid, and baseless colonial historiography, whereas settlers in the United States, Canada, Australia, and Palestine-Israel do come from elsewhere and are part, although variedly, of the Euro-American colonial project is not a difference that can be subordinated to another greater factor (i.e., the modern colonial coupling of the nation-state), but is rather a defining kind of difference.

For example, and very briefly, it is highly doubtful that a strategy to eradicate the Indigenous-settler distinction in Canada will yield an improvement in the lived realities of Indigenous peoples. In fact, it would likely do the opposite and contribute to the silencing, eradication, and cultural genocide of Indigenous peoples by suffocating their decolonial movements. Define and rule is certainly operative in Canada and the United States, and Mamdani is correct to challenge how some Indigenous political groups and organizations have come to accept colonial historiography and grammar. However, this is not lost on Indigenous scholars and activists (from the American Indian Movement to Idle No More for example) who advocate a strategy to redefine Indigenous identity (by engaging with Indigenous ways of knowing, theorizing, and living in order to reject colonial definitions) for the sake of establishing Indigenous sovereignty (which would operate alongside or parallel to, but not under or through, settler sovereignty), as opposed to an outright eradication of the Indigenous-settler distinction as political identities.[6] There are similar issues and difficulties in the case of Australia.[7] These decolonial alternatives that are advocated and articulated in Indigenous resistance are far deeper and more complex than Mamdani allows for in his critique of Audra Simpson's work. Certainly, Indigenous activists and scholars would agree that "self-identification is not the same as self-determination," that Indigenous decolonization is about more than reclaiming cultural identities, and that the mere "proclamation of Indian identity is not a solution."[8] Nowhere is the critique of these points more penetrating and deeper than in Indigenous activism and scholarship: for example, critiques of strategies and ideologies that sacrifice land, resources, and sovereignty for the sake of some multicultural liberal notion of cultural autonomy; or critiques of Indigenous political associations and institutions that have been established through settler colonial law, and so on.

The point that Simpson and many others have emphasized is that Indigenous identity is in itself part of the regeneration of a decolonial alternative: that their identities are not merely national identities that operate within the logic of the Euro-American nation-state but are rather identities that engender a new kind of political community, the likes of which Mamdani calls for. As to Mamdani's point that "America will never decolonize while the colonized themselves tell us they are sovereign," one needs to distinguish here between what kind of sovereign claim is being made and the context in which it is being made.[9] For instance, my reading of Simpson is not that she is claiming that Indigenous sovereignty is alive and well in the lives of the Mohawks of Kahnawà:ke, but rather, that an element of Indigenous sovereignty (which is a distinct form of sovereignty—more on this later in this book) has survived the settler colonial attempt to completely eradicate it. This element, akin to Dabashi's notion of the sovereignty of the nation, is not blind to the existential threat against it. In fact, it is because it is so reflexively and critically aware of the existential threat against it that it proclaims its existence. Far from standing in the way of decolonization, this element is what remains to oppose the complete and utter success of the settler colonial project. This excess is decolonization—it is decolonial sovereignties.

I briefly engage here with these debates because they are relevant to the question of decolonizing Palestine-Israel. As has been established in the fields of Settler Colonial Studies and Indigenous Studies, the case of Palestine-Israel is foundationally settler colonial, but it also has features that are similar to postcolonial contexts in parts of Africa and Asia (as indeed all settler colonial contexts do). With the postcolonial context (e.g., postcolonial Sudan), it shares an important similarity: one of the key problems of the postcolonial world revolves around the question of how to deal with the historical movement and intertwinement of different cultures, which have intermingled and migrated in these regions for thousands of years, without attributing authenticity and originality to just one group.[10] Because of this important similarity, where this land is rich with a complex intertwinement and movement of peoples, cultures, and ideas, this book takes seriously Mamdani's challenge and considers it one of the most difficult aspects of theorizing the Palestinian-Israeli case.[11]

To be clear, against this contrapuntal history that should be celebrated, Zionist settler colonialism has superimposed settler colonial homogeneity on that long history of intermixture for the purposes of eradicating the edifice of hybridity, alterity, and heterogeneity. It is a historical fact, and one that ought to be contrapuntally celebrated, that certain Jewish communities have lived on this land and called it home for thousands of years, and in the modern world, prior to Zionism, identified as Palestinian Jews. It is also true that historically, among other peoples and groups, Jewish people who were Indigenous to this land practiced forms of ancient sovereignty that are very different from modern ones. To conclude from these facts the fantastical claim that Israel is the reemergence and continuation of the ancient kingdom of Judea, the return of the "original" inhabitants of the land, and that this land belongs exclusively to Jews and Jewish history, is inaccurate, invalid, and violent.[12] The establishment of Israel is a modern phenomenon we know as settler colonialism. It is this foundation that the case of Palestine-Israel shares with failed settler colonial projects in places like Algeria and ongoing settler colonial projects in places that are today called Canada, Australia, and the United States.

So, how do we conceptually approach Palestine-Israel by combining these postcolonial insights into this settler colonial context?

The Problem of Essence and Origins

A well-known difficulty of decolonial struggles is to launch a countermovement that is already based in and constitutive of an alternative worldview, to counter colonialism without falling back into the colonial logic or grammar. One of the more difficult questions in the case of Palestine-Israel is this: How can decolonial movements in Palestine-Israel claim and reclaim a peoples' place in the face of elimination and replacement without essentializing the peoples or the place, or the relation between them? How does the Indigenous oppose the settler without depending on a stark Indigenous-settler distinction, but in a way that does not conceal the fact of the settler's existence as one that is predicated on the continuous expulsion of the Indigenous?

In Zionist ideology, the two categories of settler and Indigenous are not permitted to coexist: one must supplant the other in order to survive and exist. This Zionist zero-sum perspective (which takes the shape of Jews versus non-Jews) seeks to foreclose as opposed to acknowledge (much less recognize) an Indigenous Palestinian sovereignty.[13] In its settler colonial project, "Zionism aimed to create a society that could never be anything but 'native,' " in the sense of expelling and displacing the Indigenous Palestinian population and replacing them with new (supposedly "original") natives.[14] For Lorenzo Veracini, this project is precisely what ensures that the Zionist settler collective will never be able to fully resolve the Indigenous-settler distinction or move beyond it: they will forever remain on the road to indigenizing without becoming Indigenous.[15]

Against this argument, some scholars, like Raef Zreik have wondered how long it may take for settlers to become Indigenous in an effort to move beyond the Indigenous-settler distinction. For Zreik, Palestinians should reject Jewish supremacy and open the door for Jewish equality, rights, and safety.[16] This platform would signal the normalization of "national Jewish existence in Israel/Palestine" at the same time that it would entail the defeat of supremacist Jewish projects.[17] The Jewish settlers must, in turn, directly address the dispossession of the Palestinians and commence on a road of reparations: "Only facing history, not running from it, will allow the settler to settle down, and allows him to move from conquest to contract."[18] Veracini does not regard Zreik's question as a logical one, and he argues that the idea of *becoming* Indigenous "is a logical impossibility": you are either already Indigenous or you are not.[19] Similarly, Mamdani whose question Zreik is reasking, still asserts that the settler can never become Indigenous since both categories are produced as intertwined opposites in the settler colonial nation-state.[20] Although the overall gesture of Zreik's argument in this article points us toward the necessity for overcoming the Indigenous-settler dichotomy, his argument fails to properly deal with the zero-sum nature of, and the logic of abandonment in, Zionist logic and thinking. We end up, more or less, with a call for a civic nationalism, but that does not address, as I argued in chapter 1, how this nationalism cannot terminate the settler colonial foundations of the so-called civic national state.

Rana Barakat also agrees and asserts that from an Indigenous political perspective, the settler can never become Indigenous. Barakat, though, takes issue with Veracini's earlier work, which frames this question of becoming Indigenous within the conceptual framework of triumph/defeat.[21] For Barakat, Veracini's differentiation between the colonial occupation of 1967 and the settler colonization of 1948 on the basis that the former retains the colonizer/colonized distinction whereas the latter seeks to eliminate that distinction hence normalizing the settler as Indigenous, misses how (a) the colonial occupation of 1967 is still settler colonial insofar as it engenders policies and mechanisms of transfer and elimination, and (b) repeats settler narratives (particularly liberal ones) that differentiate between the two events across the categories of triumph (1948) and failure (1967).[22] This is important because, while it is not the intention of scholars like Veracini and Mamdani, Barakat argues that an emphasis on the settler (i.e., how the settler perceives the success/failure of the settler colonial project, attempts to redeem the settler's morality and ethical promise through a reckoning with the settler colonial past, etc.) produces the effect of epistemologically eliminating the Indigenous.

Instead, Barakat argues that we must work from the basis of an Indigenous sovereignty, which highlights and foregrounds Indigenous resistance to elimination, Indigenous connection to the land, Indigenous history and culture, and so on; and only then can we usefully use the lens and conceptual tools of settler colonialism in our historiography. Thus, for Barakat, in agreement with and building on

Patrick Wolfe's work, the binary of settler vs. Indigenous is necessary for a proper accounting of the ongoing violences of settler colonialism. Succinctly put, "the scholarship that abstracts or avoids or outright denies the primary and enduring Native/settler divide must be read as a blatant denial of native histories and indigenous sovereignty."[23] For Barakat, it is often settlers, and rarely natives, who are uncomfortable with a paradigm that centers and foregrounds that binary: the main reason being that settlers are uncomfortable with a paradigm that reminds them of their failure to become Indigenous. The paradigm, in other words, is a reminder that Indigenous people still endure, resist, and offer an alternative to the settler.

Barakat's warnings against the danger of blurring this binary are well founded, but I do not believe that these warnings present a full picture of the settler view of and approach toward the binary. Yes, the settler does fear the binary because it prevents the normalization of their settlement, and this is why the Indigenous-settler distinction remains implicit and hidden in much of Israeli scholarship.[24] But what the settler fears the most, I argue, is the *dissolution of their settlement as lordship*. This explains why settlers and the state will inevitably shift their discourse toward one where they claim to be the "original" and "first" inhabitants. When their positionality as settlers becomes a source of questioning their presence on the land, settlers do not seek to join the Indigenous people, becoming one of them, and they do not seek conciliation with the Indigenous people because such approaches would threaten their lordship. Instead, they double down on their elimination project, and assert themselves as the "original" and "first" inhabitants in order to secure the binary distinction as absolute and pure, striving to ensure their racial supremacy and absolute indivisible sovereignty. In short, the settler will sometimes respond to the Indigenous-settler binary that reveals settler colonial domination by holding onto the binary in a way that conceals it, not by dissolving the binary.

It is important to emphasize that the settler's claim of being the "original" and the "first" is different from the Indigenous claim of being the "first." Within the decolonial binary that reveals settler colonial power, the Indigenous as the "original" and "first" denotes Simpson's sense of "prior to" and an "alternative of," which assumes and invites relationality with alterity and heterogeneity, whereas within the colonial binary that conceals and thus entrenches and advances settler colonial power, the Indigenous as the "original" and "first" denotes the sense of the absolute, omnipresent, and indivisible sovereign voice over everything, molding all heterogeneity into the selfsame substance.[25] Put differently, the "first" is not the pre-political that gives authority and the authorial potency to the enunciator of the constructed political, as is the case with settler colonial sovereignty. Rather, the "first" here is a complex social, political, cultural, economic, and legal pluriverse that is silenced, suppressed, eliminated, and/or destined for elimination. This "first" is what is removed from even the "pre-political" of the settler colonial state when it attempts to eliminate and replace the Indigenous. This Indigenous "first" is therefore fundamentally in excess of the settler sovereign claim, and in many cases, it constitutes an alternative to it: decolonial sovereignties.

Thus, the settler is much more committed and wedded to the binary distinction of Indigenous-settler than may appear on the surface. One approach is to then clearly distinguish between the settler colonial and decolonial versions of that binary distinction and emphasize the latter over the former on the path of decolonization while maintaining the distinction. Another approach would be to follow the decolonial potentiality of the Indigenous version of the distinction, while also dissolving the binary distinction. In this book, I am following the second path. Let me be clear that my approach to the binary does not represent a universal claim toward it and does not discard the binary altogether. My position on this question will be specific to Palestine-Israel: in this struggle, the settler is Jewish-Israeli and the Indigenous is Palestinian. This is a fundamental ground that is not seriously disputed, and hence why political ideologies that wish to flip that reality on its head must refer to a supernatural deity that supposedly has decided the opposite of this basic ground, utilize complex legal mechanisms of citizenship that gain their validity only because they were established through force, and so on.[26] Moreover, we must also avoid the settler liberal approach to the dissolution of the binary, which as Barakat shows, eliminates Indigenous epistemology, history, and aspirations. To this, I add that the distinction of Indigenous-settler is not the natural or raw material upon which violence arises; but rather, it is itself a feature of the violence of expulsion—a manifestation of each dimension of violence that allows us to better observe the simultaneity of the four-dimensional operation of violence. To find a path or movement beyond this four-dimensional violence, then, we must first acknowledge that Zionist settler colonialism displaces Indigenous Palestinians and examine the violences of expulsion through that prism, and second work to dismantle the distinction by insisting that the decolonial path cannot be traveled through or along with even a "reformed" Zionism that listens to the Indigenous perspective only as an ethnographic fact (to go back to the second epigraph from Said's work).[27] Rather, it is a path that can only be led by the Indigenous. It cannot be achieved through force and the elimination of Indigenous people and *their claim to decolonial sovereignties*, but *through* these decolonial sovereignties. This is a long and painful road to be sure, but one that must be traveled.

Before I follow this path and expand on these points in the analysis of violence and decolonial sovereignties, I draw on the existing academic literature in the next section to unpack the nature of the Zionist project in terms of how it constitutes the Indigenous-settler distinction in Zionist settler nationalism and explain why even a reformed Zionism cannot lead to decolonization. I argue that it does not much matter whether Zionist settler nationalism posits the Israeli Jew as either settler or Indigenous, but rather how violence creates and sustains a racialized casing of the Indigenous-settler distinction as pure, absolute, and hierarchized in Zionist settler nationalism.

THE RACIALIZED INDIGENOUS-SETTLER DISTINCTION IN ZIONIST SETTLER COLONIAL NATIONALISM

All the means we need, we ourselves must create them, like Robinson Crusoe on his island—your readers will surely understand this hint.

—Theodor Herzl in an interview to the London Zionist journal, *Young Israel*, July 1898, quoted in Gabriel Piterberg, *The Returns of Zionism*

This desire to have been a Prussian Junker is highly significant for . . . this was the social type whose acceptance Herzl sought for himself and for the Jews.

—Gabriel Piterberg, The Returns of Zionism

In his important book, Gabriel Piterberg draws on the ever-expansive critical scholarship (Israeli, Palestinian, and international) in order to usefully summarize the three main parts of the Zionist foundational myth that creates the Israeli Jewish people, and which revolves around the Indigenous-settler distinction: the "negation of exile," the "return to the land of Israel," and the "return to history."[28] Briefly, the first part of the mythology renders an entire history of Jewish existence in especially Europe as "unnatural," "undesirable," and in need of a radical solution which would not reform, augment, or improve exilic existence but (to varying degrees) negate it.[29] This part basically first reduces practically all Jewish existence in Europe as "exilic," and second makes of exile a weak, miserable, and docile existence that is not worthy of adulation or pursuit. The second part asserts that the only "natural" or "organic" existence is one where a people establish political sovereignty over a specific territory and thus realize the "true" existence of the people—the "organic" expression of the people's "spirit"—and indeed of the land itself.[30] The third part posits that only when a people have established their national political sovereignty over a territory they have truly entered history—or in this case "*re*-entered" and "*re*turned" to the history that they once belonged to in ancient Israel—and be seen as part of the civilized world.[31]

Within Zionist ideology, sovereignty is seen to resolve the fragmented condition of Jewish life—sovereignty is seen as the "negation of exile." Amnon Raz-Krakotzkin emphasizes in his analysis the important notion of an "emptying of Jewish time" that takes place in the opposition between "exile" and "sovereignty" in Zionist ideology.[32] The idea that 2,000+ years of Jewish history, experience, and tradition is "empty" is nonsensical. I need not rehearse all the details of critiques like Raz-Krakotzkin's and Piterberg's (among many others, such as Ilan Pappé and his body of work) that have convincingly illustrated the shallowness of these ideas of "emptiness" and other elements of Zionist mythology.

Importantly for my purposes is that engendered in and through this mythology, the Zionist sovereign self, operating both before and beyond the settler colonial state, carries in itself the mark, not just of the sovereignty of the settler state, but of the indivisible sovereign as such. The development and assertion of this primordial sovereignty began well before the establishment of the Israeli state in 1948. Theodor Herzl was obsessed with gaining acceptance from white Christian Europe—not acceptance of his existence within Europe (i.e., as belonging to and being of Europe as a Jew), but acceptance of his sovereign Jewish self as that which is outside of Europe, as a sovereign coming from elsewhere, standing before and next to Europe, and thus equal in status to the sovereign European self. In particular, it was the worldview of Prussian Junkers, powerful landlords who embodied the land/people fusion as lordship, that Herzl sought to emulate and mirror. Zionist leaders sought to become a masculine, civilized, and properly historical "Man" who asserts "His" will and writes "His" own story (History) by successfully colonizing and settling the East.[33] It is no coincidence, as we can see in the epigraph, that Herzl's political and moral imagination relates the Zionist story to his European audience through *Robinson Crusoe*. We've already seen how Jacques Derrida draws out the element of *re*invention in his reading of *Crusoe*. This element seeks to summon the power of the indivisible sovereign, which separates man from beast, as a primordial sovereignty that underpins a "Historical" social and political sovereignty. The posited primordial sovereignty of "man's reinvention of civilized life" serves to provide a natural and naturalized power and potency to the social and political sovereignty that are built on top of it and through it. This is what I mean by the settlers as carrying the mark of the indivisible sovereign as such.

Both Herzl and *Robinson Crusoe* share the colonial imaginary: the assertion of the unalloyed sovereign self, as that which both precedes and exceeds the state (i.e., the excess of sovereignty as creation itself), by making as national (and thus civilized and productive) what was perceived as a pristine, prehistoric (in the sense of being outside of proper human history), virgin, and empty land. Emphasizing the prefix "re," the labor of reproducing and recreating by "ourselves," without help or need of help, all of the marks of civilization is also, in Herzl and in Zionist ideology, what makes "Zionists who they are": the expression of the organic spirit of a people as the only true and authentic Jews who have reestablished the sovereign Israeli state and returned Jews to the status of a civilized people.[34]

The autochthonous setter self that has been produced in Zionist ideology and praxis is, at its foundation, a notion of ethnic purity.[35] It separates the "self" from the "other" in absolute and fixed terms. This separation is not explained by modern nationalism but primarily by the settler colonial violence of expulsion. Specifically, Zionist violences operate around a racially constructed Indigenous-settler distinction, within which we can understand the element of Zionist settler nationalism.[36]

The specific contents of the Indigenous-settler distinction in Zionist settler nationalism have shifted and changed over the years. In the early parts of the twentieth century alone, there were multiple ways in which the Zionist movement regarded the Indigenous Palestinians: the Indigenous as uncivilized and must be removed, as uncivilized but could be developed and civilized with the aid of Jewish incomers, as the true racial ally of European Jewry, as the new anti-Semite, and so on.[37] The way the Indigenous was conceived is not as crucial for my purposes as is the fact that the Indigenous-settler distinction as a stark racialized distinction took hold in Zionist ideology. This is the case even when we examine the dubious Zionist claim that Jews and Israelis are the real Indigenous people to the land and that the Palestinians are somehow the usurpers of Jewish land—again here the distinction holds, even though who occupies which category is flipped on its head. The reversal of who occupies which category is not simply a matter of relativity (i.e., who is "Indigenous" is relative to X or Y perspective) but is very much a matter of violence that first and foremost assigns superiority to the Jewish identity no matter where it is posited on the distinction. The constitution of these racialized categories has been and continues to be constructed through military, legal, political, cultural, and economic violence and force.

Similar to other settler colonial ideologies, then, the land becomes in Zionist ideology a scene of battle between Indigenous and settler as racial categories that are integral to social and political structures.[38] This ideological construction is not solely a problem of baseless knowledge that can be corrected with valid knowledge, but to go back to my earlier theoretical discussion on ideology and violence, *it is itself violence and force rooted in the racialization and racial logics of colonial modernity.* In other words, *it is violence that gives validity to the racialized distinction, and not the ideological substance that articulates the "purity," "superiority," and "absoluteness" of the Zionist story of Jewish identity and nationalism.* The violent racialized casing of the content is more significant than the content, and this casing is settler colonial root and branch. This is where the racial logics of colonial modernity, the "absolutist" discourse on ethnicity and race that Paul Gilroy elucidates, are most visible in Zionism.[39] In its assertion of a settler sovereign Jewish self, separate from and always separating the Palestinian as that which does not belong to the land and can never even belong to the political or the historical as such, Zionism merely continues colonial modernity's absolutist discourse on race and racialization. There is nothing unique in Zionism's articulation of settler nationalism to suggest that it springs from a context that is opposed to colonial modernity. Zionism replicates the basic tenets of colonial modernity, foremost among them absolutist racialization logics that are (re)produced through settler colonial and colonial violences.

The nationalist impulse is not what explains Zionist notions of racial purity, superiority, and absolute distinctions across racial and ethnic identities, because that very construction of race is always already embedded in colonial modernity. Without colonialism and indeed especially without settler colonialism in the "New World," these nationalist impulses never emerge in the racialized way that they did across Europe.[40] In that regard, modern political Zionism—which is by far the most dominant form of Zionism since the early parts of the twentieth century—was settler colonial even before it established a settler colony: its racial logics of purity, superiority, and absoluteness give it away as part and parcel of colonial modernity.

Speaking to Zionism's rootedness in the racializing logics of colonial modernity, Achille Mbembe suggests that Israel's efforts to separate itself from Palestinians falls within the general defining features of our present epoch, namely, the separation of a racialized enemy with whom no recognition, dialogue, exchange, hospitality, or sharing is possible. One of the key elements of this separation is that "the anxiety of annihilation is . . . at the heart of contemporary projects of separation."[41] Mbembe argues that a new "security state," made operational through complementary "nanoracism" and "hydraulic racism" (to oversimplify, everyday banal racism that is embedded in the social fabric and state/institutional racism, respectively), emerges in contemporary liberal democracies with the promise of killing, maiming, torturing, encamping, exploiting, surveilling, dehumanizing, deporting, and encasing the "enemy-other" and protecting the "self." Within these racializing logics, certain bodies are rendered as unwanted, surplus, and as a threat to the very existence of the self, and hence must be separated, controlled, cleansed, and/or annihilated.

The impulse toward this kind of separation is not new in human history, but for Mbembe, the "anxiety of annihilation" distinguishes it from historical cases of separation, and is what (among other things, such as scale and scope—e.g., the massive movement and (re)settlement of peoples) marks out the European colonial project from "old settler colonies" such as those established by African, Arab, Chinese, and Mongol empires.[42] In Israeli practices toward the Palestinians, which in addition to the colonial/apartheid Wall and settlements include home and business demolitions, targeted assassinations, persistent and total surveillance, checkpoints, imprisonment, control of critical resources, the (non)issuing of permits, and so on, all of these practices amount to an effort "aimed at transforming the life of Palestinians into a heap of ruins or a pile of garbage destined for cleansing."[43] The body of the Palestinian is rendered an "evil object" that continuously threatens the very existence of the Israeli self.

But this colonial project of isolation, dehumanization, and fragmentation always falls short of its ultimate objective: it can never fully eradicate or separate the "evil object" because "short of total extermination, the Other can never be external to us: it is within us, under the double figure of the alter ego and the altered ego . . ., each mortally exposed to the other and to itself."[44] While written through a psychoanalytic lens, this insight is not very different from my notion of enemy-siblings (which emerges from an engagement with postcolonial, poststructural, psychoanalytic, critical hermeneutic, and mimetic theories of the "self-other," favoring and emphasizing the postcolonial), especially when Mbembe asserts that "the 'evil object' (the object that has survived from initial destruction) can never be thought of as completely exterior from the self."[45] Here is the affirmation of the notion that *"the evil object and I can never be entirely separated*. At the same time, however, *we can never be entirely one and the same.*"[46] This is again what I mean by the interlocking of enemy-siblings: despite the efforts at separation, the self cannot in fact exterminate or separate the "evil object" that is the enemy-other. I do not explain this failure to exterminate and separate through a critique of the politics of our epoch (Mbembe does question whether or not our epoch is really that different from others in the beginning of his essay), but rather it is in violence, in the violent efforts to fragment, isolate, and dehumanize that we can find the failure of the project of separation.

Zionist raciology—following the raciology of colonial modernity in "invoking 'race' as a primary means of sorting people into hierarchies and erecting unbridgeable chasms around their discrete collective identity"—rests on a separation between Jew and Arab Palestinian.[47] Like all raciologies, it of course fails to properly, adequately, or validly describe the contrapuntal hybridity, intermixture, and interconnection of social, cultural, and political life, and like all raciologies it violently seeks (but can never in fact achieve) to establish an "absolutist discourse" of discrete and pure races.[48] Thus, Zionist raciology is about, for example, the "cleansing" of the Arab Jew/Jew

Arab of Arabness.[49] But more importantly, underneath this racist cleansing, this de-Arabizing of Mizrahi Jews, is the dehumanizing racialization of the Palestinian body, which constitutes the violent foundation and machinations of the Israeli settler colonial project. As Israeli settler sovereignty cleanses the lands of Palestinian Arabs, attempts to annihilate the Palestinian "evil object," the Palestinian remains inside the Israeli Jewish self, which then necessitates (within the logics and dynamics of settler colonial sovereignty) the use of violence to continuously secure and cleanse the self from the other. In this sense, violence both makes possible and impossible the self: on the one hand, in promising to annihilate the enemy-other, violence is believed to be able to produce sovereign selves; simultaneously, in reaching its limits in terms of totally eliminating the colonized, settler colonial violence of expulsion ensures that the expelled-but-still-there "other" is interlocked with the expeller, thus forming the interlocking of enemy-siblings, which then circles back to the promise of violence to produce the sovereign self, and so on. It is conventionally assumed that the cycle of violence is a result of the exchange and escalation of violent acts between two separate sides. What I argue is that the propagation of violence takes place within the logics and mechanisms of settler colonial sovereignty. Within the structure of settler colonial violence is found the manner in which the interaction between settler violent acts produces a cycle of violence. I will show this in my analysis in chapter 4, but this can be illuminated theoretically here.

The sovereign claim, and as such violence (we must always remember the beast and terror, to go back to Derrida) always destroys and constructs, always expels before it builds. This is not a onetime expulsion that will resolve, once and for all, the "return" of the sovereign as sovereign. This is a structure that operates by ensuring that expulsion itself will not cease. There is always more expulsion that is begotten with every act of expulsion because the people expelled and their stories do not simply disappear (hence Raz-Krakotzkin's sensible appeal to memory as discussed earlier) and can never be fully defeated and eradicated. Thus, the structure of violence that expels must engage in a constant process of expulsion. Every time it believes to have sealed the autochthonous people from the "other," the remnants remind it of its failure, and it has to unseal, so as to suck out the people and the stories and the memories that remain. And since those can never be fully or definitively eliminated, since at the very least, the voices of the dead always remain, expulsion can never stop.[50]

So, we end up in a structure of violence where there are continuous acts of unsealing in order to secure and protect the autochthonous self, then reseal, and repeat. The violence is not cyclical because of its engagement with the violence of Palestinian resistance as is often presented in Euro-American and Israeli discourses (i.e., the idea that Israeli settler violence escalates only in response to Palestinian violence). It is cyclical by its own continuous structure of expulsion, where every act of expulsion begets more expulsion. Palestinian resistance, armed and unarmed, throws a wrench into this cycle, which from time to time, disrupts its movement and slows its progress. But Palestinian resistance is not the reason that the cycle moves.

It is important to foreground this specific kind of cyclicality of violence for reading chapter 4, enhancing our ability to capture the simultaneity of the four-dimensional operation of violence. The fragmentation of the Palestinian people across space creates the conditions necessary for the expansion of settler colonial sovereignty, wherein separation is always already annexation and a continuation of the expulsion of the Indigenous people. This expansion is further cemented and advanced through the violences of isolation and dehumanization. Isolation means the political estrangement of the Palestinians who are not heard in accordance with their voice when they speak. Thus an appeal to memory assumes that the memory will be heard in accordance with its own voice (this is the limit of Raz-Krakotzkin's approach), but the violence of isolation is always about concealing that voice before it even appears. This violence of isolation basically cements the gains made—the settlement of more lands—through the expansion of settler colonial sovereignty. In addition, the violences of dehumanization prepare for the next and upcoming expansion of settler colonial sovereignty. In placing the Palestinians outside of the human, settler colonial sovereignty prepares the conditions necessary for further fragmentation and expansion. These three features of violence work in a cyclical manner where they all support and feed each other, propelling settler colonialism forward, enacting a process of expulsion that has no end.

But even as violence creates the Zionist Israeli state, violence is not forging Israel as an autochthonous national state; but rather it is forging Israel with Palestine. Meaning, Israel cannot produce sovereign autochthonous Jews but rather can only produce Israeli settlers who have expelled and must continue to expel Indigenous Palestinians. It produces subjectivities of lordship over the Palestinian.

This is the phenomenon that I think Fayez Sayegh is grappling with when in his famous essay, he writes: "Racism is not an acquired trait of the Zionist settler-state. Nor is it an accidental, passing feature of the Israeli scene. *It is congenial, essential and permanent.* For it is inherent in the very ideology of Zionism and in the basic motivation for Zionist colonisation and statehood."[51] In short, racial supremacy over the Palestinian Arab inhabitants of Palestine is a central feature of the Zionist project, which is in part why the logic of abandonment is invariably connected to the Indigenous-settler distinction. The racialized distinction must always separate the master ethnos/race, extricate the master from the hybridity and multiplicity of human existence, and then ensure the existence of the master as lord, by violently remolding the hybridity and multiplicity of human life into the selfsame substance. These are the substitutions I previously theorized and discussed in chapter 2: the logic of abandonment that seeks to secure and cement the racialized Indigenous-settler distinction, which springs, as an absolutist and indivisible claim on land/people, from the posture of lordship. The desire to separate, extract, and establish the supremacy of the master ethnos or race is realized through the violences of expulsion, specifically fragmentation, isolation, and dehumanization. Against this desire and intention, however, is the hidden operation of violence: namely, the interlocking of enemy-siblings as enemy-siblings. Understanding this interlocking is critical to a decolonial unraveling of the Indigenous-settler distinction.

THE INTERTWINEMENT OF THE PALESTINIAN AND JEWISH QUESTIONS

In the middle of the twentieth century, two critical events took place that continue to shape Palestinian and Israeli lives: the Holocaust and the Nakba. Although it is not the first attempt, the book edited by Bashir Bashir and Amos Goldberg, *The Holocaust and the Nakba*, offers a recent set of rich analyses about the relation between these two traumas.[52] Their book juxtaposes the two events within a carefully qualified comparative framework that neither collapses each event into the other nor follows the dominant paradigm of Holocaust Exceptionalism that makes any comparison with the Holocaust impossible. A critical reinterpretation of their work will allow for a presentation of what I mean by the interlocking of enemy-siblings and how this can help us reach a decolonial unraveling of the Indigenous-settler distinction.

Bashir and Goldberg suggest that the two national narratives are opposed because they are each connected to, following the work of Charles S. Maier, two opposing metanarratives that have shaped understandings of modernity and the twentieth century: "the

Holocaust narrative" and the "postcolonial narrative."[53] The Holocaust narrative is one that posits this trauma as an aberration, a slide back into barbarism, in the steady progress of the Enlightenment, modernity, and the democratic liberal state (which needs to be strengthened in order to avoid future catastrophes);[54] whereas the postcolonial narrative asserts that catastrophic violence is indeed at the very core of the Enlightenment, modernity, and the democratic liberal state.[55]

Seen from within this opposition of metanarratives, one can hardly find a point of contact or connection between the two national narratives. The Israeli national narrative views the Holocaust as one of the greatest crimes inflicted on any people anywhere in world history and views the Zionist project as the miraculous recovery of the Jewish people from wandering and exile and the Israeli state as the only means through which the Jewish people can find security and safety from elimination. The Palestinian national narrative focuses on the settler colonial nature of the Zionist project, and how this project has inflicted the greatest catastrophe in the history of the Palestinian people, who have experienced and continue to experience expulsion and displacement as a direct result of Zionism and the formation of the Israeli state, and it views the Palestinian right to national self-determination as a necessary step in securing Palestinian freedom, liberation, and autonomy.[56] So, in the first narrative, the Israeli state is the manifestation of the progressive ideals of the Enlightenment and modernity and it works to halt the catastrophically violent and destructive side of modernity from remerging; in the second narrative, the Israeli state is the manifestation of the destructive *nature* of the Enlightenment and modernity (of colonial modernity), whereby European modern states emerged only as a result of the colonial violence that was inflicted upon the majority of the world's population.

Bashir and Goldberg believe that we can find a bridge across the two national narratives as each metanarrative is necessary for understanding the Palestinian-Israeli issue. They argue that scholars must account for how Zionism operates as a settler colonial project, is founded through settler colonial logics, and (re)creates settler colonial structures; at the same time that scholars must account for the trauma of the Holocaust and European anti-Semitism as the impetus behind the formation of Zionism—for instance, we must account for not just the Nazi attempt to totally exterminate Jewry, but also how anti-Semitism meant that Jewish refugees, particularly in Eastern Europe, could not simply return to their homes and lands in post–World War II Europe.[57] This drives the authors to contextualize the wider context of modern political violence, since it encapsulates the different albeit connected imperial/colonial violences and the violences that created nation-states. According to the authors, while the Holocaust falls within the category of genocide and the Nakba falls within the category of ethnic cleansing (although this distinction is not convincing), both forms of violence are connected to the formation of the modern nation-state which, in the name of race, ethnicity, and religion, created refugees for the sake of an ethnic homogeneity: "The Nakba was the almost unavoidable consequence of the convergence of two fundamental components of Zionism, namely chauvinistic ethnonationalism and settler colonialism."[58] This new historical grammar centered on a critique of the larger context of modern political violence, the authors hope, will open the door for a fruitful accounting of the two narratives that mitigates their binary opposition and exclusivist structures.

The problem in this approach is that it accepts the conventional understanding that "chauvinistic ethnonationalism" is a separate and distinct problem from settler colonialism, and that the two *national* narratives are in fact separate.[59] Of course, they have been separat*ed* in political and much of academic discourse, but that does not speak to the interlocking of the two narratives that has been taking place for decades, despite not being named as such. This interlocking does not refer to the idea that the national narratives are identical or the same because they are not, as each operates on a different version of the national (or, at the very least, different versions of the national predominate within each narrative). For example, widespread grassroots Palestinian nationalism (not the official nationalism of the Palestinian Authority) is a liberatory nationalism in the Dabashian sense of nationalism, whereas predominant Israeli nationalism is a classic settler colonial nationalism. Putting aside the liberatory kind of nationalism for now (I come back to this in chapter 6), I want to focus here on how the narratives are interlocked in a specific direction: the continuation of settler colonial violence. The issue here is not about bridging what are separate narratives, but rather understanding how the formation and interlocking of enemy-siblings as enemy-siblings propagates a settler colonial interlocking and prevents the release of a decolonial interlocking. Thus, we need a deeper understanding of the interlocking of the Jewish and Palestinian Questions, and I believe a fruitful mode of explaining that interlocking comes in one of the chapters in the Bashir and Goldberg book.

In Gil Anidjar's chapter, which builds on his core argument in *The Jew, the Arab: A History of the Enemy*, Anidjar posits the connection between the two traumas within a postcolonial paradigm that highlights a shared underlying dynamic across the traumas.[60] Anidjar's analysis of the term "*Muselmann*" of Auschwitz—or, as Anidjar puts it, "Muslims in Auschwitz"—shows that at the heart of the European Christian political theology is a disarticulation of the Muslim and the Jew: a long history of making impossible the coming together of the Jew and the Muslim, the two enemies of Europe, internal and external respectively, which render possible the European self.[61] For Anidjar, at stake in the articulation and disarticulation of the two terms "is a complex and shared history, a common language of alleged and naturalized empiricity (nationality, race and ethnicity, or religion), analytic and political distinctions and categories (conquest and genocide, settler colonialism and apartheid, anti-Semitism and Islamophobia)."[62] Instead of distance and separation between the two traumatic events in question, he argues that we indeed find a "Gordian knot." This knot is predicated on European violence against and expulsion of the enemy, the Jew and the Muslim. And the two terms become joined at the hip, as it were, where the terms "always function together, one word joining, authorizing, or effacing the other."[63] Europe depends on their separation and distinction, it constructs two different headings "Europe and the Jews, Islam and the West, or . . . anti-Semitism and orientalism," but the two are indeed part of a shared history that ultimately makes up *"one question."*[64]

In Anidjar's work, a different and deeper line of interpretation from the conventional separation of the Holocaust vs. postcolonial narrative opens before us. Historical events are no longer compartmentalized here, each explained in accordance with particular historical structures, policies, and institutions; rather, we begin to pay attention to deeper foundations that animate historical events. As he concludes; and it is worth quoting him at length:

> Muslims in Auschwitz reminds us that history here does not mean the serial and linear occurrence of events, but rather their concatenation as "one single catastrophe which keeps piling wreckage upon wreckage." . . . Muslims in Auschwitz carry a . . . lesson for *Shoah* and *Nakba*. No analytic distinction, and certainly no geographic distance, no identity claim, will suffice to maintain the separation in which Christian Europe, along with its nationalist avatars in "the region," continues to be invested. If the protracted demise of Sykes-Picot bears the shattered form colonial imposition has taken (peoples at war, borders on fire), it is also because Europe never found the way to *answer* its own, aberrant questions. It insisted on implementing and fostering solutions and dissolutions, separations and divisions, across time and space. Much as it drew borders and created countries out of thin air, Europe

instituted other kinds of boundaries between Jews and Muslims, between Nazism and colonialism. These borders should not be conceived as analytical advances or as narrowly epistemological, even if "epistemological nationalism" has played its part very well to that effect. Muslims in Auschwitz—this names an imperative to hold together one history, one question.[65]

The focus on a fundamental underlying dynamic that piles up wreckage upon wreckage, the emphasis on colonial and settler colonial logics and structures within which nationalism operates, highlighting how it is that Europe develops/functions on the basis of exporting internal conflicts and tensions (hence the co-constitution of Europe across colonial and colonized spaces), the shared question that animates the specificities of the Jewish and Palestinian Questions, all of these elements are skillfully encapsulated in one paragraph by Anidjar. It is this book's contention that this offers a most fruitful ground for analyzing the forging of Palestine-Israel as interlocked, and not the aforementioned supposed distinction between metanarratives.

Perhaps nowhere is the intertwinement of the Palestinian Question and the Jewish Question more critically and deeply developed and analyzed than Joseph A. Massad's work. Massad is critical of efforts that encourage us to forget Semitism and Orientalism and to instead remember only anti-Semitism in international political discourse, philosophy, history, and so on.[66] Such efforts, in asserting that it is only anti-Semitism that opposes the Semite and not Semitism, basically keep hidden from our critical purview the colonial and settler colonial matrix of power in which the discourses formative of these identities emerged and to which they give rise and maintain (in particular, identities that operate on the binary opposition of Aryan vs. Semite). Instead of forgetting Semitism, Massad urges scholars to examine the way many lives became interpellated within these discourses as Semites: that is, to historicize Semites and the formation of Semites as a discrete racial category. The stakes are high since only when we fully appreciate the ways in which Europe created Semitism and the Semite within and through colonial racial logics for the sake of advancing colonial power as well as nation-state formation and consolidation within Europe, can we gain a better understanding of precisely how it came to be that the Jewish and Palestinian Questions became synonymous.[67]

In his analysis of key thinkers (e.g., Arendt, Renan), Massad asserts: "The act of inventing the Semite is the very act of inventing the carrier of that identity as other. It is indeed the act of creating the anti-Semite. In this light, *Semitism has always been anti-Semitism.*"[68] This important insight leads Massad to critique how Zionist ideology failed to properly deal with the Jewish Question—it basically accepted that there was a racial category called Semite, and that this racial category (posited as inferior to the Aryan) does not belong to Europe, is not of Europe, and therefore must leave Europe.[69] Instead of resolving the problem of race, ethnicity, nationality, and sovereignty, Zionism basically displaces the Jewish Question onto another people—the Palestinians.[70]

In his previous work, Massad argues that Zionism in a sense affirms European anti-Semitism by accepting the diasporic Jew as undesirable and as something that is to be replaced with the "sovereign" Jew (a dynamic that Herzl, among other early Zionist leaders, understood to some degree).[71] With the growth and dominance of Zionism, this dynamic is displaced onto the Palestinians, who are then rendered under the same category as the diasporic Jew who was the first "other" and target of Zionism: "Through the mechanism of expulsion, the land-based Palestinian is metamorphosed overnight into the landless wandering diaspora Jew for whom Zionism has only contempt."[72] Thus, there is a need within Zionism to continuously suppress this "other" that constitutes the "self," which began to form well before the encounter with the Palestinians: "Zionism was not entirely convinced that its colonial settler project would be sufficient to transform Jews into Europeans. Its higher objective was that Jews would be normalized only when they have become European anti-Semites, when they began to view diaspora Jewishness through the eyes of anti-Semitism."[73] As a settler-colonial project, Zionism must expel statelessness itself, whether that of the diasporic Jew or the Palestinians that it has rendered and made stateless and landless. This leads to Massad's important conclusion that "the persistence of the *Palestinian* Question . . . *is* the persistence of the *Jewish* Question. Both questions can only be resolved by the negation of anti-Semitism, which still plagues much of Europe and America and which mobilizes Zionism's own hatred of Jewish Jews *and* of the Palestinians."[74]

This is for me the clearest and most fruitful analytical path that can be taken to challenge, not just the separation of the two narratives, but relatedly the Indigenous-settler distinction. Instead of reifying, flipping on its head, or leaving intact the Indigenous-settler distinction, it is perhaps more fruitful to examine a shared fundamental question that cuts across the political identities of Indigenous and settler: and that question, I argue, concerns specifically the posture of lordship.

This path crucially does not obscure the power asymmetry insofar as the primary ground in Palestine-Israel remains (following Barakat) that of Palestinians as Indigenous (grounded in an alternative to settler colonial sovereignty) and Israelis as settlers (grounded in settler colonial sovereignty). The Jewish Question is answered by Zionism and Israel by affirming Israel's right to exist as politically sovereign in the mold of settler colonial sovereignty. Regardless of different political viewpoints that exist within Zionism, and I will expand on this in chapter 4, the foundation of the Israeli state is lordship itself—that is why the Israeli positionality is always already grounded in settler colonial sovereignty.[75]

But the effort to establish lordship can only proceed through violence and paradoxically it is in this very path that the Zionist project both makes itself real/possible as well as impossible and revealed for the chimera of reality that it is. Instead of sovereign selves, Zionist violence interlocks enemies as enemy-siblings. This interlocking is explained in the settler colonial context of asymmetrical power relations as a process wherein Zionist violent acts interact with each other in the ever-elusive and continuous chase after lordship.

CONCLUSION

Zionism as a modern political ideology is irredeemable: it can only lead to settler colonization, racism and racialization, apartheid, and ethnic cleansing—in short, to the violence of expulsion.[76] The element of Jewish refugee suffering, however, which Zionism claims to have spoken for and represented once and for all, that non-Zionist element is very much redeemable and must be redeemed if we are to challenge settler colonial sovereignty. As Judith Butler argues, this redemption must foreground the encounter with non-Jewish people. It cannot be reached through an exclusively Jewish historiography, instead locating Jewish refugeehood and "Jewishness in the moment of its encounter with the non-Jewish, in the dispersing of the self that follows from that encounter."[77] The interconnection between Palestinian suffering from Zionism and Jewish suffering from European anti-Semitism can only be properly understood within the larger context of a racializing and eliminatory colonial modernity, where we acknowledge that settler colonial violences radically transform the Israeli "self" into lords that must continuously expel the Indigenous Palestinian.

The expulsion of Jewish life from Europe was underpinned by the posture of lordship. This is the element that escapes Zionism and the

Israeli state discourse of "return" and "redemption." It is the non-Zionist excess that can point us toward a path whether the posture of lordship can be named and countered. The two questions are therefore intertwined precisely because they each spring from a posture of lordship that has devastated both questions (albeit in different ways—and an analysis of this posture in the context of European anti-Semitism is beyond the scope of this book, although important for a future project). To name and counter this posture of lordship in Palestine-Israel is to transform the interlocking of enemy-siblings into a decolonial kind of interlocking—one which follows the path of decolonial sovereignties. The only method of releasing this path's potentiality for decoloniality is to shift the analysis toward the violence of expulsion and understand the operation of four-dimensional violence.

4

THE FOUR-DIMENSIONAL OPERATION OF VIOLENCE

Fragmentation, Isolation, Dehumanization, and Lordship

> *What the discourse on terror seeks is the erasure of power relations as the central problematic of violence.*
> —Joseph A. Massad, *The Persistence of the Palestinian Question*

Power relations are a crucial part of the problematic of violence. For Massad and many critical scholars, any attempt to decentralize power relations is an attempt to mystify violence, to hide from view that the powerful Israeli state is unleashing a greater violence on a stateless Palestinian people. This is an accurate and necessary critique against the most dominant strands of public discourse in North America and Europe on violence in Palestine-Israel, which attempt to artificially equate the two sides and their violences, thus enabling the continuation of uninhibited Israeli violence against Palestinians. The equation of the sides takes place through varied discursive techniques and rhetorical mechanisms, most prominently when in both liberal and conservative mainstream discourses, Palestinian violence is framed as "terror" and Israeli violence as "righteous self-defense." This effective technique positions the Palestinian as a blood thirsty entity that kills and harms for the sake of killing and destruction, specifically targeting Jews for being Jews, thus justifying any and all acts of Israeli violence against the Palestinian.

But not every attempt to decentralize power relationships, while still paying attention to them, is bound to replicate discourses that conceal the reality of settler colonialism and justify and validate Israeli violence. I believe that the following analysis will show that we can pay attention to the four-dimensional operation of violence without losing sight of how violence allows the Israeli state to solidify and expand its settler colonial power over the Palestinian people. Power is analytically decentralized only at the point where violence escapes the ability of any political force to fully control. The Israeli state does achieve many of its instrumental goals through violence, which establish, solidify, and expand Israeli settler colonial sovereignty. But violence also produces effects that exceed those instrumental goals, and in varied respects, these effects run counter to the professed and even realized instrumental goals of the Israeli state. Of particular interest in this book is not the strategic effects that garner some attention from political analysts (e.g., Israel's instrumental goal of defeating Hamas through violence has historically strengthened Hamas's position within Palestinian politics, etc.). Rather, it is an effect that directly runs counter to the fundamental goal and drive of the Zionist project at the core of the Israeli state: the creation and enactment of settler colonial sovereignty. To illustrate this, I analyze the three observable dimensions of Israeli settler colonial violence: fragmentation (instrumental), isolation (linguistic), and dehumanization (mimetic). Throughout this analysis, we can observe the effects of the fourth transcendental dimension, the posture of lordship, which is highlighted through the Indigenous-settler distinction, and in the process keep the simultaneous operation of the four dimensions in our analytical purview.

Israel's *fragmentation* of the land of historic Palestine is well documented. From the onset of the Zionist settler colonial project in the early parts of the twentieth century to the contemporary moment, with the 1948 and 1967 wars standing out as major events, Palestinian lands and communities have been fragmented by Israeli violences. Within Zionist discourse, this fragmentation is concealed. The Israeli discourse on the creation of the State of Israel in 1948 presents a picture of the forging of a new entity that is whole and complete. This discourse centers the 1948 War as the moment in which Israel claims itself as the one true, rightful, original, and indivisible sovereign over the land of historic Palestine. But what this conceals of course is that these events are about the fragmentation of Indigenous sovereignty, people, and lands. This is evident, among other things, in the construction of the Separation/Annexation Wall. In analyzing the Wall as a form of violence, we can observe how Israel's lordship over the land can only be realized through the continuous fragmenting of the Indigenous population into small pieces that can be restricted, contained, policed, and eliminated/marked for elimination.

A necessary effect of this fragmentation is separation, which operates on two main levels: the separation of the Indigenous Palestinian population from each other, and the racialized separation of the Indigenous population from the settler population. Both separations are effectively what the violences of fragmentation seek to achieve for the settler sovereign. The instrumental goal of these violences is to create, secure, and cement the separation of the settler from the Indigenous in order to make possible the sovereign settler self in the first place, and ensure the inability of the Indigenous people to successfully resist by separating them from each other. The two separations work together in and through the violences of fragmentation.

Related to fragmentation is the violence of *isolation*, where the expelled Palestinian is isolated in their expulsion. In Zionist ideology and practice, there can only be a pure, absolute, and sovereign Jew that inhabits Israel, and as such all bodies that stand in the way must be expelled and removed, symbolically and physically. This process necessarily isolates the bodies that it marks as destined for elimination and expulsion. There are three interconnected elements in the violence of isolation: the isolation of Palestinian communities that are marked for expulsion in the short and immediate terms, the isolation of settlers as supposedly fringe movements within Israeli society and politics, and the isolation of the expelled Palestinian in the form of a political estrangement. I argue that the operation of these elements is best seen through the violences of settlement. This analysis shows how settler colonial violence produces, not autochthonous selves, but rather a subjectivity of lordship.

Finally, is the violence of *dehumanization*, where a Zionist raciology separates, not just communities from each other (Mizrahi, Ashkenazi, Palestinian, etc.), but the self from its constituent elements in the aim of producing purified sovereign Jews. In this raciology, the Palestinian is racialized along an Indigenous-settler distinction that is validated through violence and force. Part of what gives Zionism away as simply another manifestation of colonial modernity is a mode of dehumanizing racialization that makes it possible for Zionism to unleash uninhibited violence almost without fear of consequence. Exemplified in Israel's full military onslaughts on the Gaza Strip, we can see how dehumanizing violences of the Israeli state racialize Palestinians as destined for elimination and expulsion: as a nonhuman entity that is not worthy of life, death, or anything in between. Palestinians simply become an object that can be discarded through maiming and killing in the same way that inorganic material is discarded. But these violences also reveal how the voices of the dead echo long after their death, revealing the limits of the Israeli attempt to debilitate Palestinian futurity. The racialized dehumanization of Palestinians becomes an integral part of a Zionist raciology that underpins Israeli state and society, driving this raciology toward its revelation, opening the fissures that Zionism seeks to eliminate and cover over through the violences of expulsion.

Just as Israeli violences achieve instrumental results for the settler sovereign, namely the establishment and expansion of Israeli settler sovereignty, they also produce other less visible effects that run counter to the instrumental achievements and goals. Instead of forging Israel as a whole and indivisible entity, these violences forge Israel with Palestine. I do not mean Palestine here as a state or even as a political community aspiring for statehood. What Israel is forging itself with is the homeland of Palestine. The very homeland that Israel seeks to erase, completely and definitively, cannot be erased and indeed seeps into Israel challenging and unraveling the idea and project of Zionism from within, often in hidden ways, such as everyday Palestinian acts of resistance that remind the Israeli sovereign of the Palestinian connection to the land, of Palestine as homeland. What this means is that the fragmentation, isolation, and dehumanization of the Palestinian land/people, make Israel both possible and impossible.

Before proceeding, an important reminder is that in the enactment of settler colonial violence, all four dimensions operate simultaneously. Elements of isolation are visible in the instrumental dimension, elements of dehumanization are visible in the linguistic dimension, elements of lordship operate in all of the dimensions, and so on. Moreover, the focus on a specific type of Israeli violence within each dimension is for the sake of conceptual clarity. I do not claim that only the violence of settlement falls within the linguistic dimension, nor is the following analysis meant to be an exhaustive analysis of all the different types of Israeli violence. Examining each type of violence across the four dimensions is neither necessary nor practical for one book. Rather, the following should be read as an illustration of how a four-dimensional analysis unfolds, and the gaps can be filled in future works.

FRAGMENTATION: THE SEPARATION/ANNEXATION WALL

The fragmentation of the lands of historic Palestine into manageable spaces that are militarily bounded and legally, politically, socially, culturally, and economically restricted under the rule of Israeli settler sovereignty can be observed in a number of Israeli policies, architecture, infrastructural and city/town planning (across the private and public sectors), national parks, settlement projects, checkpoints, and legal regimes,[1] but perhaps most poignantly in the construction of the Separation/Annexation Wall through and around the West Bank and the Gaza Strip.[2] The naming of this object is contested, and it has been called the Wall, the Apartheid Wall, the Colonial Wall, the Separation Fence, Security Fence, and the Racial Segregation Wall.[3] The Wall (*Al-jedar*), which consists of large concrete walls, fences with barbed wires, electronic fences, and sniper/watch towers equipped with advanced surveillance equipment, constitutes a set of barriers that restrict/remove Palestinians' access to each other, critical resources, and lands.

Ariel Sharon's construction of the Wall in the West Bank (which in fact began in 1999–2000 under Prime Minister Ehud Barak) essentially builds on Israel's strategy to construct a Wall in the 1990s around the Gaza Strip (which was initiated and built by alleged "peacemakers" Yitzhak Rabin and Shimon Peres), in order to separate and enclose Palestinian communities from one another and from Israeli Jewish communities.[4] This strategy of separation, disengagement, and enclosure accomplishes many specific tactical and strategic interests for Israel: it prevents Palestinian territorial continuity and contiguity; weakens Palestinian resistance by fracturing it; fragments the Palestinian economy; limits Palestinian connections across the land so as to make the struggle different and unique for each group; secures and expands Israeli settlements in the West Bank, East Jerusalem (and initially Gaza); and accelerates and solidifies the bantustanization of Palestinian territory.[5] The Wall is basically part of Israel's long-established effort to place *maximum Arabs on minimum land* so as to ensure the ultimate goal of *maximum land with minimum Arabs*.[6] Although cumbersome for the purposes of public discourse, the name "Separation/Annexation Wall" perhaps most accurately captures this object because the Wall's primary objective is simultaneously the separation of various Palestinian communities from each other and from Israeli communities, and the annexation of lands (estimated to be 13 percent of the West Bank) and resources through various rerouting strategies under the guise of security considerations.[7]

From within Zionist ideology, Sharon's West Bank Wall and disengagement plan from Gaza have been portrayed as primarily a security measure. The Separation/Annexation Wall, they claimed, would protect Israeli citizens from Palestinian attacks and suicide bombings. It would be part of Israel's unilateral plan to protect itself from Palestinians and their violence. The Wall would build the physical barrier that would once and for all separate the two sides and protect the Israeli "self" from the Palestinian "other," which is captured in Rabin's 1992 election slogan "Us Here, Them There."[8] This Israeli rhetoric, however, does not reveal the complex operation of violence but rather continues and expands the violences of fragmentation by concealing the Wall's actual violences and indeed the Wall as violence: from land seizures, expulsions and killings, control, and total surveillance, to the creation of the world's largest open air prison that is the Gaza Strip.[9]

The reference to Gaza, which is often excluded from the public imagery and imaginary of the Wall, is critical because it highlights how the Wall always was and still is a response to the problem for Zionism from the beginning: land and demography. Tareq Baconi astutely makes the case that Sharon's 2005 disengagement plan from Gaza was not only meant to "undermine the viability of a future

Palestinian state," but more importantly the production of an isolated and Israeli controlled Palestinian population within a very small territorial boundary. The Gaza Strip is the "outcome of processes of land consolidation and demographic isolation that began in what is now Israel and continue apace in the rest of historic Palestine."[10] Far from exceptional, then, Gaza is in fact "the measure of Israel's structural engagement with Palestinians" and constitutes "the starkest manifestation of settler colonialism in Palestine, where territorial annexation, demographic isolation, land dispossession, and population pacification have been taken to their natural end point."[11] The disengagement from Gaza in 2005 was not the final outcome of Israeli decision-making, marking the Gaza Strip as forever a besieged Palestinian space. Rather, it was an action that followed what is possible at that historical juncture but is ultimately geared toward the realization of Greater Israel—of lordship over the entire land of historic Palestine.

We can observe what Baconi is describing and illuminating in a 2004 interview in the *Jerusalem Post*, where one of the Separation/Annexation Wall's chief academic supporters if not architect, demographer Arnon Soffer, discussed the uninhibited nature of the violences that would take place at the Wall, particularly in Gaza:

> First of all, the fence is not built like the Berlin Wall. *It's a fence that we will be guarding on either side.* Instead of entering Gaza, the way we did last week, we will tell the Palestinians that if a single missile is fired over the fence, we will fire 10 in response. And women and children will be killed, and houses will be destroyed. After the fifth such incident, Palestinian mothers won't allow their husbands to shoot Kassams, because they will know what's waiting for them.
>
> Second of all, when 2.5 million people live in a closed-off Gaza, *it's going to be a human catastrophe. Those people will become even bigger animals than they are today, with the aid of an insane fundamentalist Islam.*

> The pressure at the border will be awful. It's going to be a terrible war. *So, if we want to remain alive, we will have to kill and kill and kill.* All day, every day.
>
> *If we don't kill, we will cease to exist.* The only thing that concerns me is how to ensure that the boys and men who are going to have to do the killing will be able to return home to their families and be *normal human beings.*
>
> Unilateral separation doesn't guarantee "peace"—*it guarantees a Zionist-Jewish state with an overwhelming majority of Jews*; it guarantees the kind of safety that will return tourists to the country; and it guarantees one other important thing. Between 1948 and 1967, the fence was a fence, and 400,000 people left the West Bank voluntarily. This is what will happen after separation. If a Palestinian cannot come into Tel Aviv for work, he will look in Iraq, or Kuwait, or London. *I believe that there will be movement out of the area.*[12]

Soffer's words are considered extreme in liberal security discourse, but he essentially presents in blunt and graphic language what liberal discourse also says, although sometimes in more subtle and indirect ways: that Israel needs to take all necessary "security measures" to ensure that it is safe and remains a Jewish state for a Jewish majority population.[13] I do not wish to downplay the differences in how each mode of representation justifies and promotes Israeli violence (the liberal security discourse tends to be more effective in shaping international diplomatic and public opinion discourses), but what is most critical here is that although explicitly violent and graphic, Soffer's words conceal violence yet still. Graphic words do not in and of themselves reveal violence (which is why I argued that "freeing" the concept of violence—following the flux of violence—has nothing to do with discussing the gruesome details of violence).[14]

Three points are worthy of attention from Soffer's quote to illustrate how his words conceal violence. First, it is clear that annexation of land and the goal of *maximum land with minimum Arabs* ("movement out of the area") are central to the disengagement plan and the construction of the Wall. This reveals how the goal of separation is always already entangled with the aim of annexation within Israeli Zionist ideology and strategies.[15] Second, although it is very clear that Israel is in full control of both sides of the Wall ("It's a fence that we will be guarding on either side") and that Israeli settler colonial violences are responsible for the creation of the situation inside the Gaza Strip, which is "a human catastrophe" (the words "a" and "catastrophe" render this condition a "natural disaster" of sorts), this is concealed through the dehumanization of Palestinians as animals. They are only human at the point of "catastrophe," and they may be pitied the way we pity human victims of a volcano, earthquake, flood, etc., but Palestinians are always animals first. The siege of Gaza, which is never named as such, will produce "even bigger animals" because animality and beastliness is the Palestinians' natural state, driven as it is by "insane" ideas and ideologies such as "fundamentalist Islam." Third, when he proclaims that "If we don't kill, we will cease to exist," he is not referring to an actual genocide of Israeli Jews but rather what will cease to exist is "a Zionist-Jewish state with an overwhelming majority of Jews." In other words, and this is certainly concealed in his discourse, what will cease to exist is Israeli Jewish existence *as lords*.

In this graphic quote, the posture of lordship remains unsaid. This posture animates the entire discourse and the project of the Separation/Annexation Wall, but for those who proclaim violence for the purpose of instrumental goals, violence and its brutality are viewed simply as natural (à la my critique of Benny Morris).[16] Soffer and others from the Israeli Left, center, and Right continuously interpret and articulate violence, no matter how honest about their brutality in their words, as the necessary evil (e.g., Morris) or simply as necessary (e.g., Soffer) for ensuring the "security" of the Jewish people.[17]

These discourses are neither new nor hidden. For example, we can find them in several testimonies and accounts of the 1948 war and its massacres in the work of Palestinian and Israeli historians. Edward Said was discussing this kind of brutality when he cited an Israeli—Ran Kislev—writing for Haaretz in 1983, sharing the views of a random sample of young Israelis about to be conscripted, where the majority believed that Palestinian citizens ("Arabs of Israel") "should be deprived of Israeli citizenship," "be physically eliminated including the old, women, and children," "argued for South African style apartheid," and when Kislev compared "Sabra and Chatila and the Nazi extermination campaign, they voiced their approval and declared in all honesty that they were willing to do the exterminating with their own hands, without guilt feelings or hang-ups."[18] In 2014, Hamid Dabashi succinctly captured these kinds of attitudes here:

> Look at Israeli society today, when it has unleashed its gargantuan military machine against a mostly defenceless population. Rape their women, cries one Israeli to his comrades-in-arms, kill their entire population so they won't breed more "little snakes," echoes an Israeli member of parliament. Burn them alive and watch them die, then go on a hilltop to watch even more of them slaughtered by your army.
>
> Kill them as they play on the beach, kill them in the playground, kill their crippled, kill them as they pray in their mosque. Destroy their homes and flatten an entire neighbourhood, maim and murder them in UN school shelters and then gather gleefully to sing: "Tomorrow there's no school in Gaza, they don't have any children left."
>
> Just for good measure, so no one could misinterpret any of this, one Israeli newspaper published a reader's blog openly calling for the "permissible genocide" of Palestinians.[19]

In none of these accounts are those who express this brutality able to fully grasp the posture of lordship that animates their violences because all their expressions spring from that posture. When they reveal their worldview in which the Palestinian Arab is fundamentally an animal, a beast, they reveal their entrenchment in the posture of lordship from which settler colonial sovereignty, as a project of colonial modernity, cannot be divorced. They seamlessly move into the only conclusion they can reach from within this posture: the animal must be made into an even bigger animal, and to do that, you must become an even bigger animal yourself, a supreme beast that turns animals into bigger animals that then must be eliminated from the human world to which only the supreme beast belongs (i.e., Soffer's concerns for how the killers can return home and be "normal human beings"). And the goal of the supreme beast, which renders it sovereign—the sovereign is made sovereign by its supreme beastliness—is to establish, secure, and expand the sovereign's lordship. This great violence of the sovereign is meant to make the lord whole and complete, separated from the animals that they eliminate in order to create this wholeness.

The more Israel kills and dominates Palestinians in and through the Wall, the more the dehumanization of the Palestinian seeps into the very subjectivity of the killers. Soffer worried about how young Israelis who do the killing will be able to come back home and join normal life, precisely because on some level, the killers understand that killing dehumanizes them. These are not just problems that can be resolved through trauma counseling and therapy for the killers. These are much deeper problems with far-reaching consequences. The main one being that the killers become just that: killers who must continuously kill in order to secure their existence as lords of the land, as Soffer's quote and so many others like it show.

The wholeness of Israel is, in other words, predicated on fragmentation. Fragmentation inheres in the fabric of the Israeli state. In Israel's settler colonial project, the wholeness sought from the violences of the lord's fragmentation of the Indigenous people's lands is a dynamic that is also present in the state's efforts to create a people who are whole. Although Israel, as a project, understands itself as the bringing together of a fragmented diasporic Jewish existence into both an original (ancient Judea) and new (modern Israel) whole—making the fantastical connection between the two itself whole—the violences of fragmentation that it directs against the Palestinians in order to create this wholeness are defining features of Israeli state and society. The more Israel fragments Palestine, the more its wholeness is marked by fragmentation. The lord can only exist and continue to exist as whole by becoming an expert in fragmentation, which then comes to paradoxically mark the "wholeness" of the lord.

The Wall separates, but as it seeks to secure a stark "Us Here, Them There" separation, it cannot but annex since the land is already inhabited by the "Them." The annexation through the Wall has to be properly situated on the continuum of Israel's founding violences: the expulsion of the Indigenous so as to be replaced by settlers from elsewhere. In other words, the Wall separates the Indigenous people from each other, the land, and from the settler in order to establish, secure, and expand the elimination of the Indigenous people, not merely place them in a "There" as if they get to remain on their lands. The Wall as a form of violence, regardless of any instrumental function of separation, is ultimately always geared toward expulsion. There may well be temporary separations, but separation is ephemeral. It is a stage, a step, along the continuum of settler colonial expulsion. It may provide a resting place for the settler sovereign to secure its lordship, build its grip on the unruly Indigenous people, and wait for and/or create the right conditions for the next escalation, the next mass expulsion of the Indigenous people, which will become clearer as we move through the dimensions of the violence of expulsion. This separation is merely the moment in which expulsion of the Indigenous continues unabated, thus further cementing the interlocking of enemy-siblings as enemy-siblings: as a settler that must eliminate and replace Indigenous people. Indeed, that interlocking never ceased its escalation in the moments where the settler sovereign attempts to secure the conquest but can be looked at more appropriately as undergoing varying levels and intensities (in terms of visibility) of interlocking.

The consequences of this analytical shift, away from separation, and into the interlocking of enemy-siblings is critical because it shows that the "Us Here" is not an Israeli self that is whole and distinct from the "Them There" Palestinians. The "Us" is none other than what brute force and violence has rendered as master and lord. Far from serving the instrumental purpose of Jewish security, safety, and wholeness, the violences of settler colonial fragmentation, such as the Wall, are a manifestation of a posture of lordship that works to create masters and lords. No matter how much they may attempt to conceal this lordship by normalizing the fusion of land/people of lordship as "natural," "good," and "just," Palestinian resistance ensures that the situation is called and named for what it is: lordship and mastery. As Rema Hammami captures this dynamic in relation to the checkpoints (which are part and parcel of the Wall), Israel may view these increasingly technologized and bureaucratized "security" apparatuses, mechanisms, and techniques as ensuring the separation of the Israeli sovereign master from the Palestinian subject (even to the extent where technology attempts to replace face-to-face interactions), but embodied Palestinian agency and resistance is inevitable and continuously challenges this separation by reminding the Israeli soldiers that Palestinians exist and call this place their homeland, and that Israeli presence is the outcome and necessary continuation of lordship and settler colonial violence.[20]

Instrumental violence achieves strategic and tactical goals for the Israeli state, and it does attain a level of mastery and lordship for Israelis in relations of power, but absolute and indivisible control and mastery is impossible to achieve precisely because of Palestinian resistance. Violence also moves beyond the instrumental dimension of violence, and we can observe its operation in the linguistic dimension, where the events of violence (the 1948 settler colonial conquest, the Wall, etc.) move into the making of subjectivities, specifically the aforementioned racialized casing of the people.

ISOLATION: SETTLEMENT

The linguistic dimension of violence refers to the ways in which state violence never ends with the state announced "end" but rather descends into the ordinary in uncontrollable ways that continue to shape subjectivities long after the so-called end of the event. We can observe the movement of violence in the linguistic dimension by examining the ways in which *subjectivities are produced as lords*, although this largely remains concealed and unsaid on the surface. The dominant academic and political Israeli narrative on settlement practices post-1967 conceal the continuation of Israel's founding violence in 1948 and violent expansion in 1967.[21]

The post-1967 settlement project is marked by the violence of isolation, which concerns three interconnected isolations. First and closely related to the violences of fragmentation already discussed, settlement practices seek to isolate Palestinian communities in Palestine in order to enable ethnic cleansing and the expulsion of Palestinians. Settlement practices in their very construction isolate and expel to expand the "Land of Israel." Second, we find the dominant narrative that seeks to isolate the post-1967 settlement projects from "Israel proper." This is where the supposed distinction between the Israeli secular Left and the Israeli religious Right works to conceal that the founding of the settler colonial state is in fact a project of elimination and replacement of the Indigenous people—that is, a project of settlement. This second element is the most critical and I will spend most of the following analysis unpacking it. Third, settlement engenders the isolation of the Palestinians in the international arena in the sense of the political estrangement of the Palestinians. In order for expulsion and ethnic cleansing to continue unabated, albeit at a slower pace (for now) than it took in 1948 and 1967 (although just as devastating for dispossessed and expelled families and communities), settlement projects have to render the Palestinian resistance as illegitimate and invalid: in short, as anti-Semitic. This feature of isolation is indeed closely tied to dehumanization and will lead the analysis into it.

First, and very briefly since I already discussed this feature through the violences of fragmentation, it has been well-documented and studied how Israeli settlements encircle and isolate Palestinian communities, take strategic locations on hilltops, and create pressures on the encircled Palestinian communities to make life unlivable for them. Settlements essentially follow militaristic tactics and strategies to isolate targeted populations and more easily dispose of them in order to create space for the settlers. Whether it is the construction of homes, roads, playgrounds, and other public spaces, settlements are designed to isolate and then squeeze the isolated Palestinian communities. The presence of these Palestinian communities on their lands is not an obstacle that points out the dissonance between the ideologies of "return" and the reality of an already inhabited land; rather it is simply a practical obstacle that stands in the way of Zionist "return."

This brings us to the second (and more critical for this dimension) type of isolation, which separates post-1967 settlement from all Zionist settlement practices that commenced in earnest at the beginning of the twentieth century. The dominant narrative in Israel and Euro-American spaces asserts that since the 1967 war, a cleavage within Israeli society has emerged between the so-called religious right-wing settlers and settler movements exemplified in the ideology of Gush Emunim ("Bloc of the Faithful"), and the so-called secular left-wing of Israeli politics which seeks to trade land for peace.[22] This conventional liberal framing of the matter began in the 1970s and survives until today—it can be seen in various diplomatic discourses in the United States as well as academic works.[23] This discourse, which operates on the "hijacking thesis," presents a picture of a society that is being hijacked and torn apart by an extremist and sometimes fanatic faction—the settlers—that is betraying the promise of Israeli secularism, which is supposedly marked by respect for international law, human rights, social liberalism, and so on.[24] The settler movement is presented in this discourse as a nuisance to the Israeli state and as opposed in its politico-religious ideology to the modern and secular Israeli state.

This framing begins its story in the aftermath of the 1967 war, when Israel invaded the remaining lands of historic Palestine. The newly conquered lands were now under Israeli military rule, with the army commander serving as "the official sovereign in the West Bank."[25] While Israel did not declare official sovereignty over the occupied territories, it practiced sovereignty from the outset, by first declaring that there are no sovereigns and that there does not exist Indigenous sovereignty within these lands. It created a complex system of overlapping jurisdictions (Civilian Security Coordinators, the State of Israel, the IDF, Israeli settlers and settlements) that "all are part of a concerted strategy to produce a chaotic space in the Occupied Territories so as to deepen and extend the conditions of settlement."[26] This kind of unofficial Israeli sovereignty existed and continues to exist in a continuous state of exception. The Israeli legal system follows certain aspects of international law to build and maintain "a regime in the territories based on a military commander's authority and power in an occupied territory" at the same time that "it has not taken upon itself the limitations and prohibitions that obligate an occupying state, like the prohibition on transferring population from that state into the occupied territory, or the prohibition on confiscating private property."[27] In essence, and I will come back to this shortly, the Israeli state rendered the colonized territories the malleable space of sovereignty—a liquid inferno that can be molded and shaped into whatever solid form that settler sovereign power wished to create.

But back to the conventional narrative, according to which this occupation created two competing camps: the settlers and the secular Left. The settlers are cast in this narrative as a new group of people who fancied themselves as the reincarnation of the early Zionist pioneers of pre-1948 and even the ancient Israelites. The settlers believe that it is their duty to God and Judaism to retake the lands that were divinely promised to them. As far as they are concerned, the Palestinians who inhabit these lands are the real colonizers and conquerors. Taking the "land back" from Palestinians and restoring "rightful Jewish sovereignty" over the land is their mission.[28] The settlers do not portray their movement as a new epoch or stage in the development of Zionism (they are not neo-Zionists as some academics see them and certainly not post-Zionists), they rather see themselves as the true and authentic Zionists of this particular era: they are the carriers of the Zionist mission who will resuscitate the Zionist dream from what they deem as its lethargic—even anxious, self-doubting, and defeatist—path within official Israeli politics.[29] Their goal is in alignment, as they see it, with the original goal of Zionism, which is the *re*creation of Greater Israel. This Greater Israel includes at least all the Palestinian lands, but depending on the group of settlers you read, it can also include lands in modern day Jordan, Syria, Lebanon, and beyond.

The other camp, what we might call "liberal Zionism," according to the conventional narrative, consists of those who believe that Zionism achieved its purpose and goal with the establishment of Israel in 1948. The borders that were created through the 1948 war are seen here as the final borders of the Israeli state. Almost all the lands that were captured in 1967 can therefore be used as bargaining chips in negotiations with the Arab states (and not until the 1990s, with the Palestinians) in exchange for peace. This camp is often portrayed as secular, modern, bound by international law and respectful of human rights conventions, and whose demands for peace revolves mainly around internationally accepted conventions on security and human rights. The secular Left is posited then as genuinely interested in peace with the Palestinians and willing to see the creation of an independent Palestinian state.

This conventional framing of the cleavage is a weak one. While this framing certainly offers many strategic advantages to the Israeli state on the international stage by isolating settlers as a fringe movement, it cannot withstand academic scrutiny. Actively encouraging and making possible the movement of settlers into more Palestinian lands, the Israeli state has never seriously undertaken steps to finalize its borders in accordance with the outcome of the 1948 war (and we cannot forget the fact that the 1948 borders were established through settler colonial genocidal violence), and it has certainly never taken any serious steps to see the creation of a truly independent and *sovereign* Palestinian state. At best, the Oslo Accords sought to create Palestinian self-administration and Palestinian cultural autonomy over small and discontiguous territories, which would serve Israeli settler colonial interests and not the desires or aspirations of the Palestinian people for decolonial liberation. In all of the "peace" plans and proposals, the Palestinian state was never going to enjoy full or in most areas any autonomy in our normal understanding of the term, or control over its security, taxes, management of crucial resources like water and energy, borders, or law (among other things).[30] In short, the Palestinian Authority (PA) was always a "veneer of fake sovereignty" that ultimately served Israeli settler colonial strategic interests.[31] As Rashid Khalidi succinctly summarizes, Oslo and other agreements around "security coordination" solely served Israeli security concerns and interests in exchange for practically nothing but the narrow interests of a small colonized elite political class, who served as "a subcontractor for the occupation."[32]

Most importantly in terms of borders: whether we examine the Israeli efforts to annex East Jerusalem and establish an undivided Jerusalem as the capital of Israel, or Israel's active policy of expanding settlements on Palestinian lands across the West Bank, or Israel's proposals of land for peace, the Israeli state has never considered the question of its borders a closed question.[33] Zionist leaders, since the early parts of the twentieth century, sought to create a Jewish state on all the lands of historic Palestine, and this type of thinking about a Greater Israel (where "Judea and Samaria"—the West Bank—are seen as part of Israel) continued within the Israeli state well after 1948.[34]

The point here is not to say that there are not different opinions within Israeli society and politics over the issue of the 1967 occupied Palestinian lands. There are differences between left-wing liberal Israelis and right-wing religious Israelis (not to mention the differences within each group and across this spectrum) in terms of lifestyles, worldviews, beliefs, policy positions, and ideologies. Moreover, Israeli critics of the settlers and their ideology are correct in highlighting a few ideological discrepancies between the post-1967 settlers and the early Zionist settlers. These groups do emerge from different socioeconomic, political, and ideological backgrounds. For example, Gush Emunim does not view the Zionist project as an effort that will introduce Israel into the community of nations as just another nation. Rather, they view Israel as a unique nation of a unique people that is and should be isolated from the rest of the world.[35] Thus, the claims of the settlers to be the true or authentic Zionists of today is not entirely convincing. Moreover, their perceived connections to ancient Israelites are outright delusional. But they are, I argue, archZionists ("arch" has nothing to do with authenticity and true origin as Jacques Derrida's philosophy illustrates) in the sense of how they go about creating Israeli sovereignty. As Idith Zertal and Akiva Eldar put it in the more concrete terms of political strategy, "The pragmatist philosophy of 'another acre and another goat,' which had guided the pioneers of secular socialist Zionism and established the state, had now been confiscated by the new alliance of the Revisionists and the national-religious, and had become their tool."[36] This core similarity helps explain why so many on the Israeli center and Left—both in the leadership and the supporters—have a deep psychological and emotional connection to the settlers and their actions.[37]

Therefore, this cleavage cannot be properly accounted for in the language of Left vs. Right politics, the peace camp vs. the belligerent camp, secular vs. religious, or most importantly the old settler vs. the new settler, and the two sides of the cleavage are best seen as "mutually inclusive."[38] As Joyce Dalsheim puts it, the "apparent conflicts may conceal more than they reveal" and she argues that "the hatred and intolerance between these groups is fueled by the very depth of their commonality."[39] It is worth quoting at length here what Dalsheim has to say regarding the old settler vs. the new settler distinction within Israeli public discourse and her analytical approach toward it:

> In Hebrew, there are two terms denoting "settler." The term *mityashev*, meaning "settler," and the verb *hityashvut*, meaning "settlement activity," carry neutral or positive connotations and are generally used in reference to the pioneering socialist settlers in the pre-state era. The term *mitnahel* and the verb *hitnahlut* also refer to settlers and settlement activity. These terms carry negative connotations and are used in reference to Jewish settlement in the land occupied by Israel following the 1967 Six-Day War. I use the term "settler" interchangeably to disturb the separate categories that emerge in popular discourse. This article argues that the conflict at hand is best understood when situated

within the context of a society that is continually struggling with the outcomes of its settler origins and ongoing settlement activity, which takes a variety of forms on both sides of the pre-1967 Green Line. Based on this characterization, the question that emerges is how the current struggle between "settlers" on either side of the Green Line can be understood within the colonial context.[40]

Despite apparent discursive differences, then, what both groups share is settlement activity and the identity of being settlers, and more crucially I add, of being lords. The main reason behind the vitriolic disdain and anger that liberal Israelis feel toward the religious settlers is that they remind them of who they themselves really are and the true nature of the Zionist enterprise in which they exist, as a settler-colonial nationalism which must exclude and expel Palestine and Palestinians.[41] They remind them that they exist as Israelis precisely because Palestine has been destroyed by the Zionist project, and how Palestinians have been made to disappear from the Israeli liberal worldview and sense of identity and self. The word "occupation" indeed conceals that all of Palestine was and is colonized. What the settlers and their ideology signify is not the political nuisance for the Israeli state, but the foundation of the Israeli state, revealed in its naked form. Therefore, although one can argue these changes toward a more religious Zionism has transformed the implementation of settler colonial practices and specific settler colonial legal, political, and economic structures, the underlying structure of expulsion not only still operates in and through a posture of lordship across these variations, but perhaps reveals lordship in ever more stark ways.[42]

In their seminal book on the subject, Zertal and Eldar's extensive research reveals the complex politics and the social forces that underpin the settler movement as well as the important social and political developments the settlers have introduced within Israeli society since 1967. While the authors make clear some of the tensions, oppositions, and even conflicts between the settler movement and the political establishment (and hence can be critiqued for adopting the liberal "hijacking thesis"), their research does ultimately show that:

> The expansion of the settlements would not have been possible without massive aid from various state institutions, without legal sanction, and without the expedient and affective ties woven between the settlers and the military. The settlements flourished not only with the authorities' seal of approval but also with official encouragement and at the government's initiative.[43]

And according to them, this encouragement, support, and complicity came from across the political spectrum and from a variety of state institutions, although certainly the state support took on different forms and degrees depending on which political party and politicians were in power.

It is most interesting for my purposes that the authors title their book, *Lords of the Land*. The authors do not theorize what they mean by "lords," which is understandable since they are political and social analysts and not theorists. But the reader can gather what is meant by lords in the book, especially when looking at the one place where the concept is briefly defined: "The settlers saw the territories as their domain and themselves as its lords. Officers who were unable to adapt to the settlers' lordship and did not see the nurturing of their sacred project as a key element in their military role were tagged as 'leftists,' as 'defilers of Israel.'"[44]

Whether in their analysis of the relationship between the settlers and the military, politicians, elections, political parties, civil servants, and the legal system, or in their analysis of settler violence against Palestinians, Zertal and Eldar argue that the settlers always stand firm on their position that they are the one and only true owners of the land—this is an insight that other scholars have delineated as well.[45] Most revealing is how this lordship over land takes place in and through the law. The settlers are lords because they are above the law, or more properly, they are their own law, they "became a law unto themselves."[46] In this case, it is not that Israeli laws exist within definitive boundaries that determine what the settlers can and cannot do; rather, Israeli sovereignty, which I will denote here with a capitalized Israeli Law, becomes lawful and enforceable wherever the settlers move. More importantly, Israeli Law becomes lawful and enforceable only in its approval of settlement: that is, whenever Israeli laws limit the ability of the settlers to settle, they disregard these laws and fight against them, and "the Jewish settlement, at God's command and at the government's will" is created.[47] This intertwinement between secular and religious laws is a key feature of Israeli sovereignty in the form of Israeli Law. While many legal debates within Israel highlight the tension between secular and religious laws at the foundation of the Israeli state, it is critical to instead emphasize that Israeli Law is constructed foundationally as the legal justification (which sometimes shifts in content) and codification of the settlement of Palestinian lands and the forceful taking of Palestinian property.[48]

Within Zionist ideology, the theological and the political are wedded, each enabling the other. This political theology is not an invention of Gush Emunim and the new political parties of the religious Right. It has always been present in Israeli society and politics. Indeed, Zionism can be seen as an ideology that precedes the contemporary secular-religious divide in Israeli society and one that originated in the integration of these two trends: "Zionism and its overarching ideology emerged in the interaction and integration of 'religious' and 'secular' impulses and beliefs that pre-dated the Zionist movement."[49] In short, Zionism always contained within it an effort to integrate secular and religious trends, and not the imposition of one over the other as the narrative of "a secularism attacked by religious fanatics" wants to portray. Religious and secular nationalisms are not separate species of nationalism, but rather constitute in their intertwinement Zionist Israeli settler nationalism—their variety and difference does not denote opposition but rather an enforcement and reinforcement of one another in their shared goal of expelling, displacing, and excluding Palestine and Palestinians.[50]

The settler's fight against specific Israeli laws is thus done in the name of Israeli Law. I am not referring here to the use of specific Israeli laws to fight and render inapplicable other specific Israeli laws that seek to limit the actions of the settlers—this certainly happens and it takes place through the Israeli state, but that is not the most revealing element here.[51] What I am referring to is that ultimately, the settlers' opposition to specific Israeli laws is always carried out in the name of expanding the sovereignty of Israeli Law (which is both divine and secular).

This practice of creating the very validity of Israeli laws is the practice of the sovereign, as I discussed earlier through Giorgio Agamben and Derrida. The validity of the law is created, not *regardless* of how many laws are broken in the state of exception, but that validity is created precisely *because* laws are broken in the state of exception. The actions of the settlers, in their very illegality, are precisely the actions of the sovereign in the state of exception. Their actions are akin to the actions of the de facto military sovereign in the Palestinian territories. As Patrick Wolfe puts it, "Among Israelis in the Palestinian territories, it is more appropriate to assign gradations of military status than to distinguish between military and civilian occupiers."[52] The settlers are not outlaws (this title is reserved for the Palestinians as I previously argued), they are rather the validators of Israeli laws.[53] They enter a space that some have called "decentralized settler sovereignty,"[54] but is more accurately referred to as a primordial settler sovereignty, where sovereignty, as a fundamental element in the making and remaking of social, political, and legal orders, is in its hot fluid form. This is the lava that forges the "Land of Israel." In the violence of settlement, we see the formation of the crust, underneath which is an ever-burning volcanic fire that can forge more and more of Israel. The actions of the settlers are not in opposition to the state that emerged from that very same space, they rather reignite that space, to set it in motion for creating new pieces of the state. This means that the settlers are not the only group deserving the title of "lords of the land"; rather, the foundational Israeli subjectivity is that of lords of the land—this is, for example, what makes the Israeli soldier manning the checkpoints what Hammami calls "the little sovereign" who decides on a whim where a Palestinian can and cannot move, whether or not they are going to be killed or imprisoned.[55] Lords do not pay much attention to the humanity of their subjects, and consider them as outside the realm of ethics, morality, history, politics, and so on.

Therefore, the relationship between the state and the settlers is not one of opposing dynamics or faces of the Israeli state.[56] That relationship is the revelation of the core of the Israeli state as a subjectivity of lordship.[57] Indeed, this symbiotic relationship between the settlers and the state (especially the military apparatus) reaches back to the 1960s; and even more to the point, the symbiotic connection between settlements and security goes back into at least the 1930s and has a continuous genealogy through to the present.[58] Settler movements and the settlers currently eliminating and replacing Indigenous Palestinians from more and more Palestinian lands are both beneath and beyond the state. They are the foundation of the state revealed while they are expanding the state. The tension between the state and the settlers is one where the settlers want to expand and reveal, whereas the state wants to expand and conceal.

Settlement, as practices by the state is the construction of Jewish only communities, roads, public facilities: in short, autochthonous Jewish peoplehood. Ensconced in claims of Jewish "purity" and "authenticity," of being a "unique" nation among the world of nations, of existing within a seamless continuity across Jewish past-present-future from which non-Zionist Jewish life and non-Jewish life is expelled, the Israeli state inevitably turns to the charge of anti-Semitism to conceal the settler colonial violence of expulsion and oppose any and all resistance to it. This brings us to the third element of the violence of isolation, which concerns the political estrangement of Palestinians.

The framing of the Palestinian decolonial critique and opposition to the Israeli state as fundamentally anti-Semitic has long been deployed and advanced by the Israeli state and its supporters since at least the 1970s.[59] Various projects funded and developed by the Israeli state have for decades sought to delegitimatize and even criminalize Palestinian decolonial resistance and discourse, particularly in Euro-American spaces through the charge of anti-Semitism.[60] One of the simplest, yet most strategically effective, ways in which this takes place is through a question that is relentlessly directed at Palestinians in academe, politics, public discussions, media interviews, etc.: "Do you believe that Israel has the right to exist?"[61] The strategic purpose of this question is the discursive colonization of Palestinians, since Palestinians cannot give a decolonial answer to it. If they say yes, it means that first and foremost, they acquiesce to their expulsion and accept the settler colonial order that was established on the ruins of Palestinian society. If they say no, they are immediately cast as anti-Semites and the conversation moves into arenas in which the destruction of Palestine is hidden and the quest for a decolonial Palestine is subdued from the outset.

It is important to note here that this discursive colonization of Palestine and Palestinians occurs across the political spectrum of Israeli politics and within many different spheres including academe. A recent example of an academic discursive colonization is the development and advancement of definitions of anti-Semitism that center the Palestinian Question. Two such documents have garnered international attention, the International Holocaust Remembrance Alliance (IHRA) Working Definition of Antisemitism and the Jerusalem Declaration on Antisemitism (JDA). In this "battle" of definitions, the liberal JDA positions itself in opposition to the conservative IHRA.

While there are important differences between the two documents, this is no battle at all since they both share the same Orientalist ground: the political estrangement of Palestinians and Palestine. In framing "new definitions of antisemitism" around the question of Israel and Palestine, both documents institutionalize, if not in intent (IHRA) then in effect (JDA), the allegation that Palestinians ought to first and foremost be monitored for anti-Semitism. Palestinian speech and resistance (for example, through the Boycott, Divestment, Sanctions (BDS) campaign) is cast as suspicious, malicious, and always potentially (JDA) if not automatically (IHRA) anti-Semitic.

I have critiqued the substance of these documents elsewhere and need not repeat those points.[62] Most crucial here is that Palestinians are never consulted in the production of these documents. For the producers of these documents, Palestinians do not deserve to be included into discussions of what counts as legitimate and illegitimate critiques and discussions on Israel and Palestine. For example, proponents of the IHRA proclaim that only Jews can define anti-Semitism, and therefore Palestinians should not be consulted even though seven out of eleven examples of anti-Semitism that they advance concern Palestine-Israel. Only after it was completed and no longer open to edits and change, were some Palestinians "consulted" on the JDA—like the IHRA, two thirds of the JDA document is dedicated to guidelines about legitimate and illegitimate speech on Palestine-Israel. Palestinian voices are thus actively removed from the discussion on Palestine-Israel, especially when it comes to the foundation of Israel as a settler colonial project. In the case of the IHRA, this is seen in one of its examples of anti-Semitism: "Denying the Jewish people their right to self-determination, e.g., by claiming that the existence of a State of Israel is a racist endeavor."[63] In the case of the JDA, this is seen in Section B which lists five guidelines on Israel and Palestine where we find "examples that, on the face of it, are anti-semitic" where guideline number 10 declares the following as anti-Semitic: "Denying the right of Jews in the State of Israel to exist and flourish, collectively and individually, as Jews, in accordance with the principle of equality."[64] In other words, Israel as a settlement project is what is being hidden from view in both documents by labeling Palestinian critiques of the foundation of the Israeli state and society as anti-Semitic. In both documents, the "do you believe that Israel has the right to exist?" question is repackaged and formulated more bluntly (IHRA) or more subtly (JDA), but producing the same effect that it has always produced: Palestinians cannot challenge the foundations of Zionism and Israel as a racist settler colonial project and cannot advance a decolonial alternative without being labeled hateful, bigoted, violent, and uncivilized.

In these documents, Palestinians are isolated and marginalized in the international discussion on what constitutes legitimate acts and speech and what is effectively criminal hate speech when it comes to their own struggle. In this process of discursive colonization, the intertwinement of the Palestinian and Jewish Questions is completely hidden from view. Only the Israeli and Jewish voices, which effectively and wrongfully conflate the two as does Zionism, are posited as the authoritative—and in effect dictatorial—voice on how we can talk about and act on Israel and Palestine. They come to discursively occupy the position of the sovereign as lord.

Put together, we see here that the violence of isolation operates across three interconnected elements that reinforce one another. All of this can be captured in the violence that is settler colonial settlement. We often conceptualize settlement as a displacement and expulsion that casts the expelled "outside" of the settlements. To a certain extent, yes, the Indigenous Palestinians are expelled "outside," but they are not then without relation to the settlement. The settlement is that which isolates Palestinians in their expulsion. From that position of an included exclusion, or isolated expulsion, Palestinians are obstructed from even communicating their expulsion as an expulsion. Simultaneously, the settlement is about the isolation of the autochthonous Jewish sovereign self from the Indigenous Palestinian and indeed from all non-Zionist Jewish life. It is no coincidence then, that over time, this isolation became much more ideologically central and concerned all non-Jewish nations across the world; hence the idea of a unique Jewish nation that stands apart from all other nations. Within this cycle of violence that is internal to the settler colonial structure of domination, however, a mimetic dimension of the violence forms. This is where we can trace the dehumanization of the Palestinian, which is undertaken so as to complete and finalize the expulsion of the isolated enemy-other.

DEHUMANIZATION: RACIALIZATION OF THE PALESTINIAN BODY

Racial supremacy over the Palestinian Arab inhabitants of Palestine is a central feature of the Zionist project.[65] In this racial hierarchy, which springs from colonial modernity, Palestinian Arabs occupy a place that is destined for the violences of exclusion and expulsion. As Noura Erakat argues, Israel's "legalized" violence against Palestinians is not properly understood when framed as a violence of self-defense, a violence between warring sides, or as a violence under an occupation law framework; rather, it is an eliminatory violence that aims to secure settler colonial sovereignty through the political and physical elimination of the "dangerous" native.[66] Regardless of the security threat that Palestinians actually pose or might pose (which in the majority of cases, for example during the Great March of Return in Gaza, is very minimal), we find that "Israel's martial law regime incorporated a permanent structure of exception into its system of governance that racialised Palestinian bodies as 'always-already signifying violence.'"[67]

The idea that the militarist Israeli state is the entity that is under threat when confronted with largely unarmed Palestinian bodies, and hence necessitates Israeli violence, is so absurd it should not require a retort. The reason why the Palestinian body is always already dangerous and violent within the Zionist worldview is because their mere existence as Indigenous Palestinians puts into question the existence of the Israeli settler colony as sovereign lords. The racialization of the Palestinian body is not marked solely by Brownness or Blackness, violence vs. nonviolence, civilization vs. barbarity, rationality vs. irrationality, enlightenment vs. darkness, democracy vs. tyranny, and so on. It is marked by all those things, and some are more accentuated than others in specific temporal periods and spatial locations, but most importantly all of this ever-shifting ideological content is always already organized along the Indigenous-settler distinction wherein the settler is absolutely distinct from the Indigenous (or the "Indigenous" Israeli is distinct from the Palestinian "settler" in ahistorical discourses). The Palestinian becomes that which must be continuously expelled, killed, maimed, and absolutely removed from the Israeli "self."

The Indigenous-settler distinction is only, can only be, validated through violence and force, for which the dehumanization of the racialized Indigenous Palestinian body is necessary (which is why Fayez Sayegh is correct when he states that racism "is congenial, essential and permanent" to the Zionist settler state). Part of what gives Zionism away as simply a particular manifestation of colonial modernity, as previously discussed, is a mode of dehumanizing racialization that makes it possible for Zionism to unleash uninhibited violence. In Israeli violence, race, and racial logics operate in such a way that renders the racialized Palestinian Arab body as John Harfouch puts it, "inorganic": a stagnant material caught forever in the repetition of the same; unthinking, unchanging, not only incapable of development, evolution, or transformation, but indeed constitutes a negation of temporal and spatial movement of any sort.[68] This racial logic is part and parcel of settler colonial genocidal violence that does not and cannot recognize itself as genocidal or even as violent because it negates the life and death of that which "naturally" ought to be eliminated—in short, within Zionist settler colonial racial logics, their violence only eliminates "human dirt."[69] Therefore, the Palestinian becomes destined for elimination in the particular sense that the Palestinian does not even die within this racist worldview because the Palestinian never lived.

The placing of the Palestinian body on the path of elimination applies as much to the maiming of Palestinians as it does to their killing. We should not succumb to shallow and misleading state discourse that attempts to paint its maiming violence (shots to the knees instead of the head) as a sign of an increasing humanitarian concern in warfare. As Jasbir K. Puar's work shows, the "right to maim" is another vector of sovereign violence ("will not let die") that debilitates the Palestinian body for the sake of extracting capital from the debilitated body, as well as eliminating the resistance and potential resistance of the Palestinian. The vector of "will not let die" is not a sign of humanitarian concern, but the expression of the colonizer's hold on the life and death of the colonized and everything in between: it basically says, "the Palestinians are not even human enough for death."[70] In short, the "right to maim" is part and parcel of the settler sovereign project of elimination.[71]

Crucially, Puar argues that acts of Israeli violence serve to debilitate "generational time" across the spectrum of past-present-future so as to "render impotent any future resistance, future capacity to sustain Palestinian life on its own terms."[72] The right to maim—the setting of the Palestinian as "naturally" destined for debilitation—is at bottom, an attack on the ability of the Palestinian to resist as an Indigenous Palestinian. We can observe how this operates, to go back to the previous section, in settler violence, which once again mimics the state's logics and reveals them in more explicit terms. The strategic utility of maiming is captured in the words of the perpetrator of an attack on Palestinian mayors in 1980 with explosives:

> Yehuda Etzion, one of the heads of the terror organization [the Jewish Underground], testified that the attacks were planned so that they would injure the victims and not kill them. "We chose the size of the explosive charge and its placement attached to the vehicle so that people would be injured in their legs only," said Etzion. "This principle of injuring and not killing was also applied in the way the charge was placed next to Tawil's garage." The Underground, said Etzion, did not want to make the victims into martyrs by killing them but rather into "living symbols of the crime and the punishment."[73]

Using violence to injure and not kill in the quote above serves the exact same purpose that Puar analyzes in Israeli state actions: it is not indicative of a humanitarian effort to reduce harm on the victim, but to eradicate the very existence of the victim as a resisting body without eradicating the body, since the eradication of the body risks the martyrdom of the victim and thus the entrenchment of resistance on behalf of the martyr.

The merger of Israeli state and society—not just the so-called "new settlers" but society writ large—on the idea that it is congenial and essential to continuously and permanently eliminate dehumanized Palestinian bodies who are incapable of life and death, is not only visible in the violences of settlement but perhaps even more visible in—but not exclusive to—the Israeli military onslaughts on Gaza. To be clear from the outset, the settler colonial attack on the Gaza Strip began in 1948 when Palestinian refugees were forced to live in camps there and has not stopped since. The most recent stage of this larger attack can be traced to the so-called disengagement plan in 2005 and the besiegement of Gaza which became full-fledged in 2007. The besiegement itself is indeed uninhibited and not so hidden structural violence: it is deadly and destructive in design and effects. It involves, among other things, the de-development of the economy, the degradation of basic and vital infrastructure (access to clean water, electricity, health care), and complete control over what goes in and what comes out of the Gaza Strip, among other things.[74] Within this structural violence, which is concealed as violence when it is constituted as the "normal background" of the "Israeli-Palestinian conflict" in official international discourse, we also find more visible elements of what Slavoj Žižek calls "subjective" violence—violent acts that are carried out by a specific agent that disrupt the normalcy of the background context.[75] This violence is as continuous as is the structural violence of the besiegement. It comes in the form of harassment of fishermen (which includes sinking their vessels and killing/maiming), shooting and maiming protesters during the March of Return and other forms of protest, small-scale military operations, and so on.[76] Within that spectrum of agentic violence, we find the major military assaults that Israel has launched against Gaza in 2008, 2014, and 2021.

I cannot examine all these violences here and how they compound one on top of the other (that would be a book project in its own right). But a brief examination of a recent full military assault on Gaza will suffice for the purposes of this book. From May 10 to May 21, 2021, Israel launched a full military assault on the Gaza Strip. During those eleven days, 256 Palestinians were killed, including sixty-six children, and almost 2,000 Palestinians were injured, including over 600 children, 400 women, and 1,000 men, "some of whom sustained severe injury and may suffer from a long-term disability requiring rehabilitation."[77] The infrastructural damage was severe: around 2,000 housing units were either destroyed or severely damaged; 15,000 housing units suffered some damage; multiple water and sanitation facilities and infrastructure were damaged (leaving approximately 800,000 people without regular access to safe water); fifty-eight education facilities, nine hospitals and nineteen primary healthcare centers all suffered some damage.[78] There was an estimated $89 million worth of damage to the energy, agricultural, and industrial sectors.[79] This amount is cumulative from previous full military onslaughts and the continuous siege of Gaza, and is thus always growing because of limited access to electricity, water, and other crucial basic resources that are required for recovery: all of which amount to the intentional de-development of the Palestinian economy and the dependence of Palestinian life on foreign aid.

The weapons used by the Israeli military against a stateless population with limited capacities for organized violence is truly staggering. State of the art fighter jets, drones, naval ships, and tanks fire devastating bombs and missiles at largely unarmed Palestinian population centers, without having any real concern from anti-tank, anti-aircraft, or anti-ship weaponry.[80] Secured in their ability to unleash sovereign state violence without any serious military, diplomatic, or economic consequence, the Israeli state can, as Israeli strategists famously put it in 2014, "mow the lawn" without hindrance. Palestinians are a mere blade of grass in Israeli discourse and praxis, which needs to be cut down when it grows too long. As a static inorganic material, to go back to Harfouch, the idea that the grass can actually grow is intolerable to the comfort of the settler sovereign who walks on top of the grass. When Palestinians begin to annoy the lords of the land on their sovereign walk in the "Promised Land," they must simply be cut down.

The kind of violence that is continuously unleashed on besieged Palestinians can only operate when those Palestinians are dehumanized, rendered disposable, destined for maiming and killing so as to prevent them from ever arising as human. The only method of securing the "purity," "superiority," and "absoluteness" of the Jewish nation is the positing of the racialized Indigenous as nonhuman: a staple of colonial modernity's racialization of the non-European. This, and not the ever-shifting ideologies of Jewish nationalism, ought to be our analytical focus. Regardless of their plans and intentions, what Israeli strategists and politicians and indeed the Israeli public is doing to the Palestinians in Gaza directly stems from the settler colonial structure of expulsion and elimination and is geared toward achieving it.[81] The Israeli actions stated above, and many others, are clearly not necessary to achieve the stated goals of "Israeli security," but rather stem from the aspirations toward absolute, indivisible, and omnipresent power and control over the lives and deaths of the Palestinians: it stems from a posture of lordship.

Despite these aspirations, the Israeli settler colonial project cannot in practice achieve them, and that is due to Palestinian resistance. It is critical to underscore that the resistance of the Palestinian people is the primary reason that has prevented, and continues to prevent, the Zionist goal of definitively eliminating the Indigenous as Indigenous. Certainly, pressure from international institutions, states, civil societies across the world, international advocacy and social movements, liberal global mores and norms against genocide, and certain aspects of international law, have also played an important role. But ultimately, it is the resistance of ordinary Palestinians that gives impetus, form, content, and direction to this international pressure in the first place. This resistance is not always present in the form of activism (petitions, strikes, armed missions, protests, blockades, occupation of public spaces, educational activities, and so on), but can also serve the function of engendering and guiding international pressure through the words of the dead.

Immeasurable in statistics of death and destruction is the devastation of Palestinian lives. Despite the racializing discourse which conceals and eliminates them as thinking, doing, living, dying, knowing humans, the life and death stories of the Palestinians killed and maimed continue to echo long after the "end" of Israel's barrage of bombs and destruction. The words of Palestinians which describe, communicate, and reveal settler colonial violence as eliminatory violence, can never in fact be eliminated. These words can never fully capture violence because nothing can, but the limitations that they reach are precisely the point where the complex operation of violence can be traced. This is where the (un)knowability of violence becomes apparent: regardless of the efforts to silence and eliminate them, and regardless of how much investigators, journalists, and scholars can document the violence in lives lost, injuries suffered, damages, and so on, there will always be an element beyond any representation (whether that representation seeks to conceal or reveal violence)—an element which we must follow if we are to understand violence.

Take for example the harrowing story of Yayha Khalifa, a thirteen-year-old boy whose body was torn to pieces while he was simply walking to the market to buy yogurt. As reported in the *Middle East Eye*, the Israeli bombs dropped on him and many others, including other children, at around 9 p.m. on May 13, 2021. This is how his brother, eighteen-year-old Mustafa, described the scene:

> I was running in the street and people killed and injured were everywhere. The blood covered my feet, and it was too dark that I hardly found Yahya. I held him with my hands. His back was open, and part of his shoulder was dislocated. I lived 18 years, and this was the most horrific scene I have seen and will ever see in my entire life.

Since that moment, I try not to leave the house so that I won't have to remember the scene when I see that place.[82]

Yahya's mother, Asmaa, described how his younger brother, ten-year-old Moatassem, also witnessed his brother's little body torn apart by the Israeli attack. Asmaa recounts how as soon as he saw her when he walked into the house, Moatassem passed out. She has already observed serious trauma in Moatassem, from loss of appetite to how "sometimes in the midst of laughing he starts screaming angrily without a reason. He cries all the time and is still experiencing the deep shock."[83] Asmaa then recounts the unbearable that is on top of the already unbearable:

> They buried [Yahya] on the next day. When my husband [Mazen] came back from the funeral, neighbours in the street called him and told him "Your son's flesh is on the electricity pillar." He went there and saw a piece of flesh hung on the pillar, he took it with a piece of cloth and went back to Yahya's tomb and buried it.[84]

She recounts how Yahya had saved money for weeks to buy a bike two days before being killed by the Israeli state:

> He bought the bike for 60 shekels ($19). For weeks he kept himself from buying chocolate or chips like his friends, only to save his pocket money to buy it. He waited to ride his bike and bought tiny LED lights to hang them on it to celebrate the Eid. But he left before he could do any of this. Yahya could not wait for Eid. What did he do to be killed in this horrible way and prevented from celebrating it?[85]

His plans, his very futurity (not just his future, but the very ability to imagine a continuing existence) was ripped apart from Yahya *and his family* by ripping apart his flesh, his presence. Debilitation of "generational time," as Puar theorizes it, does not occur just through the maiming of the body that is now unable to resist (at least according to Israeli logic); but also in the killing of the Palestinian body, Israeli genocidal violence disrupts and debilitates an entire family's "generational time."[86] In taking away Yahya's futurity, it indeed takes away all his family's futurity—indeed the futurity of the Palestinian: the ability to even think about a future for Palestine and Palestinians. In this sense, Israeli violence is an attack on life, death, and across life and death, as it is total in its aspirations and to some extent in its practice.[87] This is the indivisibility of settler colonial sovereignty at work: this is the manifestation of lordship. Israel is not just the most supreme beast. It is also playing a role that diverse human societies, cultures, and religions have attributed only to God or the gods: it decides, as the first and final word, the dictatorial voice, on life, death, and everything in-between and beyond.

But despite these efforts, Palestinian resistance, through *Sumud* (steadfastness, or steadfast perseverance), continuously holds on to its futurity. As Rehab Nazzal, an artist who uses art therapy with traumatized children in Gaza captures it here:

> The terror inflicted on children by settler colonial and apartheid states, whether in Palestine, across Turtle Island, South Africa, Algeria, or other colonized territories, in the past or in the present, targets the future of colonized peoples and attempts to crush their resilience and their will to resist. Targeting children obstructs the possibility of a radically different future—particularly the right to reclaim stolen lands and homes. Settler entities rely on the adage that "the old will die and the young will forget." But how can children forget a history that shapes their everyday reality? Does history not teach us that trauma and difficult experiences are passed on, silently, from one generation to the next?[88]

Critical to underscore is how the colonized, even when faced with the impossible task of fully narrating their trauma, draw on that impossibility to ensure that their stories are never forgotten, and are indeed part of the well from which resistance continuously springs. Thus, it is not that Asmaa, Mazen, Moatassem, and Mustafa are incapable of fully registering their horror because nobody in their situation can, and then we as scholars, journalists, artists, activists, and concerned people can document and discuss these horrors. Their reaction, their words, their unbearable burden and pain is precisely what we all should also acknowledge as our basic standpoint for knowledge. Each one of the sixty-six children and their families, and indeed each one of the 256 Palestinians who were killed and the 2,000 Palestinians who were injured in those eleven days of uninhibited settler colonial brutality has a similar story to share. This story is one in an eleven-day window into one hundred years of the brutal settler colonial conquest of Palestine. When compounded together, one can easily see why it is critical to underscore the (un)knowability of violence. It is simply beyond our ability to comprehend this much violence and brutality—we cannot comprehend the voices of the dead.

Nonetheless, these voices of the dead scream out for justice, and they reach spaces and times far beyond their immediate space-time. It is the very unspeakability and unknowability of their pain and suffering that gives impetus to international and generational solidarity with the Palestinians. Although Palestinians are largely prevented from narrating their experiences and suffering in colonial and imperial spaces because of the racial logics of Euro-American epistemology, their words and voices can still pierce through ideological barriers and reach audiences across the world.[89] It is these Palestinian stories that are situated at the roots of international pressure on Israel, revealing the Israeli project for what is: a never-ending cycle of settler colonial violence that seeks to create and secure Israelis as lords of the land.

CONCLUSION

Fragmentation, isolation, and dehumanization work in concert to expel the Indigenous Palestinians. This is a structure of expulsion that cannot but endlessly continue because the expelled always remains, and remains as an embodiment of an alternative world to that of settler colonialism. Settler colonial sovereignty is an effort to erase the stubborn reality of that resistance and its alternative vision for society, politics, and the human. It responds to that stubbornness with a continuous effort to expel the Palestinian "other," but that very settler violence breeds resistance and the resistance ensures that the expeller remains interlocked with the expelled. Enemy-siblings, as a concept, speaks to that interlocked condition and the ways in which violence itself, even when used in a zero-sum game between so-called separate and separated identities, and perhaps precisely because it is used in a zero-sum game between identities, ensures the interlocking of enemies as enemy-siblings: as hopelessly and stubbornly interconnected in the never-ending drive to expel the colonized.

When violence interlocks enemy-siblings as enemy-siblings, the interlocking can only lead to the propagation of settler colonial violence. But this is not a destiny or the necessary fate of enemy-siblings. Efforts can be made to transform the manner and type of the interlocking. We may not be able to escape the interlocking that violence has forged, but we can work from that ground to transform it, as can be seen in my analysis of Said's representation of violence in *A Hermeneutics of Violence*. One of the key features of postcolonial theorizations of the interlocking of racialized "self-other" relations brought forth by colonial modernity is to highlight how the self is multiple and multiplying, where there is no self that is unalloyed and independent standing outside of another.

Decolonial sovereignties are different from settler colonial sovereignty insofar as they emerge from the disposition of the diversity, hybridity, and plurality of the human condition. They are modes of sovereignty that serve as a platform for the infinite multiplication of the self, and to these modes, the book now turns. It will be critical in the effort to unleash decolonial sovereignties to directly tackle, *unbearable* as it is, the violent interlocking of enemy-siblings.

5

A LITERARY CRITIQUE

Toward Decolonial Sovereignties

Dispersion is precisely the principle that must be "brought home" to Israel/Palestine in order to ground a polity where . . . sovereignty itself will be dispersed.
—Judith Butler, *Parting Ways*

I want In the Wake *to declare that we are Black peoples in the wake with no state or nation to protect us, with no citizenship bound to be respected.*
—Christina Sharpe, *In the Wake*

This chapter will begin to move the book's analytical attention into decolonial sovereignties through a critical reading of literary works. Insofar as decolonial sovereignties offer an alternative to a mode of settler colonial sovereignty that saturates our world, it is difficult to find the right language to describe and conceptualize them. This is not to say that decolonial sovereignties do not already exist and operate—they most certainly do, but because they operate within colonial modernity even as they oppose it, the task of conceptualizing this phenomenon is difficult because the risk of articulating these sovereignties through the terms and logics of settler colonial sovereignty is high.[1] To avoid concealing more than revealing their decolonial potentiality and in search of fresh decolonial conceptual thinking, specifically on time-space and the "I," I turn to decolonial literature.

My point of departure follows Gurminder K. Bhambra's argument that if we are to move beyond colonial modernity, then scholars must examine how decolonization struggles challenge colonialism from a position that is both inside and outside colonial modernity, and provide alternative modes of being, doing, and knowing. Specifically, I focus on alternative modes of knowing in two literary representations of Palestine, which present a decolonial challenge to one of the key features of settler colonialism: eliminating, or what is perhaps a better word in an analysis of literary works, *erasing* the homeland of the colonized.

The focus on literature has been a staple of postcolonial theory since the school's emergence in the field of literary criticism, most notably in Edward Said's work. What makes "postcolonial literature" distinctive is the literary works' foregrounding of the tensions between the colonizer and the colonized as well as the aim of decolonizing culture and people's perceptions of the colonial world they inhabit.[2] It is fair to argue that certain strands of literary postcolonial analysis have strayed far past the lived experiences of the colonized;[3] but this does not mean that we are to disavow such a form of analysis altogether, but rather to work more clearly toward conceptualizing a decolonial politics in literary analyses.[4] Thus the analysis here aims to locate and explore the critique of colonial ideology that is operative in the "epistemic dimension of literature" (what literature teaches about the resistance to colonial ideas and the production of decolonial alternatives) in order to present conceptual tools for analyzing decoloniality in the case of Palestine.[5] There is indeed much to be learned from Palestinian literature in regard to the Palestinian struggle—as Refqa Abu-Remaileh puts it, there is a need to "integrate discussions of literature more concretely within the broader field of Palestine studies" and "to address the pertinence of literature as a living creature shaping the discussions that preoccupy the field."[6]

In reading literature on Palestine, I am not interested, as Ambreen Hai puts it, in focusing on the politics of the text "as thematics," but instead "show how politics inheres in the aesthetics of the writings" examined.[7] Hai usefully highlights how for postcolonial writers, "the capacity of their writing to act in the world is inseparable from its ability to tell dangerous truths, to push the boundaries of the unspeakable, or to participate in the making of new truths that shape reality."[8] As opposed to Hai's analytical emphasis on the body of the author as the site of agency, more pertinent to explore in the Palestinian case where the problem of erasure is ever-present, is the manner in which the erasure of the author occurs when the subject matter is itself erasure. That is, the politics that inheres in the aesthetics of the writings in the Palestinian case is a politics of erasure, and since the aesthetics of writing is ensconced in the dynamic of erasure, I argue that there is a transformative dimension to the manner in which the erasure of the author comes to bear in certain literary representations.[9] It is this particular dynamic within Palestinian art that demands the closest attention, I argue, since it reveals a conception of space and time that is alternative to the one underpinning colonial modernity.

There are five general features of Palestinian art (visual, literary, film, etc.) that stand out when it comes to representing the loss and erasure of Palestine after 1948: (1) artworks, in their form and content, "convey a sharp and composite sense of disorientation" and fragmentation;[10] (2) an emphasis on hybridity and the deconstruction of East-West dichotomies, replacing them with an exilic energy that constantly moves across identities;[11] (3) artworks engage directly with death and loss (of Palestine, and of politics to free Palestine), not nihilistically, but toward a politics that affirms life and freedom;[12]

(4) a paradox "of being something and its opposite at the same time" (or, *the thing and its negation*) is ever-present in the representation of Palestine (e.g., writing a nation without a nation-state);[13] and (5) Palestine is not just a physical territory but also stands as a symbol for decolonial freedom and liberation that many people across the world share as an aspiration and goal.[14]

Of course, Palestinian art that deals with erasure and exhibits these features is vast and cannot be discussed in its entirety here.[15] My analysis is limited to two seminal attempts in the literature on Palestine at writing the erasure of a Palestinian homeland, which are Elias Khoury's *Gate of the Sun* and Mahmoud Darwish's *Absent Presence* (I also draw on some of Darwish's poems).[16] I chose these two seminal texts because of their unique contributions to our understanding of a decolonial space-time and the decolonial "self," or "I." Particularly, I am interested in how Khoury engages Palestinian experiences with modernist conceptions of a bounded entity of space (the nation-state), and how Darwish grapples with the Palestinian experiences of linear progressive conceptions of time—both of which are staples of the Palestinian experience with colonial modernity. The underlying posture in these works is not an opposition to colonial modernity from an outside but is transformative of it from a position that is both inside and outside the settler-colonial state and modernity. In their representations, the limits of colonial modernity become visible and where we can find, not just a writing that affirms Palestine in spite of the erasures of Palestine and Palestinians, but where an alternative decolonial trajectory of space-time is illuminated.

The question of time and space is connected to the question of self-other, insofar as the former, in probing the notion of belonging, inevitably conjures up a questioning of the latter (and vice versa). This is a well-examined feature of many forms of postcolonial literature, wherein questions about "place" and "displacement" are connected to questions about "the myths of identity" opening up the promise of a "home" that can "become the transformative habitation of boundaries."[17] These literary works reorient our understanding of the multiplicity of the "self" in terms of its relation to the multiplicity of the "other" by shattering the spatial and temporal boundaries in which the self-other dichotomy is conventionally enclosed. Once these boundaries are shattered, I argue that we are left with a self-annihilation that is simultaneously a self-creation. By rendering Palestine in a position between a space that is everything and nothing and a time that neither begins nor ends, the self dissipates in its multiplicity, and *Palestine, as a decolonial alternative to colonial modernity, becomes the potentiality, the promise of a meeting between the "sun" and "absent presence."*

The first section in this chapter focuses on Khoury's challenge to colonial-modernist conceptions of space, while the second examines Darwish's challenge to colonial-modernist conceptions of time. The third section brings together both of those interventions and amalgamates them into a decolonial trajectory, which probes the question of self-other through these alternative conceptions of time and space. Engaging with Peter Hallward's critique of postcolonial literature, the paper explores how the question of self-other can be thought through these conceptions in order to situate the literary works' "specific-singular" transformative potentiality.

Before delving into the texts, it is important to briefly position my mode of textual analysis on the question of the erasure of the writing subject and the text. Much of contemporary theory contemplates the erasure of the writing subject in lieu of the centralization of the text in literary criticism. One of the exceptions is Giorgio Agamben's work, which shifts the analytical attention to the erasure of the writing subject in lieu of the de-subjectification of the subject. Agamben presents a penetrating critique of both modern and postmodern articulations of the writing "I" as a witness to suffering and death. Modern positivist articulations posit a centered self that is in full control of its intentions and meanings, objectively relaying the facts of the suffering. Postmodern articulations, such as Roland Barthes, posit that all writing involves an erasure and the erasure of the erasure, which challenges notions of an autonomous and centered writing subject who is in control of the writing and its effects.[18]

In his analysis of testimonies from Jewish survivors of the Nazi extermination camps, Agamben reorients these postmodern articulations. He argues that the question becomes complicated when the subject matter of writing is de-subjectification or erasure, when the writing grapples with erasure. He asks: Does it necessarily erase (not just decenter) the writing subject altogether? As I read Agamben, this does not refer to the poststructuralist "death of the author" catchphrase, or to the thesis Jane Gallop advances, where deaths refer to theoretical and literal deaths, both from the reader's and the writer's perspectives;[19] rather, I read Agamben's critique as referring to an erasure of the writing subject in the sense of a necessary effect of writing erasure, which is driven by a destructive brutality that is co-constitutive of the "self." De-subjectification introduces a brutal element within and of the self that the survivor/witness can neither expiate the self from (because it is co-constitutive of the "self"), nor directly acknowledge/face (because it is destructive). One of the ways in which this difficulty becomes manifest is through a mechanism of self-annihilation—i.e., since a destructive force is always present in the "self," it comes to manifest itself through self-annihilation that begets self-creation, which becomes especially acute when the writing "I" is grappling directly with the destructive force of erasure.[20]

This dynamic is visible in Khoury's and Darwish's writing of the multiplicity of the self and the writing "I," respectively. Following this dynamic as it opens up an alternative potentiality for decolonial politics would be missed if the analysis simply proclaimed the "death of the author" in lieu of the centrality of the text, which would direct the analytical gaze toward the effects of the text itself. I will come back to the question of potentiality in the third section but next, I examine how the politics of erasure, as I cited Hai earlier, inheres in the aesthetics of the writing, wherein the analysis follows the erasure of the writing subject in lieu of de-subjectification.

THE CAVE, THE SUN

Facing the difficult task of writing exile, death, and displacement of Palestinians and loss of Palestine, Khoury employs numerous writing techniques that neither obscure nor make clear the erasure. The dominant technique is the employment of a dialogue over the erasure between two main protagonists, Dr. Khalil who is afflicted by his shattered state, and Yunes who is oblivious to his own destruction. In *Gate of the Sun*, this dialogue is effectively a monologue within a self that is not whole. Yunes, the aged freedom fighter lies in a coma in a makeshift hospital in the Shatila refugee camp where Khalil nurses him. Khalil believes that retelling stories of their past can bring Yunes back to life, recounting stories that Khalil's voice, on its own, could not have spoken.[21]

That his voice is not his but Yunes's, that he is as much a patient as he is a doctor, that they are in a hospital that is not really a hospital, a refugee camp that is not really a refugee camp, all of these and more point to the world of semblances that the protagonists inhabit.[22] In this world, the thing and its negation lie next to each other in open contradiction, and therefore the semblances constitute a space that is both everything (the thing) and nothing (its negation). Without being dragged into this continuous contradiction between everything and nothing, writing cannot begin, and this is most clearly seen in the ultimate pairing of the thing and its negation: life and death. As Khalil puts it, "writing is confusion. . . . It's a state between life and death that no one dares enter."[23] Despite himself, Khalil enters this state, and the dialogue between the oblivion of Yunes and the affliction of Khalil reveals that the unknown and malleable space between life and death from which the comatose self "speaks" makes possible the writing of the subject matter of death, displacement, and erasure. Only in the meeting between everything and nothing where the protagonists are near life and near death, can the road to writing be opened, where erasure becomes communicable, but never fully comprehensible.[24] Simply put, the writing subject does not die with the writing; the writing of erasure reveals that the writing subject has always already experienced death.[25]

Central to this engagement with death is a refusal at being imprisoned by a living death. This is best expressed in Khalil's fear of any mono-history. For Khalil, any one version of history will ossify those imprisoned in its story, and such ossification is another name for the worst kind of death, a living death.[26] To live outside this living death, Yunes created in secrecy *Bab al-Shams* (gate of the sun), the cave in which he hid and lived during his excursions from Lebanon to his destroyed village in Palestine. He created a house, a village, and a country out of it, and no one had penetrated its secret presence or the secrets behind its creator, a creator of multiple identities. No matter how hard Khalil tries, he cannot ever arrive at the "truth" of Yunes, at the reality of who he was and what he created.[27]

There is a moment toward the end, however, where Yunes, nine months after the onset of his coma, becomes a baby again and is about to die—the beginning catches up with the end as the end returns to the beginning. At this point, Khalil is ready to let Yunes die because Yunes's truth was now inside him: Yunes's death gives birth to his truth inside Khalil after their nine-month ordeal in the hospital. And the truth Khalil discovers is simple: Yunes is and was irreducible and multiple, that he was the words that created shelters and countries for himself and Khalil to inhabit, and that at this point, Yunes had entered a distant world of poetry wherein the multiplicities of Yunes do not know of his death, and "only the forest of oblivion remembers [Yunes] now."[28] That is why *Bab al-Shams*, the cave that was the "only liberated plot of Palestinian land," was closed by Yunes's sons and their sons, who were named Yunes: the multiplicities of Yunes closed the door on Yunes's secret, which was only free to operate in its multiplicity because it was hidden.[29] When the inevitable end of one's life does come, a multiplicity of Yunes must close the door on Yunes's secret in order to ensure that Yunes is moving forward as a multiplicity, forgotten as the one.

Lital Levy discusses the importance of the cave as a "symbolic space" in Palestinian literature that deals with 1948. Levy's focus on the intergenerational tensions in the Palestinian story of 1948 and the cave as an alternative "underground homeland" is interesting, but I believe a different direction of analysis that highlights the continuous experience of 1948 in Khoury's writing opens the door for a more fruitful engagement with the decolonial writing of space exemplified in the cave.[30] The cave, as a liberated Palestine, in its multiplicity of lives and forms of life was hidden so as to remain liberated and free in its operation, but when that inevitable moment of the end comes, it must be closed so as to protect the operation of multiplicity, so as not to reduce Palestine to the one—to Palestine the modern nation-state as the only salvation for Palestinians. In the process, Khoury's cave falls within the purview of postcolonial literary attempts to reimagine the topographies of the colonized lands in ways that challenge colonial topographies of owned and bounded lands (land as resource) that belong to a specific national identity.[31]

Had the cave been open, it would have been occupied by the Israeli settler colonial state. In this context of modernity and the Euro-American nation-state, self-creation can only emerge from a geographical location that is at once outside (hidden) and inside (near his erased Palestinian village) the modern settler colonial nation-state. The writing subject cannot write the colonial experience constitutive of modernity strictly from within the confines of the nation-state. Rather, from the malleable space where everything and nothing meet, a kind of writing emerges that is transformative of colonial modernity. In the secret labyrinths of the cave, lies not darkness, but the sun—the freedom and liberation, which are nowhere else found in the visible spaces of the modern nation-state, glow brightly in the darkest of places. This is not Plato's cave, where the bright truth of the Good Life awaits us outside the cave, and although closer to it, *Bab al-Shams* is not the late modern culture of imagining a dark truth outside the scarcely lit cave in which we are trapped and oppressed.[32]

The cave in this novel is much closer to the parables of the cave in nineteenth-century feminist literature, where the cave is "a female place," a "womb-shaped enclosure" that contains both "negative metaphoric potential" for annihilation and "positive mythic possibilities" of self-creation.[33] The female writer withdraws into the cave away "from those open spaces where the scorching presence of the patriarchal sun" predominates.[34] This withdrawal is not a hiding or a capitulation, but rather a promise of a utopian future: "the cave is not just the place from which the past is retrieved but the place where the future is conceived."[35] It is also closer to "black feminist thought [which] roots freedom in the darkness of the cave, in that well of feeling and wisdom from which all knowledge is recreated."[36] Similarly in Khoury, the cave—whose nature, coincidently, Khalil discovers only after a nine-month truth-birthing ordeal—is the combination of self-creation and self-annihilation. In *Bab al-Shams*, much like the womb, everything (light) and nothing (darkness) meet. But slightly different from feminist literature in this case is the location of the sun. Yunes is in the cave because the dark truth of the outside world forced him there (not the scorching sun), and in the cave, much like Black feminist thought (exemplified in Audre Lorde), Yunes creates the bright truth of freedom and liberation that cannot be allowed to escape into the outside world where it would lose its brightness.[37]

The meeting between everything and nothing marks the decoloniality of space in Khoury's writing. A decolonial Palestine reveals the shaping and bending of space—reveals the attempt in colonial modernity to control and fix the openness, malleability, and unboundedness of space as an attempt to naturalize a beginning and an end, a mono-history that imprisons the self. In contrast, the practice that follows a decolonial conception of Palestine continuously closes the cave that houses the sun so as to affirm the meeting between self-creation (a liberated Palestine) and self-annihilation (the destruction of the unified, core "self")—this meeting is the feature of liberation in a decolonial Palestine where place can never saturate or exhaust the infinite openness of space and the multiplication of the self across that plane. The truth of multiplicity is also only exposed once Yunes becomes a baby again after nine months, at the moment of his death; put differently, this truth of multiplicity is revealed only when the beginning and the end release themselves from each other's grip: accordingly, liberation in decolonial Palestine can only take shape in a fleeting time where beginning and end lose the rigid chronological structure of their relationship.

THE "I" IN TIME

Darwish's writing better reveals the question of the beginning/end by presenting it more firmly in the problematic of past-present-future and the question of the writing "I." In *Absent Presence*, Darwish places the capacity to write only at the beginning since this capacity, when exercised, can only, because of Palestine's fragmentation in 1948, scatter the "I" along the lines of the text.[38] The scattered "I" finds itself caught between two points, the beginning (life in Palestine) and the end (death of 1948 Palestine). Thus, one must go back to the beginning, just to resuscitate the capacity to write, but this capacity necessarily always ends itself in its unfolding. Darwish does not attempt to force the capacity into any other direction, since that would be an attempt to impose something that is antithetical to the nature of the capacity. His writing, therefore, does not attempt to bring together the scattered "I" into a harmonious whole. There are laments, curious explorations, and imaginations of what life would be like had the "I" been complete, but every attempt at articulating such harmony is inevitably followed with the destabilizing and scattering structure of this capacity to write, of the impossibility of a meeting between the beginning and the end in the case of Palestine, where the "I" is always "complete and nothing."[39]

The acceptance of the scattered "I" is not to be confused, however, with a submission to the existential threat toward Palestine.[40] Against attempts to deny the existence of Palestinian refugees, Darwish reclaims the 1948 events of death and erasure as a constant reminder of the absolute reality of the life and existence of the refugee. The refugee does not require any "official" proof to assert existence; the "I" in this case exists in its lived experience of the erased homeland, in its continuation in the face of erasure and death, in its witnessing of that erasure, and in its memory of the erased homeland.[41] The "I" simultaneously exists by virtue of its scattering and despite its scattering.

In Darwish, the image of the lost place can substitute for the lost place in such a way so as not to trap the "I" within its confines. Imagination and hope constitute the words that try to capture the night of the displacement in 1948—a night caught between a "collapsing world behind and a world as yet unformed before [the displaced]" where the displacement becomes "narrator, narration, and subject."[42] The conflation between the writing subject, the subject of writing, and the form of subjectivity (self-annihilation/self-creation) within the sphere of death and loss is the scattering of the "I" that makes the identity of the "I" a complex and impossible endeavor. Yet, it is a sustainable endeavor since the imagined place suffices as a substitute with which we can play in the space between the lost place and the imagined place. The imagined place does not in itself sustain the writing subject, but rather the play between the lost and the imagined that the imagined place engenders does, and this, somewhat like Yunes's cave, ensures that the writing subject does not submit to the existential threat that scattered it.

It is an altogether different story with the death of time. In Darwish, we can only feel time when it is too late, we only feel it when it is ending, after it has almost finished killing us.[43] Time constitutes a trap that we do not see until we reach the edge of time and "we are unable to dance in the barrier separating the beginning from the end."[44] Like the separation between a lost and imagined place, the beginning and the end are separated by a barrier, but the barrier in this case only becomes clear when it is too late to explore and navigate.[45] By inability to dance, I understand Darwish as referring to our inability to connect distinct eras or periods of the beginning and the end. This inability constitutes a trap in the sense that even the separation, as much as the interconnection, between beginning and end becomes incomprehensible.

Time in its past-present-future formulation becomes incomprehensible.[46] The past is created in a sudden flash that formed a stark contrast between "here" (refugee camp) and "there" (the lost homeland): "The past was born suddenly, like a fissure. . . . The past was born of absence."[47] In the fissure of time is a "past" irreconcilably separated from the present and future. This lost, dead past turns into the hidden condition of life in the present—the substitution of concepts for the lived experiences that were lost—and in the process, it creates a question that makes incomprehensible the present and therefore the future: "In what time am I?"[48] When the condition of life becomes a road with neither beginning nor end, when the condition of life hurls the writing subject inside and outside the world, rendering their presence absent and their absence present, then the present becomes not timeless but impossible to look upon.

Any journey that tries to connect past-present-future in a linear and seamless whole is always already incomplete because it begins in the condition of death, of the lives, as Darwish puts it, that never completed their supper, prayers, not even their nightmares on the night of expulsion and displacement. Any coming together of the "I" can only be fleeting—why? Because the way forward is the next day, when the journey will begin, when the day will have come to commence the final journey back to the beginning; but this is a beginning that has passed the "I" and that the "I" constantly passes when it proclaims that the journey has begun; so, the journey will not begin, because it is only the speaking about the beginning of a journey that sustains the specter of a complete "I"![49]

Put differently, when time loses its past-present-future distinction, in rigidity and structure, the "I" no longer "is." A decolonial conception of Palestine can be understood as a traversal of an indistinguishable past-present-future. The configuration is not linear, progressive, or centered on/erected from a rupture. It rather opens the writing up to the abyss of time. Time kills us; it shatters and annihilates the self, not in an entirely destructive sense, but rather in the sense that time dissipates the self, revealing its many parts. In a fleeting time that neither begins nor ends, self-creation is entangled with this self-annihilation, leading not to death, but to the insight that the self cannot liberate itself by itself; that the self can only gain liberation and freedom from a relation to the multiplicity of "others," or to the endless stream of an ever-emerging "another." Properly speaking then, this paradoxical combination of self-creation and self-annihilation means that there is no such thing as *self*-liberation, but only liberation of oneself as another. Hence, simultaneous self-creation/self-annihilation, the mark of the erasure of the writing subject in lieu of de-subjectification, is revealed also as potentially the condition of liberation.

A DECOLONIAL PALESTINE

The question of potentiality, initially raised in the beginning of this chapter through Agamben, is perhaps fruitfully approached through a critical engagement with Peter Hallward's critique of postcolonial literature. Hallward employs three concepts that can help orient scholarly analysis of postcolonial literary writing: the singular, the specific, and the specified. The singular is a self-generative force and is nonrelational as it transcends and dissolves all relations and relationality. In contrast, the specific is relational as it remains committed to the world of relations, not in the sense of reifying that world, but in creatively engaging with and transforming it (i.e., taking sides, with intentionality toward liberation, in ongoing relations with others). The specified is precisely that reified writing of the world and its relations; it presents the world as if we are bound to be a certain specified identity (national, religious, gendered, ethnic, etc.) in a naturalized world that cannot be altered.[50]

Hallward is critical of both the specified and the singular and finds the greatest transformative potential in the specific. For Hallward, the specified simply imprisons us in "what is" and thus does not deserve serious analytical attention. The singular is essentially about the eradication of the writing "I," not about isolating the "I" from other individuals and the world, but rather about dissolving all such relations in the original nothingness of creation itself, to a time before time, a space before space, where the "I" would directly speak as creation itself. For Hallward, this attempt at removing oneself from the messiness of the world can only end in an (unintentional) acquiescence to the power relations that turned the world into an unbearable colonized condition.[51]

In Hallward, the specific and the singular are mutually exclusive, and he urges analysts to focus only on the specific. While Hallward presents a valid case, I agree with Lindsey Moore that this position requires more "finesse." Instead of mutual exclusivity, Moore suggests analytical openness to the transformative potential, in ethico-political terms, of the death of the "self" within the singular.[52] This can be specifically observed in Darwish and Khoury who show that the movement toward the singular is not the escape that Hallward says it must be; but rather, in this context, the singular acts as the energy well for the change that needs to take place in the specific. These works ultimately shed light on the positions taken in relationality and encourage the readers to take the side of liberation and freedom, making them "specific." But they likewise dissolve the "I" in their questioning of space and time, rendering them "singular" as well. Instead of tracing their movements from one pole to the next and then favoring their articulations of the specific as Hallward might, I think more fruitful is an attempt to understand how the singular, which appears in response to the necessary effect of writing erasure (the dissipation of the "I"), feeds the specific in terms of its vitality, energy, and direction. A more accurate and fruitful approach to the role and place of the singular in decolonial writing is that we stare into the nothingness of it all in order to ask a critical question: How can I draw on what is unbearable to see in order to remake the unbearable that I can see? This is especially critical in the case of Palestine because for the expelled Palestinians, it is understandably unbearable to see and operate from the space of interlocking enemy-siblings, where they come face-to-face not just with "the other" but with the other who has expelled and continues to expel them. In making this argument in the writings of Darwish and Khoury, I go back to Darwish first and incorporate some of his poems into the analysis.

In one of Darwish's last poems "A Ready Scenario," two enemies fall together into a hole, cannot overcome their impasse, and as a result reach their tragic ends as murderer and murdered. Honaida Ghanim shows in her analysis of this poem that the way out of the hole is "to displace the gaze from the 'present partnership of enmity' into the 'past partnership of multiplicity.'"⁵³ Ghanim argues that Darwish's insistence on the irrevocable relation between Arabs and Jews is built on the multiplicity of past partnerships between a myriad of cultures and religions in this common place of theirs. The past in its multiplicity, therefore, is the key to our escape from the present predicament of the hole where exclusivist enmity prevails. I think this is an insightful reading of the "specific" in Darwish's poem, but I think that adding Darwish's "singular" understanding of time is necessary to push the analysis further, since multiplicity in this case does not only include "other" cultures and identities, but painfully an "other" who wants to erase and expel the Palestinian.

As previously discussed, the specter of a complete "I" is sustained by speaking about the beginning of a journey, but the fleeting glimpse of this complete "I" is built on a condition of a mimetic relation to an "other" that wants to eliminate the Palestinian but which is now nonetheless part and parcel of oneself—indeed to a multiplicity of the self that is infinitely multiplied. Any effort to absolutely separate self from other, such as the Israeli effort to build a sovereign self by silencing and murdering the Palestinian enemy-other, is bound to fail for Darwish.⁵⁴

In "Like a Hand Tattoo in the Jahili Poet's Ode," which features the theme of a split "I" that then predominates *Absent Presence*, the "I and I" are joined by a third—a "realistic one" who is the voice of their destinies and who dictates that they bid farewell to what was and what will be.⁵⁵ It is clear in these passages, I think, that the third is a "specific" kind of Israeli other (there is no "specified" mono-Israeli-Other in Darwish): the "bulldozer driver who changed the spontaneity of this place."⁵⁶ As I stated earlier through Agamben, the destructive brutality of the "other" remains within the surviving "self." That is, Darwish's writing always already includes, in a "specific" manner, the most painful other in the capacity to write—the other that scattered the self and made the very constitution of the self a never-ending and impossible "singular" journey is always already there. Thus, the approach toward the "singular" is far from an escape here, but rather an effort to deal with the difficulty of confronting the co-constitution of the "self" with the brutality of an "other": this is the interlocking of enemy-siblings that Darwish tackles directly in his writing. This effort is not acquiescence to power, but rather it is driven to revitalize the struggle against forms of power that produced this effect in the first place.

It is critical to emphasize the point here that we are indeed talking about a co-constitution and not simply the presence of two or three sides of the self. This third who joins the "I and I" does not constitute a triad of the writing subject. Rather it is, as Hamid Dabashi captures it in the poetry of Persian poet Hatef Isfahani (died ca. 1783): "the subject is neither dual nor even a triad, but circulatory, circumambulatory, always substitutional, substitutionary, not absorbed, but in fact intensified in subjection of alterity."[57] The emphasis on the subject as circumambulatory and substitutionary, the infinite multiplication of the self, is critical to underscore in the writings of Darwish and Khoury.

This is why Yunes, also, is a multiplicity of Yunes. His truth cannot be reduced to a single fixed self—not only did Khalil struggle with this truth, but also Yunes did not fully understand this truth about himself since it is difficult to look into a mirror that reveals the depth of this truth (as I discussed through Agamben, this concerns the difficulty of directly acknowledging the destructive element that is co-constitutive of the "self"). This difficulty is illuminated in a brief exchange between Yunes and his wife Nahilah, where she informs him of their children's mastery of the Hebrew language. Yunes is wary of this news since it suggests that the children will forget their Arabic language and therefore their history and will become like the occupiers. Nahilah answers Yunes's misplaced fears by stating that this is the Israelis' problem: she asserts that the Israelis do not want the Palestinians to assimilate and become Israelis since they are a society that is built on an absolute distinction between "self vs. other."[58] This exchange reveals how Yunes's fears in fact mirror Israeli fears (a specific kind of Israeli "other" similar to the bulldozer driver described in Darwish) without him ever grasping this mirroring. This mimetic relation with the enemy-others, the interlocking of enemy-siblings, while very difficult to look directly into especially for the colonized who are facing erasure and elimination, must nonetheless be addressed and tackled. This has to occur in such a way as not to continue and propagate the mimetic relation of violence (the interlocking of enemy-siblings as enemy-siblings), but to establish a new and different kind of mimetic relation (the co-constitution of the self).

Faced with a daunting task, Khoury and Darwish do not attempt to circumvent the difficulties of erasure and self-erasure, but they also do not fall into the hubris of thinking they can overcome the difficulty of writing erasure by falling back upon some generative force of the void, of the singular as such. They simply lay out for us a serious attempt to play with this difficulty. And I argue that they play with the singular because the erasure of the writing subject becomes a necessary effect of writing about erasure; and furthermore, only then can their writing reveal a decolonial conception of Palestine that can be helpful in scholarly examinations of the paths of decoloniality in Palestine, not just in literary works, but in political groups, ideologies, and social movements.

In situating Palestine between a space that is everything and nothing, and a time that neither begins nor ends (both of which are singular conceptions), Palestine (as specific) emerges as the potentiality of a meeting between the sun and absent presence. This meeting takes place in what Dabashi has called the "interstitial space of the art of protest," which is:

> Somewhere in between, somewhere between the event that has occasioned it, the art that remembers it, and the theory that seeks to

capture its enduring significance. . . . If protest, its arts, or its politics do not lead to liberation, it is an exercise in futility, whether academic or artistic. The art of protest, always in the purgatorial limbo, preempts that futility—and over which fact and phenomenon no state has any say or sovereignty.[59]

In the interstitial space, the art of protest produces, encases, and releases the revolutionary alternative to the illegitimate postcolonial and settler colonial garrison state. It is a space where the revolutionary potential flourishes away from the overpowering gaze and violence of the state apparatus, and from which it launches its decolonial liberation project.

The potentiality of Palestine in this interstitial space, following long-theorized and studied challenges to colonial modernity, begins by illustrating how space-time was molded in a specific way through colonial modernity and must be made otherwise in order for a decolonial alternative world to emerge and flourish. This is not about going to a space before space and a time before time, an approach that Hallward critiques; but rather, creating something alternative. The decoloniality of space-time here engenders a return to fundamental questions about humanity, politics, society, justice, peace, belonging, and freedom—it reignites debates that have gone stale with colonial modernity's centralization of the nation-state as *the* locus of liberty, freedom, and the means through which can be reached the so-called apex of humanity.

For my purposes, I want to emphasize the insights and generative lessons of the reimagination of space-time in these authors' works for the sake of our understanding and reimagination of sovereignty, and this can be directly seen in how these authors exhibit the "I" and what happens to the "I" in and through their writing of erasure. In remaining open to the malleability of space-time, Khoury and Darwish posit the multiplicity of the "self," not just as hybrid and interconnected, but also as a locus of self-creation/self-annihilation. From the crucible of this space-time, emerges the potentiality of a decolonial Palestine that has practically nothing to do with Palestine as a *Euro-American type of statist and/or nationalist idea* or as the salvation from the predicaments introduced by colonial modernity (this is what makes the works discussed in this chapter distinct from certain strands of mainstream nationalist art).[60] Rather, the decolonial potentiality is a Palestine that concerns, not the re-Palestinianization of space and time in the dominant nationalist sense (what Mamdani would call conservative and reactionary nationalism), but rather the re-Palestinianization of space and time in the sense of liberation of oneself as another where claims of belonging to the land are fundamentally reimagined and practiced—where the tension between the unboundedness of space and the boundedness of place is revisited, reignited, and reactivated. The re-Palestinianization of space and time in the latter sense means, first and foremost, the return of Palestinians to all the lands of historic Palestine, and crucially means a collectively sanctioned legal, political, social, and cultural acknowledgment and affirmation of Palestine and Palestinian existence in all of Palestine. *This act of collective sanctioning in the case of particular decolonial strands of Palestinian resistance is none other than an alternative decolonial mode of sovereignty—the (re)commencement of a claim of belonging that does not rest on the foundation of the dictatorial colonial sovereign "I," but rather the multiplication of a decolonial "I" that always already takes into account and directly faces the interlocking of enemy-siblings.*

This decolonial endeavor can (and probably must) constructively engage with the nation-state as a mode of social and political organization. I acknowledge that the nation-state has widespread appeal for its promise of security, stability, prosperity, etc., and that a transformation of social and political modes of organization that have taken hold in the local and international public imaginary and practice, as has the nation-state, does not occur quickly or suddenly. To place ourselves on the path of transformation, this endeavor takes as its starting point, not the idea that Palestinians and Israelis must see that their liberation is tied together where an acknowledgment of cultural multiplicity and interconnectedness is key to our escape from exclusivist enmity as I cited Ghanim earlier; but rather the idea that decolonial liberation hinges on a self-annihilation that gives birth to a new self-creation. In the words of Darwish, "Every time you die in a poem, you are born anew."[61] The self-annihilation that must take place is not to Palestinian and Israeli identities per se, but to the interlocking of enemy-siblings as enemy-siblings, *and what promises to come out of this self-annihilation is a slow transformation of the interlocking of enemy-siblings into co-constituents of the self.*

In other words, we are not discussing here the meeting between two already established and stable identities where the interlocutors acknowledge their interconnections and place themselves at the ready to be shaken. Violence has already interlocked the identities as enemy-siblings. We can only work from this interlocking in the hope of transforming it; we are not destined to repeat and propagate it. What Darwish and Khoury accomplish is to show us that a different approach to the encounter can yield an outcome different from enemy-siblings. When we view and approach the encounter as one between always already destabilized, dissipated, and shaken selves with no recourse to a bounded space-time that can house them as lords and masters, we open the door for creating a new kind of house in accordance to a more open and malleable space-time: a form of political action and consciousness that would be epoch-making, much like the path that Christina Sharpe captures in the epigraph. I realize that this is a disquieting idea, and that individuals and groups will be tempted by the *potential* recourse to the bounded space-time of the modern nation-state (for Palestinians) and will be wedded to the *existing* recourse to a bounded space-time (for Israelis), but this is perhaps the only sharp alternative to settler colonial sovereignty. I do not claim to have discovered how to convince people to join this path and how especially difficult it will be convincing and moving Israelis who enjoy overwhelming power over Palestinians and therefore believe that they have nothing to gain and everything to lose if they give up their lordship. All I can do is chart the options and present the path that can actually lead us into a new decolonial world. The path we are currently on can lead only to the propagation of settler colonial sovereignty.

The sovereign "I," which both precedes and exceeds the settler colonial state, is constituted as a realm where a "pure" and "absolute" sovereign force (re)creates social, political, and legal orders and institutions. This structure of a continuously (re)creating sovereign force certainly takes different forms within Zionist ideology (from secular to religious, from civic nationalism to ethnonationalism, etc.) but the structure itself is the same and is manifested in the operation of Israeli violence as I have shown in chapter 4. Decolonial sovereignties must therefore not just oppose ethnocracy and ethnonationalism (as is often emphasized in the liberal one-state solution model) but must more importantly challenge and unravel the very primal scene that underpins settler colonial sovereignty (and therefore, underpins democracy and liberal civic nationalism in the settler colony). This is a challenge that places Palestinian resistance within its epoch-making decolonial potential, and this potential can only be unleashed when we reimagine and reconstitute the "I" away from its constitution as the dictatorial voice and subject of settler colonial sovereignty.

Going back to *A Hermeneutics of Violence*, I argued that the analysis of the mimetic relation with the enemy-other must center around the possibility-impossibility of enemy-siblings. The multiplicities of the self—the almost infinite co-constituents of the "self" that render the "self" a set of multiplicities—point us toward a dynamic process that I called violent dialogue, whereby the conflictual character of enemy-siblings is not simply an external confrontation that takes places across separate and separated selves, but also a confrontation that takes place within the self. What decolonial resistance must contend with (and cannot avoid, even though it is unfair to ask of the colonized to deal with this challenge), is that a dash is forged in and through violence (i.e., Palestine-Israel) that makes the terms on either side of the dash both possible (as co-constituents) and impossible (as sovereign selves in the mold of colonial modernity).

Violence places the thing and its negation next to each other as we have seen in this chapter. So, the difficulty for decolonial resistance is that the coming together of the co-constituent elements is always necessarily possible (the thing) and impossible (its negation). Regardless of which political perspective one takes, the possibility-impossibility of enemy-siblings always appears. For example, from the perspective of Israeli settler colonial sovereignty, we can observe how the possibility of creating Israeli sovereign selves (what is achieved through violence: the creation of an internationally recognized Israeli state, the expulsion of Palestinians, the erasure of Palestine, and so on) is always necessarily accompanied by the impossibility of creating Israeli sovereign selves (what is produced is a subjectivity of lordship that can never cease the chase after a purity and absoluteness that it cannot in fact achieve because of the resistance of the colonized).

Having said that, there is an opening for decolonial resistance to challenge the propagation of this dynamic—of this interlocking of enemy-siblings as enemy-siblings. In the system and logics of settler colonial sovereignty, the sovereign "I" is both the driver and the goal of ever-continuous eliminatory violences. The sovereign "I" is both sustained by and itself sustains the structure of settler colonial expulsion. On the other hand, the decolonial "I" that appears in Darwish and Khoury opens the door for slowly transforming the cyclical propagation of violence in settler colonial sovereignty, where the chase after the sovereign "I" is ever-continuous (i.e., when the sovereign "I" is not achieved, more violence is called upon to achieve it). Because the decolonial "I" continuously summons multiplicity and infinite multiplication, it can throw a wrench into that cyclical movement of propagation. Precisely because the multiplying "self" can no longer be achieved through the violence of expulsion, the cycle of violence is decelerated and theoretically it can be dissipated. The decolonial "I" promises to be the most fruitful path, and since it underpins an alternative to settler colonial sovereignty, the multiplication of this self means that we cannot speak of a decolonial sovereign*ty* but rather decolonial sovereign*ties*.

CONCLUSION

I have made the case in this book that the Indigenous-settler distinction must, paradoxically, be cemented as the ground from which we then work to eventually challenge this distinction. Cementing this distinction is necessary as the only way in which we can acknowledge the interlocking of enemy-siblings as enemy-siblings. It is impossible to deal effectively with violence without tackling directly and bluntly what violence has constituted as "real," and violence in this case has constituted as "real" the Palestinian subject as destined for expulsion. Cementing the position of the Palestinian as the Indigenous who is destined for expulsion and the Israeli as the settler who is destined to (re)create settler colonial sovereignty is the only means through we which we can face the violence that must be dealt with and transformed.

Transforming the dynamics of violence cannot mean the replacement of the master with a new master. Although this is a red herring in debates about Palestinian liberation and ought to be simply dismissed and called out for its anti-Palestinian racism, I will say explicitly here what should be obvious for fair and honest readers (lest I be ludicrously charged with genocidal intent as has become the norm for anyone calling for a free Palestine): Palestinian domination over and/or expulsion of Israelis is neither desirable nor transformative of settler colonial sovereignty. What I am arguing for in this book is clearly a transformation of settler colonial sovereignty, away from the posture of lordship and into a new mode of sovereignty. Decolonial sovereignties, by virtue of their being in practice and aspiration, shared, layered, and multiplying (following the decolonial "I" that underpins them), will not only oppose and not reproduce settler colonial power and domination, but they should theoretically slowly transform the Indigenous-settler distinction. Because they do not aspire to, or seek in practice, the establishment of a pure, superior, and absolute sovereign self, and emphasize instead the co-constituency of the self, they theoretically can and should, over time, dissolve the distinction. We are probably decades away from this new world and will likely be decades away even if we commenced on this path of decolonial sovereignties this year. But we must break the cycle of settler colonial sovereignty first. This is the urgent task at hand, and there is valid theoretical reason to believe that the decolonial path we follow will indeed produce the desired results for all the people who inhabit this land and the people who yearn for their return: a homeland that offers them belonging, safety, meaning, and nourishes life.

As I mentioned at the beginning of this chapter, it is difficult to theorize decolonial sovereignties because our thinking, living, doing, knowing, has been saturated with the logics and systems of colonial modernity. But this does not mean that these sovereignties can only be imagined. They have operated across the long and rich archive of decolonial resistance in multiple geographical locations and times. There have certainly been many forms of Palestinian resistance historically and into the present that have exhibited these decolonial sovereignties. In chapter 6 I turn to one such example, the popular committees of the first intifada, to show how decolonial sovereignties offer an alternative to settler colonial sovereignty, in practice and most importantly, in their aspirations. In theory, these decolonial sovereignties can challenge and transform the Indigenous-settler distinction and chart a new decolonial path of co-constituent existence.

6

DECOLONIAL SOVEREIGNTIES

The quest for establishing a Palestinian nation-state is fraught with difficulties, particularly insofar as this potential nation-state is forced to form and operate in a fragmented Palestinian landscape. It is clear to many activists and scholars that the Palestinian Authority (PA) cannot counter settler colonial grammar and forms of power but instead replicate and serve them. The PA does this in part because, by Israeli colonial design, it is incapable of addressing the violences of fragmentation. The PA's institutions, which operate on what Tariq Da'na and Ali Jarbawi call "colonial extraterritorial autonomy," is but the latest form of colonial governmentality that follows previous Israeli plans to cement the settler colonial fragmentation of Palestine and the Palestinian people.[1]

The PA's nation-state building project has, more or less, followed what Israel and the international system has pushed the Palestinian liberation movement toward: a brokered and limited sovereignty that would serve the interests of the Israeli settler colonial project, which is itself a cog in an international system built and developed of and for the project of Euro-American imperial hegemony.[2]

There has never been a concerted international effort to establish a territorially sovereign Palestinian state that, in the mold of the modern nation-state, could determine and control its own borders, govern all the inhabitants of its territory, control its security, resources, and so on.[3] Calls for Palestinian liberation and independence in the full anti-colonial sense of those terms have been consistently shunned and rejected in the international system. It is important to underscore that settler colonial projects always and by definition reject any and all Indigenous sovereign claims.

As Joseph A. Massad's work shows, the international system's rejection of Palestinian decolonial liberation dates back to the earliest stages of the colonization of Palestine: "the British Nationality and Status of Aliens Act of 1914, and its 1918 amendments, namely, the two main definitions of the right to nationality: blood and land, or, *jus sanguinis* and *jus soli*."[4] These legal definitions were central to the establishment of a Zionist claim to Palestine, and later underpinned some of the ideologies of Palestinian resistance to Zionist settler colonialism.[5] Massad illustrates how Zionist and British authorities denied the Indigenous Palestinian population any claim or right to independence and liberation, to a sovereign life on the land, by denying them *jus sanguinis* and *jus soli* (sometimes just one, at other times, denying them both):

> Colonizing Palestine entailed a series of classic settler-colonial considerations of determining who constituted and who did not constitute a nation, who and who is not entitled to *jus soli* and *jus sanguinis*, who, through right of conquest, could establish sovereignty and possess a right to self-determination, and who could establish racialized and religious origins based on biblical scriptures and who could not.[6]

In the case of the Palestine Liberation Organization (PLO), their resistance moved from a claim based on *jus soli* (prior to the Nakba of 1948) to a combination of *jus soli* and *jus sanguinis* (post-Nakba) to a severance between *jus soli* and *jus sanguinis* in and through the 1993 Oslo Accords.[7] After Oslo, Palestinians outside discontiguous scraps of land lost all and any *jus soli*. In effect, and regardless of the debates over the intentions and strategic calculations of the Palestinian leadership, the Palestinian nation-state project in and through the Oslo path accepted a narrow and essentialist understanding of Palestinian nationality and nationhood—a brokered, fragmented, tenuous, and transient kind of "possessive nationalism" to borrow the term from Judith Butler.[8] Even prior to Oslo, the PLO's relative acceptance of the idea of partition in 1974 "signified a drift from an inclusive, largely civic, Palestinian nationalism to an ethnicized Palestinian nationalism."[9]

After the Oslo agreements solidified and expanded the violences of fragmentation (an example of how peaceful dialogue substitutes for violent dialogue), Palestinians would come to constitute a nation that practices at best very limited sovereignty (of the Euro-American nation-state type) over approximately 18 percent of the West Bank. All other Palestinians would be considered fellow nationals only symbolically, and all Palestinian lands beyond the meagre 18 percent of the West Bank would be Palestinian only in the imaginary of the Palestinian people and their supporters, but not internationally recognized or protected legally or politically as Palestinian. In other words, the collective will of the people in this situation cannot be institutionalized in any way through this replica of Euro-American sovereignty.

Against the cheap and limited copy of sovereignty in 18 percent of the West Bank "under" the PA, are decolonial sovereignties, which have been imagined and practiced in the Palestinian liberation movement for decades. I want to be clear that my critique of Palestinian nationalism is directed toward the dominant strand that gave birth to the PA which Massad and others have critiqued. We must always keep this distinguished from a different kind of Palestinian nationalism—what Nahla Abdo calls "the nationalism of a liberation movement"—that is more appropriately understood within Hamid Dabashi's notion of the nation as excess of the state project of nationalism, and which at least strives in its praxis to challenge Palestinian fragmentation and assert a kind of unity that neither conceals nor valorizes difference (e.g., it remains vigilant against the dangers of nationalism as a form of community and belonging insofar as "racism is constantly emerging out of nationalism, not only toward the exterior but toward the interior" even in national liberation struggles).[10] I am talking here about the kind of nationalism we find in the intifada as a people's uprising, where the national element emerges as a way to articulate the common experience of Palestinians under Israeli occupation, state and settler violence, economic degradation and humiliating labor conditions, restrictions on movement, patriarchy and gender power relations, imprisonment, torture, dispossession, and so on—in short, the collective experience of settler colonialism as an experience that permeates all aspects of Palestinian life comes to mark the nationalism of the people as a collective quest for liberation. It is in these spaces of popular organization and mobilization that we find decolonial sovereignties as an alternative to settler colonial sovereignty.

The rich archive of Palestinian resistance is too large to be covered in one chapter. Here, I focus on the popular committees of the first intifada as a particular configuration of decolonial sovereignties, which are marked by the practice and aspiration toward layered, shared, and multiplying sovereignties. In the first section, I argue that the underlying condition that distinguishes decolonial sovereignties from settler colonial sovereignty and cheap replicas of it is a critique of the violence of expulsion that must counter the posture of lordship. In the first subsection, I explain why I hold onto the term "sovereignty" in delineating a decolonial path. Although a change of terminology may be necessary over the long term of the struggle, I focus instead on what is substantively distinctive about decolonial sovereignties. I argue that decolonial sovereignties necessarily present an alternative configuration of the relationship between the social and the political. This is indeed embedded in the critique of the violence of expulsion. Decolonial sovereignties necessarily always engender such a critique of violence, but not only that, this critique has to include a challenge to the posture of lordship, which not every critique of the violence of expulsion accomplishes. In the second subsection, I outline the criterion that marks this condition as a *decolonial* critique of the violence of expulsion. I argue that a critical and necessary criterion for decoloniality, for the opportunity to open up a path toward decolonial sovereignties, is an opposition to the subjectivity of lordship. Without an undoing of this subjectivity and its replacement with a decolonial "I," we will be bound to replicate and propagate settler colonial sovereignty through violent dialogue—through the interlocking of enemy-siblings.

Once I have identified the condition and its criteria for decoloniality, the second section delves into the distinguishing features of decolonial sovereignties in an analysis of the popular committees of the first intifada. In contrast to settler colonial sovereignty, decolonial sovereignties are layered, shared, and multiplying in both practice and aspiration. Part of what makes these decolonial sovereignties potentially epoch-making is that we can see in them a traversal across the social-political relationship which, in contrast to what we observe in colonial modernity, does not hierarchize the relationship between the social and the political. I argue that the Palestinian women's movement provides one of the more illuminating and guiding examples of this decolonial social-political relationship.

LIBERATION AND DECOLONIAL SOVEREIGNTIES

The Undoing of Lordship

Among Palestinians, the term for sovereignty, siyādah, *is not heard as often as the obviously anticolonial* tahrīr, *liberation, or* istiqlāl, *independence. (It would be hopeful to suggest that this results from the clear patriarchal implications of the term* siyādah, *linked as it is to the term for master and lord.)*

—Amahl Bishara, "Sovereignty and Popular Sovereignty for Palestinians and Beyond"

Amahl Bishara argues that in their resistance, whether in everyday acts, the intifadas, inside Israeli prisons, and so on, Palestinians have formed and engaged in practices of popular sovereignty in which they sought to articulate and determine their politics against the oppressive structures of settler state sovereignty. As she astutely points out in the epigraph above, sovereignty's inherent connection to master and lord in the Arabic language means that Palestinian resistance has drawn on different terms to signify their resistance to mastery and lordship: *tahrīr* and *istiqlāl*.[11] While I agree that it is hopeful to suggest that this resistance to the term *siyādah* is part and parcel of resistance to patriarchal power, I argue in this chapter that the resistance to the term is rooted in an intuitive rejection of a politics that is based on lordship. It is no coincidence, as I will argue, that the women's movement in Palestine is such a critical component of decolonial sovereignties as an alternative to a politics of mastery and lordship. The women's movement does challenge patriarchal power in Palestine, and while this has not become a dominant mark of the larger Palestinian resistance movement, I argue that this larger movement reached a decolonial alternative in the popular committees of the first intifada precisely because these committees were infused with the anti-lordship politics, mobilization, and organization of the women's movement. It may be the case that the term *siyādah* must eventually be dropped if we are to move beyond lordship and settler colonial sovereignty, but for the purposes of this book, with one of its feet firmly planted in existing sociopolitical conditions, the term sovereignty remains important for three reasons.

First and most importantly, as I described in chapter 1, the concept of sovereignty is unique in how it allows us to speak to a claim of belonging between people and land. The concept is not bound to replicate the Euro-American version of sovereignty: it was/is/will be imagined and practiced differently before/during/after the age of Euro-American empire. We still need this concept to denote such a claim, which is a necessary element of social and political life historically, in the present, and into the foreseeable future. Second, it is not clear to me that the term *siyādah* specifically is going to disappear from the political grammar of Palestinians, and the term remains at least a contested one in terms of its meanings and political utility. Third, I agree with Audra Simpson who argues that even though the term sovereignty, in its Euro-American version, is an imposition on Indigenous ways of knowing and political and legal systems (following Gerald (Taiaiake) Alfred, she agrees that it is an "inappropriate concept"), even though settler sovereignty must always eliminate Indigenous sovereignty and does not recognize its claims, the term retains a certain potency in communicating an Indigenous politics of refusal (instead of a politics of recognition) in the face of settler nonrecognition. The politics of refusal are important because they critique and challenge the story of sovereignty and nationhood that settler states like to tell about themselves.[12]

Therefore, what can be called decolonial sovereignties is not necessarily an imposition of a word, *siyādah*, that would bring mastery and lordship into the domain of Palestinian decolonial resistance, but rather a rearticulation of the term away from mastery and lordship. Khaled Furani may well be correct when he argues that we must move beyond the term *siyādah* (sovereignty) in order to free ourselves from the prison of colonialism and racial domination, but I do not believe that the term must necessarily conjure and rest on the principle of indivisibility as Furani argues that it does. It only does so in the settler colonial and colonial Euro-American version of sovereignty, and sovereignty (as a particular kind of claim to the relationship between land and people) can exist without indivisibility and instead as divisible and shared. Having said that, since *siyādah* is associated in Arabic with mastery and lordship (and as such indivisibility), Furani is probably correct that we need to find a new term, and that could very well be his excellent exposition and analysis of the Qur'anic paradigm of *khalifah*, which engenders "a political imagination concerned with human flourishing" as opposed to total power and presents us with "the promise of ethico-political renewal of a shared transient existence-in-entrustment (*amanah*) leading to freedom in the land, for Palestinians and all other inhabitants."[13] In a sense, what Furani and others see as the substantive promise of *khalifah* is very similar to the promise that I outline in this chapter under the heading of decolonial sovereignties: a shared, layered, and multiplying existence.[14] Terminology debates aside, then, I will keep the focus on the substantive meaning of the term that I am after in this chapter, which concerns a decolonial imagination and practice of sovereignty in Palestinian resistance practices. To properly analyze these practices, I present in this section a general outline of what analysts can look for in delineating Palestinian aspirations and practices that we might call decolonial sovereignties. Particularly helpful in theoretically framing the distinctiveness of decolonial sovereignties is Simpson's work, which focuses on Indigenous practices of resistance that are older and longer than Palestinian resistance.

In Simpson's analysis, the Mohawks of Kahnawà:ke show us a path of resistance that refuses the imposition of settler notions, practices, and institutions of sovereignty and nationhood. Whereas settler sovereignty and nationhood are singular (in law and authority), closed, and revolve around mastery and lordship, decolonial Indigenous sovereignties are "nested," plural, open, and continuously engender a critique of settler sovereignty.[15] Or more properly, they are nested, plural, and open precisely because their underlying logic is to continuously engender this critique.

This critique is as much directed toward current modes of sovereignty that are practiced in the "reserves" as they are against settler colonial sovereignty. Simpson illustrates this in many ways throughout her analysis (perhaps most critically in her discussion on the difference between membership and citizenship from the perspective of the Mohawk community). Suffice it to say for my purposes, the openness and plurality of the Mohawks of Kahnawà:ke is evident in their political, legal, and cultural life until "biopolitics and race became unambiguous techniques of settler-state sovereignty and governance."[16] It was only after the initiation of the structure of elimination, the loss of land, resources, dispossession, killing and maiming that "race became an issue at the time when being Mohawk became being Indian and being Indian carried rights."[17] The structures of elimination that continue to be imposed on Indigenous communities (e.g., laws around gender, identity, and membership) are therefore critical to understanding how it came to be that "official" Indigenous forms of sovereignty practiced in the reserves themselves became closed, singular, and connected to lordship.

Despite that closure, however, the community and the people themselves still practice a kind of sovereignty that challenges and interrupts the dominant and official narratives and practices. Thus, even if "membership entails formal recognition by the Mohawk Council of Kahnawà:ke," then citizenship, or "feeling citizenship," concerns "a complex of social belonging, of family, of *intracommunity recognition and responsibility*."[18] The two overlap for Simpson in the lived experience and reality of the community, but I want to stress that the two operate on different registers of recognition, much like Niang's distinction between the registers of *Naam* (the political) and *Tenga* (the social), which was discussed in chapter 1. The first is a formal, official, recognition of and for the structures of the settler state, whereas the second (in being blocked from such recognition and from creating the state or state-like structures that would bestow such recognition) responds by creating an informal and communal type of recognition—an intracommunity recognition that refuses the recognition of the state. Indeed, it must refuse state recognition if it is to elevate intracommunity recognition to the level of sovereignty, that is, to the discursive and practical spheres of rights, belonging, and responsibility.

Once again, we observe that decoloniality is always enmeshed in an effort to imagine and practice a different kind of relationship between the social and the political. One of the examples from Simpson's book that can further illuminate these different registers—how a reinvigoration of the social, decolonizing the social, serves to combat the colonial separation of the social and the political—comes at the end of chapter one (the point at which she says her book begins) in her brief discussion on Mohawk activist, painter, and writer Louis Karoniaktajeh Hall. Simpson cites Hall's 1979 "Mohawk Ten Commandments," wherein he states for the tenth commandment:

> 10. ACQUIRE ADVANCED HUMAN RELATIONSHIP. Human birth is an act of Nature, and all humanity is equally subject to Nature's law of death. *No one has the right of lordship over others.* The more able only have the right to help those less able; the appointed leaders of governments only have the right to be the voice and will of the people that all may share in the bounties of Nature and know peace and happiness.[19]

Simpson states that Hall's critique of lordship here is "a direct jab at the hereditary chiefs of the Iroquois Confederacy and the hereditary process itself."[20] A marginal figure in the "larger picture of Iroquois tradition," Hall is, according to Simpson, "a critical voice in a Mohawk nation-building project," and his "critique of monarchical forms of sovereignty" refuses the politics of sovereignty as practiced by the settler state "and even traditional forms of power."[21] Hall draws on the rich Mohawk tradition in a way that activates and reinterprets that tradition, treating it as a living organism that is as much oriented toward the present and the future as it is to the past—"his mission of enlightened militancy" directs our attention, efforts, praxis, thinking into an alternative universe of meaning and living, one that pinpoints the core of that which oppresses and seeks to eliminate Indigenous sovereignty and offers an alternative and oppositional path forward. The register of "reserve" sovereignty follows in the path and footsteps of lordship, whereas the register of the intracommunity aspiration and practice of sovereignty necessarily rests on a critique of lordship.

The point that stands out for me, then, is that decolonial sovereignties must at all times engender a critique of lordship. Hall may have referred specifically in the above text to this lordship in the monarchical sovereignty of settler colonialism, but as I have already argued, it is not only the monarchical form of settler sovereignty that rests on and carries lordship, but rather settler colonial sovereignty as a whole, in all of the different shapes and forms that it has taken. Furthermore, since lordship is unthinkable without violence, since lordship is initiated, maintained, and continued through violence, then decolonial sovereignties must first and foremost be that which operates on the logic of a critique of violence. One could argue that the colonized, regardless of ideology or approach, all exhibit a critique of the violence of expulsion. But what we learn from Simpson is that what distinguishes these critiques is whether or not they critique lordship—Hall's commandments critique all lordships, including the lordship of the hereditary chiefs. Decolonial sovereignties, which operate on a decolonial construct of the relationship between the social and the political, are a kind of sovereignty that fundamentally must engender a critique of the violence of expulsion that has to include a challenge to the posture of lordship.

But if, as I have argued in this book, the interlocking of enemy-siblings is intimately connected with the violence of expulsion, then how does a critique of violence approach the interlocking of enemy-siblings in an effort to transform it? The critique, in other words, is always already planted in this interlocking, so how can we transform the interlocking without replicating the interlocking of enemy-siblings as enemy-siblings? In chapter 5, I argued that a different understanding of the "I" is required for this task. The decolonial "I" that we can glimpse in the writings of Mahmoud Darwish and Elias Khoury presents an alternative to the subjectivity of lordship, and without an undoing of this subjectivity, we can never hope to transform the interlocking of enemy-siblings as enemy-siblings. In other words, this decolonial "I" names and opposes the subjectivity of lordship (i.e., Darwish's and Khoury's critique of a mono-history that attempts to violently expel the enemy-other) and thus shows the important implications to how we theorize a decolonial undoing of the interlocking of enemy-siblings as enemy-siblings. I begin this analysis in the next section by going back to Mahmood Mamdani's work.

Transforming the Interlocking of Enemy-Siblings

What Fanon and Césaire required of their own partisans . . . was to abandon fixed ideas of settled identity and culturally authorized definition. Become different, they said, in order that your fate as colonized peoples can be *different.*
    —Edward Said, "Representing the Colonized: Anthropology's Interlocutors"

Mamdani's solution to the problem of extreme political violence is a call to focus on the victims and perpetrators of violence as *survivors* (in order to avoid the victim's and the victor's justice, which are ultimately about revenge and power), decoupling the nation-state, and decolonizing the political. At the core of decolonizing the political, then, is the effort "not to avenge the dead but to give the living a second chance."[22] The reasoning behind the shift of focus is the necessary transition for Mamdani from treating violence as criminal to treating it as political. The criminal approach has a neoliberalized human rights framework where violence is pitted on individuals (even in the thousands) and ignoring the political systems that made this violence possible in the first place. The political approach seeks to radically transform those systems. In particular, it seeks to decolonize the political where the state no longer becomes the structure that represents only a majority nationality. The criminal approach revolves around victims and perpetrators, whereas the political approach revolves around all of those left in the wake of extreme violence as survivors.[23]

Of course, Mamdani does not suggest that we ought to level out the differences between victims and perpetrators. Instead, when we label all of them as survivors, we open the door for a radical rethinking of the political, which when properly transformed can become the new groundwork for productive efforts at achieving justice for the victims. This is where social justice can be productively pursued. This means that enemies will not cease to oppose one another, but they will become adversaries in their opposition, no longer enemies.[24]

Exemplary of this political approach is the formation of the Convention for a Democratic South Africa (CODESA), which for Mamdani presented a much more fruitful path of decolonization and reconciliation than the Truth and Reconciliation Commission (TRC). While the TRC was largely reactionary to apartheid and individualized the crimes of apartheid (and thus did not fundamentally challenge apartheid), CODESA allowed all South Africans, regardless of race and ethnicity, or of their previous position on apartheid, to come together in one shared political order to resist, oppose, and transform a system of apartheid and settler colonialism which separated them.[25] In this coming together, "there were enemies who might become adversaries, if only they were enabled to participate together in the same political order."[26] This coming together is not a harmonious event, turning enemies into friends, but is designed to simply create a political order where differences, oppositions, and fierce disagreements are handled politically and not through extreme political violence. This coming together in a new political community is ultimately an effort "to recognize that the racial political identities of the past were not timeless but rather created by *political processes*" and "as such they could be dismantled by political processes as well."[27] Although CODESA was flawed and incomplete, it was nonetheless an effort "to destroy the settler and the native by reconfiguring both as survivors."[28] Mamdani suggests that CODESA provides important lessons for other contexts, such as Palestine-Israel.

Mamdani concludes that the Zionist project cannot continue if we are to witness a decolonial moment: "The South African lesson for Palestine and Israel is that historic Palestine can be a homeland for Jews, but not for Jews only."[29] When enough Israeli Jews come to believe that they will be counted as survivors of Zionism, the Palestinian moment of freedom and liberation will come, just as Israeli Jews are liberated from the violences in which Zionism has entrapped them. "De-Zionization" means that Israeli Jews would no longer be "natives or settlers in historic Palestine" but rather "immigrants . . . welcome residents in a historic homeland."[30] The Jewish nation, in short, becomes decoupled from the state, just as the Palestinian nation is a priori decoupled from the new state. There would be no Jewish state or Palestinian state, but a decolonial state that belongs to all of its inhabitants:

> The state is not the property of any nation; the nation is not sovereign. *Nations* are not sovereign; the state is no more binational or

multinational than it is committed to a single national majority. The state is home to no nation. Home is society, where multiple nations with multiple histories can coexist. The state, meanwhile, is not a coming together of nations but a coming together of citizens who share a vision for a common future.[31]

This is the coming to fruition of the decolonized political—the end of colonial modernity's nation-state: "The nation made the immigrant a settler and the settler a perpetrator. The nation made the local a native and the native a perpetrator, too. In this new history, everyone is colonized—settler and native, perpetrator and victim, majority and minority. Once we learn this history, we might prefer to be survivors instead."[32] While this can be read as a leveling of victim and perpetrator experiences, I do not think this is Mamdani's point here. He is rather pointing out how victims can themselves at certain points in history turn into perpetrators as he convincingly argued was the case in the Rwandan genocide, and as we have seen European Jewry turning from the victims of violent European anti-Semitism to perpetrators of settler colonial violence in Palestine. Moreover, the decolonized political would not obfuscate the differences between the people that inhabit a new decolonial state: "Decolonizing the political through the recognition of a shared survivor identity does not require that we all pretend we are the same; far from it. It requires that we stop accepting that our differences should define who benefits from the state and who is marginalized by it."[33] In other words, the new decolonized political community would deal with the death, suffering, and destruction, but it would do so without one national identity claiming the mantle of the state at the expense of all others. The South African model, exemplified in CODESA, showed how the decolonial moment comes when the enemy would not be the "settlers but the settler state, not whites but white power."[34] Similarly, the enemy would not be Israeli Jewish settlers but the Israeli settler state, not Jews or Israelis but Israeli Jewish supremacy.

Mamdani's approach is a useful starting point for a constructive engagement with three issues, which can help us gain a better understanding of the criteria that a critique of the violence of expulsion must meet in order to be properly decolonial (i.e., not reproduce settler colonial violence, power, and domination) opening up the path toward decolonial sovereignties. First, many segments of the Palestinian liberation struggle have framed their resistance in precisely the terms that Mamdani proposes, going back one hundred years (that the state and Jewish supremacy is the problem and the enemy—not Jews). The result has been that the majority of Israelis are not listening. Most Israelis do not just lack the knowledge about Palestine and Palestinians, they actively oppose it and/or avoid it and its lessons and consequences. So, the problem for Palestinians is not an epistemological one, at the very least, not primarily that. The reason why Israelis are foreclosed to the Palestinian perspective and vision is precisely the subjectivity of lordship. This is the structure that needs to be undone, because it always already forecloses listening and hearing Palestinians and Palestine. *Simply put, the situation is not as simple (complex as it is in its own right) as Palestinians as an identity speaking to Israelis as an identity. Rather, we are talking about a situation in which the Israelis are constituted, foundationally, as lords, and lords are not known for their listening skills when it comes to those whom they rule and lord over.*

The second is the separation of the social-political, where the social is considered home, separated from the political which is the state (this to oppose political modernity's conflation of state and society). Since as the Mamdani quote above states, sovereignty cannot reside in the social but only in the political, then it is not quite clear what it is that holds together the political. Is it solely a set of laws that determine the rules and shape of the arrangement of individual units? Is the idea of a political community of survivors that would be codified in law as a community sufficient for holding people together? What is the nature of the connection between the social and the political in this model? If we adopt the idea (and I think this is what Mamdani's book argues), of the political as the foundation upon which social life then transpires, we still need a connection between them. This is the role of national identity in the Euro-American nation-state, but since Mamdani rejects this form of identification, then something else must replace it and fulfill this function. So, what does survivorhood look like on the level of the social? How does survivorhood become part and parcel of the collectivity? I think that we must think here more carefully about the social-political relationship as equal, as opposed to hierarchical, in which the political plays a more important role. Or, because the political plays a more important role, a hierarchical relationship between the social and the political becomes inevitable, and this makes survivorhood as a *shared* social subjectivity almost impossible as it is not clear what sort of identification will hold together the social.

This problem is directly related to the third issue, which four-dimensional violence raises, where the enemies are not just enemies, but rather they are enemy-siblings. If identities are ensconced in an ongoing political project of displacement and elimination, then can we talk about sovereign enemies who belong to the same order or structure of sovereignty? Are we presented with a situation in which there exists equally sovereign Palestinian and Israeli selves who are, as it were, the players in a game of enmity? Or, are we presented with a situation where enmity—or rather the interlocking of enemy-siblings as enemy-siblings—is the outcome of the ever-continuous violent elimination and expulsion of Indigenous sovereignty and selfhood? As I argued in chapter 5, we must transform the settler colonial interlocking of enemy-siblings into the idea of interlocking as co-constituents of the self. I am not raising these questions to dismiss the necessity of reimagining Israeli and Palestinian identities, but rather to point toward how deep that reimagination needs to go, the uneven nature of that transformation, and establishing the obstacles which stand in the way of that reimagination. What are those obstacles that I am referring to?

Going back to Mamdani's point that "racial political identities of the past were not timeless but rather created by *political processes*"—while I agree that political processes are necessary for dismantling these identities, four-dimensional violence shows that these identities were created by *violent* political processes. Mamdani is aware of the immense difficulties of transforming enemies into adversaries. But the difficulties go beyond convincing the beneficiaries of Zionist settler colonial apartheid that life beyond Zionism can still be good to them, provide them safety and security, and so on. In short, it goes beyond the political. It is only when we understand the role of violence in creating these identities that the political process can properly dismantle them. Any decolonial political process must contend with a "reality" that has been constituted as "real," by violence. Meaning, the very terms of the political process are from the outset determined and guided by violences that have rendered those terms as "real." So, we must confront and transform the subjectivity of lordship, which is the biggest obstacle. If we do not, we end up with a political process where cultural Zionism, without naming or addressing Zionism as a settler colonial project, sees itself as a form of resistance in the political. Such an approach is not a true decolonial critique of the settler colonial violence of expulsion.

Indeed, we will see in the next section that we require more than just a political process upon which social justice is pursued. We see instead the need for *social and political* processes to dismantle what violence has created and developed as enemy-siblings. I am not referring here to Mamdani's promotion of Palestinian activists in the BDS movement reaching out to the Israeli social sphere in order to help put pressure on the Israeli government, but rather social processes of transformation: not just teaching people in the social sphere how the new political can be good to them, but transforming the very structure and foundations of the relationship between the social and the political.[35]

"Become different, they said, in order that your fate as colonized peoples can *be* different," to reiterate from Said's quote in the epigraph. We can agree with Mamdani, Said, Césaire, Fanon, and Dabashi that the closed, fixed, univocal, and bounded nationalism of Euro-America is the enemy in this decolonial project. The perplexing question remains: Whose path leads us away from settler colonial violence and the violence of the modern nation-state? An inclusive and common path, that's needed of course, but on whose and what terms is this path imagined and written?

Yes, certainly it is important, as Mamdani argues, to move away from revenge and "give the living a second chance." But if we only, or primarily, focus on the living and give the living a second chance, then what have we done to the memories of the dead—to what I referred to in chapter 4 as the voices of the dead? Perhaps far from favoring the living over the dead, we need to listen more closely and carefully to the voices of the dead, not necessarily for avenging the dead, but for fulfilling the promise of their struggle for a justice that both precedes and exceeds codification in law and even in the political; for the remnants, for the excess that they both reveal and leave behind— that source of vitality and direction that resists representation, yet points us toward an alternative world. And what is decolonial struggle if not the struggle for the new alternative world? For that which refuses, opposes, and transforms the terms constituted by and through the violences of the postcolonial and settler colonial nation-state.

The decolonial critique of the violence of expulsion must meet a crucial criterion to qualify as decolonial: it must unravel the subjectivity of lordship because it cannot actually speak with it. Any effort to speak with it is simply the continuation of violent dialogue and can only lead to the cementation of the posture of lordship and the propagation of violence. This is not the same thing as saying that one cannot or should not speak with Israelis. This remains critical, inevitable, and necessary: the interlocking of enemy-siblings, I will repeat, cannot be wished away. But to speak from that interlocking to *transform it* means (and this is already present and visible in the practices of Palestinian resistance, from intifadas to acts of everyday resistance to the Boycott, Divestment, Sanctions [BDS] campaign) *a refusal to speak to Israel and Israelis on the terms that violence has constituted as "real": namely, that Israelis are the lords of the land*. This is the first and primary point of contact with Israel and Israelis. We can move forward only after this condition has been undone, symbolically and materially.

This form of refusal is indispensable to the formation of decolonial sovereignties, which can only emerge with the multiplication of the "I" and the recognition of the necessary coupling of self-creation/self-annihilation on the path toward a new and daring decolonial future. But we do not have to wait for the future to glimpse these decolonial sovereignties. We need to look no further than the recent past to understand what they are and how they operate. To these I turn next.

THE POPULAR COMMITTEES

The Intifada was a spontaneous, bottom-up campaign of resistance, born of an accumulation of frustration and initially with no connection to the formal political Palestinian leadership. As with the 1936–39 revolt, the intifada's length and extensive support was proof of the broad popular backing that it enjoyed. The uprising was also flexible and innovative, developing a coordinated leadership while remaining locally driven and controlled. Among its activists were men and women, elite professionals and businesspeople, farmers, villagers, the urban poor, students, small shopkeepers, and members of virtually every other sector of society. Women played a central role, taking more and more leadership positions as many of the men were jailed and mobilizing people who were often left out of conventional male-dominated politics.

—Rashid Khalidi, *The Hundred Years' War on Palestine*

According to Khalidi, one of the stories of the first intifada is the distance it revealed between local leaders of the uprising and the higher echelons of the Palestinian leadership in exile.[36] The local leaders had a much more nuanced and experientially based understanding of the Israeli state, society, and the nature of their colonial project. As a result, they were much more effective in both devising tactics and strategies of resistance as well as a superior ability to communicate their messages to an Israeli and international audience.

What was unique about the era of the first intifada was the fact that the PLO, the Palestinian leadership in exile, had long been positioning itself in the international arena as the representative of the Palestinian people and the Palestinian cause. Yasser Arafat became jealous and even resentful of the successes of local leaders and the major advancements that the intifada was making in international public discourse. This began a long road of the PLO taking advantage of the gains made by the countless Palestinians who sacrificed lives and livelihoods during the intifada (both inside and outside of Palestine), agreeing to the Oslo Accords and other agreements thereafter, and forming what became the Palestinian Authority.[37] This tragic outcome left Palestinians at the end of the intifada with a Palestinian security subcontractor serving the settler colonial interests and strategies of the Israeli state. In a nutshell, the Palestinian Authority that came out of the so-called peace process was essentially Israel's plan to inhibit and prevent the type of mass mobilization and organization that created the first intifada.

Despite this outcome, I want to go back to the intifada here to draw out what I think is a clear manifestation of decolonial sovereignties. The uprising would not have been possible without the formation of "popular committees," which were crucial to its activities, mobilization, and momentum.[38] As Noura Erakat summarizes here:

> Though seemingly spontaneous, the eruption of the uprising came on the heels of a decade of mass-based organizing. Students, women, professionals in many areas, and laborers responded to Palestinian ambitions for independence by combining national and social liberation. The Palestinian civilians under occupation made themselves ungovernable. Decentralized popular and national committees organized communities to meet their own needs, from creating alternative economies, schooling, day-care centers, and ways of ensuring food security to promoting "social and political consciousness to sustain the intifada." Broad-based and inclusive, the uprising featured boys and girls as well as young men and women throwing stones, burning tires, and hurling Molotov cocktails.[39]

The popular committees, in other words, carried out the tasks and functions of sovereignty, such as ensuring food security, community-based conflict resolution and mediation, equitable distribution of basic resources, creating and developing an independent Palestinian economy, providing services such as education and health, and improving community safety.[40] Crucially, in all of these activities they emphasized collective well-being and the common good over and above neoliberal calculations and individualistic concerns.[41] In their aspirations and practices, they reimagined the meaning of sovereignty, and this really concerned Israeli authorities. As Glenn E. Robinson explains:

Clearly, the Israelis were concerned about the growing autonomy of the Palestinian community as it began to disengage itself from its longstanding dependence on Israel. The initial success (or, at least, excitement over the possibility of success) of popular education and other areas of informal Palestinian organization led to the outlawing of all popular committees by Israel's defense minister Yitzhaq Rabin in August 1988. In justifying this action Rabin initially responded that these committees encouraged "violent activity." However, he went on to state what was undoubtedly the underlying motive for outlawing them: the popular committees were "undermining the Israeli government apparatus and establishing an alternative apparatus in its place."[42]

This alternative apparatus was not an accidental outcome of the popular committees but the very reason they emerged. Building on years of the labor movement's and the women's movement's professed goal to provide "concrete solutions to people's daily problems" and their success in "undermining the institutional control exercised by the occupying power," these popular committees managed to build an alternative mode of sociopolitical organization.[43]

The collapse of these committees and their anti-colonial liberation framework and ethos came with the Israeli criminalization of the committees that drove Palestinian resistance increasingly into underground cells, the advancement of the quasi nation-state building project of the Oslo Accords, and the "NGOization" of Palestinian civil society where NGOs beholden to international donors and the "conflict resolution through dialogue" agenda replaced the popular committees' forms of social organization that were beholden to the Palestinian people and the national liberation agenda.[44]

Moreover, Rema Hammami shows that these committees eventually suffered from internal contradictions that marked all forms of mass mobilization and organization prior to the intifada. For better and for worse, grassroots mobilization and social organization were closely associated with political factions in the early parts of the 1980s (a shift from the 1970s), and this resulted in contradictions "between their contending aims (grassroots development versus political mobilisation), within their leadership structures (party hierarchy versus professional staff versus community participation), and over their funding base (political versus donor money versus community support)."[45] By 1990, these contradictions, along with the Israeli crackdown on the popular committees were already leading to their demise; "By 1991 many of these popular initiatives had transmogrified into professionally based, foreign-funded and development-oriented centers."[46] As Tariq Da'na succinctly puts it, we witnessed in the 1990s "the dramatic shift from an indigenously defined mass-based civil society to globally designed and promoted NGOs."[47]

Crucially, though, for the period between 1988–1989, especially 1988, Hammami states:

> At first, the intifada was able to submerge these growing contradictions. Not only was it a unifying force, but, in the first two years, it reasserted the organisations' popular and mass nature—in some ways returning them to the original voluntarist and non-factional spirit of the late 1970s.[48]

Remarkably, during their most vibrant and forceful appearance on the historical scene in 1988, popular committees, in their mass mobilization and direct challenge to Israeli settler colonial authority, left an impact on the landscape of Palestinian resistance perhaps more so than any other sociopolitical formation: the "nostalgia for the first intifada is not a question of the past, but rather a question of a particular moment that can be reproduced, a replicable event. The search for collectivity and popular participation has made the first intifada an important 'site of memory' to be visited and narrated."[49] I believe that is the case because in their practices and aspirations, these popular committees give us a glimpse of decolonial sovereignties as a true alternative to settler colonial sovereignty: this was nothing short of a glimpse into an alternative world.

There are three main features of the practice and aspiration of decolonial sovereignties: they are layered, shared, and multiplying. These three features distinguish decolonial sovereignties from settler colonial sovereignty on the critical axis of aspirations. That is, it may well be the case that in its practice, settler colonial sovereignty is also layered, shared, and multiplying, but not in its aspirations. Because settler colonial sovereignty operates upon aspirations that are absolute, omnipresent, and indivisible, its practices are always directed toward settler colonial violence, however limited that may then appear in practice (and thus carry features that could be called layered, shared, and multiplying). In contrast, decolonial sovereignties operate on aspirations that are themselves layered, shared, and multiplying and thus offer an alternative to settler colonial sovereignty and in their practices constitute a critique of settler colonial violence.

These sovereignties were *layered* in the sense that they, when appropriate, overlapped and worked with other social and political bodies that carried out the functions of sovereignty, such as political factions, trade unions, more specialized committees (health committees, agricultural committees, etc.), and community organizations. There was no aspiration here to replace any of these other bodies or place them under the umbrella of the popular committees, specifically under the Unified National Leadership of the Uprising (UNLU), which was made up of various leaders of these committees and representatives from all the political organizations that made up the PLO (many of whom had been working on the level of popular mobilization and organization for years especially in the labor movement).[50] In their communiqués (many of which from the critical year of 1988 are reprinted in Zachary Lockman and Joel Beinin's *Intifada: The Palestinian Uprising against Israeli Occupation*), the UNLU was always empowering the committees and not taking power away from them or trying to centralize sovereignty.[51] Moreover, the UNLU did not attempt to displace other social and political bodies through the popular committees, so long as the popular committees remained the main organ through which the people determined their paths of action. In other words, the popular committees did not supplant other social and political bodies, but rather cooperated with them.[52] They did, however, importantly supplant older forms of social organization that were being utilized by the Israeli state to serve its own settler colonial project.[53]

Because the aspiration directed practice toward this layering of sovereign functions, where sovereign functions were fulfilled through cooperative attempts to achieve them and no absolute political or social body laid a claim to own any particular practice, an absolute or even large separation never took place between the social and the political. Any given sovereign function did not become the exclusive domain of a particular political and/or social body. Rather, organizations, groups, political factions, and individuals based in both the social and the political spheres worked seamlessly across the spheres in a complementary fashion for the sake of fulfilling the functions of sovereignty. Thus, instructions were not centrally determined and then imposed on popular committees (the political ruling over the social), and neither was it the case that the popular committees practiced or aspired to complete autonomy and separation from the UNLU or the PLO (the social without a political).

Organically there emerged similar or even the same set of actions, instructions, techniques, tactics, and strategies, but ultimately these largely developed out of the aspirations and practices of people on the ground who created and drove the popular committees.[54] Because cooperation and coordination was organically developed between the popular committees and other social and political bodies, the relationships remained diffuse and cooperation was celebrated and applauded (as opposed to being forced upon the popular committees), as well as moving in both directions where the UNLU would acknowledge heeding the recommendation of the committees in devising some of its instructions.[55]

Second, these sovereignties were *shared* in the sense that the functions of sovereignty were determined and carried out by the people for the people. The UNLU did not attempt to announce itself or speak with that dictatorial voice of settler colonial sovereignty—rather, "the voice of this leadership is communal and anonymous."[56] For instance, the communiqués of the UNLU encouraged the people to follow the lead of their own popular committees, to participate in their popular committees, and to create popular committees.[57] The popular committees were critically seen as the antidote to the Zionist appointed municipal committees which served the occupation, and thus their voice was always the most cherished and respected voice, as a voice that represents the collective will and guides the collective toward a liberated decolonial life.[58]

Moreover, the UNLU and the PLO were almost synonymous in their communiqués in terms of their relationship to the popular committees and their actions. They were still considered separate in their roles and the UNLU never presented itself as an alternative to the PLO.[59] The communiqués would at times speak in the voice of the PLO (usually when speaking to issues outside of Palestine such as international agreements and summits where the PLO is seen as the legitimate representative of the Palestinian people) and at most times in the voice of the UNLU (usually when speaking to issues inside of Palestine such as the daily actions of the Palestinian people against the occupation), but at all times, neither voice asserted a sovereign absolute authority over the popular committees, at least not in 1988–1989. In fact, these voices of the leadership recognized the popular committees as the critical organ of the voice that matters most: the voice of the collective. Without this latter voice, there is no uprising, and this was very well understood and accepted by the leadership.[60]

The layered and shared character of these decolonial sovereignties is encapsulated in communiqué no. 22 from July 21, 1988:

> The Unified National Leadership ... emphasizes the following: Full adherence to all the previous calls for resignations, boycotts and organization of citizens' lives. The importance of continuing to set up popular committees and support them by rallying around them, seeking their help in solving all problems, and backing their implementation of their programs considering them the people's alternative authority to the occupation authority's organs and appointed committees.[61]

As the will and voice of the people, these popular committees as "innovations of our people in the uprising and natural outgrowths of their struggle," embodied the layering and sharing of decolonial sovereignties.[62]

Finally, the popular committees were *multiplying* in the sense that the sovereign was not one and absolute, but rather their communal character encouraged their multiplication across Palestine. Each community could and was encouraged to create its own popular committee. As necessity and the conditions dictated, different committees would coordinate and work together to reach certain goals, changing once again their level of coordination when it was no longer necessary to do so, and so on. At certain times, smaller committees would form out of larger ones, and such was the movement of these committees. They were constantly multiplying into different sizes and levels of coordination. Significantly, these multiplications of sovereignties were an aspiration and not a source of major conflict or tension. They worked, relatively speaking, in a harmonious way for the sake of advancing the uprising, which is why the UNLU did not fear multiplication but indeed kept encouraging the formation of more and more popular committees.[63]

One of the critical consequences of multiplication is that it staves off the stark separation of the rulers from the ruled, the governors from the governed. People are continuously engaged in running their communal and collective affairs. This becomes part of the fabric of daily life, and as such the social sphere becomes almost at one with the political. I stress this because there will always be a need for a political sphere that is distinct from the social—a sphere that is solely dedicated to debating, organizing, operationalizing, and mobilizing resources for the common good. But in the practices and aspirations of decolonial sovereignties, the absolute and decisive separation of the two spheres is prevented by this coming together of the social and the political as one in the fabric of daily life. In other words, people do not add to their daily social existence a political activity for a political faction or party. Rather, the political act of thinking about and acting for the collective and common good becomes seamlessly enmeshed in the social. That is one of the great strengths of the committees and can be particularly seen in the aspiration and practice of multiplication: the never-ending work of attending to collective affairs within what I previously theorized as a complementary form of opposition between the social and the political, where (a) communication is open, honest about differences, and vibrant precisely because it is not about strategic discourse that advances the power of individuals and political parties but rather a dialogical encounter over the common and collective good, (b) membership is inclusive to all precisely because all must compromise to the larger collective and is healthily proportional (i.e., people will have different levels and degrees of participation) precisely because all are included, and (c) the definition of "rule" or "governance" revolves around the practice of everyone being both rulers and ruled, governors and governed, where the collective common good, and not the advancement and cementation of the power of a class of rulers, is the means and the end of rule/governance.[64]

When we combine these features, we see that decolonial sovereignties can move productively across the social-political divide and, in theory, indeed across all binary distinctions and absolutist and decisive separations. One of the areas in which our observation of this decoloniality can be enhanced is in the role of women in the popular committees, or more properly in the Palestinian women's movement. Although I cannot delve into this deep and complex topic, a brief accounting of it here can help reveal why this movement is so important, not just for liberating women, but also for directing all toward a truly decolonial struggle that exposes, names, opposes, and presents an alternative to the posture of lordship and settler colonial sovereignty.

For years prior to the intifada, women's committees had been building an alternative mode of social-political organization. This experience proved integral to the structure and operation of the popular committees, in which women took a leading role, so much so that "the work of the women's committees and popular committees became indistinguishable."[65] Significantly, "women were crucial in sustaining the intifada through the networks connecting the ... UNLU with the masses."[66] Women's activism was the glue that ensured a healthy and reciprocal relationship between the UNLU and the masses who created and participated in the popular committees. I argue that the main reason they were imperative is that they staved off the stark separation of the social and the political—their mode of work prevented the UNLU from becoming a separated political sphere that rules over the life of the masses in the social sphere, because as women, they had already dissipated that kind of decisive opposition between the social and the political in their own organizing.

The women's committees infused into the popular committees the structure and operation of a complementary form of opposition between the social and the political. The women's movement that developed in the 1940s was distinguished from previous forms of the Palestinian women's movement in its incorporation of women from across socioeconomic classes and regions (rural and urban), and as we moved into the 1970s and 1980s also across political ideology and affiliation.[67] The four main committees of the women's movement in the 1980s were divided along factional lines, but they never became a scene of struggle for factional domination. This is mainly because women activists and revolutionaries invariably connected the struggle for women's liberation in the social sphere (i.e., the gender struggle against patriarchal domination) with the struggle for all Palestinians in the political sphere (i.e., the national struggle against settler colonialism).[68] Both spheres become arenas of struggle for liberation and thus necessitate the inclusion of political life in the social sphere (e.g., family structure as a matter of public debate and policy) and social life in the political sphere (e.g., the rootedness of gender power relationships in colonialism—that is, the correct insight that colonialism promotes and benefits from the spread of absolute power within the colonized community, and advancing a particular form of patriarchy being one such method).[69] By connecting the gendered struggles of daily social life with the colonial project of fragmenting, isolating, and dehumanizing the colonized population, this approach basically introduces a halting mechanism to the colonial decisive and indeed divisive separation of the social-political relationship.

An example of this halting mechanism is the sense of togetherness that this form of organizing creates. Because it names and exposes the separation of the social and the political as a manifestation of *siyādah* as lordship, the women's movement emphasizes togetherness against the violences of fragmentation that often appear, for example, in hyperpolitical factionalism. Whenever the danger of advancing a political faction appears, it is offset with the grounding that as women, they are all in this together in the struggle against lordship in the social and political spheres (*siyādah* as colonial and patriarchal mastery and domination) and must not succumb to the lure of factional dominance. It was especially women's organizations and activism in the 1970s that "managed to challenge the prevailing gender order and develop a homegrown feminism that combined the national struggle with the struggle to change the prevailing gender order."[70] This was only possible because Palestinian women cut across the various layers of the social hierarchy, meeting the specific needs and aspirations of Palestinian women across Palestinian society, and ensuring their direct involvement and contribution to the struggle. This was a form of struggle and resistance that was "based on people's initiatives and direct participation."[71] Political affiliation and factionalism was held in check through this massive and powerful feeling, aspiration, and practice of and for togetherness.

If the popular committees managed, even if momentarily over the span of two years, to submerge the contradictions of factionalism as Hammami argues they did, it is probably because the women's movement was indistinguishable from the popular committees and infused them with the ability to avoid the negative effects of factionalism by grounding the struggle in the collective experiences of the people. As Islah Jad puts it, "there is a vital need for collectivity and a sense of 'togetherness'" in the Palestinian struggle, and this sense of togetherness was especially strong in leftist associations and organizations (but was present across the political spectrum to varying levels and degrees) in which women played a crucial role and reimagined and rearticulated the struggle for liberation as occurring across the social-political divide.[72] Because women activists saw the liberation of the social (gender equality) as equally important and intimately connected to the liberation of the political (the national struggle), the two spheres in their organizing did not separate.[73]

Necessary and vibrant debates continue to take place to this day on how to best tactically and strategically approach the struggles against patriarchy and settler colonialism, but that the two forms of power are always connected for the Palestinian women's movement since the 1920s is critical to underscore.[74] As an organizer from Nablus puts it in an interview with Joost Hiltermann in 1985:

> The struggles for liberation from male oppression and national oppression are intertwined. They are one and the same struggle, because the occupation reinforces the structure of male oppression. By raising the consciousness of women, they will be able to join men in the struggle for national liberation while at the same time liberating themselves from male oppression in the process.[75]

To be clear, it is not the case that factionalism must not appear at all if the movement is to survive as a collective grassroots and popular initiative and endeavor—in many ways, Islamist women's activism aligned largely with Hamas proves that.[76] Rather, a healthy and complementary opposition between the social and the political can keep the destructive side of factionalism at bay. In other words, as in the example of the Islamist women's movement after Oslo, there was no separation in these women's activism across the political and social spheres. Although there were serious limitations for them in the political sphere, and although they pushed for a vision of women's liberation that was different from (but engaged with) the secular and Left visions, these women worked in both spheres nonetheless because they understood the intimate interconnections between the two.[77]

Certainly, for Hamas as a governing political party, this served a utilitarian purpose: without a social sphere that is mobilized for liberation, there can never be political liberation; without grassroots and mass support that is based in the services provided to the masses by women and women's organizations, Hamas would lose its popularity in Palestinian politics, and there were other similar political calculations. Also, and to be clear, I am not suggesting that Hamas has, unlike the PA, effectively dealt with the separation of the social-political. This question needs a much deeper analysis, but there are many features of Hamas's governance and ideology that suggests it does not effectively deal with the separation and does in fact replicate it, when for example Hamas, just as Fatah does, gives itself the mantle of the only faction that represents the path of true national liberation.[78] But my point here is that many of the Islamist women working within these structures were not simply pawns in this political game but pushed the envelope on women's issues and sought to redress many of the oppressive structures that women face in both the social and political spheres, pushing a vision, with varying and uneven degrees of success, where women across socioeconomic status could and should be "active in all spheres of public life," which is effectively an effort to redress the separation of the social-political and oppose *siyādah* as lordship.[79]

We should neither downplay nor valorize the advancements that were made and continue to be made by the women's movement. There are gains and losses that are ongoing in this struggle. As I think Abdo's body of work teaches, Palestinian women do not have to meet the standard of complete gender equality in order to be considered successful, nor do we want to celebrate their achievements to the extent that we conceal the ongoing nature of the women's project of liberation from the interconnected (a) patriarchal structures that are imbedded in the national liberation movement itself, (b) widespread social conservatism in Palestinian society which is supported by the settler colonial power for the sake of dividing the Palestinian social sphere, as well as (c) liberation from Israeli settler colonial domination.

What I want to highlight, then, for the sake of illuminating decolonial sovereignties and the decolonial form of the social-political is that the Palestinian women's movement changed the direction, logic, and grammar of the struggle during the first intifada by creating and developing an alternative economy (e.g., enforcing and supporting boycotts of the Israeli economy, creating new markets for Palestinian produced goods, etc.), decolonizing education, building networks for childcare services, recruitment across class and region, and a mode of grassroots mobilization that remained grounded in and committed to the masses and moved in a complementary fashion across the social and political spheres. Equally important to understanding decoloniality is how these efforts were countered, which was to reestablish the stark and decisive separation of the social-political. This can be seen in the limitations and obstacles that women faced, such as how women and women's issues were largely marginalized in the structure and the communiqués of the UNLU, the pressure on women activists to join the quasi-state structures of the PA and abandon grassroots mobilization, the blockage women faced to reaching meaningful leadership positions and decision-making roles, and of course the structures of Israeli settler colonial domination that actively block women's emancipation as women and as Palestinians.[80]

As anti-colonial and critical feminists like Abdo and Jad have shown, the foundation of colonial modernity is a sexual contract which creates a decisive opposition between the social and the political. In dividing gender roles along the social-political distinction, this sexual contract places women in the social sphere serving the function of social reproduction whereas men become the rulers in the political sphere organizing the politics and the laws of the collective. Whether secular or Islamist (the PLO, PA, Hamas), mainstream and dominant structures of Palestinian nationalism has followed this separation of the social-political in and through the sexual contract.[81] These structures, often unwittingly but perhaps in some cases wittingly (a question for another kind of analysis), follow and feed Euro-American imperial interests in Palestine and the region.

This can be observed, among other things, in the phenomenon of NGOization that I mentioned earlier as one of the reasons that explain the demise of the popular committees. One of the key features of NGOization is the separation of political structures from the social sphere into which the masses are restricted. Notwithstanding some of the positive changes that the work of women NGOs has made and continue to make in Palestine, it is critical to point out that Euro-American donors are funding such NGOs precisely because they frame women's issues as only or primarily "social" and "cultural," not "political," thus serving the interests of Euro-American imperial hegemony.[82] Abdo explains:

> Removing NGOs from the sphere of political activism and change, from the actual concerns of the masses, and placing them in the sphere of "soft politics," where they deal with individual issues and internal cultural phenomena (women's issues, honor killing, Sharia laws, etc.), is not an innocent act but a global strategy with a highly political agenda. As Hanafi and Tabar have rightly observed in the Palestinian context: "It is the banality of aid systems and their 'conceptual maps,' which envision the social field as neatly divided up into political and civil societies, subsumed under and embedded within [the] public sphere, which is in need of questioning." I argue that these NGOs and the aid institutions that fund them are necessarily political, choosing not to affiliate with Palestinian national agendas and, if possible, to drive Palestinians outside of their national context and struggle.[83]

In short, Euro-American imperial hegemony, of which the Israeli settler colony is a critical component, must continuously keep the spheres of the political and the social separate and oppositional in order to establish, cement, and expand their colonial domination and lordship. The response to this approach, is not to frame and ignore women's issues as products of cultural imperialism or "Western values," etc., but rather to insist, just as the women's committees did in the first intifada, on articulating the deep interconnections between the women's struggle and the national liberation struggle. That is, to insist on bridging the social and the political and operating in a complementary form of relation between the two spheres.

That is why the women's movement is so critical—not only because it names and opposes patriarchal violence, power, and domination, but also because it challenges the larger context of colonial modernity in and through which modern patriarchal power came to be formed. That is why the women's movement, especially since it also cuts across other categories such as class in its foundations, structures, and mobilization, presents a critique of the posture of lordship in the social and political spheres and provides insights into decolonial alternatives and paths to decolonial sovereignties (perhaps) like no other movement does.

CONCLUSION

But the fellah, the unemployed and the starving do not lay claim to truth. They do not say they represent the truth because they are the truth in their very being.
—Frantz Fanon, *The Wretched of the Earth*

As this epigraph from Fanon states, the colonized "are the truth in their very being." The truth of colonized Palestinians is rather simple: across their fragmented land and people, against their isolation from one another and from the world, and despite their dehumanization, Palestinians remain a people who claim and practice decolonial sovereignties that refute lordship. In this chapter I examined the popular committees as a particularly promising formation of decoloniality, exemplified by the women's movement and the critical role they played in creating and shaping the popular committees. The demise of the popular committees does not mean the demise of the Palestinian commitment to decolonization and the effort to bring about an alternative decolonial world. So long as Israeli settler colonial violence and domination continues to colonize Palestine and Palestinians, the Palestinian people will remain the truth of decolonization and decoloniality in their very being.

To accentuate the ongoing nature of Palestinian decolonial resistance and Palestinians' continued embodiment of the truth of decoloniality, I want to conclude this chapter by briefly highlighting how we saw this truth manifest in the spring of 2021 in what Palestinians have called the "Unity Intifada." Palestinians crossed colonial borders, walls, barriers, and asserted decolonial sovereignties, not on, but of the land. Even if for brief moments, Palestinians in lands colonized in 1948, the Gaza Strip, the West Bank, and Jerusalem, descendants of Palestinian refugees and exiles in Lebanon, Jordan, Canada, the United Staes, the United Kingdom, and across the world, all joined together through marches, demonstrations, crossings, advocacy campaigns, and actions, in expressing their, not claim to the land, but their very existence as being of the land.

Palestinians in the Gaza Strip affirmed that their struggle is not unique but is rather the same as the struggle of all Palestinians against fragmentation, isolation, and dehumanization. Their demand for "collective Palestinian rights" across all the fragmented and isolated lands and people were critical in "exposing Israel's long-standing strategy of exceptionalizing Gaza's difference as an attempt to disconnect the territory from the wider Palestinian struggle."[84] Palestinians in the West Bank and Jerusalem, in calling for the revitalization of the national movement, the reunification of political factions, and the redemocratization of the PLO, named, exposed, and opposed the

Palestinian "infrastructure of struggle" that has been tragically turned through the PA to a tool that is used "to contain anti-colonial capacities and aspirations rather than to cultivate and develop them" as this infrastructure was built to do over many decades.[85] The language and actions of Palestinians in Jerusalem and beyond also captured the ongoing nature of the Nakba, and therefore the ongoing character of Palestinian resistance: their refusal to be erased and colonized, refusal to participate in their own subjugation and colonization, and refusal to simply being recognized, and instead articulated their place in the long continuum of the Palestinian desire and aspiration for decolonial liberation.[86] In their actions, slogans, manifestos, and demonstration, 1948 Palestinians rejected what Lana Tatour rightly calls the liberal path which seeks to incorporate Palestinian "citizens" of Israel "within the ambit of Israeli politics," and instead formulated and followed a decolonial path that emphasized the necessary unity of all Palestinians in their joint "effort to dismantle Israeli settler colonialism."[87]

Historically, "land for Palestinians," argues Abdo, "was the space on and from which they produced and reproduced themselves as an agricultural people."[88] Land remains for Palestinians, even as many are no longer like the agricultural people of the past, that which allows for their (re)production as a people.

The enduring nature of Palestinian longing and belonging to the land across their fragmentation, isolation, and dehumanization under lordship sent a clear message of defiance and rejection of the violences of expulsion. After decades of overwhelming Israeli violence and force, bare Palestinian bodies remain Indigenous to the land, even when and where they no longer remain on the land. This is what being of the land means: the connection between people and land need not be forged through force and violence, it simply exists. It is there, enduring, steadfast, in defiance of the settler colonial violences that have expelled the people from the land. There is nothing manufactured in this connection. State structures, empires, and global (neo)colonial orders are not required to build and sustain the relationship to the land. No advanced armies or nuclear arsenals are necessary to cement the relationship. No official papers and international legal regimes are needed to officiate the existence of the relationship or the manner of its operation. In short, there does not exist a need for a claim to indivisible sovereignty; but not only that, such an indivisible claim is revealed for the real chimera that it is in decolonial sovereignties.

It is not a chimera because the practice of sovereignty fails to reach the mythical ideals of settler colonial sovereign aspirations toward indivisibility, absoluteness, and omnipresence. As I argued in chapter 1, this misses the structure of expulsion in settler colonial sovereignty, whose aspiration for indivisibility, absoluteness, and omnipresence continuously engenders, drives, and animates its divisible and limited operations. In remaining intact, the aspiration ensures the continuous violences of expulsion, making such a claim far from a chimera insofar as it continuously leads to violent expulsions. In decolonial sovereignties, the chimera of settler colonial sovereignty is revealed as a claim that is based on a shallow and empty relationship to the land, even if and when this relationship is achieved or rendered achievable—why? Because it is a claim that is only possible through force, war, and ever-continuous settler colonial violence. In contrast, decolonial sovereignties are simply of the land and do not require, need, or necessitate a settler colonial type of sovereign claim.

In letting go of the aspirations toward absolute, indivisible, and omnipresent power and domination, decolonial sovereignties engender a critique of the settler colonial violence of expulsion, challenging fragmentation, isolation, dehumanization, and lordship. Decolonial sovereignties are not an external force that shapes and molds the land/people fusion, as does settler colonial sovereignty; rather, they remain the foundational unsaid beneath life on the land, or land as life.

There are two main objections to this argument that can be briefly answered here: (1) does the argument that I advance suggest that Palestinians hold a connection to the land that was not, at some point in history, also forged in violence? And relatedly, (2) do any other people that have called this land home both historically and in the present hold a form of decolonial sovereignty on this land? The answer to the first is that this argument does not need a nonviolent world to hold true, and for the second, the simple answer is yes, they do.

One does not need to be a specialist in the history of the land to know that wars and violences of all forms and types have existed on this land for centuries, as is also the case almost everywhere else in the world. It is probably a worthwhile project, but one beyond the scope of this book, to engage in a comparative analysis of these wars and violences across historical epochs and eras. But regardless of the specific peoples and lands concerned, it is clear to historical sociologists that the violences of the modern era dwarf those of previous ones, and are marked by forms, scales, and scopes of violence never imagined before.[89] What makes Palestinians today the holders of decolonial sovereignties is their positionality in modern history as the victims of this modern settler colonial violence and settler colonial sovereignty. It is not culture, ethnic or racial identity, or nationality per se as independent categories that shape the Palestinian's positionality as Indigenous and as practicing decolonial sovereignties. Rather, foundationally speaking, it is the positionality of the colonized in this particular project of settler colonial sovereignty, this particular manifestation of colonial modernity that then informs cultural practices and productions, identity, nationality, and so on in a decolonial direction. In his recent commentary on Ghassan Kanafani's brilliant novella *Returning to Haifa*, Massad succinctly elucidates this point here:

> The central question Kanafani's novel poses is that of origins. Are human beings to be defined according to who their parents are, their

race and blood, their geographic origins, or by some other criteria? Kanafani's questioning of biological descent as determinant of one's identity is his questioning of what academic theorists call "essentialism." As some indigenous Palestinians, in the context of the novella, can become colonising Jews and kill other Palestinians, and oppressed European Jews can become oppressors and conquerors of the Palestinians, are biological origins, genes, and geography then what is relevant in determining identity or is it ideology and power? Kanafani's conclusion is far reaching in its scope. He has Sa'id ask "What is a homeland?" and then concludes that "A human being is a cause and not flesh and blood that he inherits across generations." For Kanafani, it is here that the Palestinian is transformed from someone who is an original native of Palestine, or one who is biologically determined through birth to Palestinian parents, into someone who is a holder of liberatory and just principles that are contained within and constitute the word "cause" or "qadiyyah."[90]

This means that indigeneity is about a positionality that names, resists, and provides an alternative to settler colonial power.[91] It means that indigeneity as this positionality is not restricted to Palestinians or bound by Palestinian-ness, but rather open to many other identities, including Israelis, so long as the latter is no longer wedded to the Zionist settler colonial project and settler colonial sovereignty. It is not just Jewish supremacy in Palestine-Israel that must be disbanded through civic nationalism, but the very settler colonial claim that underpins Israeli settler colonial nationalism.

One of the main features that distinguishes Palestinian decolonial sovereignties from Zionist settler colonial sovereignty is that the former "does not obviate Jewish belonging" whereas the latter "is incommensurable with Palestinian presence."[92] Whereas Zionist sovereignty operates on the logic of lordship and mastery, Palestinian decolonial sovereignties operate on the logic of belonging and a layered, shared, and multiplying habitation.

At this temporal and spatial juncture, only Palestinians can practice and advance decolonial sovereignties, but it is when they are joined by de-Zionized Jewish Israelis that these decolonial sovereignties can be cemented and advanced, built and developed, coming to shape a new decolonial world that supplants the settler colony. How we get to this path, where the powerful colonizers transform themselves along the terms of those they colonize, along with the colonized, remains the most difficult challenge ahead. What this chapter shows is that the problem is not that there are no alternatives. The real difficulty lies in how we come to commit everyone involved to take the path toward an alternative mode of social and political life.

CONCLUSION

History will laugh at both of us. It doesn't have time for Jews and Arabs.
　　　—Mahmoud Darwish, "Exile Is So Strong Within Me,
　　　　I May Bring It to the Land"

Give Kabol to Mehrab, but keep your spear points dipped in poison, for wherever there is a kingdom, there is warfare.
　　　—Abolqasem Ferdowsi, *Shahnameh*

If I may reformulate Darwish's line in the epigraph, the *land* "will laugh at both of us"; the *land* as it passes through time "doesn't have time for Jews and Arabs." Put differently, in decolonial sovereignties, only the land is sovereign. This simple enough principle can be seen in the lives, values, symbols, beliefs, economic, political, and social structures of Palestinians prior to and enduring through Zionist settler colonialism, as resistance to and an alternative of settler colonialism. This is an organizing principle of a decolonial relationship between the land and the people that appears in different manifestations and formations across temporalities and spatial locations.

The different manifestations could be studied as moments in which the decolonial alternative erupts onto the surface in a particular form or shape, only to be attacked by the overwhelming force of settler sovereignty, and although made to retreat, is never fully eliminated. Much like Deleuze and Guattari's "war machine," this force "scatters itself everywhere, and then awaits its moment to rise again in metamorphosis."[1] Or as Abdel Razzaq Takriti puts it following Marx's understanding of revolution, we can understand Palestinian decolonial resistance as "an old mole hard at work, emerging unexpectedly out of the depths of the underground."[2]

The popular committees are one of the most promising manifestations of a decolonial formation, and it is critical to point out that their appearance in 1988 was not the first such occasion. The national and popular committees of the Great Revolt (1936–1939) (especially the popular committees of the 1936 general strike) similarly operated on decolonial sovereignties that worked "to delegitimize the colonial state while proffering an alternative vision of an incipient popular sovereignty, materialized through everyday practices and struggle."[3] Not only did these committees directly counter fragmentation, isolation, and dehumanization of British and Zionist colonialism, but also lordship and the larger problem of an absolutist, decisive, and divisive opposition between the social and the political. Like the popular committees of the first intifada, they were crushed by the factionalism that was encouraged by colonial powers separating once again the social from the political, in addition to of course the overwhelming violence of the imperial state.[4] Or rather, as this book has shown, we should understand those violences as the moments in which fragmentation, isolation, dehumanization, and lordship initiate, cement, expand, validate, and secure as "real" the colonial separation of the social and the political.

Settler colonial violence seeks to eliminate and replace, and it can achieve this instrumental goal, sometimes to a great deal of effectiveness, but it can never fully control the movement of violence. We must follow this movement of violence because it is the only way to reveal the four-dimensional operation of violence, and crucially the posture of lordship. Only in a direct opposition to lordship is there an opportunity, an opening, for a truly decolonial alternative to settler colonial sovereignty. This is the terrain of the real battle against settler colonialism. The battle can be waged on the level of fragmentation, isolation, and dehumanization, but it can never be won there. Transforming the posture of lordship is *the* critical terrain of battle. Much like the battle of the stenches that I articulate in the prelude of this book, we must wage this battle on our own terms and shift the terrain. We must move from the terrain where the stench of blood reigns supreme to a terrain guided by the stench of our sweat mixing with the soil, becoming one in our bodies with the soil, with the land. This means a radical shift in understanding, thinking, and knowing. Decolonial sovereignties, as I argued in chapters 5 and 6, give us a fighting chance to transform as opposed to reproducing settler colonial power and domination.

Some may find the language that I am using here to be a strange choice given my emphasis in this book on a critique of violence: *eruption* of decoloniality, *battle* of the stenches, a *fighting* chance. I am not being careless here and have intentionally used these words for two reasons. First, words and concepts are inherently re-signifiable. Of course, some words have become so entrenched in serving status quo power relations that they effectively can no longer be re-signified in the struggle for liberation and freedom. Thus, discussions on specific terms need to pay attention to context specific conditions, from moral to strategic considerations. That aside, I believe that it is appropriate to use words that have been associated with political violence, such as battle and fighting, in the struggle against the violence of settler colonial expulsion. But in doing so, we must be committed to re-signifying the meaning of those words. Not a battle for domination, but a battle against domination. Not fighting that propagates settler colonial violence but fighting that disrupts the cyclical movement of settler colonial violence. Our decoloniality erupts not to destroy for the sake of destruction, but to create an alternative world. I am not making any original re-significations here. Indeed, these have been the ways in which Palestinian resistance has, by and large, re-signified these terms.

Second, and relatedly, although I wish it were the case, we cannot politely ask settler colonial sovereignty to move into the dustbin of history. It must be forcibly transformed, and if it ever disappears, it will not go quietly. The structures and mechanisms that I have been attempting to delineate and illuminate in this book are entrenched and deeply rooted. Countless individuals, groups, corporations, nation-states, international and multinational organizations, institutions, multibillion-dollar initiatives, projects, investments, etc., are committed to settler colonial sovereignty. I have no illusions about the odds against a decolonial alternative. But what choice do we have? Settler colonial sovereignty is unlivable not just for Palestinians, but to billions of people across the world. Settler colonial sovereignty is directly connected to the colonial global economy, and we cannot think of the plight of the world's majority, crushed under the weight of empire and colonial modernity, without settler colonial sovereignty. The only option is to fight this system, and decolonial sovereignties must be our guide and goal.

I am not claiming that decolonial sovereignties, in and of themselves, can bring down the system of settler colonial violence. Other techniques and strategies must be employed to counter this system. In my view, this system can only be attacked through people-power across the world, mobilizing for unarmed disruptive actions such as boycotts, divestments, and sanctions against the Israeli state. Only when weakened economically and politically will the Israeli people be forced to reckon with their settler colonial sovereignty and be moved away from their lordship and toward a new decolonial path—a process that Ariella Aïsha Azoulay refers to as "unlearning imperialism." And if Palestinians and Israelis, given the worldwide attention that this struggle garners, begin a movement in and through decolonial sovereignties—my goodness, the ripple effects in its wake will be felt far and wide.

What is crucially shown in this book's analysis is that an alternative exists, and not only that—this alternative can and should offer Israelis a better future. A future that is safer, more sustainable, humane, economically productive, and I cannot stress this point enough: it is the only path that can signify a truly epoch-making contribution to the rich tradition of human life. Despite its claims, the Zionist idea of a "return to history" is anything but that; the Zionist project is simply the propagation of more of the same as just another player in the game of colonial modernity. In contrast, a Palestinian-Israeli decolonial formation would make this land and people a course of inspiration and aspiration the world over, including people who are of colonial Euro-America and are yearning for a different path, many of whom will certainly find similarities between the decolonial sovereignties I am describing in this book and the notion of popular sovereignty (which some scholars I cited earlier such as Amahl Bishara and Charles W. Anderson use to describe what I call decolonial sovereignties). But we should not conflate decolonial sovereignties with popular sovereignty in part because the latter operates on a specific conception of the "people" that was made possible in and through colonial and imperial violence (e.g., the "people" as citizens who benefit from a regime of citizenship that is based on the wealth extracted in and through the imperial and colonial project).[5] Popular sovereignty therefore does not directly name and critique settler colonial sovereignty. What distinguishes decolonial sovereignties from the conventional understanding of popular sovereignty is the direct naming and opposition to lordship as a posture of violence. Decolonial sovereignties as a concept is necessary for emphasizing this posture, but nonetheless the close connections to the notion of popular sovereignty can be a useful starting point of connecting struggles for liberation from modern territorial sovereignty across the world.

It is true that nothing is certain about transformation—but what is certain is that the current path has one ending: the propagation of colonial modernity and the violence of expulsion. This propagation has certainly served Zionist Israeli interests and goals, but nothing lasts forever. Birthed, developed, sustained, and expanded through violence, Zionism as a settler colonial project in perpetuity is none other than the never-ending propagation of violence. For millennia, we have known that violence begets violence, and we know where this ends: in more violence, destruction, and blood—as Ferdowsi captures it in the epigraph, "wherever there is a kingdom, there is warfare." It is inevitable that in this violence, positions shift and change and the vanquished becomes the victor and the victor the vanquished. It is in the interests of Zionists to de-Zionize and transform if they are to avoid this inevitability of history.

It is possible that we are already so far down this settler colonial path that we cannot change it. But it is worth the effort to transform it. This book, in combining academic insights with lessons and insights from the long history of Palestinian resistance, presents an analytical framework that can help us understand and plan this transformation, as well as guide our movement on this path, directing it toward a decolonial alternative that promises a better world. Even if we fail at this historical juncture, let us at least leave behind an example and a guide to an alternative decolonial world for future generations.

POSTSCRIPT

"What is certain is that the current path has one ending: the propagation of colonial modernity and the violence of expulsion." When I wrote these words in this book's conclusion prior to October of 2023, I did not know that the world would witness their brutal reality in a few short weeks. Indeed, I had written out these ideas before in an opinion piece for *Al Jazeera* in 2021 where I asked if "another violent mass expulsion of Palestinians [was] on the horizon" and concluded that "it is hard to deny that, if and when the right conditions materialise, the Israeli state will not hesitate to do what is necessary, including embarking on a mass expulsion of the Palestinians, to expand its sovereignty."[1] Admittedly, I have been personally preparing myself psychologically and emotionally for the horrors that have been visited upon the Palestinian people in the last twelve months for some time. But nothing can prepare you for the experience of witnessing your people's genocide unfolding on your screen, while you helplessly shout for it to stop. What Palestinians are going through in this moment will be the subject of many scholarly books, art works, public discourse, and policy discussions for years to come. What is certain is that this experience has changed something deep and fundamental in the lives of Palestinians and the collective story of Palestinians as a people. What is also certain is that this genocide has changed many non-Palestinians as well.

Today, millions of people around the world are radically changing their political consciousness as a result of this experience. The time is ripe for an alternative path to take hold and spread among the multitudes of people. But many obstacles remain, blocking people from following this path. States around the world, especially in Western Europe and North America, are not responding to their peoples' aspirations and demands, and instead are using various forms of violence to repress those aspirations. Powerful social forces that stand to lose their wealth and power from a radical transformation of social, political, legal, and economic structures are using all of their assets to maintain the status quo and defeat the oppressed and repressed social forces seeking that transformation. For example, grassroots efforts to disrupt the military-industrial complex are being met with severe punishment. Laws are being introduced that make it more difficult for people to engage in economic, political, and cultural disruptions.

Politically, the U.S. government is not budging or changing its policy position on Palestine. U.S. imperialism has too much invested in Israeli settler colonialism and remains committed to it. Despite significant internal public pressure, and indeed building diplomatic pressure, the U.S. government is refusing to change its course. The upcoming 2024 presidential elections offer little difference between a Trump or a Harris administration. Both will remain committed to the Israeli settler colonial project and provide unconditional support to it. There will be rhetorical differences between the two administrations, and there may even be small differences in terms of the level of unconditionality of their support to Israel, but it is looking like unconditional support nonetheless.

Many of the Arab states are also not changing their fundamental position. They continue to work closely with the U.S. empire, satisfying the interests of empire and a small class of economic and political elites at the expense of their people's well-being, freedom, and sovereignty as well as the liberation of the Palestinian people. Other states in the Global South remain largely symbolic in their support for the Palestinian struggle for liberation, and when more serious actions are taken, such as partially cutting ties with the Israeli state (by Türkiye, Colombia) or charging the Israeli state with crimes at the International Court of Justice (by South Africa), these actions are tied to the very limited idea of a "two-state solution." In other words, such efforts do not truly decolonize Palestine-Israel but rather attempt to resolve the struggle by offering Palestinians a seat at the table of states, where Palestinians can practice forms of self-determination and sovereignty that are grounded in colonial modernity, and over just 22 percent of historic Palestine.

There are many problems with this approach. First, even if we accept that this is the only possible path forward to stop genocide and the further expulsion of the Palestinian people, then states will have to contend with the fact that the Israeli state outrightly rejects this path. Not only in policies and practices, as was clearly determined in the ICJ's Advisory Opinion, but also in Israeli state legislation that has officially rejected the idea of a Palestinian state. So, in reality, what Israel and its imperial sponsor, the United States, fully and well understand is that a Palestinian "state" will only be in reality, Palestinian self-administration, not self-determination, in approximately just 5 to 8 percent of historic Palestine, with Israel practicing official settler colonial sovereignty over the rest, and in effect practicing settler colonial sovereignty over the entirety of the land. So, any state anywhere in the world that proclaims its support for a two-state solution must clearly indicate how it is going to force the Israeli state and the United States to accept full Palestinian sovereignty over 22 percent of historic Palestine.

Second, and more importantly, this book has argued that even that kind of sovereignty over 22 percent of historic Palestine will not yield justice or decolonization. Not only does this book predict that such a Palestinian state will not emerge since the more powerful Israeli state, in accordance with the logics of settler colonial sovereignty, will not allow that to happen; but also that should such a state emerge, it will not deal with the injustice of Israeli settler colonial violence and hence ensure the propagation of the cycle of violence that is internal to settler colonial violence. This means that even with the emergence of a Palestinian state, we are highly likely to witness more violence, not its end. Only decolonial justice can bring this cycle of settler colonial violence to an end; if not complete end, then at least, to its massive diminishment in intensity and scope.

The task ahead seems daunting. It seems like a lost cause. But I have said this before and will say it again, the Palestinian decolonial struggle may be a losing cause, but it is not a lost cause. It cannot become a lost cause, we cannot afford to let it become a lost cause, because a decolonized Palestine-Israel is precisely the spark that can ignite massive transformations everywhere around the world and direct us toward a new age that finally leaves the destruction of colonial modernity behind. These will be transformations that are for the good of the majority of the world's population across all the geographical regions of the world. A decolonized Palestine-Israel is the promise of decolonization everywhere, the end of the age of the Euro-American empire, and the establishment of a democratic world order among all the sovereign peoples of the world.

(Written October 9, 2024)

NOTES

INTRODUCTION

1. M. Muhannad Ayyash, *A Hermeneutics of Violence: A Four-Dimensional Conception* (Toronto: Toronto University Press, 2019).
2. As Rinaldo Walcott puts it, "We might have to think indigeneity as a more flexible process of critique and resistance to modernity rather than as an organic identity . . . to invoke indigeneity as an 'other' identity is already to accede to Europe's Enlightenment and the modernist anthropological project of categorizing humanness on its terms and logics." Rinaldo Walcott, *The Long Emancipation: Moving Toward Black Freedom* (Durham, NC: Duke University Press, 2021), 57.
3. Ayyash, *A Hermeneutics of Violence*.
4. Gurminder K. Bhambra, *Rethinking Modernity: Postcolonialism and the Sociological Imagination* (New York: Palgrave Macmillan, 2007).
5. Walter D. Mignolo and Catherine E. Walsh, *On Decoloniality: Concepts, Analytics, Praxis* (Durham, NC: Duke University Press, 2018), 100.
6. Gurminder K. Bhambra, "Postcolonial and Decolonial Dialogues," *Postcolonial Studies* 17, no. 2 (2014b): 115.
7. Gurminder K. Bhambra, *Connected Sociologies* (New York: Bloomsbury, 2014a), 117–39.
8. Jacques Derrida, *The Beast and the Sovereign, Volume I*, trans. Geoffrey Bennington, ed. Michel Lisse, Marie-Louise Mallet, and Ginette Michaud (Chicago: The University of Chicago Press, 2009), 92–95, 317, 330.
9. Derrida, *The Beast and the Sovereign, Volume I*, 92. For Derrida, and I agree, "If there are 'firsts,' I would be tempted to think on the contrary that they

never present themselves as such." Derrida, *The Beast and the Sovereign, Volume I*, 95.
10. For a similar argument, see Ariella Aïsha Azoulay, *Potential History: Unlearning Imperialism* (London: Verso, 2019), 20–30.
11. Hamid Dabashi, *Can Non-Europeans Think?* (London: Zed Books, 2015), 11.
12. Dabashi, *Can Non-Europeans Think?*, 5; Dabashi, *Can Non-Europeans Think?*, 22–29.
13. Joseph A. Massad "Forget Semitism!," in *Living Together: Jacques Derrida's Communities of Violence and Peace*, ed. E. Weber (New York: Fordham University Press, 2013), 59–79.
14. Judith Butler, *Parting Ways: Jewishness and the Critique of Zionism* (New York: Columbia University Press, 2014).
15. Mahmood Mamdani, *Citizen and Subject: Contemporary Africa and the Legacy of Late Colonialism* (Princeton, NJ: Princeton University Press, 1996), 11; Mamdani, *Citizen and Subject*, 13.
16. Mahmood Mamdani, *Define and Rule: Native as Political Identity* (Cambridge, MA: Harvard University Press, 2012), 81.
17. Mamdani, *Define and Rule*, 82.
18. Ayyash, *A Hermeneutics of Violence*.
19. Frantz Fanon, *The Wretched of the Earth*, trans. Richard Philcox (New York: Grove Press, 2004 [1961]).
20. As I will argue later in the book, the binary as a racialized absolute distinction still holds and plays the same role in the structure of expulsion even when Zionist ideology attempts to flip the terms and makes the absurd claim that the Palestinian is the settler, and the Israeli is the Indigenous.
21. Ayyash, *A Hermeneutics of Violence*.
22. Veena Das and Arthur Kleinman, "Introduction," in *Violence and Subjectivity*, ed. Veena Das et al., (Berkeley: University of California Press, 2000), 1.
23. Das and Kleinman, "Introduction"; Veena Das, *Life and Words: Violence and the Descent into the Ordinary* (Berkeley: University of California Press, 2007); Ayyash, *A Hermeneutics of Violence*, 81–84.
24. Hamid Dabashi, *The Emperor Is Naked: On the Inevitable Demise of the Nation-State* (London: Zed Books, 2020), 6.
25. Mignolo and Walsh, *On Decoloniality*, 125.
26. Hamid Dabashi, *The Arab Spring: The End of Postcolonialism* (New York: Zed Books, 2012).

INTRODUCTION ⚹ 275

27. This goes beyond intellectual traditions as well. For example, as Karuna Mantena puts it in the case of India, "if we take the nation-state to exhaust the political imagination of anti-colonialism, we are very likely to leave out of view an understanding of projects of sovereignty that were popular and anti-imperial but not necessarily *national* and *statist* as their post-war settlements." (Karuna Mantena, "Popular Sovereignty and Anti-Colonialism," in *Popular Sovereignty in Historical Perspective*, ed. Richard Bourke and Quentin Skinner (Cambridge: Cambridge University Press, 2016), 300). Mantena presents several examples of these anti-colonial projects, which emphasized self-rule, direct participation, and localized forms and practices of politics and rule. Mantena, "Popular Sovereignty," 312–13.
28. Fanon, *The Wretched of the Earth*.
29. Edward Said, *Culture and Imperialism* (New York: Vintage Books, 1994), 268, 276.
30. Mignolo and Walsh, *On Decoloniality*, 135–51, 223, 228.
31. Sari Nusseibeh, *What is a Palestinian State Worth?* (Cambridge, MA: Harvard University Press, 2011); Noura Erakat, *Justice for Some: Law and the Question of Palestine* (Stanford, CA: Stanford University Press, 2019); Mahmood Mamdani, *Neither Settler nor Native: The Making and Unmaking of Permanent Minorities* (Cambridge, MA: The Belknap Press of Harvard University Press, 2020).
32. Dabashi, *The Emperor Is Naked*, 196.
33. Dabashi, *The Emperor Is Naked*, 17.
34. Dabashi, *The Emperor Is Naked*, 111. This view of nationalism is important to underscore because as Benedict Anderson argues, nationalism, nationality, and nation-ness are not going to simply disappear from social and political life; they remain integral and still "command such profound emotional legitimacy." Benedict Anderson, *Imagined Communities: Reflections on the Origin and Spread of Nationalism*, revised edition (New York: Verso, 2016 [1983]), 4. I take the position that this is as true today as it was when Anderson published his book in 1983.
35. Dabashi, *The Emperor Is Naked*, 36–37.
36. Dabashi, *The Emperor Is Naked*, 38, 40.
37. Dabashi, *The Emperor Is Naked*, 41.
38. Dabashi, *The Emperor Is Naked*, 95.
39. Dabashi, *The Emperor Is Naked*, 99–101.

40. Dabashi, *The Emperor Is Naked*, 117.
41. Dabashi, *The Emperor Is Naked*, 192.
42. Dabashi, *The Emperor Is Naked*, 163.
43. Dabashi, *The Emperor Is Naked*, 87.
44. Mamdani, *Neither Settler nor Native*, 1–6.
45. Mamdani, *Neither Settler nor Native*, 9–14.
46. Mamdani, *Neither Settler nor Native*, 33–35.
47. Mamdani, *Neither Settler nor Native*, 23, 329.
48. Mamdani, *Neither Settler nor Native*, 250–51.
49. Mamdani, *Neither Settler nor Native*, 28.
50. Mamdani, *Neither Settler nor Native*, 36.
51. Mamdani, *Neither Settler nor Native*, 328.
52. Mamdani, *Neither Settler nor Native*, 334.
53. Mamdani, *Neither Settler nor Native*, 33–34, 347.
54. 'Abd al-Rahman Ibn Khaldûn, *The Muqaddimah: An Introduction to History*, 3 vols., trans. Franz Rosenthal (London: Routledge and Kegan Paul, 1958 [1378]).
55. M. Muhannad Ayyash, "Rethinking the Social-Political through Ibn Khaldûn and Aristotle," *Interventions* 19, no. 8 (2017): 1193–1209.
56. David Lloyd, "Settler Colonialism and the State of Exception: The Example of Palestine/Israel," *Settler Colonial Studies* 2, no. 1 (2012): 59–80.

1. SETTLER COLONIAL SOVEREIGNTY

1. Jens Bartelson, *A Genealogy of Sovereignty* (New York: Cambridge University Press, 1995).
2. Bartelson, *A Genealogy*, 21.
3. Bartelson, *A Genealogy*, 29. He is referring specifically to the question of the "scope" of sovereignty.
4. Bartelson, *A Genealogy*, 30.
5. Bartelson, *A Genealogy*, 41.
6. Bartelson, *A Genealogy*, 48–52.
7. Jens Bartelson, "The Concept of Sovereignty Revisited," *The European Journal of International Law* 17, no. 2 (2006): 463–74. It was always a critical feature of early modern theory (Bodin, Rousseau, Hobbes among others) to distinguish between sovereignty and government, that is, between the foundational legitimacy of a polity and the day-to-day administration of

that polity, respectively. Grotius was the main challenger to this distinction (Richard Tuck, "Democratic Sovereignty and Democratic Government: The Sleeping Sovereign," in *Popular Sovereignty in Historical Perspective*, ed. Richard Bourke and Quentin Skinner (Cambridge: Cambridge University Press, 2016), 127–28). Grotius notwithstanding, I would argue that most scholars who use sovereignty in a way where concepts like autonomy and power would suffice, fail to accentuate this distinction. Instead of following this old debate by focusing on questions of monarchy, democracy, the division of government, etc., I will later highlight something like this distinction through Derrida's account of divisibility-indivisibility and the force of law.

8. Edward Said, *Orientalism* (New York: Vintage Books, 2003 [1979]).
9. See Amy Niang's critique of Eurocentric approaches. Amy Niang, *The Postcolonial African State in Transition: Stateness and Modes of Sovereignty* (New York: Rowman & Littlefield International, 2018), 10–19.
10. Khaled Furani, "Khalifah and the Modern Sovereign: Revisiting a Qur'anic Ideal from within the Palestinian Condition," *Journal of Religion* 102, no. 4 (2022): 482–83.
11. Niang, *The Postcolonial African State*, 19.
12. Jean Bodin, *On Sovereignty: Four Chapters from the Six Books of the Commonwealth*, ed. & trans. Julian H. Franklin (Cambridge: Cambridge University Press, 1992 [1576]), Book I, Chapter 10.
13. Richard Bourke, "Introduction," in *Popular Sovereignty in Historical Perspective*, ed. Richard Bourke and Quentin Skinner (Cambridge: Cambridge University Press, 2016a), 2; Bodin believed that sovereignty was an ancient idea, but he claimed that it was never fully understood in previous cultures (Bourke, "Introduction"). This of course is a questionable claim. For example, Kinch Hoekstra argues that many early modern thinkers, like Bodin, owe their understanding of sovereignty as uncontrolled (a sovereign power cannot have a higher sovereign power overlooking it), supreme, and indivisible not to the ancient Greek understanding of sovereignty per se, but to Greeks' understanding of the concept of tyranny. Kinch Hoekstra, "Athenian Democracy and Popular Tyranny," in *Popular Sovereignty in Historical Perspective*, ed. Richard Bourke and Quentin Skinner (Cambridge: Cambridge University Press, 2016), 15–51.
14. John Agnew, *Globalization and Sovereignty* (Lanham, MD: Rowman & Littlefield, 2009), 49; also see Wouter G. Werner and Jaap H. de Wilde, "The

1. SETTLER COLONIAL SOVEREIGNTY

Endurance of Sovereignty," *European Journal of International Relations* 7, no. 3 (2001): 285–86, 299–306.
15. Robbie Shilliam, "What about Marcus Garvey? Race and the Transformation of Sovereignty Debate," *Review of International Studies* 32, no. 3 (2006): 380–81.
16. Shilliam, "What about Marcus Garvey?," 400.
17. Steve Nutt, "Pluralized Sovereignties: Autochthonous Lawmaking on the Settler Colonial Frontier in Palestine," *Interventions* 21, no. 4 (2019): 511. As Jane Burbank and Frederick Cooper put it in their massive study of world empires, "The pragmatic, interactive, accommodating capacity of empires makes us skeptical of arguments that assume a fundamental redefinition of sovereignty, usually dated to the seventeenth century, when Europeans are said to have created a new system of potentially national and separate states. . . . The history of empires allows us instead to envision sovereignty as shared out, layered, overlapping." (Jane Burbank and Frederick Cooper, *Empires in World History: Power and the Politics of Difference* (Princeton, NJ: Princeton University Press, 2010), 16–17). This complex history is always entangled with the control and expansion of power and sovereignty over space, which does not always take the form of the modern territorial state (Burbank and Cooper, *Empires*, 8, 182–83).
18. Niang, *The Postcolonial African State*, 25–27.
19. Niang, *The Postcolonial African State*, 28–29, 121–24, 187.
20. Niang, *The Postcolonial African State*, 27.
21. Niang, *The Postcolonial African State*, 23, 88, 141.
22. Niang, *The Postcolonial African State*, 20–21, 53, 78–80, 143, 157–80.
23. Niang, *The Postcolonial African State*, 132.
24. Werner and de Wilde, "The Endurance of Sovereignty," 286–90.
25. J. Samuel Barkin, "The Evolution of the Constitution of Sovereignty and the Emergence of Human Rights Norms," *Millennium: Journal of International Studies* 27, no. 2 (1998): 229–52.
26. This idea is similar to what Ford calls, "perfect settler sovereignty." Lisa Ford, *Settler Sovereignty: Jurisdiction and Indigenous People in America and Australia, 1788–1836* (Cambridge, MA: Harvard University Press, 2011), 2, 183–203.
27. Jacques Derrida, *The Beast and the Sovereign, Volume I*, trans. Geoffrey Bennington, ed. Michel Lisse, Marie-Louise Mallet, and Ginette Michaud (Chicago: University of Chicago Press, 2009), 18.

28. Derrida, *The Beast and the Sovereign, Volume I*, 18.
29. Derrida, *The Beast and the Sovereign, Volume I*, 46.
30. Derrida, *The Beast and the Sovereign, Volume I*, 26.
31. Derrida, *The Beast and the Sovereign, Volume I*, 19–20, 208–9, 217–18; Jacques Derrida, *The Beast and the Sovereign, Volume II*, trans. Geoffrey Bennington, ed. Michel Lisse, Marie-Louise Mallet, and Ginette Michaud (Chicago: The University of Chicago Press, 2011), 259–61. Analyzing the Euro-American legal claims to dominion over what is now the United States of America, Mamdani writes, "What underlay the claim of dominion was neither discovery nor civilization. Rather, might made right." (Mahmood Mamdani, *Neither Settler nor Native: The Making and Unmaking of Permanent Minorities* (Cambridge, MA: The Belknap Press of Harvard University Press, 2020), 48). And so the story goes for all other (settler) colonial projects.
32. Derrida, *The Beast and the Sovereign, Volume I*, 39.
33. Derrida, *The Beast and the Sovereign, Volume I*, 43. Despite the fact that the Lockean tradition limits the power of the sovereign, it still assigns to the sovereign the task of maintaining the very social/political order in which its power and violence (fear and terror) are then limited. In other words, accountability of the sovereign, or holding the sovereign to account has been one of the features of sovereignty throughout history, but this does not take away from the notion that the ability/task of the sovereign to maintain the social/political order as such coexists with varying forms of accountability.
34. This is why we can see the coupling of the sovereign and the beast paradoxically as "a duo or even a duel, but also an alliance." Derrida, *The Beast and the Sovereign, Volume I*, 32; Derrida, *The Beast and the Sovereign, Volume I*, 40, 41.
35. C. Heike Schotten, *Queer Terror: Life, Death, and Desire in the Settler Colony* (New York: Columbia University Press, 2018), xiv.
36. Schotten, *Queer Terror*, xv–xvii, 33–35, 49–59, 129, 144–45, 149–50, 161–68.
37. Derrida, *The Beast and the Sovereign, Volume I*, 14.
38. Derrida, *The Beast and the Sovereign, Volume I*, 70–71, 76–77.
39. Derrida, *The Beast and the Sovereign, Volume II*, 21.
40. For key passages see Derrida, *The Beast and the Sovereign, Volume II*, 21–24, 30, 38, 55, 277–79.
41. Derrida, *The Beast and the Sovereign, Volume II*, 79.
42. Derrida, *The Beast and the Sovereign, Volume II*, 82.
43. Derrida, *The Beast and the Sovereign, Volume II*, 277.

280   1. SETTLER COLONIAL SOVEREIGNTY

44. Derrida, *The Beast and the Sovereign, Volume II*, 279.
45. Derrida, *The Beast and the Sovereign, Volume I*, 67.
46. Aileen Moreton-Robinson, ed., *Sovereign Subjects: Indigenous Sovereignty Matters* (New York: Routledge, 2007); Circe Sturm, "Reflections on the Anthropology of Sovereignty and Settler Colonialism: Lessons from Native North America," *Cultural Anthropology* 32, no. 3 (2017): 344.
47. Derrida, *The Beast and the Sovereign, Volume I*, 270.
48. Derrida, *The Beast and the Sovereign, Volume I*, 215.
49. Derrida, *The Beast and the Sovereign, Volume I*, 257–59. This is different from the Hobbesian view of the sovereign from its highest point, which was critiqued in Foucault. Schotten, *Queer Terror*, 77.
50. Derrida, *The Beast and the Sovereign, Volume I*, 257.
51. Audra Simpson, *Mohawk Interruptus: Political Life across the Borders of Settler States* (Durham, NC: Duke University Press, 2014), 18.
52. Derrida, *The Beast and the Sovereign, Volume I*, 47.
53. Derrida, *The Beast and the Sovereign, Volume I*, 49.
54. Derrida, *The Beast and the Sovereign, Volume I*, 49, 50.
55. M. Muhannad Ayyash, *A Hermeneutics of Violence: A Four-Dimensional Conception* (Toronto: University of Toronto Press, 2019), 105–6.
56. Derrida, *The Beast and the Sovereign, Volume I*, 53.
57. Derrida, *The Beast and the Sovereign, Volume I*, 55.
58. Derrida, *The Beast and the Sovereign, Volume I*, 55.
59. Ayyash, *A Hermeneutics of Violence*, 104–6.
60. Derrida, *The Beast and the Sovereign, Volume I*, 42–43.
61. For example, Derrida writes this about Aristotle's text when he is exploring some of Aristotle's ideas alongside biblical assertions, stories, and ideas: "Aristotle's text comes before the Gospels and above all remains the more political, in truth the only one that is explicitly and literally political . . . the only one that conjugates *logos* with the political." Derrida, *The Beast and the Sovereign, Volume I*, 314.
62. See Wise's critique of Derrida's Abrahamic-centric philosophy. Christopher Wise, *Derrida, Africa, and the Middle East* (New York: Palgrave Macmillan, 2009).
63. Georges Bataille sees in this description of indivisible sovereignty the elements of a transgressive or revolutionary sovereignty, which is unalloyed to any kind of anticipation or servitude to an end. In Bataille, the sovereignty

1. SETTLER COLONIAL SOVEREIGNTY ❧ 281

that we can trace in feudal, bourgeois, and Soviet communist societies is in a sense a cheapening of the godly or godlike sovereignty that exists within all human beings in a diffuse manner (Georges Bataille, *The Accursed Share: An Essay on General Economy, Volumes II and III*, trans. Robert Hurley (New York: Zone Books, 1989 [1976]), 214–23). This sovereignty can only be sovereign when it is not displayed (197), does not anticipate the future (199), is not subordinate or subject to utility (204), is "life delivered from its servitude" (207) and constraints including the constraints imposed on us by the anguish of death (219), and is "not reducible to a means" (315). He argues that "only unknowing is *sovereign*" (208) and that "sovereignty is NOTHING" (430) insofar as it separates itself from the world of things and the pursuit of accumulation (428). For the sovereign, "the world of practice" smells badly, but not from the odor of death, rather from a life that is filled with the anguish of death, with the desire to expel the death that it cannot in fact banish (222–23). This sovereignty is not produced through the enslavement and exploitation of people—that would be the historical forms of sovereignty—but comes before and exceeds these forms (285). But what is missed in Bataille and other critical theorists, especially those following a Nietzschean philosophy, is that the cheapened forms of sovereignty that we can point to in the body of the king (although not for Bataille the "first kings" whose sovereignty was supposedly godlike before we attributed to the gods what was first in the human—319–22), the feudal lords, the state, is only possible precisely because of this godly or godlike sovereignty. Bataille tells us that this godly or godlike sovereignty was first in the human before it was transposed onto a divine entity, rendering this godlike sovereignty as something that already exists within all human beings and which we can and should unleash. But this approach still creates a binary between two opposing sovereignties, locating a point of origin on the one hand and cheapened manifestations of it on the other hand. But instead of a fixation on origins and originality, we need to examine the operation of sovereignty through *différance*: to oversimplify, as a paradoxical play between opposing forces that makes possible and impossible these forces. Bataille's attempt to locate a revolutionary, transgressive, unalloyed, true sovereignty as the "original" sovereignty of the so-called "first kings"—a Nietzschean style "overman," an "original" figure par excellence—Bataille is perhaps more enwrapped with a settler colonial sovereignty than he could see.

282 ∽ 1. SETTLER COLONIAL SOVEREIGNTY

64. As Schotten puts it, "in Hobbes, sovereign is he who produces life itself, both its existence and its content." Schotten, *Queer Terror*, 41.
65. Derrida, *The Beast and the Sovereign, Volume I*, 282. In his analysis of the American founding, popular sovereignty, and the legal debates around Royalist vs. authorization (through voting) theories of representation, Nelson makes a similar general point regarding the American Revolution, when he concludes "that if popular sovereignty in America does not rest on the Royalist theory of representation, it rests on nothing." Eric Nelson, "Prerogative, Popular Sovereignty, and the American Founding," in *Popular Sovereignty in Historical Perspective*, ed. Richard Bourke and Quentin Skinner (Cambridge: Cambridge University Press, 2016), 211.
66. The conceptual (if not, strictly speaking, existent) changes are summed up here by Anderson in reference to the context of the Americas: "Out of the American welter came these imagined realities: nation-states, republican institutions, common citizenships, popular sovereignty, national flags and anthems, etc., and the liquidation of their conceptual opposites: dynastic empires, monarchical institutions, absolutisms, subjecthoods, inherited nobilities, serfdoms, ghettoes, and so forth." Benedict Anderson, *Imagined Communities: Reflections on the Origin and Spread of Nationalism*, rev. ed. (New York: Verso, 2016 [1983]), 81.
67. Derrida, *The Beast and the Sovereign, Volume I*, 296.
68. Derrida, *The Beast and the Sovereign, Volume I*, 290–91. If we are to deconstruct the architecture of sovereignty, then we cannot rely or call upon nonsovereignty, but rather we must question "the modalities of transfer and division of a sovereignty said to be indivisible—said and supposed to be indivisible but always divisible" (Derrida, *The Beast and the Sovereign, Volume I*, 291). This is one of the reasons that I hold onto the term sovereignty and utilize a concept of decolonial sovereignties, although I do not follow Derrida's deconstructions and instead draw on an explicitly decolonial path in this task.
69. J. Samuel Barkin and Bruce Cronin, "The State and the Nation: Changing Norms and the Rules of Sovereignty in International Relations," *International Organization* 48, no. 1 (1994): 108.
70. Barkin and Cronin, "The State and the Nation," 111.
71. Barkin and Cronin, "The State and the Nation," 111. The types and shapes that this can take across contemporary world politics are numerous, often in the name of one form or another of national self-determination (Benyamin Neuberger, "National Self-Determination: A Theoretical Discussion,"

Nationalities Papers 29, no. 3 [2001]: 391–418). None of these conceptions of national self-determination, however, operate in a pure moral or ethical vacuum (i.e., the idea that the adoption and declaration of national self-determination is a mark of humanity's progress), but are ideologically articulated, politically shaped, and legally constructed most often to benefit colonial, neocolonial, and especially in the contemporary era settler colonial powers at the expense of the world's colonized populations (Jospeh A. Massad, "Against Self-Determination," *Humanity: An International Journal of Human Rights, Humanitarianism, and Development* 9, no. 2 [2018]: 161–91).

72. Patrick Wolfe, "Settler Colonialism and the Elimination of the Native," *Journal of Genocide Research* 8, no. 4 (2006): 393.

73. Patrick Wolfe, *Settler Colonialism and the Transformation of Anthropology: The Politics and Poetics of an Ethnographic Event* (London: Cassell, 1999), 167. Also see Wolfe, "Settler Colonialism and the Elimination of the Native," 390–93. As Wolfe shows in his later works, "settler invasion typically combines a shifting balance of official and unofficial strategies, initially to seize Native territory and subsequently to consolidate its expropriation." Patrick Wolfe, *Traces of History: Elementary Structures of Race* (London: Verso, 2016), 41.

74. Wolfe, *Traces of History*, 144–45.

75. Wolfe, *Traces of History*, 41.

76. Michael Biggs, "Putting the State on the Map: Cartography, Territory, and European State Formation," *Comparative Studies in Society and History* 41, no. 2 (1999): 374–76, 385, 390–91, 398–99; Robert Jackson, *Sovereignty: Evolution of an Idea* (Cambridge: Polity Press, 2007); Neil Brenner and Stuart Elden, "Henri Lefebvre on State, Space, Territory," *International Political Sociology* 3 (2009): 353–77.

77. Burbank and Cooper, *Empires*; Radhika Mongia, *Indian Migration and Empire: A Colonial Genealogy of the Modern State* (Durham, NC: Duke University Press, 2018).

78. Mongia, *Indian Migration*, 1–4, 11–15; also see Ford, *Settler Sovereignty*, 13–29; Arie M. Dubnov and Laura Robson, eds, *Partitions: A Transnational History of Twentieth-Century Territorial Separatism* (Stanford, CA: Stanford University Press, 2019); Ariella Aïsha Azoulay, *Potential History: Unlearning Imperialism* (London: Verso, 2019), 386.

79. Gurminder K. Bhambra, *Rethinking Modernity: Postcolonialism and the Sociological Imagination* (New York: Palgrave Macmillan, 2007), 77. Colonialism and settler-colonialism are to be examined, not as the so-called dark side

of modernity (i.e., as an unintended consequence of modernity), but as a historical experience that is integral to and constitutive of modernity. This is a process that Barlow refers to as "colonial modernity," (Tani E. Barlow, ed., *Formations of Colonial Modernity in East Asia* (Durham, NC: Duke University Press, 1997), and Aníbal Quijano refers to as "coloniality/modernity," Aníbal Quijano, "Coloniality of Power, Eurocentrism, and Latin America," trans. Michael Ennis, *Nepantla: Views from South* 1, no. 3 (2000): 533–80; Aníbal Quijano, "Coloniality and Modernity/Rationality," *Cultural Studies* 21, no. 2–3 (2007): 168–78. Following the work of Quijano, Mignolo and Walsh build the concept of the "colonial matrix of power." Although Mignolo utilizes the terminology of the "darker side of modernity," he nonetheless ensures that the reader understands by this an undivorceable (and co-constitutive) relation between coloniality and modernity. Walter D. Mignolo and Catherine E. Walsh, *On Decoloniality: Concepts, Analytics, Praxis* (Durham, NC: Duke University Press, 2018).

80. The antecedents to this moment are often located in the 1648 Peace of Westphalia where "the inception of a new multi-state system . . . characterized by the simultaneous centralization and impersonalization of political power," and "the separation between religion and state, as well as the emergence of theories of sovereignty, has been seen as uniquely European and as constituting a key aspect of European identity." Bhambra, *Rethinking Modernity*, 91; also see, 106–8.

81. Bhambra, *Rethinking Modernity*, 109–12.

82. Bhambra, *Rethinking Modernity*, 49.

83. Bhambra, *Rethinking Modernity*, 115. For a critique of this narrative that asserts a revolutionary change in sovereignty from one based in the monarchical ruler to one based in "the people," see Burbank and Cooper, *Empires*, 219–50.

84. Karuna Mantena, "Popular Sovereignty and Anti-Colonialism," in *Popular Sovereignty in Historical Perspective*, ed. Richard Bourke and Quentin Skinner (Cambridge: Cambridge University Press, 2016).

85. Bhambra, *Rethinking Modernity*, 118–22.

86. Mongia, *Indian Migration*, 21.

87. As Mongia puts it, "A blurring of the vocabularies of nationality and race is a founding strategy of the modern nation-state that makes it impossible to inquire into the modern state without attending to its creation in a global

context of colonialism and racism." Mongia, *Indian Migration*, 107–11, 113, 117–39.
88. This is what scholars like Mann argue. Michael Mann, *The Dark Side of Democracy: Explaining Ethnic Cleansing* (New York: Columbia University Press, 2005).
89. Mongia, *Indian Migration*, 139.
90. Mongia, *Indian Migration*, 143.
91. Mongia, *Indian Migration*, 150.
92. Glen Coulthard, *Red Skin, White Masks: Rejecting the Colonial Politics of Recognition* (Minneapolis: University of Minnesota Press, 2014).
93. Audra Simpson, "The State is a Man: Theresa Spence, Loretta Saunders and the Gender of Settler Sovereignty," *Theory and Event* 19, no. 4 (2016).
94. Mahmood Mamdani, "Settler Colonialism: Then and Now," *Critical Inquiry* 41, no. 3 (2015): 598–602, 612–13; Mamdani, *Neither Settler nor Native*, 86–96.
95. Mignolo and Walsh, *On Decoloniality*, 57–58.
96. For example, see Kauanui for her masterful analysis of this process of erasure in the case of Hawaii. J. Kēhaulani Kauanui, *Hawaiian Blood: Colonialism and the Politics of Sovereignty and Indigeneity* (Durham, NC: Duke University Press, 2008); Jodi A. Byrd, *The Transit of Empire: Indigenous Critiques of Colonialism* (Minneapolis: University of Minnesota Press, 2011); Roxanne Dunbar-Ortiz, *An Indigenous Peoples' History of the United States* (Boston: Beacon Press, 2014).
97. Gurminder K. Bhambra, *Connected Sociologies* (New York: Bloomsbury, 2014), 153.
98. Joseph A. Massad, *Islam in Liberalism* (Chicago: The University of Chicago Press, 2015); Said, *Orientalism*; Edward Said, *Culture and Imperialism* (New York: Vintage Books, 1994).
99. Indeed, it is more accurate to situate the emergence of the nation-state within a much longer and interconnected set of histories of "empire states" spanning the entire globe. In their work, Burbank and Cooper define empire states (Rome, China, Mongols, Ottomans, British, etc.) as "large political units, expansionist or with a memory of power extended over space, polities that maintain distinction and hierarchy as they incorporate new people" whereas the nation-state "is based on the idea of a single people in a single territory constituting itself as a unique political community" (Burbank and Cooper, *Empires*, 8). They show that the nation-state is

not the natural or evolutionary successor of empire states, but rather as a relatively recent (twentieth century) outcome of the interaction between empire states and changes/developments within them, and as such the nation-state, as a specific mode of social and political organization, continues to ask questions and propose solutions that are situated within (or at least shaped and influenced by) the political imagination that has been constituted in and through empire for centuries (Burbank and Cooper, *Empires*, 20–22, 443–59).

100. Bhambra, *Connected Sociologies*, 141–56.
101. Bhambra, *Connected Sociologies*, 155.
102. Mignolo and Walsh, *On Decoloniality*, 7.
103. Bhambra, *Rethinking Modernity*, 22.
104. There is a limit (perhaps an insurmountable one) to how much rehabilitation can be done to such entrenched historiographies and therefore social and political theories. As a result, scholars may be better served by simply transcending them altogether. Bhambra, *Rethinking Modernity*, 11.

2. LORDSHIP AS VIOLENCE IN THE SETTLER COLONY

1. For example, Michael Mann, *The Sources of Social Power Volume 2: The Rise of Classes and Nation States, 1760–1914* (Cambridge: Cambridge University Press, 1993); Hendrik Spruyt, *The Sovereign State and its Competitors: An Analysis of Systems Change* (Princeton, NJ: Princeton University Press, 1994); Gianfranco Poggi, *The State: Its Nature, Development, and Prospects* (Stanford, CA: Stanford University Press, 1990); Charles Tilly, ed., *The Formation of National States in Western Europe* (Princeton, NJ: Princeton University Press, 1975); Charles Tilly, *Coercion, Capital and European States AD 990–1990* (Cambridge: Blackwell, 1990).
2. Norbert Elias, *The Civilizing Process: Sociogenetic and Psychogenetic Investigations*, rev. ed., trans. Edmund Jephcott, ed. Eric Dunning, Johan Goudsblom, Stephen Mennell (Malden, MA: Blackwell Publishing, 2000 [1939]), 214.
3. Elias, *The Civilizing Process*, 215.
4. Elias, *The Civilizing Process*, 215.
5. Elias, *The Civilizing Process*, 216.
6. Elias, *The Civilizing Process*, 217.

7. Elias, *The Civilizing Process*, 217–18; also see Jane Burbank and Frederick Cooper, *Empires in World History: Power and the Politics of Difference* (Princeton, NJ: Princeton University Press, 2010), 88–89.
8. Elias, *The Civilizing Process*, 218; Burbank and Cooper, *Empires*, 90.
9. Elias, *The Civilizing Process*, 218.
10. Elias, *The Civilizing Process*, 219–20.
11. M. Muhannad Ayyash, "Rethinking the Social-Political Through Ibn Khaldûn and Aristotle," *Interventions* 19, no. 8 (2017).
12. Elias, *The Civilizing Process*, 230–233.
13. Elias, *The Civilizing Process*, 236; also see 204–8.
14. Elias, *The Civilizing Process*, 204–5.
15. Elias, *The Civilizing Process*, 260–61, 312–17.
16. Elias, *The Civilizing Process*, 263, 305.
17. Burbank and Cooper, *Empires*, 120; Elias, *The Civilizing Process*, 268–70, 289–302.
18. Elias, *The Civilizing Process*, 311.
19. Elias, *The Civilizing Process*, 343.
20. This is also, more or less, the accepted turning point in the emergence of popular sovereignty that accompanied the transition to the modern state, which most trace specifically to the American and French Revolutions. There are of course variances in how scholars understand this took place, some of which are highlighted in my discussion (the decolonial critique in particular), but I need not deeply delve into this question. Moreover, there are ongoing debates on how this shift from absolutism to revolution took place in the theorization of sovereignty—from Hobbes/Bodin to Rousseau for instance. See for example, Richard Bourke, "Popular Sovereignty and Political Representation: Edmund Burke in the Context of Eighteenth-Century Thought," in *Popular Sovereignty in Historical Perspective*, ed. Richard Bourke and Quentin Skinner (Cambridge: Cambridge University Press, 2016b), 212–35.
21. Elias, *The Civilizing Process*, 353.
22. Elias, *The Civilizing Process*, 272–77, 354.
23. Elias, *The Civilizing Process*, 275.
24. Elias, *The Civilizing Process*, 268.
25. Otto Brunner, *Land and Lordship: Structures of Governance in Medieval Austria*, 4th rev. ed., ed. and trans. Howard Kaminsky and James Van Horn Melton (Philadelphia: University of Pennsylvania Press, 1992).

26. Brenna Bhandar, *Colonial Lives of Property: Law, Land, and Racial Regimes of Ownership* (Durham, NC: Duke University Press, 2018), 8, 77–108.
27. Carole Pateman and Charles W. Mills, *Contract and Domination* (Malden, MA: Polity Press, 2007), 53–73; Gurminder K. Bhambra, *Rethinking Modernity: Postcolonialism and the Sociological Imagination* (New York: Palgrave Macmillan, 2007), 38–45, 143; Eve Tuck and K. Wayne Yang, "Decolonization is not a Metaphor," *Decolonization: Indigeneity, Education & Society* 1, no. 1 (2012): 24; also see, Rinaldo Walcott, *The Long Emancipation: Moving Toward Black Freedom* (Durham, NC: Duke University Press, 2021); Gurminder K. Bhambra, "Colonial Global Economy: Towards a Theoretical Reorientation of Political Economy," *Review of International Political Economy* 28, no. 2 (2021): 307–22; Andrew Phillips and J. C. Sharman, *Outsourcing Empire: How Company-States made the Modern World* (Princeton, NJ: Princeton University Press, 2020); Sven Beckert, *Empire of Cotton: A Global History* (New York: Vintage Books, 2015); Sven Beckert and Seth Rockman, eds., *Slavery's Capitalism: A New History of American Economic Development* (Philadelphia: University of Pennsylvania Press, 2016).
28. Elias, *The Civilizing Process*, 428–29.
29. Robert J. C. Young, *Empire, Colony, Postcolony* (Malden, MA: Wiley Blackwell, 2015), 40. It is important to also add the significant role of the transatlantic slave trade and slavery within the colonies in the creation, development, and advancement of capitalism, the Industrial Revolution, and the wealth of colonizing nations. Eric Williams, *Capitalism and Slavery* (Chapel Hill: University of North Carolina Press, 1944); David Eltis and David Richardson, *Atlas of the Transatlantic Slave Trade* (New Haven, CT: Yale University Press, 2010). Not to mention the advance of modernity. Paul Gilroy, *The Black Atlantic: Modernity and Double Consciousness* (Cambridge, MA: Harvard University Press, 1993); Walcott, *The Long Emancipation*.
30. Eqbal Ahmad, "Postcolonial Systems of Power," in *The Selected Writings of Eqbal Ahmad*, ed. Carollee Bengelsdorf, Margaret Cerullo, and Yogesh Chandrani (New York: Columbia University Press, 2006 [1980]), 138.
31. Ahmad, "Postcolonial Systems of Power"; Eqbal Ahmad, "The Neofascist State," in *The Selected Writings of Eqbal Ahmad*, ed. Carollee Bengelsdorf, Margaret Cerullo, and Yogesh Chandrani (New York: Columbia University Press, 2006 [1981]), 142–53. This insight has been shown in numerous studies throughout the postcolonial world. Benoit Challand, "Citizenship

and Violence in the Arab Worlds: A Historical Sketch," in *The Transformation of Citizenship, Volume 3: Struggle, Resistance and Violence*, ed. Juergen Mackert and Bryan Turner (London: Routledge, 2017), 93–112; Mahmood Mamdani, *Define and Rule: Native as Political Identity* (Cambridge, MA: Harvard University Press, 2012), 2, 122–25. I follow such assessments and agree that the stark separation between ruler and ruled, and the ruler's control over the monopoly of violence through the mechanism of the state of exception, which was introduced and cemented by colonial power, continues to plague much of the postcolonial world, and that the postcolonial state cannot function without the divisions it creates and sustains in the social order (Ayyash, "Rethinking the Social–Political.")

32. Western colonial expansion involved a propriety claim over the oceans and seas in addition to land. Lincoln Paine, *The Sea and Civilization: A Maritime History of the World* (New York: Vintage Books, 2013), 388.

33. Wolfe clarifies in his later writings that while "colonialism came before race," race and racialization play a central role in the development of colonialism and settler colonialism, particularly as settler societies enter a stage where they seek to continue the elimination of Indigenous peoples through means other than war and physical violence (e.g., through assimilation policies). Patrick Wolfe, *Traces of History: Elementary Structures of Race* (London: Verso, 2016), 5, 14–15, 101, 388.

34. Patrick Wolfe, "Settler Colonialism and the Elimination of the Native," *Journal of Genocide Research* 8, no. 4 (2006): 395.

35. Pateman and Mills, *Contract and Domination*, 36.

36. Wolfe, *Traces of History*, 100–101.

37. Yuval Evri and Hagar Kotef, "When Does A Native Become a Settler? (With Apologies to Zreik and Mamdani)," *Constellations* 29, no. 1 (2020): 3–18.

38. Pateman and Mills, *Contract and Domination*, 46; Patrick Wolfe, *Settler Colonialism and the Transformation of Anthropology: The Politics and Poetics of an Ethnographic Event* (London: Cassell, 1999), 27.

39. Wolfe, *Settler Colonialism and the Transformation of Anthropology*, 25–29, 163; Wolfe, "Settler Colonialism and the Elimination of the Native," 396–97.

40. Wolfe, *Settler Colonialism and the Transformation of Anthropology*, 203; also see Lisa Ford, *Settler Sovereignty: Jurisdiction and Indigenous People in America and Australia, 1788–1836* (Cambridge, MA: Harvard University Press, 2011).

41. Wolfe, "Settler Colonialism and the Elimination of the Native," 388; also see Pateman and Mills, *Contract and Domination*, 67.
42. Pateman and Mills, *Contract and Domination*, 59, 68–73.
43. Audra Simpson, "The State Is a Man: Theresa Spence, Loretta Saunders, and the Gender of Settler Sovereignty," *Theory and Event* 19, no. 4 (2016).
44. Wolfe, *Traces of History*, 34.
45. Wolfe, *Traces of History*, 34. One of the key distinguishing features of the Indigenous framework is "its commitment to collective ownership" (Wolfe, *Traces of History*, 171). This is similar to the fellahin notion of ownership, which I have discussed elsewhere, M. Muhannad Ayyash, "An Assemblage of Decoloniality? Palestinian Fellahin Resistance and the Space-Place Relation," *Studies in Social Justice* 12, no. 1 (2018): 21–37.
46. Wolfe, *Traces of History*, 34–39.
47. Wolfe, *Traces of History*, 139, 188.
48. Mamdani captures here why extending the defining feature of the warrior class beyond the particularity of that class and how it can illuminate European (settler)colonial projects: "Norbert Elias writes of a Chinese visitor to Europe during the Middle Ages, who remarked on how 'civilized' Europeans used miniature weapons to eat at the table. This visitor noted on the basis of his observations that the warrior class appeared to set the model of European culture. That view may be reductionist, but something in it rings true. Europeans have spent hundreds of years spreading civilization with the power of arms." Mahmood Mamdani, *Neither Settler nor Native: The Making and Unmaking of Permanent Minorities* (Cambridge, MA: The Belknap Press of Harvard University Press, 2020), 330.
49. For example, see Brunner, *Land and Lordship*, 294–364.
50. Bhambra, *Rethinking Modernity*, 24–30.
51. Glen Coulthard, *Red Skin, White Masks: Rejecting the Colonial Politics of Recognition* (Minneapolis: University of Minnesota Press, 2014), 6–7.
52. Coulthard, *Red Skin, White Masks*, 7.
53. Yezid Sayigh, *Armed Struggle and the Search for State: The Palestinian National Movement, 1949–1993* (Institute for Palestine Studies, Washington, D.C.: Oxford University Press, 1997), 46–47. Although of course proletarianization eventually does emerge in Palestine as it does in other settler colonial contexts, Nahla Abdo states: "Unlike in the Western European countries, especially Britain, where expropriation turned peasants or farmers into a mass of wage labourers required by the emerging capitalist relations, in the

Palestinian case the Zionist colonial project had a different end in mind: turning Palestinian land into exclusively Jewish land and employing only Jewish labour to work it" (Nahla Abdo, *Women in Israel: Race, Gender and Citizenship* [London: Zed Books, 2011], 67). In addition, while his book mainly falls within a political-economy–centric approach that unconvincingly challenges the settler colonial paradigm, even Gershon Shafir's earlier work acknowledges the following in the case of Palestine-Israel: "In a reversal of historical patterns, the period of 'primitive accumulation' was less violent than the completion of the 'transformation of Palestine'" (Gershon Shafir, *Land, Labour and the Origins of the Israeli-Palestinian Conflict, 1882–1914*, updated ed. [Berkeley: University of California Press, 1996 (1989)], 43). The latter transformation concerns the 1948 War.
54. Coulthard, *Red Skin, White Masks*, 11–12, 59–60.
55. Coulthard, *Red Skin, White Masks*, 13. Similarly, in Palestine, dispossession takes precedence and is indeed the condition of proletarianization—"The proletarianization of Palestinians was accelerated by land dispossession: between 1967 and 1974, land confiscation by Israeli authorities caused the area of cultivated land to fall by one-third—in the Jordan Valley alone, 87 percent of all irrigated land owned by Palestinians became off-limits." Sobhi Samour, "Covid-19 and the Necroeconomy of Palestinian Labor in Israel," *Journal of Palestine Studies* 49, no. 4 (2020): 58.
56. Wolfe, *Traces of History*, 21–22.
57. Coulthard, *Red Skin, White Masks*, 13–15.
58. Bhambra, "Colonial Global Economy," 3.
59. I will later delve deeper into the question of identity within the Indigenous-settler distinction as this takes shape in Palestine-Israel. But it is worth noting here that the question of national/ethnic identity in the settler colonial context is a complex one and cannot be reduced to the (often privileged) imperative of moving beyond narrowly defined nationalist/ethnic identities for the sake of a "progressive" politics. Coulthard excellently captures this point here: "no discourse on identity should be prematurely cast as either inherently productive or repressive prior to an engaged consideration of the historical, political, and socioeconomic contexts and actors involved. . . . This is particularly relevant from the perspective of Indigenous peoples' struggles, where activists may sometimes employ what appear to outsiders as essentialist notions of culture and tradition in their efforts to transcend, not reinforce, oppressive structures and practices" (Coulthard, *Red Skin, White*

Masks, 103). J. Kēhaulani Kauanui further explains, "indigenous peoples' assertions of distinction and cultural differences are often heard as merely essentialist and therefore resembling static identities based on fixed inherent qualities. As such, what remains for some scholars as well as national and international governmental actors is the question as to whether indigeneity has any substance that can be used as a foundation to make a claim. In terms of both cultural and political struggles, one of the tenets of any claim to indigeneity is that indigenous sovereignty—framed as a responsibility more often than a right—is derived from original occupancy, or at least prior occupancy. Like race, indigeneity is a socially constructed category rather than one based on the notion of immutable biological characteristics" (J. Kēhaulani Kauanui, "'A Structure, not an Event': Settler Colonialism and Enduring Indigeneity," *Lateral: Journal of the Cultural Studies Association* 5, no. 1 Spring (2016)). These are critical points that are missed by many postcolonial and decolonial scholars who mistakenly flatten the differences between the settler colony, the postcolony, and the colony (direct and indirect rule), and thus end up making the grave mistake of flattening the difference between autochthonic ethnonationalism and Indigenous identity, sovereignty, and nations (e.g., Nandita Sharma, "Against National Sovereignty: The Postcolonial New World Order and the Containment of Decolonization," *Studies in Social Justice* 14, no. 2 [2020]: 391–409).

60. Lorenzo Veracini, *Settler Colonialism: A Theoretical Overview* (New York: Palgrave Macmillan, 2010), 6.
61. Veracini, *Settler Colonialism*, 8–9, 33–52.
62. Wolfe, "Settler Colonialism and the Elimination of the Native," 402–3.
63. Veracini, *Settler Colonialism*, 72.
64. Veracini, *Settler Colonialism*, 53.
65. Veracini, *Settler Colonialism*, 53.
66. Jacques Derrida, *The Beast and the Sovereign, Volume II*, trans. Geoffrey Bennington, ed. Michel Lisse, Marie-Louise Mallet, and Ginette Michaud (Chicago: University of Chicago Press, 2011), 30, 280–90. Derrida here is engaged in a deconstruction of Heidegger's work and his use of the German word, *walten*.
67. Veracini, *Settler Colonialism*, 60–61.
68. The mechanisms of transfer and elimination are varied in the settler colony and not always necessarily genocidal in the conventional understanding of the term. As Wolfe puts it, "settler colonialism is inherently eliminatory but

not invariably genocidal" (Wolfe, "Settler Colonialism and the Elimination of the Native," 387). In regard to the point on imperial sovereignties, Veracini does not agree that feudalism is a useful analytical tool for understanding the relation between the settler communities and the distant sovereign in European metropoles. For him, settler colonial sovereignty "is not a leftover from transplanted political traditions, it is the beginning of a distinct political tradition and its sovereignty." (Veracini, *Settler Colonialism*, 59). I follow this reading, and again to be clear, my use of the feudal notion of land ownership that I began with is undertaken so as to outline a posture of lordship as violence.

69. Veracini, *Settler Colonialism*, 73.
70. Veracini, *Settler Colonialism*, 73–74.
71. Wolfe, *Settler Colonialism and the Transformation of Anthropology*, 3, 34, 163–64, 183–90, 203–4, 211. Some examples of how Wolfe articulates his emphasis on ideology include the following statements: "Analytically, to recap, it can be seen how the logic of elimination, *most crudely manifest in the initial massacres*, has persisted into the present by way of a number of strategic transformations" (Wolfe, *Settler Colonialism and the Transformation of Anthropology*, 204; emphasis added); in reference to political and legal changes in the 1990s, he states: "Yet such developments make it easier for my argument, which is *most pressed to accommodate the subtler manifestations of the logic of elimination*" (Wolfe, *Settler Colonialism and the Transformation of Anthropology*, 211; emphasis added).
72. M. Muhannad Ayyash, *A Hermeneutics of Violence: A Four-Dimensional Conception* (Toronto: University of Toronto Press, 2019).
73. Yasmeen Abu-Laban and Abigail B. Bakan, "The Racial Contract: Israel/Palestine and Canada," *Social Identities* 14, no. 5 (2008): 637–60; Abigail B. Bakan and Yasmeen Abu-Laban, "The Israel/Palestine Racial Contract and the Challenge of Anti-Racism: A Case Study of the United Nations World Conference Against Racism," *Ethnic and Racial Studies* 44, no. 12 (2021): 2167–89; Nadera Shalhoub-Kevorkian, "Human Suffering in Colonial Contexts: Reflections from Palestine," *Settler Colonial Studies* 4, no. 3 (2014): 277–90.
74. Jens Bartelson, *A Genealogy of Sovereignty* (Cambridge: Cambridge University Press, 1995); Robin Wagner-Pacifici, *The Art of Surrender: Decomposing Sovereignty at Conflict's End* (Chicago: The University of Chicago Press, 2005).

75. This is what Erakat in *Justice for Some: Law and the Question of Palestine* (Stanford, CA: Stanford University Press, 2019) has emphasized in her analysis of the colonial state of exception. In the settler colonial context, the abandoned Indigenous Palestinian is estranged from the political and politics by virtue of being that which the Israeli settler has expelled and continues to expel. The Indigenous is always already confined by the settler even when expelled—or more properly, precisely because they are expelled, they are confined (to varying degrees of course).
76. Ayyash, "Rethinking the Social-Political."
77. Giorgio Agamben, *Homo Sacer: Sovereign Power and Bare Life*, trans. Daniel Heller-Roazen (Stanford, CA: Stanford University Press, 1998 [1995]), 15.
78. Agamben, *Homo Sacer*, 17–25.
79. Agamben, *Homo Sacer*, 27.
80. Agamben, *Homo Sacer*, 83.
81. Agamben, *Homo Sacer*, 28.
82. Agamben, *Homo Sacer*, 29.
83. Agamben, *Homo Sacer*, 90.
84. Jacques Derrida, *The Beast and the Sovereign, Volume I*, trans. Geoffrey Bennington, ed. Michel Lisse, Marie-Louise Mallet, and Ginette Michaud (Chicago: University of Chicago Press, 2009), 17.
85. Derrida, *The Beast and the Sovereign, Volume I*, 316.
86. Derrida, *The Beast and the Sovereign, Volume I*, 330.
87. See Schotten's astute critique on this and other points. C. Heike Schotten, *Queer Terror: Life, Death, and Desire in the Settler Colony* (New York: Columbia University Press, 2018), 3, 17–30, 63–65.
88. Derrida, *The Beast and the Sovereign, Volume I*, 333–334.
89. Hans-Herbert Kögler, *The Power of Dialogue: Critical Hermeneutics After Gadamer and Foucault*, trans. Paul Hendrickson (Cambridge, MA: The MIT Press, 1999 [1992]), 230.
90. Kögler, *The Power of Dialogue*, 239.
91. Kögler, *The Power of Dialogue*, 256–57.
92. Kögler, *The Power of Dialogue*, 262.
93. M. Muhannad Ayyash, "Hamas and the Israeli State: A 'Violent Dialogue,'" *European Journal of International Relations* 16, no. 1 (2010): 103–23; M. Muhannad Ayyash, "Jerusalem and Violence: The Transformation of Secular and Sacred Interpretations," in *Cultural Violence and Destruction of*

Communities: New Theoretical Perspectives, ed. Fiona Greenland and Fatma Müge Göçek (London: Routledge, 2020), 95–115.
94. Jacques Derrida, "Force of Law: The 'Mystical Foundation of Authority,'" in *Acts of Religion*, trans. M. Quaintance, ed. Gil Anidjar (New York: Routledge, 2002 [1990]), 228–98.
95. Much of the discussion on four-dimensional violence is replicated verbatim (with slight editorial changes) from my first book, particularly my discussion on the transcendental dimension of violence. Ayyash, *A Hermeneutics of Violence*, 132–78.

3. THE INDIGENOUS-SETTLER DISTINCTION AND THE INTERLOCKING OF ENEMY-SIBLINGS

1. Hans-Herbert Kögler, *The Power of Dialogue: Critical Hermeneutics After Gadamer and Foucault*, trans. Paul Hendrickson (Cambridge, MA: MIT Press, 1999 [1992]); Hans-Georg Gadamer, *Truth and Method*, 2nd rev. ed., trans. Joel Weinsheimer and Donald G. Marshall (New York: Continuum, 2004 [1960]).
2. Patrick Wolfe, *Traces of History: Elementary Structures of Race* (London: Verso, 2016), 255.
3. Mahmood Mamdani, *Citizen and Subject: Contemporary Africa and the Legacy of Late Colonialism* (Princeton, NJ: Princeton University Press, 1996); Mahmood Mamdani, "Beyond Settler and Native as Political Identities: Overcoming the Political Legacy of Colonialism," *Comparative Studies in Society & History* 43, no. 4 (2001): 651–64; and Mahmood Mamdani, *Define and Rule: Native as Political Identity* (Cambridge, MA: Harvard University Press, 2012), 6.
4. Mahmood Mamdani, *When Victims Become Killers: Colonialism, Nativism, and the Genocide in Rwanda* (Princeton, NJ: Princeton University Press, 2001).
5. Mamdani, *Define and Rule*, 4, 107.
6. For example, see Glen Coulthard, *Red Skin, White Masks: Rejecting the Colonial Politics of Recognition* (Minneapolis: University of Minnesota Press, 2014); Audra Simpson, *Mohawk Interruptus: Political Life Across the Borders of Settler States* (Durham, NC: Duke University Press, 2014); Leanne

Betasamosake Simpson, "Land as Pedagogy: Nishnaabeg Intelligence and Rebellious Transformation," *Decolonization: Indigeneity, Education & Society* 3, no. 3 (2014): 1–25; Kevin Bruyneel, *The Third Space of Sovereignty: The Postcolonial Politics of U.S.-Indigenous Relations* (Minneapolis: University of Minnesota Press, 2007).

7. Patrick Wolfe, *Settler Colonialism and the Transformation of Anthropology: The Politics and Poetics of an Ethnographic Event* (London: Cassell, 1999), 166–68, 179–83.
8. Mahmood Mamdani, *Neither Settler nor Native: The Making and Unmaking of Permanent Minorities* (Cambridge, MA: Belknap Press of Harvard University Press, 2020), 97.
9. Mamdani, *Neither Settler nor Native*, 98.
10. Mamdani, *Define and Rule*, 85–106; see also Amy Niang, *The Postcolonial African State in Transition: Stateness and Modes of Sovereignty* (New York: Rowman & Littlefield, 2018), 35, 49, 125.
11. Donald B. Redford, *Egypt, Canaan, and Israel in Ancient Times* (Princeton, NJ: Princeton University Press, 1992); Victor Kattan, *From Coexistence to Conquest: International Law and the Origins of the Arab-Israeli Conflict, 1891–1949* (New York: Pluto Press, 2009), 1–2; Nur Masalha, *Palestine: A Four Thousand Year History* (London: Zed Books, 2020).
12. Nadia Abu El-Haj, *Facts on the Ground: Archaeological Practice and Territorial Self-Fashioning in Israeli Society* (Chicago: University of Chicago Press, 2001); Nadia Abu El-Haj, *The Genealogical Science: The Search for Jewish Origins and the Politics of Epistemology* (Chicago: University of Chicago Press, 2012); Nur Masalha, *The Bible and Zionism: Invented Traditions, Archeology and Post-Colonialism in Israel-Palestine* (London: Zed Books, 2007).
13. Edward Said, "Zionism from the Standpoint of Its Victims," *Social Text* 1 (Winter 1979): 44.
14. Said, "Zionism from the Standpoint of Its Victims," 33.
15. Lorenzo Veracini, "Israel-Palestine Through a Settler-Colonial Studies Lens," *Interventions* 21, no. 4 (2018): 578–80.
16. It must be noted here that many Palestinian groups and scholars have already articulated this message and pushed for it. See for example, Said, "Zionism from the Standpoint of Its Victims"; Ali Abunimah, *One Country: A Bold Proposal to End the Israeli-Palestinian Impasse* (New York: Metropolitan Books, 2006); Omar Barghouti, "A Secular Democratic State in Historic

Palestine: Self-Determination through Ethical Decolonisation," in *After Zionism: One State for Israel and Palestine*, ed. Antony Lowenstein and Ahmed Moore (London: Saqi Books, 2012), 194–209; Haidar Eid, "The Zionist-Palestinian Conflict: An Alternative Story," *Nebula* 5, no. 3 (2008): 122–39; Haidar Eid, "Edward Said and the Re-Drawing of the (Post)colonial Political Map of Palestine," *Decolonization: Indigeneity, Education & Society* 6, no. 1 (2017): 64–78. For an overview of this movement, see Cherine Hussein, *The Re-Emergence of the Single State Solution in Palestine/Israel: Countering an Illusion* (New York: Routledge, 2015). Although polls will vary depending on a variety of factors, including how the question is framed, some have argued that even public opinion for Palestinians inside and outside of Palestine has moved in favor of a one-state solution and away from the two-state disaster that was begun in the Oslo Accords (Eid, "Edward Said," 75). Unfortunately, these voices are not particularly embraced or welcomed in Israeli society and the Israeli state has shown and continues to show outright hostility to Palestinians advancing this position.

17. Raef Zreik, "When Does a Settler Become a Native? (with Apologies to Mamdani)," *Constellations* 23, no. 3 (2016): 360. In regard to Zreik's point about Palestinians needing to address Jewish rights: it is not accurate to state that Palestinians have not done that—because they have across history. If Zreik wants to make the point that this kind of recognition is not widespread and spoken with one voice across the Palestinian community, then that is technically valid, but that is a very challenging task to ask of any national grouping let alone one that is under settler colonial domination.

18. Zreik, "When does a Settler become a Native?," 360.

19. Veracini, "Israel-Palestine," 577–78, note 12.

20. Mamdani, *Neither Settler nor Native*, 144.

21. Lorenzo Veracini, "The Other Shift: Settler Colonialism, Israel and the Occupation," *Journal of Palestine Studies* 42, no. 2 (2013): 26–42.

22. Rana Barakat, "Writing/Righting Palestine Studies: Settler Colonialism, Indigenous Sovereignty and Resisting the Ghost(s) of History," *Settler Colonial Studies* 8, no. 3 (2018): 350–51.

23. Barakat, "Writing/Righting Palestine," 356.

24. Areej Sabbagh-Khoury, "Tracing Settler Colonialism: A Genealogy of a Paradigm in the Sociology of Knowledge Production in Israel," *Politics & Society* 50, no. 1 (2022): 44–83.

25. Simpson, *Mohawk Interruptus*.
26. For the point on this being a fundamental ground, see Rashid Khalidi, *The Hundred Years' War on Palestine: A History of Settler Colonialism and Resistance, 1917–2017* (New York: Metropolitan Books, 2020), 246; for the point on referring to a supernatural deity, see Veracini, "Israel-Palestine"; for the point on legal mechanisms, see Lana Tatour, "Citizenship as Domination: Settler Colonialism and the Making of Palestinian Citizenship in Israel," *Arab Studies Journal* 27, no. 2 (2019): 8–39; Noura Erakat, "The Sovereign Right to Kill: A Critical Appraisal of Israel's Shoot-to-Kill Policy in Gaza," *International Criminal Law Review* 19, no. 5 (2019): 783–818.
27. Said, "Zionism from the Standpoint of its Victims," 40.
28. Gabriel Piterberg, *The Returns of Zionism: Myths, Politics and Scholarship in Israel* (London: Verso, 2008), 94. Wolfe astutely observes that "the genius of return" is that "it allowed a non-state, a diffuse transnational metropole, to colonize." Wolfe, *Traces of History*, 246–247.
29. Piterberg, *The Returns of Zionism*, 96–133.
30. Piterberg, *The Returns of Zionism*, 140–51.
31. Piterberg, *The Returns of Zionism*, 155–87, 208–39.
32. Amnon Raz-Krakotzkin, "Exile within Sovereignty: Critique of the 'Negation of Exile' in Israeli Culture," in *The Scaffolding of Sovereignty: Global and Aesthetic Perspectives on the History of a Concept*, ed. Zvi Ben-Dor Benite, Stefanos Geroulanos, and Nicole Jerr (New York: Columbia University Press, 2017 [1993–1994]), 404.
33. Piterberg, *The Returns of Zionism*, 34–36, 39–42, 138.
34. Piterberg, *The Returns of Zionism*, 246–48.
35. Piterberg, *The Returns of Zionism*, 272–82.
36. Nadia Abu El-Haj, "A 'Common Space'? The Impossibilities of a New Grammar of the Holocaust and Nakba," *Journal of Genocide Research* 22, no. 1 (2020): 142–47.
37. For example, see Joseph Massad, *The Persistence of the Palestinian Question: Essays on Zionism and the Palestinians* (New York: Routledge, 2006), 13–40.
38. Said situates the colonial roots of Zionism as follows: "For although it coincided with an era of the most virulent Western anti-Semitism, Zionism also coincided . . . with the period of unparalleled European territorial acquisition in Africa and Asia, and it was as part of this general movement of acquisition and occupation that Zionism was launched initially by Herzl. During

the latter part of the greatest period in European colonial expansion Zionism also made its crucial first moves along the way to getting what has now become a sizeable Asiatic territory." Said, "Zionism from the Standpoint of Its Victims," 22–23.

39. Paul Gilroy, *The Black Atlantic: Modernity and Double Consciousness* (Cambridge, MA: Harvard University Press, 1993).

40. Attempts to separate nationalism from settler colonialism as two distinct paradigms entirely misses how the settler colonial paradigm always already speaks to nationalism and crucially misses the fact that modern nationalism emerged in the settler colony and the project of empire, not in modern European states as separate from the colonial project. Benedict Anderson, *Imagined Communities: Reflections on the Origin and Spread of Nationalism*, rev. ed. (New York: Verso, 2016 [1983]), xiii, 46–65, 191; Arie M. Dubnov and Laura Robson, eds. *Partitions: A Transnational History of Twentieth-Century Territorial Separatism* (Stanford, CA: Stanford University Press, 2019).

41. Achille Mbembe, "The Society of Enmity," trans. G. Menegalle, *Radical Philosophy* 200, (Nov/Dec 2016): 23.

42. Mbembe, "The Society of Enmity," 23–26.

43. Mbembe, "The Society of Enmity," 24.

44. Mbembe, "The Society of Enmity," 25.

45. Mbembe, "The Society of Enmity," 25; M. Muhannad Ayyash, *A Hermeneutics of Violence: A Four-Dimensional Conception* (Toronto: University of Toronto Press, 2019), 115–27.

46. Mbembe, "The Society of Enmity," 26.

47. Paul Gilroy, *Against Race: Imagining Political Culture Beyond the Color Line* (Cambridge, MA: Harvard University Press, 2000), 28.

48. Edward Said, *Culture and Imperialism* (New York: Vintage Books, 1994); Gilroy, *The Black Atlantic*; This is why albeit constructive critiques of the settler colonial paradigm such as Evri and Kotef are not convincing. When they argue that in the case of Zionism, "racial division is at best blurred" (Yuval Evri and Hagar Kotef, "When Does a Native Become a Settler? (With Apologies to Zreik and Mamdani)," *Constellations* 29, no. 1 (2020): 13), they are missing the point that racial divisions are always at best blurred. Colonial and settler colonial ideologies can never, in any case, achieve their delusional, baseless, fictive, yet violent and destructive raciologies. The contrapuntal

human condition is the only one that is supported by historical evidence, not the absolutist and pure ideologies of race.

49. Nahla Abdo, *Women in Israel: Race, Gender, and Citizenship* (London: Zed Books, 2011); Abu El-Haj, *The Genealogical Science*; Hakem Al-Rustom, "Returning to the Question of Europe: From the Standpoint of the Defeated," in *The Arab and Jewish Questions: Geographies of Engagement in Palestine and Beyond*, ed. Bashir Bashir and Leila Farsakh (New York: Columbia University Press, 2020), 122–47; Evri and Kotef, "When does a Native become a Settler?," 6–12; Mamdani, *Neither Settler nor Native*; Ella Shohat, "Sephardim in Israel: Zionism from the Standpoint of Its Jewish Victims," *Social Text* 19/20 (Autumn 1988): 1–35; Ella Shohat, "The Invention of the Mizrahim," *Journal of Palestine Studies* 29, no. 1 (1999): 5–20; Ella Shohat, "On Orientalist Genealogies: The Split Arab/Jew Figure Revisited," in *The Arab and Jewish Questions: Geographies of Engagement in Palestine and Beyond*, ed. Bashir Bashir and Leila Farsakh (New York: Columbia University Press, 2020), 89–121.

50. Ayyash, *A Hermeneutics of Violence*, 56–64.

51. Fayez Sayegh, "Zionist Colonialism in Palestine (1965)," *Settler Colonial Studies* 2, no. 1 (2012): 214.

52. See Edward Said, "Afterword: The Consequences of 1948," in *The War for Palestine: Rewriting the History of 1948*, ed. Eugene L. Rogan and Avi Shlaim (Cambridge: Cambridge University Press, 1999), 206–19; Edward Said, *The End of the Peace Process: Oslo and After* (New York: Vintage Books, 2001), 12, 120–23, 205–9, 282–86; Massad, *The Persistence*, 129–42.

53. Bashir Bashir and Amos Goldberg, "Introduction: The Holocaust and the Nakba: A New Syntax of History, Memory, and Political Thought," in *The Holocaust and the Nakba: A New Grammar of Trauma and History*, ed. Bashir Bashir and Amos Goldberg (New York: Columbia University Press, 2018), 3.

54. Timothy Snyder's work stands out in making this case. Timothy Snyder, *Black Earth: The Holocaust as History and Warning* (New York: Tim Duggan Books, 2015).

55. Bashir and Goldberg, "Introduction," 3–4.

56. Bashir and Goldberg, "Introduction," 4–5.

57. Bashir and Goldberg, "Introduction," 15–16.

58. Bashir and Goldberg, "Introduction," 20; For a critique of the distinction between genocide and ethnic cleansing, see Nahla Abdo and Nur Masalha, eds, *An Oral History of the Palestinian Nakba* (London: Zed Books, 2018).

59. For a critique of this separation, see Muhannad Ayyash, "Zionism, Nationalism, and Settler Colonialism: On Motivations and Violence," *Middle East Critique* 33, no. 2 (2024): 195–210.
60. Gil Anidjar, *The Jew, the Arab: A History of the Enemy* (Stanford, CA: Stanford University Press, 2003).
61. Gil Anidjar, "Muslims (Shoah, Nakba)," in *The Holocaust and the Nakba: A New Grammar of Trauma and History*, ed. Bashir Bashir and Amos Goldberg (New York: Columbia University Press, 2018), 71. Raz-Krakotzkin's chapter in the book supports and builds on Anidjar's work. Amnon Raz-Krakotzkin, "Benjamin, the Holocaust, and the Question of Palestine," in *The Holocaust and the Nakba: A New Grammar of Trauma and History*, ed. Bashir Bashir and Amos Goldberg (New York: Columbia University Press, 2018), 79–91.
62. Anidjar, "Muslims," 68.
63. Anidjar, "Muslims," 71.
64. Anidjar, "Muslims," 71, 72.
65. Anidjar, "Muslims," 76; The words in quotations are Walter Benjamin's words.
66. Massad argues that Derrida's notion of the Abrahamic is especially guilty of this. Joseph A. Massad, "Forget Semitism!," in *Living Together: Jacques Derrida's Communities of Violence and Peace*, ed. E. Weber (New York: Fordham University Press, 2013), 68–79.
67. Massad, "Forget Semitism!," 61.
68. Massad, "Forget Semitism!," 64.
69. Massad, "Forget Semitism!," 65.
70. As Wolfe puts it when discussing how Zionism embraced Eurocolonial discourse as opposed to opposing it and resolving the Jewish Question: "In preference to the traditional alternatives of either confining Jews to bounded spaces within or expelling them to boundless space without, Zionism provided for a bounded space without." Wolfe, *Traces of History*, 110.
71. See Piterberg, *The Returns of Zionism*, 8–9.
72. Massad, *The Persistence*, 172.
73. Massad, *The Persistence*, 176.
74. Massad, *The Persistence*, 178.
75. Ayyash, "Zionism, Nationalism, and Settler Colonialism."
76. Judith Butler, *Parting Ways: Jewishness and the Critique of Zionism* (New York: Columbia University Press, 2014), 19, 24.
77. Butler, *Parting Ways*, 26.

4. THE FOUR-DIMENSIONAL OPERATION OF VIOLENCE: FRAGMENTATION, ISOLATION, DEHUMANIZATION, AND LORDSHIP

1. For examples, see Tareq Baconi, "Gaza and the One-State Reality," *Journal of Palestine Studies* 50, no. 1 (2021): 77–90; Brenna Bhandar, *Colonial Lives of Property: Law, Land, and Racial Regimes of Ownership* (Durham, NC: Duke University Press, 2018), 108–48; Rema Hammami, "Destabilizing Mastery and the Machine: Palestinian Agency and Gendered Embodiment at Israeli Military Checkpoints," *Current Anthropology* 60, (Supplement 19) (2019): 87–97; Rashid Khalidi, *The Hundred Years' War on Palestine: A History of Settler Colonialism and Resistance, 1917–2017* (New York: Metropolitan Books, 2020); Sari Makdisi, *Palestine Inside Out: An Everyday Occupation* (New York: Norton, 2010); Edward Said, *The Politics of Dispossession: The Struggle for Palestinian Self-Determination, 1969–1994* (New York: Vintage Books, 1995); Omar Jabary Salamanca et al., eds, "Past is Present: Settler Colonialism in Palestine," *Settler Colonial Studies* 2, no. 1 (2012); Rafi Segal and Eyal Weizman, eds, *A Civilian Occupation: The Politics of Israeli Architecture* (London: Verso, 2003); Eyal Weizman, *Hollow Land: Israel's Architecture of Occupation* (London: Verso, 2007); Haim Yacobi and Elya Milner, "Planning, Land Ownership, and Settler Colonialism in Israel/Palestine," *Journal of Palestine Studies* 51, no. 2 (2022): 43–56.
2. Although some of the specific details have changed since this article was written and have indeed become worse, see Pike for a succinct overview of the Wall's construction, dimensions, violences, and the displacing and suffocating conditions it creates for Palestinians living within its confines. Deborah J. Pike, "Sharon's Wall and the Dialectics of Inside/Outside," *Borderlands E-Journal: New Spaces in the Humanities* 5, no. 3 (2006).
3. Pike, "Sharon's Wall."
4. Graham Usher, "Unmaking Palestine: On Israel, the Palestinians, and the Wall," *Journal of Palestine Studies* 35, no. 1 (2005): 31, 33; Weizman, *Hollow Land*, 164; Idith Zertal and Akiva Eldar, *Lords of the Land: The War over Israel's Settlements in the Occupied Territories, 1967–2007*, trans. Vivian Eden (New York: Nation Books, 2009), 332; Peter Lagerquist, "Fencing the Last Sky: Excavating Palestine after Israel's 'Separation Wall,'" *Journal of Palestine Studies* 33, no. 2 (2004): 6–10.

5. Leila Farsakh, "Independence, Cantons, or Bantustans: Wither the Palestinian State?," *Middle East Journal* 59, no. 2 (2005): 230–45; Lagerquist, "Fencing the Last Sky"; indeed, Sharon uses the term "bantustans" to describe his vision for the Palestinian territories (Zertal and Eldar, *Lords of the Land*, 336).
6. Nur Masalha, *Land Without a People: Israel, Transfer, and the Palestinians, 1949–1996* (London: Faber and Faber, 1997); Darryl Li, "The Gaza Strip as Laboratory: Notes in the Wake of Disengagement," *Journal of Palestine Studies* 35, no. 2 (2006): 39; Tariq Da'na and Ali Jarbawi, "Whose Autonomy? Conceptualising 'Colonial Extraterritorial Autonomy' in the Occupied Palestinian Territories," *Politics* 43, no. 1 (2023): 106–21.
7. Noura Erakat, *Justice for Some: Law and the Question of Palestine* (Stanford, CA: Stanford University Press, 2019), 211; Dina Jadallah, "Colonialist Construction in the Urban Space of Jerusalem," *Middle East Journal* 68, no. 1 (2014): 84; David Newman, "From *Hitnachalut* to *Hitnatkut*: The Impact of Gush Emunim and the Settlement Movement on Israeli Politics and Society," *Israel Studies* 10, no. 3 (2005): 209; Weizman, *Hollow Land*, 161–82.
8. It is crucial to keep in mind that the Israeli Right and Left do not much differ on this point since it is the staple feature of Zionism. As Peter Lagerquist puts it, both the Right and the Left in the 1990s and early 2000s "followed the lead of Rehevam Ze'evi, the founder of Israel's Moledet (Transfer) party, who eight years earlier had campaigned on the slogan 'Us Here, Them There, and Peace in Israel.' 'If there is disagreement, it is only about where is there?' Ze'evi concluded." Lagerquist, "Fencing the Last Sky," 19.
9. The International Criminal Court (ICC) delivered an "Advisory Opinion" in 2004 which declared that "not only did its construction impose unnecessary hardship upon Palestinians in the Occupied Territory of the West Bank, but its very route, often cutting deep into Palestinian land was, the Court argued, dictated as much by political as security considerations." Clive Jones, "The Writing on the Wall: Israel, the Security Barrier and the Future of Zionism," *Mediterranean Politics* 14, no. 1 (2009): 3.
10. Baconi, "Gaza and the One-State Reality," 84.
11. Baconi, "Gaza and the One-State Reality," 84, 85.
12. Arnon Soffer, "It's the Demography, Stupid," interview by Ruthie Blum, *Jerusalem Post*, May 20, 2004, http://free--expression.blogspot.ca/2009/01/arnon-soffer-on-palestine-israel-and.html. (Emphasis added.) The original

link from the *Jerusalem Post* was broken due to the public relations storm that these comments created, but not before the transcript was copied and posted on various websites. Soffer is a very well-known and influential Israeli demographer who met with Sharon (and various other political leaders) on several occasions, pushing him toward the disengagement plan and unilateral separation.

13. For examples, see Daphne Barak-Erez, "Israel: The Security Barrier—Between International Law, Constitutional Law, and Domestic Judicial Review," *International Journal of Constitutional Law* 4, no. 3 (2006): 540–52; Efraim Inbar and Eitan Shamir, "'Mowing the Grass': Israel's Strategy for Protracted Intractable Conflict," *Journal of Strategic Studies* 37, no. 1 (2014): 65–90.
14. M. Muhannad Ayyash, *A Hermeneutics of Violence: A Four-Dimensional Conception* (Toronto: University of Toronto Press, 2019), 12, 187.
15. Zertal and Eldar, *Lords of the Land*, 316–18, 334–41.
16. Ayyash, *A Hermeneutics of Violence*, 184–207.
17. Benny Morris, *Righteous Victims: A History of the Zionist-Arab Conflict, 1881–2001* (New York: Vintage Books, 2001).
18. Said, *The Politics of Dispossession*, 92–93.
19. Hamid Dabashi, "Gaza: Poetry after Auschwitz," *Al-Jazeera*, August 8, 2014, http://www.aljazeera.com/indepth/opinion/2014/08/gaza-poetry-after-auschwitz-201487153418967371.html.
20. Hammami, "Destabilizing Mastery and the Machine."
21. Areej Sabbagh-Khoury, "Tracing Settler Colonialism: A Genealogy of a Paradigm in the Sociology of Knowledge Production in Israel," *Politics & Society* 50, no. 1 (2022): 48–55.
22. The group was established in 1974 (Kevin A. Avruch, "Traditionalizing Israeli Nationalism: The Development of Gush Emunim," *Political Psychology* 1, no. 1 (1979): 48–49) and "while the movement as such ceased to exist in the 1980s, it gave birth to a large number of settlement, political, and ideological organizations which continue to implement the basic ideology laid out by the movements founders, focusing, above all else, on the Greater Land of Israel ideology and spearheaded through its West Bank and Gaza settlement policy" (Newman, "From *Hitnachalut* to *Hitnatkut*," 192). My interest here is in the ideology of the movement and not the particular group, Gush Emunim.

23. For example, see then-Secretary of State John Kerry's speech just before the end of the Obama administration in 2016 where he (a) downplays the issue of settlements as a side issue that is not helping the peace process, as opposed to the core problem that it is, and (b) paints the settlement movement as separate from, and in some respects, in opposition to the Israeli state. John Kerry, "Israeli Settlements and a Two-State Solution," *Time*, December 28, 2016, https://time.com/4619064/john-kerrys-speech-israel-transcript/. For academic examples, see Giora Goldberg and Efraim Ben-Zadok, "Gush Emunim in the West Bank," *Middle Eastern Studies* 22, no. 1 (1986): 52–73; Newman, "From *Hitnachalut* to *Hitnatkut*"; Ines Gabel, "Historical Memory and Collective Identity: West Bank Settler Reconstruct the Past," *Media, Culture & Society* 35, no. 2 (2013): 250–59.
24. Zertal and Eldar, *Lords of the Land*, 11–13; For a critique of this discourse, see Joyce Dalsheim, "Ant/agonizing Settlers in the Colonial Present of Israel-Palestine," *Social Analysis* 49, no. 2 (2005): 122–43; Claudia Baumgart-Ochse, "Opposed or Intertwined? Religious and Secular Conceptions of National Identity in Israel and the Israeli-Palestinian Conflict," *Politics, Religion & Ideology* 15, no. 3 (2014): 401–20.
25. Zertal and Eldar, *Lords of the Land*, 230.
26. Steve Nutt, "Pluralized Sovereignties: Autochthonous Lawmaking on the Settler Colonial Frontier in Palestine," *Interventions* 21, no. 4 (2019): 525.
27. Zertal and Eldar, *Lords of the Land*, 271.
28. Gabel, "Historical Memory," 252–54.
29. Newman, "From *Hitnachalut* to *Hitnatkut*," 217; Avruch, "Traditionalizing Israeli Nationalism," 53; Newman, "From *Hitnachalut* to *Hitnatkut*," 196; Zertal and Eldar, *Lords of the Land*, 156.
30. Da'na and Jarbawi, "Whose Autonomy?"
31. Jadallah, "Colonialist Construction," 95.
32. Khalidi, *The Hundred Years' War*, 200–206; also see 198–99.
33. Zertal and Eldar, *Lords of the Land*, 249–50. See Zertal and Eldar for how "the settlements and the settlers were the factor that dictated more than any other element the positions of the State of Israel in the first official negotiations with the Palestinians on permanent borders" (Zertal and Eldar, *Lords of the Land*, 152–53). In contrast to Ehud Barak's version and spin on the breakdown of the negotiations, Haidar Eid shows that "The Zionist left is prepared to negotiate with the Palestinians in order to give them an advanced

form of self-rule that will be called a state, and through which the Palestinians will be enabled to possess certain selected features of 'independence,' such as a Palestinian flag, a national anthem, and a police force. Nothing more! This was Barak's 'generous' offer in Camp David in 2000" (Haidar Eid, "Edward Said and the Re-Drawing of the (Post)colonial Political Map of Palestine," *Decolonization: Indigeneity, Education & Society* 6, no. 1 (2017): 66). Also, see Khalidi's critique of Barak's and Clinton's spin on the negotiations and what really caused the failure of the talks (i.e., Israel's insistence on exclusive sovereignty over a "unified" Jerusalem) (Khalidi, *The Hundred Years' War*, 210–11).

34. Avruch, "Traditionalizing Israeli Nationalism," 47; Zertal and Eldar, *Lords of the Land*, 24–43.
35. Zertal and Eldar, *Lords of the Land*, 181–82.
36. Zertal and Eldar, *Lords of the Land*, 57.
37. Zertal and Eldar, *Lords of the Land*, 147–49.
38. Da'na and Jarbawi, "Whose Autonomy?," 112.
39. Dalsheim, "Ant/agonizing Settlers," 124.
40. Dalsheim, "Ant/agonizing Settlers," 125; Newman describes "hitnahlut" from the perspective of the religious settlers here, "Unlike the rest of Israeli society, which distinguishes between the self ascribed positive notion of 'hityashvut' (settlement) as contrasted with the negative notion of 'hitnachalut' (squatting) the settlers themselves view this latter term as denoting the tradition of continuity between the biblical narrative of a Promised Land and its translation into new tangible realities expressed through contemporary political notions of Zionism, statehood, and sovereignty." Newman, "From *Hitnachalut* to *Hitnatkut*," 207.
41. Dalsheim, "Ant/agonizing Settlers," 136–39.
42. For the argument on how a more religious Zionism has transformed the implementation of settler colonial practices, see Sabbagh-Khoury, "Tracing Settler Colonialism," 61.
43. Zertal and Eldar, *Lords of the Land*, 12–13. When it comes to the question of funding, the authors summarize the state relation to the settlement movement as follows: "Deception, shame, concealment, denial, and repression have characterized the state's behavior with respect to the flow of funds to the settlements" (Zertal and Eldar, *Lords of the Land*, 16). This goes to show the degree of care the state undertook to conceal its support to settlers and

4. THE FOUR-DIMENSIONAL OPERATION OF VIOLENCE ⋘ 307

maintain its image in the international arena of settlements as nuisance to the Israeli state. For a critique of Zertal and Eldar as promoting the liberal "hikacking thesis" see Baumgart-Ochse, "Opposed or Intertwined?," 408.
44. Zertal and Eldar, *Lords of the Land*, 239.
45. For example, Segal and Weizman, *A Civilian Occupation*; Yacobi and Milner, "Planning, Land Ownership."
46. Zertal and Eldar, *Lords of the Land*, 309.
47. Zertal and Eldar, *Lords of the Land*, 272.
48. Nadim N. Rouhana, "'Constitution by Consensus': By Whose Consensus?," *Adalah's Newsletter* 7 (November 2004), http://www.adalah.org/newsletter/eng/nov04/ar1.pdf; Nadim N. Rouhana, "Decolonization as Reconciliation: Rethinking the National Conflict Paradigm in the Israeli-Palestinian Conflict," *Ethnic and Racial Studies* 41, no. 4 (2018): 651; Bhandar, *Colonial Lives of Property*.
49. Avruch, "Traditionalizing Israeli Nationalism," 50–51.
50. David Lloyd, "Settler Colonialism and the State of Exception: The Example of Palestine/Israel," *Settler Colonial Studies* 2, no. 1 (2012): 64–66; Baumgart-Ochse, "Opposed or Intertwined?," 402–5, 409, 412–17.
51. Zertal and Eldar, *Lords of the Land*, 249–64, 271–311; Erakat, *Justice for Some*, 61–93.
52. Patrick Wolfe, *Traces of History: Elementary Structures of Race* (London: Verso, 2016), 249; also see, Nutt, "Pluralized Sovereignties," 519–25.
53. M. Muhannad Ayyash, "Hamas and the Israeli State: A 'Violent Dialogue.'" *European Journal of International Relations* 16, no. 1 (2010).
54. Nutt, "Pluralized Sovereignties."
55. Hammami, "Destabilizing Mastery and the Machine," 89.
56. As Tareq Baconi puts it, "the settlement enterprise is one of the Israeli government's largest budget items, and various decisions related to governance of those territories, from defense to construction, are made by ministerial departments, and not the military regime. The military regime is but a facade masking the fact that annexation has already happened, de facto." Baconi, "Gaza and the One-State Reality," 79.
57. As Steve Nutt puts it, "Where the cases of North America and Australia show an *ad hoc* chaos of sovereignty and jurisdiction enabling the processes of structural invasion, the case of the Israeli State, the IDF, and the settlers themselves in the Occupied Territories indicates an example of such a

process that has become a conscious and instrumentalized strategy of conquest." Nutt, "Pluralized Sovereignties," 519.
58. Zertal and Eldar, *Lords of the Land*, 228–34
59. Muhannad Ayyash, "Liberal Zionism: A Pillar of Israel's Settler Colonial Project," *Al-Shabaka: The Palestinian Policy Network*, June 14, 2023, https://al-shabaka.org/briefs/liberal-zionism-a-pillar-of-israels-settler-colonization-project/.
60. Hil Aked, *Friends of Israel: The Backlash against Palestine Solidarity* (London: Verso, 2023); Ben White, "Delegitimizing Solidarity: Israel Smears Palestine Advocacy as Anti-Semitic," *Journal of Palestine Studies* 49, no. 2 (2020): 65–79.
61. Steven Salaita, *Inter/Nationalism: Decolonizing Native America and Palestine* (Minneapolis: University of Minnesota Press, 2016).
62. Muhannad Ayyash, "The IHRA Definition will not Help Fight Antisemitism," *Al-Jazeera*, November 23, 2020, https://www.aljazeera.com/opinions/2020/11/23/the-ihra-and-the-palestinian-struggle-for/; Muhannad Ayyash, "The Jerusalem Declaration on Antisemitism is an Orientalist Text," *Al-Jazeera*, April 21, 2021, https://www.aljazeera.com/opinions/2021/4/21/the-jerusalem-declaration-on-antisemitism-is-an-orientalist-text; Muhannad Ayyash, "The Toxic Other: The Palestinian Critique and Debates about Race and Racism," *Critical Sociology* 49, no. 6 (2022): 953–66.
63. International Holocaust Remembrance Alliance, "The Working Definition of Antisemitism," May 26, 2016, https://holocaustremembrance.com/resources/working-definition-antisemitism.
64. Jerusalem Declaration on Antisemitism, 2020, https://jerusalemdeclaration.org/.
65. Fayez Sayegh, "Zionist Colonialism in Palestine (1965)," *Settler Colonial Studies* 2, no. 1 (2012): 214–18.
66. Noura Erakat, "The Sovereign Right to Kill: A Critical Appraisal of Israel's Shoot-to-Kill Policy in Gaza," *International Criminal Law Review* 19, no. 5 (2019):790; also see Khalidi, *The Hundred Years' War*, 225–26.
67. Erakat, "The Sovereign Right to Kill," 794; also see 793, 796–801, 809–15.
68. John Harfouch, "The Arab That Cannot be Killed: An Orientalist Logic of Genocide," *Radical Philosophy Review* 20, no. 2 (2017): 231–37.
69. Harfouch, "The Arab That Cannot be Killed," 236.

4. THE FOUR-DIMENSIONAL OPERATION OF VIOLENCE ○○ 309

70. Jasbir K. Puar, *The Right to Maim: Debility, Capacity, Disability* (Durham, NC: Duke University Press, 2017), 141.
71. M. Muhannad Ayyash, "Vaccine Apartheid and Settler Colonial Sovereign Violence: From Palestine to the Colonial Global Economy," *Distinktion: Journal of Social Theory* 23, no. 2–3 (2022): 304–26.
72. Puar, *The Right to Maim*, 152.
73. Zertal and Eldar, *Lords of the Land*, 76.
74. For example, see Sara Roy, *The Gaza Strip: The Political Economy of De-Development*, expanded third edition (Washington, D.C.: Institute for Palestine Studies, 2016); Omar Jabary Salamanca, "Unplug and Play: Manufacturing Collapse in Gaza," *Human Geography* 4, no. 1 (2011): 22–37; Helga Tawil-Souri, "Digital Occupation: Gaza's High-Tech Enclosure," *Journal of Palestine Studies* 41, no. 2 (2012): 27–43; Erika Weinthal and Jeannie Sowers, "Targeting Infrastructure and Livelihoods in the West Bank and Gaza," *International Affairs* 95, no. 2 (2019): 319–40.
75. Slavoj Žižek, *Violence* (New York: Picador, 2008), 1–10.
76. For example, see Khalid Manzoor Butt and Anam Abid Butt, "Blockade on Gaza Strip: A Living Hell on Earth," *Journal of Political Studies* 23, no. 1 (2016): 157–82; Noura Erakat, "Five Israeli Talking Points on Gaza—Debunked," *The Nation*, July 25, 2014, https://www.thenation.com/article/archive/five-israeli-talking-points-gaza-debunked/.
77. The United Nations Office for the Coordination of Humanitarian Affairs (OCHA), "Situation Report," no. 1: 21–27, May 2021: https://reliefweb.int/sites/reliefweb.int/files/resources/Occupied%20Palestinian%20Territory%20%28oPt%29%20-%20Response%20to%20the%20escalation%20in%20the%20oPt%20-%20Situation%20Report%20No.%201%2C%2021%20-%2027%20May%202021.pdf.
78. OCHA, "Situation Report."
79. Nidal Al-Mughrabi and Jonathan Saul, "Palestinians, Israelis Count Cost of 11-day Fight," *Reuters*, May 20, 2021, https://www.reuters.com/world/middle-east/palestinians-israelis-count-cost-11-day-fight-2021-05-20/.
80. Sebastien Roblin, "Israel's Bombardment of Gaza: Methods, Weapons, and Impact," *Forbes*, May 26, 2021, https://www.forbes.com/sites/sebastienroblin/2021/05/26/israels-bombardment-of-gaza-methods-weapons-and-impact/?sh=588d5d312f44.

81. Most of the Israeli public supports these campaigns. In the case of the 2021 attack on Gaza, when the ceasefire came into effect, a poll published on Israel's Channel 12 "indicated that 72 percent of Israelis thought the air campaign in Gaza should continue, whereas 24 percent said Israel should agree to a cease-fire." Cited from: Isabel Kershner and Adam Rasgon, "'Nothing Has Changed.' Truce Prompts Israelis to Voice Frustrations," *New York Times*, May 22, 2021.
82. Maha Hussaini, "Gaza: Families of Two Boys Killed in Israeli Attack Left Traumatised," *Middle East Eye*, June 10, 2021, https://www.middleeasteye.net/news/Gaza-Israel-air-strike-boys-killed-family-traumatised.
83. Hussaini, "Gaza."
84. Hussaini, "Gaza."
85. Hussaini, "Gaza."
86. Puar, *The Right to Maim*, 150–53.
87. Ayyash, "Vaccine Apartheid."
88. Rehab Nazzal, "Palestinian Children: Art Therapy and Intergenerational Trauma," *Society for the Diffusion of Useful Knowledge* 12 (May 2022): 25.
89. M. Muhannad Ayyash, "Racial Logics and the Epistemological Space of Palestine," *Culturico*, March 14, 2021, https://culturico.com/2021/03/14/racial-logics-and-the-epistemological-space-of-palestine/.

5. A LITERARY CRITIQUE: TOWARD DECOLONIAL SOVEREIGNTIES

1. Ariella Aïsha Azoulay, *Potential History: Unlearning Imperialism* (London: Verso, 2019), 380–83.
2. Bill Ashcroft, Gareth Griffiths, and Helen Tiffin, eds., *The Empire Writes Back: Theory and Practice in Post-Colonial Literatures*, 2nd ed. (New York: Routledge, 2002 [1989]), 2, 28–30, 194–95.
3. Peter Hallward, *Absolutely Postcolonial: Writing Between the Singular and the Specific* (New York: Manchester University Press, 2001), xiv.
4. Anna Bernard, Ziad Elmarsafy, and Stuart Murray, eds, *What Postcolonial Theory Doesn't Say* (New York: Routledge, 2016), 1–9; also see Ashcroft et al., *The Empire Writes Back*, 205; Hallward, *Absolutely Postcolonial*, xix.
5. Hallward, *Absolutely Postcolonial*, xx, 44–45; Satya P. Mohanty, ed, *Colonialism, Modernity, and Literature: A View from India* (New York: Palgrave

Macmillan, 2011), 2–6; For the role that literature, or "culturalism" generally, can play in opening up alternatives against the political deadlocks that have permeated the history of the Palestinian-Israeli conflict, see Bart Moore-Gilbert, "Palestine, Postcolonialism and Pessoptimism," *Interventions* 20, no. 1 (2018): 7–40.
6. Refqa Abu-Remaileh, "The Three Enigmas of Palestinian Literature," *Journal of Palestine Studies* 48, no. 3 (2019): 22.
7. Ambreen Hai, *Making Words Matter: The Agency of Colonial and Postcolonial Literature* (Athens: Ohio University Press, 2009), 11.
8. Hai, *Making Words Matter*, 19.
9. For more on the politics of erasure, see Najat Rahman, *In the Wake of the Poetic: Palestinian Artists after Darwish* (Syracuse, NY: Syracuse University Press, 2015), 2.
10. Gannit Ankori, *Palestinian Art* (London: Reaktion Books, 2006), 22, 47; Rahman, *In the Wake of the Poetic*, 22–23, 76–80.
11. Ankori, *Palestinian Art*, 22, 90–92, 154; Rahman, *In the Wake of the Poetic*, 20–21, 25.
12. Rahman, *In the Wake of the Poetic*, 10–12.
13. Abu-Remaileh, "The Three Enigmas," 21.
14. Edward Said, *The Politics of Dispossession: The Struggle for Palestinian Self-Determination, 1969–1994* (New York: Vintage Books, 1995); Edward Said, *After the Last Sky: Palestinian Lives*, photographs by J. Mohr (New York: Columbia University Press, 1999).
15. For overview and analysis, see Kamal Boullata, *Palestinian Art: From 1850 to the Present* (London: Saqi, 2009).
16. While Khoury is a Lebanese writer, his work certainly exhibits the main features of Palestinian literature discussed earlier.
17. Ashcroft et al., *The Empire Writes Back*, 9, 218–19.
18. Roland Barthes, "The Death of the Author," in *The Book History Reader*, ed. David Finkelstein and Alistair McCleery (New York: Routledge, 2002 [1967]), 221–24.
19. Jane Gallop, *The Deaths of the Author: Reading and Writing in Time* (Durham, NC: Duke University Press, 2011).
20. Giorgio Agamben, *Remnants of Auschwitz: The Witness and the Archive*, trans. Daniel Heller-Roazen (New York: Zone Books, 2005 [1999]), 129–35, 151–59.

21. Elias Khoury, *Gate of the Sun*, trans. Humphrey Davies (New York: Picador, 2006 [1998]), 15, 238.
22. Khoury, *Gate of the Sun*, 116, 142.
23. Khoury, *Gate of the Sun*, 214; also see 154–60, 312.
24. This does not mean that it cannot be described and documented. Elsewhere, Khoury enumerates what the Palestinians lost in 1948: land, cities, names, and the ability to tell their story. Moreover, the circular place of the *Nakba* in stories speaks to Khoury's critical point that the *Nakba* is not some event of the past but is rather a continuous process that continues to shape the present moment for Palestinians and Palestine, which is why "*Gate of the Sun* is an unfinished novel." Elias Khoury, "Rethinking the Nakba," *Critical Inquiry* 38, no. 2 (2012): 265–66.
25. This is also literally the case for Darwish who experienced two cardiovascular deaths in 1984 and 1999.
26. Khoury, *Gate of the Sun*, 290–91. Khoury argues this point elsewhere when discussing the work of Ghassan Kanafani, when he states: "that the Palestinian story . . . would not be hostage to a single, closed narrative." Elias Khoury, "Remembering Ghassan Kanafani, or How a Nation was Born of Story Telling," *Journal of Palestine Studies* 42, no. 3 (2013): 89.
27. Khoury, *Gate of the Sun*, 379–80, 393.
28. Khoury, *Gate of the Sun*, 504.
29. Khoury, *Gate of the Sun*, 514–15.
30. Lital Levy, "Nation, Village, Cave: A Spatial Reading of 1948 in Three Novels of Anton Shammas, Emile Habiby, and Elias Khoury," *Jewish Social Studies: History, Culture, Society* 18, no. 3 (2012): 10–26.
31. Jonathan Bishop Highfield, *Imagined Topographies: From Colonial Resource to Postcolonial Homeland* (New York: Peter Lang, 2012).
32. Slavoj Žižek, "The 'Matrix' or Malebranche in Hollywood," *Philosophy Today* 43 (1999): 11–26.
33. Sandra M. Gilbert and Susan Gubar, eds, *The Madwoman in the Attic: The Woman Writer and the Nineteenth-Century Literary Imagination*, 2nd ed. (New Haven, CT: Yale University Press, 2000 [1979]), 93–95.
34. Gilbert and Gubar, *The Madwoman*, 101–2.
35. Gilbert and Gubar, *The Madwoman*, 102.
36. Eve Tuck and K. Wayne Yang, "Decolonization Is Not a Metaphor," *Decolonization: Indigeneity, Education & Society* 1, no. 1 (2012): 20.

37. Audre Lorde, *Sister Outsider: Essays and Speeches* (Trumansburg, NY: Crossing Press, 1984).
38. Mahmoud Darwish, *Absent Presence*, trans. Mohammad Shaheen (London: Hesperus, 2010 [2006]), 3, 119. Similar to the "I" in the English language, the Arabic "ana" "divides the self from itself and from its 'people'. . . . The self can no longer adhere to an imposed logic of monolingualism but reflects the reality of dispersion." Rahman, *In the Wake of the Poetic*, 35. For an analysis of Darwish's oeuvre and the evolution of his poetry in search of a "poetic agency," see Khaled Mattawa, *Mahmoud Darwish: The Poet's Art and his Nation* (Syracuse, NY: Syracuse University Press, 2014).
39. Darwish, *Absent Presence*, 4–6.
40. See Habib for an analysis of this resistance to negation in Darwish and others, showing how "Palestinians confront in their writing both Israeli discourse and their existential predicament in the present" (Maha F. Habib, "Writing Palestinian Exile: The Politics of Displacement in the Narratives of Mahmoud Darwish, Mourid Barghouti, Raja Shehadeh and Fawaz Turki," *Holy Land Studies* 12, no. 1 [2013]: 84). Unlike Habib's analysis that situates Darwish's writing within a general Palestinian aspiration toward "a return of the self to the self" (89), this paper explores how Darwish's writing does not engender a complete self, or a self reconciled with itself.
41. Darwish, *Absent Presence*, 5, 22.
42. Darwish, *Absent Presence*, 24.
43. There is a similar theme in Khoury, *Gate of the Sun*, 37.
44. Darwish, *Absent Presence*, 10.
45. Darwish, *Absent Presence*, 64.
46. Darwish, *Absent Presence*, 13.
47. Darwish, *Absent Presence*, 30.
48. Darwish, *Absent Presence*, 104.
49. Darwish, *Absent Presence*, 56.
50. Hallward, *Absolutely Postcolonial*, 2–4, 48–51, 250–53.
51. Hallward, *Absolutely Postcolonial*, 18, 21–22, 26–27, 130–32.
52. Lindsey Moore, *Narrating Postcolonial Arab Nations: Egypt, Algeria, Lebanon, Palestine* (New York: Routledge, 2017), 19–20.
53. Honaida Ghanim, "The Urgency of a New Beginning in Palestine: An Imagined Scenario by Mahmoud Darwish and Hannah Arendt," *College Literature* 38, no. 1 (2011): 90.

54. Darwish, *Absent Presence*, 46–49.
55. Mahmoud Darwish, *If I Were Another*, trans. Fady Joudah (New York: Farrar, Straus and Giroux, 2009), 177–79.
56. As Farsakh puts it, "Darwish often reminded us of entangled relation with the 'other,' of the Israeli who oppresses, dispossesses, and kills, but who also loves, as his early poem 'Between Rita and Me is a Rifle' already said" (Leila Farsakh, "Darwish and the Meaning of Palestine," *Human Architecture: Journal of the Sociology of Self-Knowledge* 7, no. 5 (2009): 104). Darwish also captures this here: "It is impossible for me to evade the place that the Israeli has occupied in my identity. He exists, whatever I may think of him. He is a physical and psychological fact. The Israelis changed the Palestinians and vice versa." Helit Yeshurun, " 'Exile is so Strong Within Me, I May Bring it to the Land': A Landmark 1996 Interview with Mahmoud Darwish," *Journal of Palestine Studies* 42, no. 1 (2012): 68; Darwish, *If I Were Another*, 177.
57. Hamid Dabashi, *The Emperor Is Naked: On the Inevitable Demise of the Nation-State* (London: Zed Books, 2020), 129.
58. Khoury, *Gate of the Sun*, 411–12.
59. Dabashi, *The Emperor Is Naked*, 130.
60. Darwish's earlier poetry can be called nationalist art, but certainly his "later poetry shows how the conception of the 'political' changed. Henceforth, it would be a poetry preoccupied with *rethinking the future, subjectivity, and the self's relations to others*." (Rahman, *In the Wake of the Poetic*, 33; also see 130–35).
61. Yeshurun, "Exile Is so Strong Within Me," 58.

6. DECOLONIAL SOVEREIGNTIES

1. Tariq Da'na and Ali Jarbawi, "Whose Autonomy? Conceptualising 'Colonial Extraterritorial Autonomy' in the Occupied Palestinian Territories," *Politics* 43, no. 1 (2023):112–16.
2. For example, see Joel Beinin and Rebecca L. Stein, eds, *The Struggle for Sovereignty: Palestine and Israel, 1993–2005* (Stanford, CA: Stanford University Press, 2006); Rashid Khalidi, *The Hundred Years' War on Palestine: A History of Settler Colonialism and Resistance, 1917–2017* (New York: Metropolitan Books, 2020).

6. DECOLONIAL SOVEREIGNTIES ✼ 315

3. As Ardi Imseis summarizes here, "Despite widespread belief, Israel has never formally agreed to the establishment of a Palestinian state in the OPT. In return for PLO recognition of Israel and its right 'to exist in peace and security', Israel has only recognized 'the PLO as the representative of the Palestinian people'. While recognition of a people perforce implies recognition of its right to self-determination, Israel has consistently adopted an emaciated view of the 'sovereignty' it would allow the Palestinians, if at all. This Palestinian 'state' would be deprived of a military, control over its air space, territorial sea, borders, the Jordan valley and territorial contiguity—akin to the Bantustans of Apartheid South Africa. Doubtless, this would fall short of the attributes of statehood under international law." Ardi Imseis, "Negotiating the Illegal: On the United Nations and the Illegal Occupation of Palestine, 1967–2020," *European Journal of International Law* 31, no. 3 (2020): 1077.
4. Jospeh A. Massad, "Against Self-Determination," *Humanity: An International Journal of Human Rights, Humanitarianism, and Development* 9, no. 2 (2018): 175. There are other mechanisms, such as certain components of the international humanitarian law (IHL), Dirk A. Moses, "Empire, Resistance, and Security: International Law and the Transformative Occupation of Palestine," *Humanity: An International Journal of Human Rights, Humanitarianism, and Development* 8, no. 2 (2017): 379–409.
5. For the role of these legal definitions in establishing a Zionist claim to Palestine, see Khalidi, *The Hundred Years' War*, 244.
6. Massad, "Against Self-Determination," 179.
7. Massad, "Against Self-Determination," 179–81.
8. Judith Butler and Athena Athanasiou, *Dispossession: The Performative in the Political* (Malden, MA: Polity, 2013), 8–9.
9. Bashir Bashir and Leila Farsakh, "Three Questions that Make One," in *The Arab and Jewish Questions: Geographies of Engagement in Palestine and Beyond*, ed. Bashir Bashir and Leila Farsakh (New York: Columbia University Press, 2020), 4.
10. Nahla Abdo, "Women of the Intifada: Gender, Class and National Liberation," *Race & Class* 32, no. 4 (1991): 22; Étienne Balibar, "Racism and Nationalism," in *Race, Nation, Class: Ambiguous Identities*, ed. Étienne Balibar and Immanuel Wallerstein, trans. C. Turner (London: Verso, 1991), 53

11. Amahl Bishara, "Sovereignty and Popular Sovereignty for Palestinians and Beyond," *Cultural Anthropology* 32, no. 3 (2017): 349–50.
12. Audra Simpson, *Mohawk Interruptus: Political Life Across the Borders of Settler States* (Durham, NC: Duke University Press, 2014), 16, 22–24, 105, 112–14, 144–45, 177–78.
13. Khaled Furani, "Khalifah and the Modern Sovereign: Revisiting a Qur'anic Ideal from Within the Palestinian Condition," *Journal of Religion* 102, no. 4 (2022): 505–6.
14. Mohamed Abdou, *Islam and Anarchism: Relationships and Resonances* (London: Pluto Press, 2022).
15. Simpson, *Mohawk Interruptus*, 10–12, 20, 129.
16. Simpson, *Mohawk Interruptus*, 59.
17. Simpson, *Mohawk Interruptus*, 59.
18. Simpson, *Mohawk Interruptus*, 188; emphasis added.
19. Simpson, *Mohawk Interruptus*, 28; emphasis added.
20. Simpson, *Mohawk Interruptus*, 28.
21. Simpson, *Mohawk Interruptus*, 26–27, 29.
22. Mahmood Mamdani, *Neither Settler nor Native: The Making and Unmaking of Permanent Minorities* (Cambridge, MA: Belknap Press of Harvard University Press, 2020), 195.
23. Mamdani, *Neither Settler nor Native*, 14–17, 101–43, 192–95.
24. Mamdani, *Neither Settler nor Native*, 333.
25. Mamdani, *Neither Settler nor Native*, 147–49, 180–88, 192.
26. Mamdani, *Neither Settler nor Native*, 349.
27. Mamdani, *Neither Settler nor Native*, 149; emphasis added.
28. Mamdani, *Neither Settler nor Native*, 144.
29. Mamdani, *Neither Settler nor Native*, 352.
30. Mamdani, *Neither Settler nor Native*, 354.
31. Mamdani, *Neither Settler nor Native*, 318.
32. Mamdani, *Neither Settler nor Native*, 355.
33. Mamdani, *Neither Settler nor Native*, 23.
34. Mamdani, *Neither Settler nor Native*, 176.
35. For Mamdani's view on BDS tactics and why they should target "nonpolitical Israelis," see Mamdani, *Neither Settler nor Native*, 324.
36. Khalidi, *The Hundred Years' War*, 173–76.
37. This road is summarized succinctly in Khalidi, *The Hundred Years' War*, 168–206.

38. Rema Hammami and Salim Tamari, "Populist Paradigms: Palestinian Sociology," *Contemporary Sociology* 26, no. 3 (1997): 275–79.
39. Noura Erakat, *Justice for Some: Law and the Question of Palestine* (Stanford, CA: Stanford University Press, 2019), 135–36.
40. See the essays in Zachary Lockman and Joel Beinin, eds, *Intifada: The Palestinian Uprising against Israeli Occupation* (Toronto: Between The Lines, 1989).
41. Tariq Da'na, "Disconnecting Civil Society from its Historical Extension: NGOs and Neoliberalism in Palestine," in *Human Rights, Human Security, and State Security: The Intersection*, ed. Saul Takahashi (Oxford: Praeger, 2014), 117–38; Layth Hanbali, "Reimagining Liberation through the Popular Committees," *Al-Shabaka: The Palestinian Policy Network*, February 16, 2022: https://al-shabaka.org/briefs/reimagining-liberation-through-the-palestinian-popular-committees/.
42. Glenn E. Robinson, *Building a Palestinian State: The Incomplete Revolution* (Bloomington: Indiana University Press, 1997), 103.
43. Joost R. Hiltermann, *Behind the Intifada: Labor and Women's Movements in the Occupied Territories* (Princeton, NJ: Princeton University Press, 1991), 126–27.
44. For the point on underground cells, see Rema Hammami, "NGOs: The Professionalisation of Politics," *Race & Class* 37, no. 2 (1995): 51–63, and "Palestinian NGOs since Oslo: From NGO Politics to Social Movements?," *Middle East Report* 214, (Spring) (2000): 16–19, 27, 48; For the point on the quasi nation-state, see Hanbali, "Reimagining Liberation"; For the point on NGOization, see Islah Jad, "NGOs: Between Buzzwords and Social Movements," *Development in Practice* 17, no. 4–5 (2007): 622–29; Islah Jad, *Palestinian Women's Activism: Nationalism, Secularism, Islamism* (Syracuse, NY: Syracuse University Press, 2018); Da'na, "Disconnecting Civil Society." In a nutshell, "The new [NGO] professionals tend to treat the 'grassroots' in a patronizing and condescending manner, perceiving them as social groups in need of instruction, rather than as constituencies from which they take their direction and legitimacy." Hammami, "Palestinian NGOs," 19.
45. Hammami, "NGOs," 55; also see Hiltermann, *Behind the Intifada*, 192, 214.
46. Hammami, "Palestinian NGOs," 16–17.
47. Da'na, "Disconnecting Civil Society," 134.
48. Hammami, "NGOs," 55.

49. Ala Alazzeh, "Seeking Popular Participation: Nostalgia for the First Intifada in the West Bank," *Settler Colonial Studies* 5, no. 3 (2015): 254.
50. Hiltermann, *Behind the Intifada*, 53, 119, 177.
51. Lockman and Beinin, *Intifada*, 327–94.
52. Communiqué no. 24 on August 22, 1988 (Lockman and Beinin, *Intifada*, 376–80).
53. Edward Said, "Intifada and Independence," in *Intifada: The Palestinian Uprising against Israeli Occupation*, ed. Zachary Lockman and Joel Beinin (Toronto: Between The Lines, 1989), 20l; Alazzeh, "Seeking Popular Participation."
54. Hiltermann, *Behind the Intifada*, 211.
55. Communiqué no. 15 on April 30, 1988 (Lockman and Beinin, *Intifada*, 349–52); also see Hiltermann, *Behind the Intifada*, 178–180.
56. Penny Johnson, Lee O'Brien, and Joost Hiltermann, "The West Bank Rises Up," in *Intifada: The Palestinian Uprising against Israeli Occupation*, ed. Zachary Lockman and Joel Beinin (Toronto: Between The Lines, 1989), 38.
57. Communiqué no. 19 ca. June 6, 1988 (Lockman and Beinin, *Intifada*, 360–61); Communiqué no. 3 on January 18, 1988 (Lockman and Beinin, *Intifada*, 333); Communiqué no. 6 on February 2, 1988 (Lockman and Beinin, *Intifada*, 334).
58. Communiqué no. 13 on April 10, 1988 (Lockman and Beinin, *Intifada*, 345).
59. Hiltermann, *Behind the Intifada*, 211.
60. Communiqué no. 7 or 8 ca. February 18, 1988 (Lockman and Beinin, *Intifada*, 337).
61. Communiqué no. 22 on July 21, 1988 (Lockman and Beinin, *Intifada*, 369).
62. Communiqué no. 24 on August 22, 1988 (Lockman and Beinin, *Intifada*, 376).
63. Communiqué no. 17 on May 24, 1988 (Lockman and Beinin, *Intifada*, 356); Communiqué no. 24 on August 22, 1988 (Lockman and Beinin, *Intifada*, 377).
64. M. Muhannad Ayyash, "Rethinking the Social-Political Through Ibn Khaldûn and Aristotle," *Interventions* 19, no. 8 (2017): 1206–7. In Euro-American scholarship, there is an assertion, which was perhaps cemented most clearly in the work of Foucault, that "rule" and "governance" are two very different forms of power, authority, sovereignty, and politics. I believe that this distinction overstates the transformation from "sovereign power" to "biopower"—a distinction that Foucault himself questions later in his career. Regardless, I do not believe that this distinction is helpful when it comes to

understanding settler colonial sovereignty. How the distinction may take shape in decolonial future(s) is another topic for another analysis.
65. Hiltermann, *Behind the Intifada*, 194.
66. Jad, *Palestinian Women's Activism*, 24.
67. Jad, *Palestinian Women's Activism*, 1, 18–25; Hiltermann, *Behind the Intifada*, 126–72.
68. Abdo, "Women of the Intifada."
69. Nahla Abdo, *Women in Israel: Race, Gender, and Citizenship* (London: Zed Books, 2011).
70. Jad, *Palestinian Women's Activism*, 159.
71. Jad, *Palestinian Women's Activism*, 159.
72. Jad, *Palestinian Women's Activism*, 22.
73. Concrete examples of this can be found in several organizations, initiatives, projects, and even ministries. See Jad, *Palestinian Women's Activism*, 46–53, 134–39.
74. Abdo, *Women in Israel*, 60–61.
75. Hiltermann, *Behind the Intifada*, 172.
76. Jad, *Palestinian Women's Activism*, 134–39.
77. Jad, *Palestinian Women's Activism*, 140–50.
78. Somdeep Sen, *Decolonizing Palestine: Hamas between the Anticolonial and the Postcolonial* (Ithaca, NY: Cornell University Press, 2020).
79. Jad, *Palestinian Women's Activism*, 153.
80. For marginalization of women and women's issues in the UNLU, see Hiltermann, *Behind the Intifada*, 199–205; For the pressure on women activists to abandon grassroots mobilization, see Jad, *Palestinian Women's Activism*, 26, 54–58, 70; For the point on women being blocked from leadership positions, see Nahla Abdo, "Gender and Politics under the Palestinian Authority," *Journal of Palestine Studies* 28, no. 2 (1999): 41–43; Jad, *Palestinian Women's Activism*, 50–55, 113–14; For the role of Israeli settler colonialism, see Abdo, *Women in Israel*, 29–30; Jad, *Palestinian Women's Activism*, 29–30.
81. Jad, *Palestinian Women's Activism*, 85–86.
82. Joseph A. Massad, *Islam in Liberalism* (Chicago: University of Chicago Press, 2015), 110–212.
83. Nahla Abdo, "Imperialism, the State, and NGOs: Middle Eastern Contexts and Contestations," *Comparative Studies of South Asia, Africa and the Middle East* 30, no. 2 (2010): 245–46.

84. Safa Joudeh, "Defying Exception: Gaza After the 'Unity Uprising,'" *Journal of Palestine Studies* 50, no. 4 (2021): 75.
85. Abdel Razzaq Takriti, "'Who Will Hang the Bell?' The Palestinian *Habba* of 2021," *Journal of Palestine Studies* 50, no. 4 (2021): 81; also see Abdel Razeq Farraj, "Palestine Rises in Rebellion," *Journal of Palestine Studies* 50, no. 4 (2021): 68–72.
86. Rana Barakat, "'Ramadan Does Not Come for Free': Refusal as New and Ongoing in Palestine," *Journal of Palestine Studies* 50, no. 4 (2021): 90–95.
87. Lana Tatour, "The 'Unity Intifada' and '48 Palestinians: Between the Liberal and the Decolonial," *Journal of Palestine Studies* 50, no. 4 (2021): 84, 88; also see Nadim N. Rouhana and Areej Sabbagh-Khoury, "Settler-Colonial Citizenship: Conceptualizing the Relationship between Israel and its Palestinian Citizens," *Settler Colonial Studies* 5, no. 3 (2015): 205–25, and "Memory and the Return of History in a Settler-Colonial Context: The Case of the Palestinians in Israel," *Interventions* 21, no. 4 (2019): 527–50.
88. Abdo, *Women in Israel*, 37.
89. Siniša Malešević, "Forms of Brutality: Towards a Historical Sociology of Violence," *European Journal of Social Theory* 16, no. 3 (2013): 273–91.
90. Josheph A. Massad, "Ghassan Kanafani, Zionism and Race: What Determines the Fate of a People," *Middle East Eye*, July 29, 2022, https://www.middleeasteye.net/opinion/palestine-ghassan-kanafani-message-inspire-how.
91. Ilan Pappé, "Indigeneity as Resistance," in *Rethinking Statehood in Palestine: Self-determination and Decolonization Beyond Partition*, ed. Leila Farsakh (Oakland: University of California Press, 2021), 276–94.
92. Erakat, *Justice for Some*, 237.

CONCLUSION

1. M. Muhannad Ayyash, *A Hermeneutics of Violence: A Four-Dimensional Conception* (Toronto: University of Toronto Press, 2019), 54.
2. Abdel Razzaq Takriti, "'Who Will Hang the Bell?' The Palestinian *Habba* of 2021," *Journal of Palestine Studies* 50, no. 4 (2021): 80.
3. Charles W. Anderson, "State Formation from Below and the Great Revolt in Palestine," *Journal of Palestine Studies* 47, no. 1 (2017): 43.
4. Anderson, "State Formation," 48–50.

5. Ariella Aïsha Azoulay, *Potential History: Unlearning Imperialism* (London: Verso, 2019), 387.

POSTSCRIPT

1. Muhannad Ayyash, "The Path to Peace in Israel-Palestine is through Decolonisation," *Al-Jazeera*, February 17, 2021, https://www.aljazeera.com/opinions/2021/2/17/the-path-to-peace-in-israel-palestine-is-through-decolonisation.

BIBLIOGRAPHY

Abdo, Nahla. "Gender and Politics under the Palestinian Authority." *Journal of Palestine Studies* 28, no. 2 (1999): 38–51.

———. "Imperialism, the State, and NGOs: Middle Eastern Contexts and Contestations." *Comparative Studies of South Asia, Africa, and the Middle East* 30, no. 2 (2010): 238–49.

———. *Women in Israel: Race, Gender, and Citizenship.* London: Zed Books, 2011.

———. "Women of the Intifada: Gender, Class and National Liberation." *Race & Class* 32, no. 4 (1991): 19–34.

Abdo, Nahl, and Nur Masalha, eds. *An Oral History of the Palestinian Nakba.* London: Zed Books, 2018.

Abdou, Mohamed. *Islam and Anarchism: Relationships and Resonances.* London: Pluto Press, 2022.

Abu El-Haj, Nadia. "A 'Common Space'? The Impossibilities of a New Grammar of the Holocaust and Nakba." *Journal of Genocide Research* 22, no. 1 (2020): 142–47.

———. *Facts on the Ground: Archaeological Practice and Territorial Self-Fashioning in Israeli Society.* Chicago: University of Chicago Press, 2001.

———. *The Genealogical Science: The Search for Jewish Origins and the Politics of Epistemology.* Chicago: University of Chicago Press, 2012.

Abu-Laban, Yasmeen, and Abigail B. Bakan. "The Racial Contract: Israel/Palestine and Canada." *Social Identities* 14, no. 5 (2008): 637–60.

Abunimah, Ali. *One Country: A Bold Proposal to End the Israeli–Palestinian Impasse.* New York: Metropolitan Books, 2006.

Abu-Remaileh, Refqa. "The Three Enigmas of Palestinian Literature." *Journal of Palestine Studies* 48, no. 3 (2019): 21–25.

Agamben, Giorgio. *Homo Sacer: Sovereign Power and Bare Life*. Trans. Daniel Heller-Roazen. Stanford, CA: Stanford University Press, 1998 [1995].

——. *Remnants of Auschwitz: The Witness and the Archive*. Trans. Daniel Heller-Roazen. New York: Zone Books, 2005 [1999].

Agnew, John. *Globalization and Sovereignty*. Lanham, MD: Rowman & Littlefield, 2009.

Ahmad, Eqbal. "The Neofascist State." In *The Selected Writings of Eqbal Ahmad*, ed. Carollee Bengelsdorf, Margaret Cerullo, and Yogesh Chandrani, 142–53. New York: Columbia University Press, 2006 [1981].

——. "Postcolonial Systems of Power." In *The Selected Writings of Eqbal Ahmad*, ed. Carollee Bengelsdorf, Margaret Cerullo, and Yogesh Chandrani, 128–41. New York: Columbia University Press, 2006 [1980].

Aked, Hil. *Friends of Israel: The Backlash Against Palestine Solidarity*. London: Verso, 2023.

Alazzeh, Ala. "Seeking Popular Participation: Nostalgia for the First Intifada in the West Bank." *Settler Colonial Studies* 5, no. 3 (2015): 251–67.

Al-Mughrabi, Nidal, and Jonathan Saul. "Palestinians, Israelis Count Cost of 11-Day Fight." *Reuters*, May 20, 2021. https://www.reuters.com/world/middle-east/palestinians-israelis-count-cost-11-day-fight-2021-05-20/.

Al-Rustom, Hakem. "Returning to the Question of Europe: From the Standpoint of the Defeated." In *The Arab and Jewish Questions: Geographies of Engagement in Palestine and Beyond*, ed. Bashir Bashir and Leila Farsakh, 122–47. New York: Columbia University Press, 2020.

Anderson, Benedict. *Imagined Communities: Reflections on the Origin and Spread of Nationalism*. Rev. ed. New York: Verso, 2016 [1983].

Anderson, Charles W. "State Formation from Below and the Great Revolt in Palestine." *Journal of Palestine Studies* 47, no. 1 (2017): 39–55.

Anidjar, Gil. *The Jew, the Arab: A History of the Enemy*. Stanford, CA: Stanford University Press, 2003.

——. "Muslims (Shoah, Nakba)." In *The Holocaust and the Nakba: A New Grammar of Trauma and History*, ed. Bashir Bashir and Amos Goldberg, 66–78. New York: Columbia University Press, 2018.

Ankori, Gannit. *Palestinian Art*. London: Reaktion Books, 2006.

Ashcroft, Bill, Gareth Griffiths, and Helen Tiffin, eds. *The Empire Writes Back: Theory and Practice in Post–Colonial Literatures*. 2nd ed. New York: Routledge, 2002 [1989].

Avruch, Kevin A. "Traditionalizing Israeli Nationalism: The Development of Gush Emunim." *Political Psychology* 1, no. 1 (1979): 47–57.

Ayyash, M. Muhannad. "An Assemblage of Decoloniality? Palestinian Fellahin Resistance and the Space-Place Relation." *Studies in Social Justice* 12, no. 1 (2018): 21–37.

———. "Hamas and the Israeli State: A 'Violent Dialogue.'" *European Journal of International Relations* 16, no. 1 (2010): 103–23.

———. *A Hermeneutics of Violence: A Four-Dimensional Conception*. Toronto: University of Toronto Press, 2019.

———. "The IHRA Definition Will Not Help Fight Antisemitism." *Al-Jazeera*, November 23, 2020. https://www.aljazeera.com/opinions/2020/11/23/the-ihra-and-the-palestinian-struggle-for/.

———. "Jerusalem and Violence: The Transformation of Secular and Sacred Interpretations." In *Cultural Violence and Destruction of Communities: New Theoretical Perspectives*, ed. Fiona Greenland and Fatma Müge Göçek, 95–115. London: Routledge, 2020.

———. "The Jerusalem Declaration on Antisemitism Is an Orientalist Text." *Al-Jazeera*, April 21, 2021. https://www.aljazeera.com/opinions/2021/4/21/the-jerusalem-declaration-on-antisemitism-is-an-orientalist-text.

———. "Liberal Zionism: A Pillar of Israel's Settler Colonial Project." *Al-Shabaka: The Palestinian Policy Network*, June 14, 2023. https://al-shabaka.org/briefs/liberal-zionism-a-pillar-of-israels-settler-colonization-project/.

———. "The Path to Peace in Israel–Palestine is through Decolonisation." *Al-Jazeera*, February 17, 2021. https://www.aljazeera.com/opinions/2021/2/17/the-path-to-peace-in-israel-palestine-is-through-decolonisation.

———. "Racial Logics and the Epistemological Space of Palestine." *Culturico*, March 14, 2021. https://culturico.com/2021/03/14/racial-logics-and-the-epistemological-space-of-palestine/.

———. "Rethinking the Social-Political Through Ibn Khaldûn and Aristotle." *Interventions* 19, no. 8 (2017): 1193–1209.

———. "The Toxic Other: The Palestinian Critique and Debates About Race and Racism." *Critical Sociology* 49, no. 6 (2022): 953–66.

———. "Vaccine Apartheid and Settler Colonial Sovereign Violence: From Palestine to the Colonial Global Economy." *Distinktion: Journal of Social Theory* 23, no. 2–3 (2022): 304–26.

———. "Zionism, Nationalism, and Settler Colonialism: On Motivations and Violence." *Middle East Critique* 33, no. 2 (2024): 195–210.

Azoulay, Ariella Aïsha. *Potential History: Unlearning Imperialism.* London: Verso, 2019.

Baconi, Tareq. "Gaza and the One-State Reality." *Journal of Palestine Studies* 50, no. 1 (2021): 77–90.

Bakan, Abigail B., and Yasmeen Abu-Laban. "The Israel/Palestine Racial Contract and the Challenge of Anti-Racism: A Case Study of the United Nations World Conference Against Racism." *Ethnic and Racial Studies* 44, no. 12 (2021): 2167–89.

Balibar, Étienne. "Racism and Nationalism." In *Race, Nation, Class: Ambiguous Identities*, ed. Étienne Balibar and Immanuel Wallerstein, 37–67. Trans. C. Turner. London: Verso, 1991.

Barak-Erez, Daphne. "Israel: The Security Barrier—Between International Law, Constitutional Law, and Domestic Judicial Review." *International Journal of Constitutional Law* 4, no. 3 (2006): 540–52.

Barakat, Rana. "'Ramadan Does Not Come for Free': Refusal as New and Ongoing in Palestine." *Journal of Palestine Studies* 50, no. 4 (2021): 90–95.

———. "Writing/Righting Palestine Studies: Settler Colonialism, Indigenous Sovereignty and Resisting the Ghost(s) of History." *Settler Colonial Studies* 8, no. 3 (2018): 349–63.

Barghouti, Omar. "A Secular Democratic State in Historic Palestine: Self-Determination through Ethical Decolonisation." In *After Zionism: One State for Israel and Palestine*, ed. Antony Lowenstein and Ahmed Moore, 194–209. London: Saqi Books, 2012.

Barkin, J. Samuel. "The Evolution of the Constitution of Sovereignty and the Emergence of Human Rights Norms." *Millennium: Journal of International Studies* 27, no. 2 (1998): 229–52.

Barkin, J. Samuel, and Bruce Cronin. "The State and the Nation: Changing Norms and the Rules of Sovereignty in International Relations." *International Organization* 48, no. 1 (1994): 107–30.

Barlow, Tani E., ed. *Formations of Colonial Modernity in East Asia.* Durham, NC: Duke University Press, 1997.

Bartelson, Jens. *A Genealogy of Sovereignty.* Cambridge: Cambridge University Press, 1995.

———. "The Concept of Sovereignty Revisited." *European Journal of International Law* 17, no. 2 (2006): 463–74.

Barthes, Roland. "The Death of the Author." In *The Book History Reader*, ed. David Finkelstein and Alistair McCleery, 221–24. New York: Routledge, 2002 [1967].

Bashir, Bashir, and Amos Goldberg. "Introduction: The Holocaust and the Nakba: A New Syntax of History, Memory, and Political Thought." In *The Holocaust and the Nakba: A New Grammar of Trauma and History*, ed. Bashir Bashir and Amos Goldberg, 1–42. New York: Columbia University Press, 2018.

Bashir, Bashir, and Leila Farsakh. "Three Questions That Make One." In *The Arab and Jewish Questions: Geographies of Engagement in Palestine and Beyond*, ed. Bashir Bashir and Leila Farsakh, 1–22. New York: Columbia University Press, 2020.

Bataille, Georges. *The Accursed Share: An Essay on General Economy, Volumes II and III*. Trans. Robert Hurley. New York: Zone Books, 1989 [1976].

Baumgart–Ochse, Claudia. "Opposed or Intertwined? Religious and Secular Conceptions of National Identity in Israel and the Israeli-Palestinian Conflict." *Politics, Religion & Ideology* 15, no. 3 (2014): 401–20.

Beckert, Sven. *Empire of Cotton: A Global History*. New York: Vintage Books, 2015.

Beckert, Sven, and Seth Rockman, eds. *Slavery's Capitalism: A New History of American Economic Development*. Philadelphia: University of Pennsylvania Press, 2016.

Beinin, Joel, and Rebecca L. Stein, eds. *The Struggle for Sovereignty: Palestine and Israel, 1993–2005*. Stanford, CA: Stanford University Press, 2006.

Bernard, Anna, Ziad Elmarsafy, and Stuart Murray, eds. *What Postcolonial Theory Doesn't Say*. New York: Routledge, 2016.

Bhandar, Brenna. *Colonial Lives of Property: Law, Land, and Racial Regimes of Ownership*. Durham, NC: Duke University Press, 2018.

Bhambra, Gurminder K. "Colonial Global Economy: Towards a Theoretical Reorientation of Political Economy." *Review of International Political Economy* 28, no. 2 (2021): 307–22.

——. *Connected Sociologies*. New York: Bloomsbury, 2014.

——. "Postcolonial and Decolonial Dialogues." *Postcolonial Studies* 17, no. 2 (2014): 115–21.

——. *Rethinking Modernity: Postcolonialism and the Sociological Imagination*. New York: Palgrave Macmillan, 2007.

Biggs, Michael. "Putting the State on the Map: Cartography, Territory, and European State Formation." *Comparative Studies in Society and History* 41, no. 2 (1999): 374–405.

Bishara, Amahl. "Sovereignty and Popular Sovereignty for Palestinians and Beyond." *Cultural Anthropology* 32, no. 3 (2017): 349–58.

Bodin, Jean. *On Sovereignty: Four Chapters from the Six Books of the Commonwealth*. Ed. and trans. Julian H. Franklin. Cambridge: Cambridge University Press, 1992 [1576].

Boullata, Kamal. *Palestinian Art: From 1850 to the Present*. London: Saqi, 2009.

Bourke, Richard. "Introduction." In *Popular Sovereignty in Historical Perspective*, ed. Richard Bourke and Quentin Skinner, 1–14. Cambridge: Cambridge University Press, 2016.

———. "Popular Sovereignty and Political Representation: Edmund Burke in the Context of Eighteenth-Century Thought." In *Popular Sovereignty in Historical Perspective*, ed. Richard Bourke and Quentin Skinner, 212–35. Cambridge: Cambridge University Press, 2016b.

Brenner, Neil, and Stuart Elden. "Henri Lefebvre on State, Space, Territory." *International Political Sociology* 3 (2009): 353–77.

Brunner, Otto. *Land and Lordship: Structures of Governance in Medieval Austria*. 4th rev. ed. Ed. and trans. Howard Kaminsky and James Van Horn Melton. Philadelphia: University of Pennsylvania Press, 1992.

Bruyneel, Kevin. *The Third Space of Sovereignty: The Postcolonial Politics of U.S.-Indigenous Relations*. Minneapolis: University of Minnesota Press, 2007.

Butler, Judith. *Parting Ways: Jewishness and the Critique of Zionism*. New York: Columbia University Press, 2014.

Butler, Judith, and Athena Athanasiou. *Dispossession: The Performative in the Political*. Malden, MA: Polity Press, 2013.

Burbank, Jane, and Frederick Cooper. *Empires in World History: Power and the Politics of Difference*. Princeton, NJ: Princeton University Press, 2010.

Butt, Khalid Manzoor, and Anam Abid Butt. "Blockade on Gaza Strip: A Living Hell on Earth." *Journal of Political Studies* 23, no. 1 (2016): 157–82.

Byrd, Jodi A. *The Transit of Empire: Indigenous Critiques of Colonialism*. Minneapolis: University of Minnesota Press, 2011.

Challand, Benoit. "Citizenship and Violence in the Arab Worlds: A Historical Sketch." In *The Transformation of Citizenship, Volume 3: Struggle, Resistance and Violence*, ed. Juergen Mackert and Bryan Turner, 93–112. London: Routledge, 2017.

Coulthard, Glen. *Red Skin, White Masks: Rejecting the Colonial Politics of Recognition*. Minneapolis: University of Minnesota Press, 2014.

Dabashi, Hamid. *The Arab Spring: The End of Postcolonialism*. New York: Zed Books, 2012.

———. *Can Non-Europeans Think?* London: Zed Books, 2015.

———. *The Emperor Is Naked: On the Inevitable Demise of the Nation-State.* London: Zed Books, 2020.

———. "Gaza: Poetry After Auschwitz." *Al-Jazeera*, August 8, 2014. http://www.aljazeera.com/indepth/opinion/2014/08/gaza-poetry-after-auschwitz-201487153418967371.html.

Dalsheim, Joyce. "Ant/agonizing Settlers in the Colonial Present of Israel-Palestine." *Social Analysis* 49, no. 2 (2005): 122–43.

Da'na, Tariq. "Disconnecting Civil Society from its Historical Extension: NGOs and Neoliberalism in Palestine." In *Human Rights, Human Security, and State Security: The Intersection*, ed. Saul Takahashi, 117–38. Oxford: Praeger, 2014.

Da'na, Tariq, and Ali Jarbawi. "Whose Autonomy? Conceptualising 'Colonial Extraterritorial Autonomy' in the Occupied Palestinian Territories." *Politics* 43, no. 1 (2023): 106–21.

Darwish, Mahmoud. *Absent Presence.* Trans. Mohammad Shaheen. London: Hesperus, 2010 [2006].

———. *If I Were Another.* Trans. Fady Joudah. New York: Farrar, Straus and Giroux, 2009.

Das, Veena. *Life and Words: Violence and the Descent into the Ordinary.* Berkeley: University of California Press, 2007.

Das, Veena, and Arthur Kleinman. "Introduction." In *Violence and Subjectivity*, ed. Veena Das, Arthur Kleinman, Mamphela Ramphele, and Pamela Reynolds, 1–18. Berkeley: University of California Press, 2000.

Derrida, Jacques. *The Beast and the Sovereign, Volume I.* Trans. Geoffrey Bennington. Ed. Michel Lisse, Marie-Louise Mallet, and Ginette Michaud. Chicago: University of Chicago Press, 2009.

———. *The Beast and the Sovereign, Volume II.* Trans. Geoffrey Bennington. Ed. Michel Lisse, Marie-Louise Mallet, and Ginette Michaud. Chicago: University of Chicago Press, 2011.

———. "Force of Law: The 'Mystical Foundation of Authority.'" In *Acts of Religion*, trans. M. Quaintance, ed. Gil Anidjar, 228–98. New York: Routledge, 2002 [1990].

Dubnov, Arie M., and Laura Robson, eds. *Partitions: A Transnational History of Twentieth-Century Territorial Separatism.* Stanford, CA: Stanford University Press, 2019.

Dunbar-Ortiz, Roxanne. *An Indigenous Peoples' History of the United States.* Boston: Beacon Press, 2014.

Eid, Haidar. "Edward Said and the Re-Drawing of the (Post)colonial Political Map of Palestine." *Decolonization: Indigeneity, Education & Society* 6, no. 1 (2017): 64–78.

———. "The Zionist-Palestinian Conflict: An Alternative Story." *Nebula* 5, no. 3 (2008): 122–39.

Elias, Norbert. *The Civilizing Process: Sociogenetic and Psychogenetic Investigations*. Rev. ed. Trans. Edmund Jephcott. Ed. Eric Dunning, Johan Goudsblom, and Stephen Mennell. Malden, MA: Wiley Blackwell, 2000 [1939].

Eltis, David, and David Richardson. *Atlas of the Transatlantic Slave Trade*. New Haven, CT: Yale University Press, 2010.

Erakat, Noura. "Five Israeli Talking Points on Gaza—Debunked." *The Nation*, July 25, 2014. https://www.thenation.com/article/archive/five-israeli-talking-points-gaza-debunked/.

———. *Justice for Some: Law and the Question of Palestine*. Stanford, CA: Stanford University Press, 2019.

———. "The Sovereign Right to Kill: A Critical Appraisal of Israel's Shoot-to-Kill Policy in Gaza." *International Criminal Law Review* 19, no. 5 (2019): 783–818.

Evri, Yuval, and Hagar Kotef. "When Does a Native Become a Settler? (With Apologies to Zreik and Mamdani)." *Constellations* 29, no. 1 (2020): 3–18.

Fanon, Frantz. *The Wretched of the Earth*. Trans. Richard Philcox. New York: Grove Press, 2004 [1961].

Farraj, Abdel Razeq. "Palestine Rises in Rebellion." *Journal of Palestine Studies* 50, no. 4 (2021): 68–72.

Farsakh, Leila. "Darwish and the Meaning of Palestine." *Human Architecture: Journal of the Sociology of Self-Knowledge* 7, no. 5 (2009): 101–4.

———. "Independence, Cantons, or Bantustans: Wither the Palestinian State?" *Middle East Journal* 59, no. 2 (2005): 230–45.

Ford, Lisa. *Settler Sovereignty: Jurisdiction and Indigenous People in America and Australia, 1788–1836*. Cambridge, MA: Harvard University Press, 2011.

Furani, Khaled. "Khalifah and the Modern Sovereign: Revisiting a Qur'anic Ideal from Within the Palestinian Condition." *Journal of Religion* 102, no. 4 (2022): 482–506.

Gabel, Ines. "Historical Memory and Collective Identity: West Bank Settlers Reconstruct the Past." *Media, Culture & Society* 35, no. 2 (2013): 250–59.

Gadamer, Hans-Georg. *Truth and Method*. 2nd rev. ed. Trans. Joel Weinsheimer and Donald G. Marshall. New York: Continuum, 2004 [1960].

Gallop, Jane. *The Deaths of the Author: Reading and Writing in Time.* Durham, NC: Duke University Press, 2011.

Ghanim, Honaida. "The Urgency of a New Beginning in Palestine: An Imagined Scenario by Mahmoud Darwish and Hannah Arendt." *College Literature* 38, no. 1 (2011): 75–94.

Gilbert, Sandra M., and Susan Gubar, eds. *The Madwoman in the Attic: The Woman Writer and the Nineteenth-Century Literary Imagination.* 2nd ed. New Haven, CT: Yale University Press, 2000 [1979].

Gilroy, Paul. *Against Race: Imagining Political Culture Beyond the Color Line.* Cambridge, MA: Harvard University Press, 2000.

——. *The Black Atlantic: Modernity and Double Consciousness.* Cambridge, MA: Harvard University Press, 1993.

Goldberg, Giora, and Efraim Ben-Zadok. "Gush Emunim in the West Bank." *Middle Eastern Studies* 22, no. 1 (1986): 52–73.

Habib, Maha F. "Writing Palestinian Exile: The Politics of Displacement in the Narratives of Mahmoud Darwish, Mourid Barghouti, Raja Shehadeh, and Fawaz Turki." *Holy Land Studies* 12, no. 1 (2013): 71–90.

Hai, Ambreen. *Making Words Matter: The Agency of Colonial and Postcolonial Literature.* Athens: Ohio University Press, 2009.

Hallward, Peter. *Absolutely Postcolonial: Writing Between the Singular and the Specific.* New York: Manchester University Press, 2001.

Hammami, Rema. "Destabilizing Mastery and the Machine: Palestinian Agency and Gendered Embodiment at Israeli Military Checkpoints." *Current Anthropology* 60 (Supplement 19) (2019): 87–97.

——. "NGOs: The Professionalisation of Politics." *Race & Class* 37, no. 2 (1995): 51–63.

——. "Palestinian NGOs Since Oslo: From NGO Politics to Social Movements?" *Middle East Report* 214 (Spring 2000): 16–19, 27, 48.

Hammami, Rema, and Salim Tamari. "Populist Paradigms: Palestinian Sociology." *Contemporary Sociology* 26, no. 3 (1997): 275–79.

Hanbali, Layth. "Reimagining Liberation Through the Popular Committees." *Al-Shabaka: The Palestinian Policy Network*, February 16, 2022. https://al-shabaka.org/briefs/reimagining-liberation-through-the-palestinian-popular-committees/.

Harfouch, John. "The Arab That Cannot Be Killed: An Orientalist Logic of Genocide." *Radical Philosophy Review* 20, no. 2 (2017): 219–41.

Highfield, Jonathan Bishop. *Imagined Topographies: From Colonial Resource to Postcolonial Homeland*. New York: Peter Lang, 2012.

Hiltermann, Joost R. *Behind the Intifada: Labor and Women's Movements in the Occupied Territories*. Princeton, NJ: Princeton University Press, 1991.

Hoekstra, Kinch. "Athenian Democracy and Popular Tyranny." In *Popular Sovereignty in Historical Perspective*, ed. Richard Bourke and Quentin Skinner, 15–51. Cambridge: Cambridge University Press, 2016.

Hussaini, Maha. "Gaza: Families of Two Boys Killed in Israeli Attack Left Traumatised." *Middle East Eye*, June 10, 2021. https://www.middleeasteye.net/news/Gaza-Israel-air-strike-boys-killed-family-traumatised.

Hussein, Cherine. *The Re-Emergence of the Single State Solution in Palestine/Israel: Countering an Illusion*. New York: Routledge, 2015.

Ibn Khaldûn, 'Abd al–Rahman. *The Muqaddimah: An Introduction to History*. 3 vols. Trans. Franz Rosenthal. London: Routledge and Kegan Paul, 1958 [1378].

Imseis, Ardi. "Negotiating the Illegal: On the United Nations and the Illegal Occupation of Palestine, 1967–2020." *European Journal of International Law* 31, no. 3 (2020): 1055–85.

Inbar, Efraim, and Eitan Shamir. "'Mowing the Grass': Israel's Strategy for Protracted Intractable Conflict." *Journal of Strategic Studies* 37, no. 1 (2014): 65–90.

International Holocaust Remembrance Alliance. "The Working Definition of Antisemitism." May 26, 2016. https://holocaustremembrance.com/resources/working-definition-antisemitism.

Jackson, Robert. *Sovereignty: Evolution of an Idea*. Cambridge: Polity Press, 2007.

Jad, Islah. "NGOs: Between Buzzwords and Social Movements." *Development in Practice* 17, nos. 4–5 (2007): 622–29.

———. *Palestinian Women's Activism: Nationalism, Secularism, Islamism*. Syracuse, NY: Syracuse University Press, 2018.

Jadallah, Dina. "Colonialist Construction in the Urban Space of Jerusalem." *Middle East Journal* 68, no. 1 (2014): 77–98.

Jerusalem Declaration on Antisemitism. 2020. https://jerusalemdeclaration.org/.

Johnson, Penny, Lee O'Brien, and Joost Hiltermann. "The West Bank Rises Up." In *Intifada: The Palestinian Uprising Against Israeli Occupation*, ed. Zachary Lockman and Joel Beinin, 29–41. Toronto: Between the Lines, 1989.

Jones, Clive. "The Writing on the Wall: Israel, the Security Barrier, and the Future of Zionism." *Mediterranean Politics* 14, no. 1 (2009): 3–20.

Joudeh, Safa. "Defying Exception: Gaza After the 'Unity Uprising.'" *Journal of Palestine Studies* 50, no. 4 (2021): 73–77.

Kattan, Victor. *From Coexistence to Conquest: International Law and the Origins of the Arab-Israeli Conflict 1891–1949*. New York: Pluto Press, 2009.

Kauanui, J. Kēhaulani. " 'A Structure, not an Event': Settler Colonialism and Enduring Indigeneity." *Lateral: Journal of the Cultural Studies Association* 5, no. 1 Spring (2016).

———. *Hawaiian Blood: Colonialism and the Politics of Sovereignty and Indigeneity*. Durham, NC: Duke University Press, 2008.

Kerry, John. "Israeli Settlements and a Two-State Solution." *Time*, December 28, 2016. https://time.com/4619064/john-kerrys-speech-israel-transcript/.

Khalidi, Rashid. *The Hundred Years' War on Palestine: A History of Settler Colonialism and Resistance, 1917–2017*. New York: Metropolitan Books, 2020.

Khoury, Elias. *Gate of the Sun*. Trans. Humphrey Davies. New York: Picador, 2006 [1998].

———. "Remembering Ghassan Kanafani, or How a Nation Was Born of Story Telling." *Journal of Palestine Studies* 42, no. 3 (2013): 85–91.

———. "Rethinking the Nakba." *Critical Inquiry* 38, no. 2 (2012): 250–66.

Kögler, Hans-Herbert. *The Power of Dialogue: Critical Hermeneutics After Gadamer and Foucault*. Trans. Paul Hendrickson. Cambridge, MA: MIT Press, 1999 [1992].

Lagerquist, Peter. "Fencing the Last Sky: Excavating Palestine After Israel's 'Separation Wall.'" *Journal of Palestine Studies* 33, no. 2 (2004): 5–35.

Levy, Lital. "Nation, Village, Cave: A Spatial Reading of 1948 in Three Novels of Anton Shammas, Emile Habiby, and Elias Khoury." *Jewish Social Studies: History, Culture, Society* 18, no. 3 (2012): 10–26.

Li, Darryl. "The Gaza Strip as Laboratory: Notes in the Wake of Disengagement." *Journal of Palestine Studies* 35, no. 2 (2006): 38–55.

Lloyd, David. "Settler Colonialism and the State of Exception: The Example of Palestine/Israel." *Settler Colonial Studies* 2, no. 1 (2012): 59–80.

Lockman, Zachary, and Joel Beinin, eds. *Intifada: The Palestinian Uprising Against Israeli Occupation*. Toronto: Between the Lines, 1989.

Lorde, Audre. *Sister Outsider: Essays and Speeches*. Trumansburg, NY: Crossing Press, 1984.

Makdisi, Sari. *Palestine Inside Out: An Everyday Occupation*. New York: Norton, 2010.

Malešević, Siniša. "Forms of Brutality: Towards a Historical Sociology of Violence." *European Journal of Social Theory* 16, no. 3 (2013): 273–91.

Mamdani, Mahmood. "Beyond Settler and Native as Political Identities: Overcoming the Political Legacy of Colonialism." *Comparative Studies in Society & History* 43, no. 4 (2001): 651–64.

———. *Citizen and Subject: Contemporary Africa and the Legacy of Late Colonialism.* Princeton, NJ: Princeton University Press, 1996.

———. *Define and Rule: Native as Political Identity.* Cambridge, MA: Harvard University Press, 2012.

———. *Neither Settler nor Native: The Making and Unmaking of Permanent Minorities.* Cambridge, MA: Belknap Press of Harvard University Press, 2020.

———. "Settler Colonialism: Then and Now." *Critical Inquiry* 41, no. 3 (2015): 596–614.

———. *When Victims Become Killers: Colonialism, Nativism, and the Genocide in Rwanda.* Princeton, NJ: Princeton University Press, 2001.

Mann, Michael. *The Dark Side of Democracy: Explaining Ethnic Cleansing.* New York: Columbia University Press, 2005.

———. *The Sources of Social Power, Volume 2: The Rise of Classes and Nation States, 1760–1914.* Cambridge: Cambridge University Press, 1993.

Mantena, Karuna. "Popular Sovereignty and Anti-Colonialism." In *Popular Sovereignty in Historical Perspective*, ed. Richard Bourke and Quentin Skinner, 297–319. Cambridge: Cambridge University Press, 2016.

Masalha, Nur. *The Bible and Zionism: Invented Traditions, Archeology and Post-Colonialism in Israel-Palestine.* London: Zed Books, 2007.

———. *Land Without a People: Israel, Transfer, and the Palestinians, 1949–1996.* London: Faber and Faber, 1997.

———. *Palestine: A Four Thousand Year History.* London: Zed Books, 2020.

Massad, Joseph A. "Against Self-Determination." *Humanity: An International Journal of Human Rights, Humanitarianism, and Development* 9, no. 2 (2018): 161–91.

———. "Forget Semitism!" In *Living Together: Jacques Derrida's Communities of Violence and Peace*, ed. E. Weber, 59–79. New York: Fordham University Press, 2013.

———. "Ghassan Kanafani, Zionism and Race: What Determines the Fate of a People." *Middle East Eye*, July 29, 2022. https://www.middleeasteye.net/opinion/palestine-ghassan-kanafani-message-inspire-how.

———. *Islam in Liberalism*. Chicago: University of Chicago Press, 2015.

———. *The Persistence of the Palestinian Question: Essays on Zionism and the Palestinians*. New York: Routledge, 2006.

Mattawa, Khaled. *Mahmoud Darwish: The Poet's Art and His Nation*. Syracuse, NY: Syracuse University Press, 2014.

Mbembe, Achille. "The Society of Enmity." Trans. G. Menegalle. *Radical Philosophy* 200 (Nov/Dec 2016): 23–35.

Mignolo, Walter D., and Catherine E. Walsh. *On Decoloniality: Concepts, Analytics, Praxis*. Durham, NC: Duke University Press, 2018.

Mohanty, Satya P., ed. *Colonialism, Modernity, and Literature: A View from India*. New York: Palgrave Macmillan, 2011.

Mongia, Radhika. *Indian Migration and Empire: A Colonial Genealogy of the Modern State*. Durham, NC: Duke University Press, 2018.

Moore, Lindsey. *Narrating Postcolonial Arab Nations: Egypt, Algeria, Lebanon, Palestine*. New York: Routledge, 2017.

Moore-Gilbert, Bart. "Palestine, Postcolonialism, and Pessoptimism." *Interventions* 20, no. 1 (2018): 7–40.

Moreton-Robinson, Aileen, ed. *Sovereign Subjects: Indigenous Sovereignty Matters*. New York: Routledge, 2007.

Morris, Benny. *Righteous Victims: A History of the Zionist–Arab Conflict, 1881–2001*. New York: Vintage Books, 2001.

Moses, A. Dirk. "Empire, Resistance, and Security: International Law and the Transformative Occupation of Palestine." *Humanity: An International Journal of Human Rights, Humanitarianism, and Development* 8, no. 2 (2017): 379–409.

Nazzal, Rehab. "Palestinian Children: Art Therapy and Intergenerational Trauma." *Society for the Diffusion of Useful Knowledge* 12 (May 2022): 24–26.

Nelson, Eric. "Prerogative, Popular Sovereignty, and the American Founding." In *Popular Sovereignty in Historical Perspective*, ed. Richard Bourke and Quentin Skinner, 187–211. Cambridge: Cambridge University Press, 2016.

Neuberger, Benyamin. "National Self-Determination: A Theoretical Discussion." *Nationalities Papers* 29, no. 3 (2001): 391–418.

Newman, David. "From *Hitnachalut* to *Hitnatkut*: The Impact of Gush Emunim and the Settlement Movement on Israeli Politics and Society." *Israel Studies* 10, no. 3 (2005): 192–224.

Niang, Amy. *The Postcolonial African State in Transition: Stateness and Modes of Sovereignty*. New York: Rowman & Littlefield, 2018.

Nusseibeh, Sari. *What Is a Palestinian State Worth?* Cambridge, MA: Harvard University Press, 2011.

Nutt, Steve. "Pluralized Sovereignties: Autochthonous Lawmaking on the Settler Colonial Frontier in Palestine." *Interventions* 21, no. 4 (2019): 510–26.

Paine, Lincoln. *The Sea and Civilization: A Maritime History of the World.* New York: Vintage Books, 2013.

Pappé, Ilan. "Indigeneity as Resistance." In *Rethinking Statehood in Palestine: Self-determination and Decolonization Beyond Partition*, ed. Leila Farsakh, 276–94. Oakland: University of California Press, 2021.

Pateman, Carole, and Charles W. Mills. *Contract and Domination.* Malden, MA: Polity Press, 2007.

Pike, Deborah J. "Sharon's Wall and the Dialectics of Inside/Outside." *Borderlands E-Journal: New Spaces in the Humanities* 5, no. 3 (2006).

Piterberg, Gabriel. *The Returns of Zionism: Myths, Politics and Scholarship in Israel.* London: Verso, 2008.

Phillips, Andrew, and J. C. Sharman. *Outsourcing Empire: How Company-States Made the Modern World.* Princeton, NJ: Princeton University Press, 2020.

Poggi, Gianfranco. *The State: Its Nature, Development, and Prospects.* Stanford, CA: Stanford University Press, 1990.

Puar, Jasbir K. *The Right to Maim: Debility, Capacity, Disability.* Durham, NC: Duke University Press, 2017.

Quijano, Aníbal. "Coloniality and Modernity/Rationality." *Cultural Studies* 21, nos. 2–3 (2007): 168–78.

——. "Coloniality of Power, Eurocentrism, and Latin America." Trans. Michael Ennis. *Nepantla: Views from South* 1, no. 3 (2000): 533–80.

Rahman, Najat. *In the Wake of the Poetic: Palestinian Artists After Darwish.* Syracuse, NY: Syracuse University Press, 2015.

Raz-Krakotzkin, Amnon. "Benjamin, the Holocaust, and the Question of Palestine." In *The Holocaust and the Nakba: A New Grammar of Trauma and History*, ed. Bashir Bashir and Amos Goldberg, 79–91. New York: Columbia University Press, 2018.

——. "Exile within Sovereignty: Critique of the 'Negation of Exile' in Israeli Culture." In *The Scaffolding of Sovereignty: Global and Aesthetic Perspectives on the History of a Concept*, ed. Zvi Ben–Dor Benite, Stefanos Geroulanos, and Nicole Jerr, 393–420. New York: Columbia University Press, 2017 [1993–1994].

Redford, Donald B. *Egypt, Canaan, and Israel in Ancient Times.* Princeton, NJ: Princeton University Press, 1992.

Robinson, Glenn E. *Building a Palestinian State: The Incomplete Revolution.* Bloomington: Indiana University Press, 1997.

Roblin, Sebastien. "Israel's Bombardment of Gaza: Methods, Weapons, and Impact." *Forbes*, May 26, 2021. https://www.forbes.com/sites/sebastienroblin/2021/05/26/israels-bombardment-of-gaza-methods-weapons-and-impact/?sh=588d5d312f44.

Rouhana, Nadim N. "'Constitution by Consensus': By Whose Consensus?" *Adalah's Newsletter* 7 (November 2004). http://www.adalah.org/newsletter/eng/nov04/ar1.pdf.

———. "Decolonization as Reconciliation: Rethinking the National Conflict Paradigm in the Israeli–Palestinian Conflict." *Ethnic and Racial Studies* 41, no. 4 (2018): 643–62.

Rouhana, Nadim N., and Areej Sabbagh-Khoury. "Memory and the Return of History in a Settler-Colonial Context: The Case of the Palestinians in Israel." *Interventions* 21, no. 4 (2019): 527–50.

———. "Settler-Colonial Citizenship: Conceptualizing the Relationship Between Israel and Its Palestinian Citizens." *Settler Colonial Studies* 5, no. 3 (2015): 205–25.

Roy, Sara. *The Gaza Strip: The Political Economy of De-Development.* Expanded 3rd ed. Washington, D.C.: Institute for Palestine Studies, 2016.

Sabbagh-Khoury, Areej. "Tracing Settler Colonialism: A Genealogy of a Paradigm in the Sociology of Knowledge Production in Israel." *Politics & Society* 50, no. 1 (2022): 44–83.

Said, Edward. *After the Last Sky: Palestinian Lives.* Photographs by J. Mohr. New York: Columbia University Press, 1999.

———. "Afterword: The Consequences of 1948." In *The War for Palestine: Rewriting the History of 1948*, ed. Eugene L. Rogan and Avi Shlaim, 206–19. Cambridge: Cambridge University Press, 1999.

———. *Culture and Imperialism.* New York: Vintage Books, 1994.

———. *The End of the Peace Process: Oslo and After.* New York: Vintage Books, 2001.

———. "Intifada and Independence." In *Intifada: The Palestinian Uprising Against Israeli Occupation*, ed. Zachary Lockman and Joel Beinin, 5–22. Toronto: Between the Lines, 1989.

———. *Orientalism.* New York: Vintage Books, 2003 [1979].

———. *The Politics of Dispossession: The Struggle for Palestinian Self-Determination, 1969–1994.* New York: Vintage Books, 1995.

———. "Zionism from the Standpoint of Its Victims." *Social Text* 1 (Winter 1979): 7–58.

Salaita, Steven. *Inter/Nationalism: Decolonizing Native America and Palestine.* Minneapolis: University of Minnesota Press, 2016.

Salamanca, Omar Jabary. "Unplug and Play: Manufacturing Collapse in Gaza." *Human Geography* 4, no. 1 (2011): 22–37.

Salamanca, Omar Jabary, Mezna Qato, Kareem Rabie, and Sobhi Samour, eds. "Past Is Present: Settler Colonialism in Palestine." *Settler Colonial Studies* 2, no. 1 (2012). (Journal special issue).

Samour, Sobhi. "Covid–19 and the Necroeconomy of Palestinian Labor in Israel." *Journal of Palestine Studies* 49, no. 4 (2020): 53–64.

Sayegh, Fayez. "Zionist Colonialism in Palestine (1965)." *Settler Colonial Studies* 2, no. 1 (2012): 206–25.

Sayigh, Yezid. *Armed Struggle and the Search for State: The Palestinian National Movement, 1949–1993.* Washington, D.C.: Oxford University Press, 1997.

Schotten, C. Heike. *Queer Terror: Life, Death, and Desire in the Settler Colony.* New York: Columbia University Press, 2018.

Segal, Rafi, and Eyal Weizman, eds. *A Civilian Occupation: The Politics of Israeli Architecture.* London: Verso, 2003.

Sen, Somdeep. *Decolonizing Palestine: Hamas Between the Anticolonial and the Postcolonial.* Ithaca, NY: Cornell University Press, 2020.

Shafir, Gershon. *Land, Labour and the Origins of the Israeli–Palestinian Conflict, 1882–1914.* Updated ed. Berkeley: University of California Press, 1996 [1989].

Shalhoub-Kevorkian, Nadera. "Human Suffering in Colonial Contexts: Reflections from Palestine." *Settler Colonial Studies* 4, no. 3 (2014): 277–90.

Sharma, Nandita. "Against National Sovereignty: The Postcolonial New World Order and the Containment of Decolonization." *Studies in Social Justice* 14, no. 2 (2020): 391–409.

Shilliam, Robbie. "What About Marcus Garvey? Race and the Transformation of Sovereignty Debate." *Review of International Studies* 32, no. 3 (2006): 379–400.

Shohat, Ella. "The Invention of the Mizrahim." *Journal of Palestine Studies* 29, no. 1 (1999): 5–20.

———. "On Orientalist Genealogies: The Split Arab/Jew Figure Revisited." In *The Arab and Jewish Questions: Geographies of Engagement in Palestine and Beyond,* ed. Bashir Bashir and Leila Farsakh, 89–121. New York: Columbia University Press, 2020.

———. "Sephardim in Israel: Zionism from the Standpoint of Its Jewish Victims." *Social Text* 19/20 (Autumn 1988): 1–35.

Simpson, Audra. *Mohawk Interruptus: Political Life Across the Borders of Settler States*. Durham, NC: Duke University Press, 2014.

———. "The State Is a Man: Theresa Spence, Loretta Saunders, and the Gender of Settler Sovereignty." *Theory and Event* 19, no. 4 (2016).

Simpson, Leanne Betasamosake. "Land as Pedagogy: Nishnaabeg Intelligence and Rebellious Transformation." *Decolonization: Indigeneity, Education & Society* 3, no. 3 (2014): 1–25.

Snyder, Timothy. *Black Earth: The Holocaust as History and Warning*. New York: Tim Duggan Books, 2015.

Soffer, Arnon. "It's the Demography, Stupid." Interview by Ruthie Blum. *Jerusalem Post*, May 20, 2004. http://free--expression.blogspot.ca/2009/01/arnon-soffer-on-palestine-israel-and.html.

Spruyt, Hendrik. *The Sovereign State and Its Competitors: An Analysis of Systems Change*. Princeton, NJ: Princeton University Press, 1994.

Sturm, Circe. "Reflections on the Anthropology of Sovereignty and Settler Colonialism: Lessons from Native North America." *Cultural Anthropology* 32, no. 3 (2017): 340–48.

Takriti, Abdel Razzaq. "'Who Will Hang the Bell?': The Palestinian *Habba* of 2021." *Journal of Palestine Studies* 50, no. 4 (2021): 78–83.

Tatour, Lana. "Citizenship as Domination: Settler Colonialism and the Making of Palestinian Citizenship in Israel." *Arab Studies Journal* 27, no. 2 (2019): 8–39.

———. "The 'Unity Intifada' and '48 Palestinians: Between the Liberal and the Decolonial." *Journal of Palestine Studies* 50, no. 4 (2021): 84–89.

Tawil-Souri, Helga. "Digital Occupation: Gaza's High-Tech Enclosure." *Journal of Palestine Studies* 41, no. 2 (2012): 27–43.

United Nations Office for the Coordination of Humanitarian Affairs (OCHA). "Situation Report." No. 1: 21–27, May 2021. https://reliefweb.int/sites/reliefweb.int/files/resources/Occupied%20Palestinian%20Territory%20%28oPt%29%20-%20Response%20to%20the%20escalation%20in%20the%20oPt%20-%20Situation%20Report%20No.%201%2C%2021%20-%2027%20May%202021.pdf.

Tilly, Charles. *Coercion, Capital, and European States, AD 990–1990*. Cambridge: Blackwell, 1990.

Tilly, Charles, ed. *The Formation of National States in Western Europe*. Princeton, NJ: Princeton University Press, 1975.

Tuck, Eve, and K. Wayne Yang. "Decolonization Is Not a Metaphor." *Decolonization: Indigeneity, Education & Society* 1, no. 1 (2012): 1–40.

Tuck, Richard. "Democratic Sovereignty and Democratic Government: The Sleeping Sovereign." In *Popular Sovereignty in Historical Perspective*, ed. Richard Bourke and Quentin Skinner, 115–41. Cambridge: Cambridge University Press, 2016.

Usher, Graham. "Unmaking Palestine: On Israel, the Palestinians, and the Wall." *Journal of Palestine Studies* 35, no. 1 (2005): 25–43.

Veracini, Lorenzo. "Israel-Palestine Through a Settler-Colonial Studies Lens." *Interventions* 21, no. 4 (2018): 568–81.

———. "The Other Shift: Settler Colonialism, Israel, and the Occupation." *Journal of Palestine Studies* 42, no. 2 (2013): 26–42.

———. *Settler Colonialism: A Theoretical Overview*. New York: Palgrave Macmillan, 2010.

Walcott, Rinaldo. *The Long Emancipation: Moving Toward Black Freedom*. Durham, NC: Duke University Press, 2021.

Wagner-Pacifici, Robin. *The Art of Surrender: Decomposing Sovereignty at Conflict's End*. Chicago: University of Chicago Press, 2005.

Weinthal, Erika, and Jeannie Sowers. "Targeting Infrastructure and Livelihoods in the West Bank and Gaza." *International Affairs* 95, no. 2 (2019): 319–40.

Weizman, Eyal. *Hollow Land: Israel's Architecture of Occupation*. London: Verso, 2007.

Werner, Wouter G., and Jaap H. de Wilde. "The Endurance of Sovereignty." *European Journal of International Relations* 7, no. 3 (2001): 283–313.

White, Ben. "Delegitimizing Solidarity: Israel Smears Palestine Advocacy as Anti-Semitic." *Journal of Palestine Studies* 49, no. 2 (2020): 65–79.

Williams, Eric. *Capitalism and Slavery*. Chapel Hill: University of North Carolina Press, 1944.

Wise, Christopher. *Derrida, Africa, and the Middle East*. New York: Palgrave Macmillan, 2009.

Wolfe, Patrick. "Settler Colonialism and the Elimination of the Native." *Journal of Genocide Research* 8, no. 4 (2006): 387–409.

———. *Settler Colonialism and the Transformation of Anthropology: The Politics and Poetics of an Ethnographic Event*. London: Cassell, 1999.

———. *Traces of History: Elementary Structures of Race*. London: Verso, 2016.

Yacobi, Haim, and Elya Milner. "Planning, Land Ownership, and Settler Colonialism in Israel/Palestine." *Journal of Palestine Studies* 51, no. 2 (2022): 43–56.

Yeshurun, Helit. "'Exile Is So Strong Within Me, I May Bring It to the Land': A Landmark 1996 Interview with Mahmoud Darwish." *Journal of Palestine Studies* 42, no. 1 (2012): 46–70.

Young, Robert J. C. *Empire, Colony, Postcolony.* Malden, MA: Wiley Blackwell, 2015.

Zertal, Idith, and Akiva Eldar. *Lords of the Land: The War Over Israel's Settlements in the Occupied Territories, 1967–2007.* Trans. Vivian Eden. New York: Nation Books, 2009. Retrieved (July 29, 2020) from ProQuest Ebook Central. https://ebookcentral.proquest.com/lib/mtroyal-ebooks/detail.action?docID=688716.

Žižek, Slavoj. "The 'Matrix' or Malebranche in Hollywood." *Philosophy Today* 43 (1999): 11–26.

———. *Violence.* New York: Picador, 2008.

Zreik, Raef. "When Does a Settler Become a Native? (with Apologies to Mamdani)." *Constellations* 23, no. 3 (2016): 351–64.

INDEX

Page locators in italics indicate figures.

abandonment, sovereign, 74, 95–102, 108, 111–12; in Zionist ideology, 125, 138–39. *See also* sovereignty
Abdo, Nahla, 222, 252–54, 290–91n53
Absent Presence (Darwish), 194, 201–4, 207–9
Abu-Remaileh, Refqa, 192–93
Africa, 15; postcolonial, 119–20; South Africa, 231–32, 233; Voltaic region, 46–48
Agamben, Giorgio, 12, 50, 52, 60, 96–101, 173, 195–96, 205, 208
"Age of Absolutism," 77–79, 85
Ahmad, Eqbal, 81–82
Alfred, Gerald (Taiaiake), 225
Algeria, 123
amanah (existence-in-entrustment), 226
Anderson, Benedict, 275n34, 282n66
Anderson, Charles W., 267
Anidjar, Gil, 142–44
anti-colonialism, 18–19, 66–67, 275n27
anti-Palestinian racism, 215–16

anti-Semitism, 141–46; settler violence concealed by charge of, 175–77, 216
Arab states, 270–71
Arafat, Yasser, 239
Aristotle, 45, 99–100, 280n61
Aryan vs. Semite binary, 144
aspirations of decolonial sovereignties, 226, 243–47
aspirations of settler colonial sovereignty, 33–34, 48–49, 60, 243; for indivisibility, absoluteness, purity, and omnipresence, 133, 184, 214, 242, 258
Australia, 121, 123
Azoulay, Ariella Aisha, 267

Baconi, Tareq, 155–56, 307n56
ban, sovereign, 96–101. *See also* bare life; *homo sacer*
Barak, Ehud, 154, 305–6n33
Barakat, Rana, 125–26, 146
bare life, 97–98, 100

Bartelson, Jens, 41, 42, 65
Barthes, Roland, 196
Bashir, Bashir, 139–42
Bataille, Georges, 280–81n63
beast and sovereign analogy,
    50–55, 58–59, 99, 131, 136, 160,
    279n34
Beinin, Joel, 243–44
belonging, claim to, 13, 40, 43, 80;
    Indigenous understanding of, 6,
    69, 257
Bhambra, Gurminder K., 10, 65–66,
    71, 192
biopolitics, 53, 99–100, 318n64
bios (natural life), 99–100
Bishara, Amahl, 224, 267
Bodin, Jean, 44–45, 57, 277n13
body, Palestinian: as always-already
    signifying violence, 179;
    debilitated/maimed, 152, 180–83;
    dehumanizing of, 135–36; as "evil
    object," 134–36; as "inorganic," 180,
    183; isolation of, 151–52;
    racialization of, 178–88
Bourdieu, Pierre, 103, 109
Boycott, Divestment, Sanctions
    (BDS) campaign, 176, 236–37, 238,
    265
British Nationality and Status of
    Aliens Act of 1914, 220
Brunner, Otto, 79, 88
Burbank, Jane, 76, 278n17, 285–86n99
Butler, Judith, 15, 147, 191, 221

Canada, 67–68, 90, 123
capitalism, 74; capital-labor relations,
    90; primitive accumulation, 89,
    291n53; proletarianization,
    290–91n53, 291n55
cave, as symbolic space, 199–201
centralization, 77–79
Césaire, Aimée, 230
children, Palestinian, trauma to,
    185–88
citizenship, 27–28, 128, 159, 191, 267;
    liberal path, 257; Mohawk
    perspective, 227
civic nationalism, 40, 64, 66–70, 125,
    221; constituted through ideas of
    "purity," 69; enslaved peoples
    ejected from, 67; Indigenous
    critique of, 69–70; limits of, 67–68
civilization, 50, 53, 60, 131
The Civilizing Process (Elias), 72–82,
    88; historical sociology framework
    of, 74–75, 77
civil society, "NGOization" of,
    241–42, 254
claim: of being the "first," 13, 118,
    125–26; to belonging, 6, 13, 40, 43,
    69, 80, 257; Indigenous, on land,
    84; on land and people, 44, 48, 50,
    139, 225, 258, 279n31, 289n32; to
    sovereignty, 39–40, 48–50
co-constitution: of colony, 80, 112–13,
    144, 284n75; of self, 6, 109, 196,
    208–9, 212–17, 235
colonialism: "colonial extraterritorial
    autonomy," 219; colonial matrix of
    power, 11, 43, 144, 284n75; of
    Crusades, 75–76, 82; decolonial
    critiques of, 11–12; differentiated
    from settler colonialism, 90–91;
    European, 8, 15, 24, 81, 134,

298–99n38; historiography and grammar of accepted by Indigenous movements, 120–21; institutionalization of, 27; "internal," 83; state as relic of European colonial project, 24. *See also* settler colonialism; settler colonial sovereignty

colonized: critique of violence, 229; as included exclusion, 97–100, 108, 115, 136, 178; outside (colony) as backward, 53, 60, 68–70; reality revealed by, 197; as survivors, 230–35; as target of claim to sovereignty, 49; truth of, 255–56; as unit of analysis, 15. *See also* Palestinians

complementary opposition, 5, 6, 31–32, 36, 46–48, 244, 247, 249–55

"conflict resolution through dialogue" agenda, 241

Convention for a Democratic South Africa (CODESA), 231–32, 233

Cooper, Frederick, 76, 278n17, 285–86n99

Coulthard, Glen, 89–91, 291nn55, 59

criminalization, 99, 231; of Palestinian speech, 175–77; of popular committees, 241

critical hermeneutics, 9, 34, 103–4, 115–16, 135. *See also* dialogical analytic

Crusades, 75–76, 82

Dabashi, Hamid, 14, 21, 118, 208, 222; "interstitial space of the art of protest," 209–10; on Israeli attitudes, 159; nation-state, view of, 24–30

Dalsheim, Joyce, 169–70

Da'na, Tariq, 219, 242

Darwish, Mahmoud, 36, 201–4, 263, 312n25, 313n38, 314nn56, 60; challenges to colonial-modernist conceptions of time, 195; monohistory critiqued by, 230; on poetry and self-creation, 212; *Works: Absent Presence*, 194, 201–4, 207–9; "Like a Hand Tattoo in the Jahili Poet's Ode," 207–8; "A Ready Scenario," 206–7

dead, voices of, 107, 137, 152, 237; as incomprehensible, 187–88. *See also* memory

death, 281n63; living, 198; Palestinians not human enough for, 180; writer's engagement with, 197–98

decolonial alternatives, 11, 22, 31–32, 192, 237–38; to Indigenous-settler distinction, 119–21; knowing, modes of, 192; Palestine as, 195, 205–15; pathways of, 4–8, 270; people-power, 266; problem of essence and origins, 123–29; settler colonial countering of, 253; "unlearning imperialism," 267. *See also* popular committees of first intifada

decolonial approach: long-established tradition of, 22; to nation-state, 23–24, 211–12; sovereignty, critique of, 45–46; violence of expulsion, critique of, 222–23, 229–30, 234, 236–38

decoloniality: as break with colonialism, 11; decolonial Palestine, 175, 201, 205–15; decolonization differentiated from, 23; Eurocentric discourses against, 10–11; multiple paths, 24; positionality of, 8
decolonialization, 116; settler colonialism versus, 9
decolonial liberation: and social-political relationship, 23–32; as struggle for new alternative world, 107
decolonial path, 7–8
decolonial sovereignties, 36–37, 189–90, 215–16, 282n68; *amanah* (existence-in-entrustment), 226; articulated through literary works, 191–97; aspirations of, 226, 243–47; cooperation and interdependence, 56; exhibited in resistance, 36–37, 216–17; Indigenous, 56, 227; *khalifah* (human flourishing), 226; as of the land, 257–59; as layered, shared, and multiplying, 243–47, 260–61; and liberation, 224–38; lordship critiqued by, 228–30; Palestinian, 48; Palestinian women's movement, 223, 224–25; refusal, politics of, 225, 238, 257; re-signification of terms, 265–66; social-political opposition not required for, 31–32; transformation of posture of lordship as critical battle terrain for, 264–65; in United States, 121–22. See also Indigenous sovereignty; intifada, first

decolonial theory, 7–74; integral to not concede to European "origin," 71; and master's tools concept, 71. *See also* Indigenous theory
decolonization: Arab uprisings, 23; and cementing of Indigenous-settler distinction, 116; critiques of, 26; decoloniality differentiated from, 23; of political sphere, 27–30, 231–33; social and political processes needed for, 236–37; of social sphere, 30–31
define and rule, 120–21
dehumanization (mimetic dimension of violence), 17–18, 33, 35, 150, 152–53, 207; of Israeli killers, 160; Mizrahi Jews, dehumanizing of, 136, 152; of Palestinians as animals, 156, 158–60; racialization of the Palestinian body, 178–88
Deleuze, Gilles, 264
"democratic regimes": emergence of, 79, 82
Derrida, Jacques, 9, 12–13, 14–15, 39, 45, 168, 173, 273–74n9; beast and sovereign analogy, 50–55, 58–59, 99, 131, 136, 279n34; divine sovereignty, view of, 57–58; Force of Law, 108, 277n7; on French Revolution, 61–62; Hobbes deconstructed by, 51–52, 57, 59; individual sovereignty, view of, 54–56, 92; *Robinson Crusoe*, reading of, 54–55, 131; transfer of power from monarch to public, 61–62, 65–66, 85
Derrida-Gadamer encounter, 9

de-subjectification, 195–97, 204
dialogical analytic, 9, 94–95, 103–9, 247; asymmetry in framing of, 105; critical hermeneutics, 9, 34, 103–4, 115–16, 135; and formation of enemy-siblings, 109; peaceful dialogue substituted for violent dialogue, 108, 221; violent dialogue, 95, 106–9, 213–14, 221, 223, 238
diaspora, 145–46
dictatorial agency, 56–57, 113
dictatorial sovereign voice, 10–17, 36, 177, 187, 211, 213, 245. *See also* isolation (linguistic dimension of violence)
dispossession, 68, 83, 87, 89–91; of Palestinians, 124; and proletarianization, 89–90, 291n55
domination: dispossession, 89; as expulsion, 88–96

"Eastern" postcolonial school, 11
Eid, Haidar, 305n33
either/or opposition, 31–32, 37
Eldar, Akiva, 169, 170–72, 305n33, 306–7n43
Elias, Norbert, 72–82, 85, 88; on Crusades, 75
elimination, 292–93n68, 293n71; imposed on Mohawk communities, 227; logic of, 91, 93–94, 293n71. *See also* dispossession; expulsion; genocide
empire states, 285–86n99
enemy-siblings, 7, 206–9; formation of at the foundation of settler colonial state, 20; and four-dimensional violence, 17–18; interlocking of, 17–18; interlocking of as enemy-siblings, 38, 109, 139, 142, 161–62, 209, 212, 214–15, 230, 235; mimetic relation of, 208–9; possibility-impossibility of, 20, 147, 213–14; present and past partnerships, 206–7; self-annihilation to interlocking of, 212; transforming the interlocking of, 230–38; violent dialogue in formation of, 109. *See also* decolonial alternatives; Indigenous-settler distinction; interlocking framework; self
enslaved peoples: ejected from civic nationalism, 67
Erakat, Noura, 178, 240, 294n75
erasure, 38, 149, 192–93; of author, 193; continuation in the face of, 202; in writing, 196–97
estrangement, political, 95–96, 137, 152, 164, 175–76, 294n75133
ethnic cleansing, 68, 164; Nakba, 139–43, 220–21, 257, 312n24; by state, 29–30; state monopoly on, 29–30
ethnic nationalism, 40, 64, 66–70, 221; "chauvinistic ethnonationalism," 141; in postcolonial Africa, 119
Etzion, Yehuda, 181
Euro-American paradigms, 16–17, 188, 211, 219; nation-state, 121, 199, 221, 235, 237; and "NGOization" of civil society, 241–42, 254; sexual contract, 253–54; sovereignty, 43, 220–21, 225–26

Eurocentric discourses: flawed positions on Palestine, 14–15; metropole versus colony, 69–70; "origins" and "firsts," 10–14, 21; role of in explaining colonial and settler colonial systems, 15; on sovereignty, 41

Europe: "Age of Absolutism," 77–79, 85; anti-Semitism of, 141; colonialism, 8, 15, 24, 81, 134, 298–99n38; Crusades, 75–76, 82; decentering of, 65, 71–72; Enlightenment, 66, 140, 273n2; feudal system, 21, 66, 76–80, 85, 293n68; French Revolution, 61–62, 65–66; "internal colonization" of land, 83; Jew and Muslim as enemies of, 142–44; Jewish existence in as "exilic," 129–30; Jewish Question of, 118; peasantry, 15, 83, 88–89, 290n53; Semitism created by, 144–45

"evil object," 7, 134–36

"evolutionary" development models, 90

exception, state of, 52, 60, 96–98, 165, 173, 289n31, 295n75179; lordship as never-ending structure of expulsion, 7, 35, 73; as permanent structure, 179

excess, 55–56, 92, 127, 131

expulsion, 19, 32–38, 274n20, 290–91n53; continuous violence of, 106, 108, 124, 136–37, 230, 258; and cycle of violence, 136–37; decolonial critique of violence of, 222–23, 229–30, 234, 236–38; erasure of Palestine through, 38; four-dimensional violence of, 102–12; isolated, 178; of Jewish life from Europe, 147–48; lack of access to the political and politics, 294n75; land appropriation as goal of, 83–84; lordship as never-ending structure of, 7, 35–36, 73, 115, 188–89, 235; never fully accomplished, 7, 35–36, 134–35; settler domination as, 88–96; of statelessness, 146; structure of, *33*; three observable dimensions of violence of, 35, 74, 110–11, 150. *See also* structure of expulsion; violence, settler colonial

factionalism, 241–42, 249–51
Fanon, Frantz, 19, 23, 26, 230, 255
Farsakh, Leila, 314n56
Fatah, 252
fear and terror, correlation with sovereign, 51–52, 279n33
feminist thought, 200, 253
Ferdowsi, Abolqasem, 3, 8, 263, 268
feudalism, 66, 76–80, 85, 293n68; acquisitive urge in, 76; centralization, 77–79; "liege lords" and "vassals," 77

"firsts" and "origins," 10–14, 21, 70, 273–74n9; binary distinction secured by, 123; and decolonial alternatives, 123–29; inaccurate Zionist claims, 123; Indigenous claims, 125–26; not conceded by decolonial critique, 71; positionality of indigeneity,

259–60; as "prior to" and an "alternative of," 127
force, 49
Foucault, Michel, 318n64
four-dimensional violence, 16–22, 235; of expulsion, 102–12; fear and terror, 52; fourth dimension as unobservable, 18, 19, 102, 107–10; fragmentation, isolation, and dehumanization linked, 19–20, 34; Indigenous-settler distinction, *33*, 34–35; lordship as fourth dimension, 40; operation of in settler colony, 73–74; simultaneous operation of dimensions, 17, 19–20, 34, 111, 113, 119, 128, 137, 150, 153; three observable dimensions, 35, 74, 110–11, 150. *See also* dehumanization (mimetic dimension of violence); fragmentation (instrumental dimension of violence); isolation (linguistic dimension of violence); posture of lordship; transcendental dimension of violence (posture of incommensurability); violence; violence, settler colonial
fragmentation (instrumental dimension of violence), *33*, 35, 74, 154–63, 222; in artworks, 193; concealed in Israeli discourse, 151, 155–58, 163; history of, 150–51; in hyperpolitical factionalism, 249–50; separation as effect of, 133, 151, 154; wholeness of Israel predicated on, 160–62. *See also* Separation/Annexation Wall

French Revolution, 61–62, 65–66
Furani, Khaled, 44, 226
futurity, 31, 200, 229, 233; foreclosed by settler colonial project, 4, 6, 26, 152, 155–56, 186–87; past-present-future spectrum, 175, 180–81, 201–4; temporalization of desire, 53; through *Sumud*, 187–88

Gadamer, Hans Georg, 9, 103
Gallop, Jane, 196
Gate of the Sun (Khoury), 194, 197–201
Gaza Strip, 154–55; casualties since May 21, 2021, 182–83; casualties since October 9, 2024, 3–4; dehumanization, violences of, 35; disengagement from, 155–56; full military onslaughts on, 111, 152, 183; Great March of Return, 179, 182; as starkest manifestation of settler colonialism, 156; and "Unity Intifada," 256; as world's largest open air prison, 155. *See also* Separation/Annexation Wall
Gaza Strip, Israeli settler colonial genocidal operation in, 35, 111, 181–82; disengagement plan (2005), 182; genocidal operation of October 7, 2023-current, 3–4, 269–72, 310n81; May 10 to May 21, 2021, 182–83. *See also* genocide, Israeli
genocide: in Americas, 27; legal concept of, 94; state monopoly on, 29–30; structural, 91

genocide, Israeli: discussion of root causes needed, 4–5; non-Palestinian responses to, 269–70; public support of in Israel, 159, 310n81. *See also* Gaza Strip, Israeli settler colonial genocidal operation in
Ghanim, Honaida, 206–7, 212
Gilroy, Paul, 133
God, figure of, 50, 55, 57–60, 281n63
Goldberg, Amos, 139–42
Gramsci, Antonio, 53
Great March of Return (Gaza), 179
Greek thought, 99–100
Green Line, 170
Guattari, Félix, 264
Gush Emunim, 164, 168, 172, 304n22

Habib, Maha F., 313n40
Hai, Ambreen, 193, 197
Hall, Louis Karoniaktajeh, 228–29
Hallward, Peter, 195, 205–6, 210
Hamas, 150, 251–52
Hammami, Rema, 162, 174, 241–42, 250
Harfouch, John, 180, 183
Hatef Isfahani, 208
Heidegger, Martin, 54, 55
Hermeneutics of Violence, A (Ayyash), 16–18, 105, 110–11, 189; "(un)knowability of violence" in, 9, 102; possibility-impossibility of enemy-siblings, 213; possibility of identity transformation in, 7, 16; on voices of the dead, 107
Herzl, Theodor, 129, 130–31, 145, 298–99n38

heterogeneity: attempt to mold into homogeneity, 6, 13, 56–57, 63, 101, 111–13, 122–23, 127; relationality invited by, 127
"hijacking thesis," 165, 171
Hiltermann, Joost, 251
hitnahlut, 169, 306n40
hityashvut, 169, 306n40
Hobbes, Thomas, 51–52, 57, 59, 280n49
Hoekstra, Kinch, 277n13
Holocaust, 139–44; Muslims in Auschwitz, 142–44
Holocaust and the Nakba, The (Bashir and Goldberg), 139–42
homeland, 260; cave as alternative underground, 199; elimination/erasure of Indigenous Palestinians from, 94, 192, 194, 202; "home," 194–95; Palestine as, 153, 216, 232. *See also* land; land and people
homo sacer, 60, 97–100
Homo Sacer (Agamben), 12, 60, 97–100
human rights, 28, 51, 167, 231

"I," 36, 192, 194, 313n38; "ana," 313n38; beginning/end, question of, 198, 201–4, 207; decolonial, 211, 214–16, 230; multiplying, 36, 201, 204, 215; scattered, 201–4, 207–8; and singular, specific, and specified, 205–10; sovereign, 211–15; in time, 201–4; writing "I" as a witness to suffering and death, 195–96. *See also* self
Ibn Khaldûn, 30

ideological (super)structures, 94–95, 112
Imseis, Ardi, 315n3
included exclusion, 97–100, 108, 115, 136, 178. *See also* selfsame substance incommensurability. *See* transcendental dimension of violence (posture of incommensurability)
Indian migrants to plantation colonies, 67
Indigenous peoples, 273n2, 290n45, 291–92n59; Australia, 121; in Canada, 120; multiculturalism as attempt to pacify and co-opt, 69; political orders of, 84; positionality of, 8, 259–60; "purity" of, 69; United States, 121
Indigenous-settler distinction, 19, *33*, 33–35, 74, 274n20; and abandonment logic, 101–2, 108; cementing of in service to decolonialization, 116; critical hermeneutic reading of, 115–16; decolonial alternatives to, 119–21; define and rule, 120–21; denial of, 126; and dispossession, 90–91; dissolution of, 116, 119–20, 126–28; distinction between 1948 and 1967 projects, 125; hidden in Israeli scholarship, 126; as marquee feature of the violence of expulsion, 113; in Palestine-Israel, 118–23; "political identities" not capable of destruction, 119–20; racialized in Zionist settler colonial nationalism, 129–39, 152; settler colonial and decolonial versions of, 127; settler never able to become Indigenous, 124–25; settler state served by, 116; shared question of lordship, 146; validated through violence and force, 152, 179; zero-sum perspective of Zionism, 124–25, 189. *See also* enemy-siblings; Zionism
Indigenous sovereignty, 121–22, 151, 165, 220; attempts to eliminate, 84, 110; claims of being the "first," 125–26; forms of, 56; intracommunity recognition, 227–28; Iroquois Confederacy, 228–29; Mohawk, 226–29; openness and plurality, 227. *See also* decolonial sovereignties
Indigenous theory, 73–74; civic nationalism critiqued, 69–70. *See also* decolonial theory; Simpson, Audra
indivisibility: claim on land and people, 44, 48, 50, 139, 258; dictatorial agency summoned by, 113; as feature of lordship, 40; and figure of God, 50, 55, 57–60, 281n63; formed in intertwinement of colonialism and settler colonialism, 44; of sovereignty, 13, 32–33, 36, 40, 50–65, 226; sovereignty as divisible and nonabsolute, 59–60. *See also* settler colonialism
instrumental dimension of violence. *See* fragmentation (instrumental dimension of violence)

interlocking framework, 7, 36, 189; contrapuntal approach, 17, 71, 122–23; decolonial versus settler colonial, 141, 148; Euro-American ideas in, 17; included exclusion, 97–100, 108, 115, 136, 178; opposing metanarratives of modernity, 139–42; as opposite of settler sovereign goal, 117; Palestine-Israel as, 37–38; Palestinian and Jewish Questions intertwined, 139–47, 175–76; self-other dichotomy, 135, 189, 194–95; and Separation/Annexation Wall, 161–62; sovereign self not established by, 112–13; transforming, 230–38. *See also* enemy-siblings

International Court of Justice, 271

International Criminal Court (ICC), 303

International Holocaust Remembrance Alliance (IHRA) Working Definition of Antisemitism, 176–77

international law, 49, 51, 165–67, 315n4; *jus sanguinis* and *jus soli*, 220–21

international political system, 49, 63, 95, 164, 219–20; isolation of the Palestinians in, 164; Palestinian decolonial liberation rejected by, 220; Palestinian liberation rejected by, 219–20

international political theory, 41–43, 49, 66, 72, 129

intifada, first: between 1988–1989, 242; collective and common good emphasized, 241, 246–48; nostalgia for, 242; outcome of so-called peace process, 239–40; as people's uprising, 222. *See also* popular committees of first intifada

Intifada: The Palestinian Uprising against Israeli Occupation (Lockman and Beinin), 243–44

intifada: "Unity Intifada," 256–57

Iroquois Confederacy, 228–29

Islamophobia, 142–44

isolation (linguistic dimension of violence), 17–18, *33*, 35, 74, 111, 150–52; and cyclical violence, 137–38; dead, voices of, 107, 137, 152, 188, 237; discursive colonization of Palestinians, 175–76; exclusion of Palestinians from discussions, 176; "hijacking thesis," 165, 171; isolated expulsion, 178; of Israel as unique, 168, 174–75; prevention of Palestinian speech, 175–77, 188; settlement, 163–78; and silencing of voice, 137–38; surveillance of Palestinian speech, 176. *See also* dictatorial sovereign voice

Israel: borders, refusal to finalize, 167–68, 170; de-Zionized Jewish Israelis, 261; forged with Palestine, 138; inability to completely control violence, 106–7; international pressure on, 183–85, 188, 237; Left versus Right politics, 158, 163–73, 303n8, 305–6n33; legal system, 165–66; lordship as foundation of, 146, 170, 174; merger of state and society, 181–82; modern establishment of as settler colonialism, 123; overlapping jurisdictions, 165; Palestinian rejection of "peace proposals" as excuse for violence, 108; second-class Palestinian citizens of, 28; wholeness of predicated on fragmentation, 160–62. *See also* Gaza Strip, Israeli settler colonial genocidal operation in; genocide, Israeli; Palestine-Israel; settler colonial project, Israeli; violence, settler colonial; Zionism

Israeli settler colonial conquest of Palestine, 1948, 108, 130, 157, 159, 163–68; and cave symbolism, 199; differentiated from colonial occupation of 1967, 125; and intergenerational tensions, 199; Israeli discourse of sovereignty concealed, 151; Nakba, 139–43, 220–21, 257, 312n24; in Palestinian art and literature, 193, 199, 201–2, 312n24; protests, 256–57; refugees forced to live in camps, 182, 202, 256

Israeli settler colonial occupation of Palestine, 1967, 125, 151, 157, 163–67

istiqlāl (independence), 224

Jad, Islah, 250, 253
Jarbawi, Ali, 219
Jerusalem, occupied, 108
Jerusalem Declaration on Antisemitism (JDA), 176–77

Jew, the Arab: A History of the Enemy, The (Anidjar), 142
Jewish life, non-Zionist, 117, 147–48, 175, 178
Jewish people: "emptying of Jewish time" as nonsensical, 130; Palestinian Jews, 123
Jewish Question, 139–47, 175–76; of anti-Semitic Europe, 118; displaced onto Palestinians, 145
jus sanguinis and *jus soli*, 220–21

Kanafani, Ghassan, 259–60, 312n25
Kauanui, J. Kēhaulani, 292n59
Kerry, John, 305n23
Khalidi, Rashid, 167–68, 238–39
Khalifa, Yayha, 185–87
khalifah (human flourishing), 226
Khoury, Elias, 36, 194–95, 312nn24, 26; mono-history critiqued by, 198, 201, 230; *Works: Gate of the Sun*, 194, 197–201
Kislev, Ran, 159
knowledge: always based on Palestinian experiences, 106; decolonial modes of, 192; Israeli opposition to/avoidance of, 234; (un)knowability of violence, 9–10, 18, 102–3, 106–7, 109, 185, 188; knowledge/power complex, 64; and misrecognition, 103
Kögler, Hans-Herbert, 103–4, 107

labor movement, Palestinian, 241, 243
Lagerquist, Peter, 303n8

land: appropriation as goal of expulsion, 83–84; bantustanization of, 155; being of, 256–58; communal ownership, 6; decolonial sovereignties as of, 257–59; decolonial topographies of, 199; erasure of homeland, 192; European "internal colonization," 83; fragmentation of, 154–63; Indigenous claim on, 84; separation between lost and imagined place, 202–3; as sovereign, 263; wars and violences in, 259. *See also* homeland

land and people, 5, 113, 115, 255, 267; claim on, 44, 48, 50, 63, 139, 225, 258, 289n32; as divisible and shared, 226; fusion of as lordship, 21, 40–41, 63, 70–71, 73, 74–88, 130–31; and lens of space/spatialization, 39–40; as selfsame substance, 70–71

"Latin American" coloniality/decoloniality school, 11

law: being-above/outside, 58, 99–101, 172; Derrida's Force of Law, 108, 277n7; international, 49, 51, 165–67; Israeli Law, 172–73; suspension of, 58, 97–99

Leviathan, 51

Levinas, Emanuel, 15

Levy, Lital, 199

liberal settler narratives, 125; people, conception of, 67–69; social sphere mobilized for, 251–52

liberation, 23–32; and cave symbolism, 199; and decolonial sovereignties, 224–38; and de-subjectification, 196; national, 26; nationalism of, 222; sun imagery, 197–201

life and death, politics of, 92, 180–82, 185, 187, 197–98

linguistic dimension of violence. *See* isolation (linguistic dimension of violence)

literary works/literature, 128, 311n5, 314n56; ability to act in the world, 193; author, erasure of, 193; capacity to write, 201–2; cave as symbolic space in, 199; contradiction between everything and nothing in, 197–203, 209; "death of the author," 196; decolonial sovereignties articulated through, 191–97; "epistemic dimension" of, 192; erasure in, 196; feminist literature, 200; five general features of Palestinian art, 193–94; "home" in, 194–95; "postcolonial," 192–95, 205; and potentiality, 195–97, 205–6; singular, specific, and specified, 205–10; space-time in, 194–95, 199–201

living death, 198

local settler communities, 92–93

Lockean tradition, 52, 279n33

Lockman, Zachary, 243–44

lordship, *33*; continuous and perpetual violence required to secure positionality, 21, 73, 106, 108, 112, 229; as core feature of settler colonial sovereignty, 39, 64; decolonial critique of, 228–30; as foundation of Israeli state, 146, 170,

174; as fourth dimension of violence, 40, 109–10; fusion of land and people as, 21, 40–41, 63, 70–71, 73, 74–88, 130–31; indivisibility as feature of, 40; in interlocking framework, 17; listening skills lacking in, 234; lord *as* lord, 85–86; lords of the land, 6, 35; as never-ending structure of expulsion, 7, 35–36, 73, 115, 188–89, 235; politics of, 76, 79, 85; as posture of incommensurability, 18–19, 33–34; put into question by existence of Palestinian bodies, 179; as shared question, 146; as social-political type, 6; undoing of, 224–30. *See also* posture of lordship; subjectivity of lordship
Lords of the Land (Zertal and Eldar), 171

macrosociology, 41–43, 62, 65
Maier, Charles S., 139–40
maiming, 152, 180–83; "right to maim," 180–81
Mamdani, Mahmood, 14–16, 116, 119–20, 211, 279n31, 290n48; nation-state, view of, 24, 26–30; racial political identities created by political processes, 232, 236–37; settler can never become Indigenous, 124; survivors, focus on, 230–35
Mantena, Karuna, 275n27
Marxist political economy, 88–89, 264
Massad, Joseph A., 118, 144–46, 149, 220

master ethnos/race, 29, 138–39
Mbembe, Achille, 133–35
memory, 130, 137–38, 187–88, 202, 237, 242–43. *See also* dead, voices of
Metaphysics (Aristotle), 99–100
metropole, 63, 64, 69, 80, 293n68; in settler colonialism, 91–93
Middle Ages, 76–77
Middle East Eye, 185–86
Mignolo, Walter D., 23–24
migration, 75, 83, 122; racialized, 67–68
mimetic dimension of violence. *See* dehumanization (mimetic dimension of violence)
minorities, national, 27–28
Mizrahi Jews, 135
modernity: colonial relationship in formation of, 65; linear progressive conceptions of time, 194; opposing metanarratives of, 139–42; postcolonial critique of, 65; racialization, 178
modernity, colonial, 5–6, 11, 44, 273n2, 283–84n79; absolutist discourse on race and racialization, 133; challenged by decolonization struggles, 192; defined, 8; events of 1492, 27; limits of, 194; literary transformation of, 199–200; posture of lordship linked with, 18–19; racialization of the non-European, 184; sexual contract, 253–54; social-political relationship of, 32; Zionism as manifestation of, 117, 133, 152, 179–80

Mohawks of Kahnawa:ke, 226–29; "Mohawk Ten Commandments," 228

monarchy, 77–79; Castilian, 27; Iroquois Confederacy, 228–29; transfer of power to public from, 61–62, 65–66, 85. *See also* lordship

Mongia, Radhika, 64, 67, 284–85n87

monopolization, 77–79

Moore, Lindsey, 205–6

Morris, Benny, 158

multiculturalism, 29, 67–69, 121

municipal committees, Zionist appointed, 244

Muslim, as enemy of Europe, 142–44

Naam (political sphere), 46–47, 228

Nakba, 139–43, 220–21, 257, 312n24

nation, 23–32; constituted through and because of racialized bodies, 68; decoupling from state, 232–33; and de-Zionization, 232–33; and first intifada, 222; sovereignty of, 26, 29–30; state in need of decoupling from, 25, 27–29

national consciousness, 25–26

national identity, 27–28, 121, 199, 233–35, 291n59

nationalism, 275n34; conservative and reactionary, 211; Jewish, shifting ideologies of, 184; of liberation movement, 222; liberatory versus settler colonial, 141; of the people, 222; "possessive," 221; as settler colonial nationalism, 68, 299n40; two kinds of interconnected across a continuum of violence, 70; Zionist settler colonial nationalism, 117, 129–39. *See* civic nationalism; ethnic nationalism

"nationality," 67–68

national self-determination, 282–83n71

national sovereignty, 26, 62–64

nation-state, 23–32, 275n27, 278n17; alternative geographical locations both outside and inside, 199–200; birth of in 1492, 27; blurring of the vocabularies of nationality and race, 284–85n87; as bounded entity of space, 194, 212–13; colonial genealogy of, 64, 67; decolonial approaches to, 23–24, 211–12; and "empire states," 285–86n99; Euro-American, 121, 199, 221, 235, 237; inevitable demise of, 24; majoritarian and minoritarian nationalities, 27–28; modern, and sovereignty, 65–70; modernist conceptions of, 194; Palestinian Authority project, 219; Westphalian, 17, 40, 44, 46, 72, 284n80

Nazi Germany, 141; Auschwitz, 142–44; survivors of extermination camps, 196

Nazzal, Rehab, 187

necropolitics of "death," 53

Neither Settler nor Native (Mamdani), 119–20

Nelson, Eric, 282n65

neoliberal approaches, 28, 116, 231
"new human," 23–24
Newman, David, 306n40
"NGOization" of civil society, 241–42, 254
Niang, Amy, 46–48, 228
nongovernmental organizations (NGOs), 317n44
Nutt, Steve, 307–8n56

Occupied Territories, 165, 303n9, 307–8n57. *See also* East Jerusalem; Gaza Strip; settlement, Israeli; West Bank
Orientalism, 144; and anti-Semitism charges, 176–77
Oslo Accords, 108, 167–68, 221, 239, 241, 297n16
"other": brutality of, 207–8; Israeli, 207; multiplicity of, 195, 204; Palestinian as target of Zionism, 145; separation of "self" from, 7, 118, 131–36, 145–46, 189
ownership: communal, 6, 290n45; of land, 76–77; of "origins" and "firsts," 10–11; private, 6

Palestine: 1936–39 revolt, 238; capitalism in, 290–91n53; as collectivity of the people, 25; decolonial, 175, 201, 205–15; as decolonial alternative, 195, 205–15; dispossession in, 89–90, 124; earliest stages in colonization of, 220; East Jerusalem, 154; erasure of, 38; as homeland, 153, 162, 216, 232; homeland of, 153; idea partition (1974), 221; leadership in exile, 239; limited sovereignty, 220–21, 315n3; quasi nation-state building project in, 241, 253; right of return, 108; settler colony illuminated by, 26; as symbol for decolonial freedom and liberation, 194; (un)knowability of violence as opening to alternatives, 106–7; writing a nation without a nation-state, 194. *See also* Gaza Strip; Israeli settler colonial conquest of Palestine, 1948; West Bank
Palestine-Israel: dominant strands of public discourse on, 149–50; European dimensions, 72; as foundationally settler colonial, 34–35; Indigenous people interpolated into settler colonial project, 84; Indigenous-settler distinction in, 118–23; indivisibility as force underpinning claim to land/people, 45; as interlocking framework, 37–38; nationalisms connected across continuum of violence, 70; one-state solution, 213, 297n16; specific case of, 116; two-state solution, 271, 297n16
Palestine Liberation Organization (PLO), 220–21, 239, 243, 315n3
Palestinian Authority (PA), 167, 219, 221, 239–40, 253
Palestinian Jews, 123

Palestinian Question, 118, 139–47, 175–76

Palestinians: attempt to expel physical, symbolic, and political existence of, 96, 133; dehumanized as animals, 156, 158–60; discursive colonization of, 175–76; as "evil object," 7, 134–36; fragmentation, isolation, and dehumanization of, 19; international and generational solidarity with, 188; national consciousness, 25–26; political estrangement of, 95–96, 133, 137, 152, 164, 175–76, 294n75; racialized as nonhuman, 152, 184; rootedness of in land and national home, 25; second-class citizens of Israel, 28; as truth of decolonization and decoloniality, 255–56. *See also* colonized

Pappé, Ilan, 130

Pateman, Carole, 83

patriarchal power, 11, 200, 222, 224, 249–52, 255

peaceful dialogue, social and political life, 40, 107–8, 221

peasantry, European, 15, 83, 88–89, 290n53

people, the, 67–69

Peres, Shimon, 154

Piterberg, Gabriel, 129

PLO, 315n3

"political lives," 25

political orders, 84, 91–92

political sphere: decolonization of, 27–30, 231–33; *Naam*, 46–47, 228; sovereignty in, 31, 47, 51, 54–55, 130–31, 234–35; state as, 27–28, 234–35; women in, 248–53

popular committees: of 1936 general strike, 264; of Great Revolt (1936–1939), 264

popular committees of first intifada, 8, 37, 217, 222–25, 238–56; alternative apparatus established by, 241–43; collapse of, 241–42; criminalization of, 241; and factionalism, 241–42, 249–51; internal contradictions, 241–42; local leaders, 239; and "NGOization" of civil society, 241–42, 254; older forms of social organization supplanted by, 244; outlawed by Rabin, 241; and Palestinian women's movement, 223–25, 239, 241, 248–55; and Unified National Leadership of the Uprising (UNLU), 243–48, 253. *See also* decolonial alternatives; intifada, first

popular sovereignty, 62–66, 224, 264, 267–68; United States, 282nn65, 66, 287n20

positionality: of beast and sovereign as above law, 50, 99; continuous and perpetual violence required to secure, 21, 73, 106, 108, 112, 229; of decoloniality, 8; of sovereign as above law, 50, 57, 99, 172

"postcolonial narrative," 139–40, 143

postcolonial state, 24–26, 289n31

postcolonial theory, 10, 15, 89, 192

postcolony, 116, 118–23

post/neo/settler, 11–12
posture of lordship, 6; colonial
    modernity linked with, 18–19;
    contextual approach, 21–22;
    critique needed, 22, 32; decolonial
    sovereignties as challenge to, 223;
    as fourth dimension of violence,
    40, 109–10; inability to grasp,
    159–60; killing required for, 156,
    158; legal machinations of, 87;
    manifestation of in specific
    contexts, 21–22; and Separation/
    Annexation Wall project, 156, 158;
    and shared dispositions, 18–19,
    109; as substitution of violence
    the "thing itself," 108; as
    transcendental violence, 17–19;
    transformation of as critical battle
    terrain, 264–65; warrior class
    linked with, 73, 87–88, 129,
    290n48. *See also* four-dimensional
    violence; lords of the land;
    transcendental dimension of
    violence (posture of
    incommensurability)
potentiality, 195–97, 212; singular,
    specific, and specified, 205–10
power relations, 103–5;
    decentralization discourse, 149–50;
    revealed by oppressed social
    agents, 106–7; unintentional
    acquiescence to, 205
primitive accumulation, 89, 291n53
private property, 8, 74, 84–85,
    165–66
proletarianization, 89–90, 290–91n53,
    291n55

Prussian Junkers, 129, 131
Puar, Jasbir K., 180–81
public opinion, 296–97n16
"purity," 13, 17, 69, 131–33, 174, 184

Rabin, Yitzhak, 154, 155, 241
racialization, 289n33; of enemy,
    133–34; of Indigenous-settler
    distinction, 117, 129–39, 152; master
    ethnos/race, 29, 138–39; and
    migration, 67–68; "nanoracism"
    and "hydraulic racism," 134; of the
    non-European, 184; of the
    Palestinian body, 178–88;
    Palestinian body as "inorganic,"
    180, 183; of Palestinians, 19; of
    Palestinians as nonhuman, 152, 184;
    Semite, creation of, 144–45;
    Zionist, 117, 129–39
raciologies, 135, 152–53, 299–300n48
Raz-Krakotzkin, Amnon, 130,
    137–38
"reality," 94, 101, 107, 112; constituted
    by violence, 20, 87, 236, 238
recognition, politics of, 68, 225
refugees: Jewish, 141, 147–48;
    Palestinian, 182, 202, 256
refusal, politics of, 225–29, 237–38,
    257
reinvention, 54–55, 92, 131
resistance: Arabic terms for, 224;
    everyday acts of, 153, 184–85, 224;
    forms of, 8, 215–17, 220–22;
    international pressure as, 183–85,
    188, 237; weakened by
    fragmentation, 154; weakened by
    maiming, 180–81

resistance, decolonial, 7–8, 32, 273n2; Boycott, Divestment, Sanctions (BDS) campaign, 176, 236–37, 265; decolonial sovereignties manifested in, 36–37, 216–17; discourse of escalation in response to Palestinian, 137; embodied Palestinian agency, 162; impossibility of eradication, 47, 49; "interstitial space of the art of protest," 209–10; Marx's understanding of revolution, 264; and memory, 187–88; predicated on liberating nation from state, 26; rendered illegitimate, 164, 175–76; *Sumud* (steadfastness, or steadfast perseverance), 187. *See also* intifada, first; popular committees of first intifada; women's movement, Palestinian

"return," discourse of, 129, 136, 148, 164, 267, 298n28

Returning to Haifa (Kanafani), 259–60

Robinson, Glenn E., 240–41

Robinson Crusoe (Defoe), 54–55, 129, 131

Rousseau, Jean-Jacques, 54

"rule" and "governance," distinction between, 247–48, 318–19n64

Rwanda, 27, 119–20, 233

Said, Edward, 23–24, 71, 115, 128, 159, 298–99n38; on becoming different, 230, 237; contrapuntal approach, 17, 71; focus on literature, 192

Sayegh, Fayez, 138, 179

Schmitt, Carl, 60

scholarship: on foundational myth of Zionism, 129–30; Indigenous Studies, 122; postcolonial theory, 10, 15, 89, 192; Settler Colonial Studies, 122

Schotten, C. Heike, 52–53

secularism: in settler-Left discourse, 164–68; and sovereignty, 58–60

"security coordination," 167–68

security discourse, 155–58, 162, 178–79, 184; "security state," 134

self: "ana," 313n38; "anxiety of annihilation," 134; civilized, in opposition to "savage" or "terrorist," 60–61; "cleansing" of other from, 136; co-constitution of, 6, 109, 196, 208–9, 212–17, 235; effort to separate from enemy "other," 7, 118, 131–36, 145–46, 189; Euro-American, 17; and four-dimensional violence, 17; interlocking of enemy-siblings, 17–18; Israeli, Palestinian body as threat to, 179; Israeli Jewish made impossible by settler colonial sovereignty, 7, 35, 106, 136; multiplicity of, 195, 196, 198–99, 201, 215; self-annihilation/self-creation, 195–204, 211–12, 238; self-identity of sovereign, 50, 54; separated from constituent elements, 152; sovereign Jewish, 7, 130–33; as unalloyed, 17, 20, 55–56, 61, 73, 131, 189; violent dialogue within, 213–14. *See also* enemy-siblings; "I"; subjectivity of lordship self, settler colonial: as always on the road of expelling the Indigenous, 20–21; as autochthonous, 131–32, 137–38, 152, 166; as ethnically pure, 131–32, 174

self-determination, 66, 89, 104, 140, 177, 220, 271, 282–83n71, 315n3; and self-identification, 121

self-liberation, 36, 204

selfsame substance, 115, 117, 139; fusion of land and people as, 70–71, 108; heterogeneity molded into, 6, 13, 56–57, 63, 101, 111–13, 127; and state of exception, 97–98. *See also* included exclusion

Semitism, 144–45

Separation/Annexation Wall, 9, 111, 134, 154–63, 302n2, 303n9; annexation entangled with separation, 158, 161; checkpoints, 162, 174; concealment of violences, 155–58, 163; description of planned violences, 156–57; expulsion as goal of, 161–62; as form of violence, 151; Israeli Jewish existence as lords, 156, 158; maximum Arabs on minimum land, goal of maximum land with minimum Arabs, 155, 157–58; naming of, 154, 155; portrayed as security measure, 155–57; technologized and bureaucratized apparatus, 162; "Us Here, Them There" slogan, 155, 161–62. *See also* fragmentation (instrumental dimension of violence)

settlement, Israeli, 35, 111; concealment of, 151, 163–64, 174–75, 182; concerted strategy to produce chaotic space, 165–66; de facto military sovereign, 173, 174; Israeli settler colonial occupation of Palestine, 1967, 125, 151, 157, 163–67; militaristic tactics and strategies, 164; Palestinian isolated in their expulsion, 178; "peace" plans, 166–68; post-1967 settlement projects, 163, 164; unofficial Israeli sovereignty, 165–66. *See also* Israeli settler colonial conquest of Palestine, 1948

settler colonialism: claim of being the "first" as attribute of, 13, 118; colonialism differentiated from, 90–91; decolonization versus, 9; as eliminatory, 292–93n68, 293n71; expulsion, structure of, 19, *33*, 38, 64, 73–74, 86, 88–112; futurity for Palestinians foreclosed by, 4, 6, 26, 152, 155–56, 186–87; Indigenous people interpolated into, 84; as land-centered project, 63–64; normalization of, 90, 124–26, 162, 182; "old settler colonies" differentiated from European, 134, 285n99; settler and native distinction, 24; settler domination as expulsion, 88–96; settler invasion, 283n73; settlers always from elsewhere, 83–84; state relationship to, 63–64; territoriality as irreducible element of, 83. *See also* colonialism; indivisibility; land as life; lordship; violence, settler colonial settler colonial sovereignty: as always an imposition, 48; biopolitical and necropolitical operations of, 53; breaking the cycle of, 137, 188, 215–16, 272; as closed and singular, 227; death drive of, 84, 86; forged in the colonies, 44; ideological apparatus of, 52–54, 60–61; Israeli Jewish self made impossible by, 7, 35, 106, 136; life and death, politics of, 92, 180–82, 185, 187, 197–98; local operation of, 91–93; lordship as core feature of, 39, 64; mobility of, 92–93, 172; primal scene of, 36, 61, 213; propagation of violence within logics and mechanisms of, 146; social-political separated by, 7, 31–32, 234–35, 249, 253–55; violence as foundation of, 52, 92. *See also* aspirations of settler colonial sovereignty; lordship; sovereignty

sexual contract, 253–54

Shafir, Gershon, 291n53

Sharon, Ariel, 154–56

Sharpe, Christina, 191, 212

Shilliam, Robbie, 45

Simpson, Audra, 121–22, 127, 225–29

siyādah (colonial and patriarchal sovereignty), 224–26, 249–50, 252

slavery and transatlantic slave trade, 81, 288n29

social agents, 103–7

social justice, 30–31

social-political relationship: of colonial modernity, 32; complementary opposition, 5, 6, 31–32, 36, 46–48, 244, 247, 249–55; complexity of, 9; and decolonial liberation, 23–32; decolonial sovereignties as alternative configuration, 223, 229–30, 247; as Mouffeian style agonism, 31, 79; and nation-state, 22; separated by settler colonial sovereignty, 7, 31–32, 234–35, 249, 253–55, 264; sexual contract, 253–54; and survivorhood, 235; in Voltaic region of Africa, 46–48

social sphere, 46–48; BDS outreach to Israeli, 236–37; collective "we" (`asabiyyah), 30; decolonization of, 30–31; masses restricted to, 254; mobilized for liberation, 251–52; nation as, 25; *Tenga*, 46–47, 228; transnationality of, 42; women in, 247–49, 251

Soffer, Arnon, 156–58, 160, 303–4n12

South Africa, 231–32, 233

sovereign: accountability of, 52, 279n33; as one who declares the state of exception, 52, 60; as outside and inside the juridical order, 96–98; positionality of as above law, 50, 57, 99, 172; "return" of as sovereign, 136, 148, 164; self-identity of, 50, 54

sovereignties, Indigenous, 56, 93, 110, 125–26, 151, 165, 220, 227, 292n59; claim of being the "first" as means of eliminating, 13; claim on land, 84, 87; not recognized by Zionism, 124; political communities, 121–22; scholarship from basis of, 125–26

sovereignties, plurality of, 36, 43–44. *See also* decolonial sovereignties sovereignty: Abrahamic-centric approach, 59, 301n66; alternative form of, 32; beast and sovereign analogy, 50–55, 58–59, 99, 131, 136, 160, 279n34; belonging, claim to, 13, 40, 43, 80; claim on land and people, 44, 48, 50, 63, 139, 225, 258, 279n31; claim to, 39–40, 48–50; colonized as target of claim to, 49; decolonial critique of, 45–46; deconstructive critique of, 41; desire for acceptance of Jewish self as outside Europe, 130–31, 145–46; dictatorial sovereign voice, 10–17, 36, 177, 187, 211, 213, 245; divine, 50, 57–58; as divisible and nonabsolute, 59–60, 282n68; early modern theory, 276–77n7, 277n13; Euro-American paradigm, 43, 220–21, 225–26; and excess, 55–56, 92, 127, 131; failures of, 126, 135, 137; fear and terror as correlate of, 51–52, 279n33; generalized understanding of, 43–45; government distinguished from, 276–77n7; as "inappropriate concept," 225; individual, 54–56, 92; indivisibility of, 13, 32–33, 36, 40, 50–65, 226; of land, 263; "little sovereign," 174; modern, 58, 64; and modern nation-state, 65–70; monarchist, 61–62; of nation, 26, 29–30; national, 26, 62–64; "national" versus "statist," 62–63; nonresponsiveness and nonresponsibility, 58, 60; not possible for national minorities, 28; as not timeless, 41; paradox of, 50; political, 31, 47, 51, 54–55, 130–31, 234–35; popular, 62–66, 224, 264, 267–68, 282n65, 287n20; primordial, 86, 130–31, 173–74; and protection function, 51–52; Prussian Junkers as model for Jewish, 129, 131; reinvention of, 54–55, 92, 131; secular, 58–60; *siyādah*, 224–26, 249–50, 252; social, 46–47, 54; source, scope, and locus, questions of, 41, 49–50; and space, 41–50; as supreme question in settler colony, 84; theorizations of, 39–43, 287n20; transferred from monarch to public, 61–62, 65–66, 85; transgressive or revolutionary, 280–81n63. *See also* abandonment, sovereign; decolonial sovereignties; decolonial sovereignties; Indigenous sovereignty; popular sovereignty; settler colonial sovereignty; state

space/spatialization, 39–40; "nonpolitical" spheres in Africa, 46–47; politicization of, 42; and sovereignty, 41–50; territory-sovereignty debate, 41–43; territory/territorialization as part of larger issue of, 48. *See also* territory/territorialization

space-time, 194–95, 199–201; beginning/end, question of, 198, 201–4, 207; as bounded, 194, 212–13; death of time, 203; linear conceptions of time, 194, 204; multiplicity of past, 207; reimagination of, 199, 210–11

Spivak, Gayatri, 89
state, 23–32; actual practices of, 45; attempt to rule over and against societies, 48; decoupling from nation, 232–33; empire states, 67, 284–86n99; ethnic cleansing and genocide, monopolization of, 29–30; "garrison states," 25; monopoly on violence, 29–30; in need of decoupling from nation, 25, 27–29; "other" as "outside" of, 69; as political sphere, 27–28, 234–35; postcolonial, 24–26, 289n31; predicated on violence, 25–26, 181; reified concept of, 40, 44, 62, 65, 72, 74–75; "security state," 134; settler colonialism, relationship to, 63–64; sociogenesis of in Middle Ages, 77–78; sovereignty transferred from monarch to public, 61–62, 65–66, 85; tensions exported by, 81–82; territorial, 47, 60, 64, 72, 278n17; terror exerted by, 52; "total states," 25. *See also* nation; nation-state; sovereignty; territory/territorialization

stateless populations, 25–26, 46, 146, 149; stateless sovereignty, 26; weapons used against, 183; writing a nation without a nation-state, 194

state of exception, 96–98, 289n2, 294n75; continuous, 165; sovereign as one who declares, 52, 60; and validity of the law, 173

state sovereignty, 45–47, 57, 62, 224, 227; emergence in context of colonialism and racism, 67, 284–85n87; Westphalian, 72

structure of expulsion, 19, *33*, 38, 64, 73–74, 86, 88–112; four main elements of, 95–99; orientation of, 95; and sovereign abandonment, 74, 95–102, 111–12; as a structure of violence, 95. *See also* expulsion

subjectivity: de-subjectification of the subject, 195–97, 204; transformations in, 17–18. *See also* isolation (linguistic dimension of violence)

subjectivity of lordship, 20, 35, 163; closed to knowledge of Palestinian perspective, 234; continuous expulsion required for, 106, 108; decolonial unraveling of, 237–38; produced by settler colonial violence, 152; refusal to speak with, 237–38. *See also* self

Sudan, 27, 120

Sumud (steadfastness, or steadfast perseverance), 187

survivorhood, 196, 230–35

taḥrīr (liberation), 224
Takriti, Abdel Razzaq, 264
Tatour, Lana, 257
Tenga (social sphere), 46–47, 228
terra nullius, 83, 131
territory/territorialization, 39, 46; bounded, 42, 47–48; and mobility of settler sovereignties, 93; and "nationality," 67–68; as part of larger issue of space/spatialization, 48; as settler colonialism's

irreducible element, 83; territorial state, 47, 60, 64, 72, 278n17; territory-sovereignty debate, 41–43. *See also* space/spatialization; state terror, 51–52, 136, 149, 279n33
"thing itself," 107, 214
transcendental dimension of violence (posture of incommensurability), 17–19, 21, *33*, 33–35; and abandonment logic, 101–2; deep postures, 107–8; as observable through effects, 107, 109–10; posture of lordship as, 40, 109–10; as unobservable, 18, 19, 102, 107–10. *See also* posture of lordship
Truth and Reconciliation Commission (TRC), South Africa, 231

Unified National Leadership of the Uprising (UNLU), 243–48, 253
United Nations Office for the Coordination of Humanitarian Affairs, 3
United States: as beast and rogue in international law, 51; decolonial sovereignties in, 121–22; Euro-American legal claims to, 279n31; ongoing settler colonial project, 123; policy position on Palestine, 270–71; popular sovereignty, 282nn65, 66, 287n20
"Unity Intifada" (2021), 256–57
universalism, 14–15; de-universalization of Europe, 71; Eurocentric rendering of provincialized forms, 43–44

"Us Here, Them There" slogan, 155, 161–62

Veracini, Lorenzo, 91–92, 124–25, 293n68
violence: (un)knowability of, 9–10, 86, 102–3, 106–9, 185, 188, 198; as political, 231; re-signification of terms, 265–66
violence, settler colonial, 1, 6–10; alternative pathway needed, 4–5, 270; asymmetry in, 105; casualties, 3–4, 182–83; concealment of, 151, 155–58, 163, 175, 182; continuum of, 70, 94; cycle of, 107, 136–38, 178, 188, 214–16, 266, 272; decolonial critique of, 228–30, 234; discussion of root causes needed, 4–5; documentation of, 9–10; effects of, 105–7, 112, 150, 153; elusive subject matter of, 9, 103, 107; enemy-siblings interlocked by, 7, 20; force, 49; as foundation of settler colonial sovereignty, 52, 92; ideological (super)structures linked with, 94–95, 112; ideology linked with, 52–54, 60–61; inequality, relationships of, 86; (un)knowability of, 9–10, 18, 102–3, 106–7, 109, 185, 188; maiming, 152, 180–83; naturalization of, 156, 158, 162, 182; Palestinian rejection of "peace proposals" as excuse for, 108; posture of, 40–41; and power relations, 103–5; and racialization of Palestinian body, 178–79; "real," 20, 87, 236; revealed by Palestinian

violence, settler colonial (*continued*)
words, 185; self-propagation of, 35; social agents' inability to comprehend, 103–7; of sovereign self, 60–61, 92, 136; state-announced "end" of, 163; state monopoly on, 29–30; state predicated on, 25–26, 181; and subjectivity of perpetrators, 20–21; subject matter of, 9, 103, 107; as the "thing itself," 102–3, 107–8; unbearability of, 9, 36, 103, 106, 186, 188, 190, 205–6; uninhibited, molded into validity of law, 97–98, 113, 133, 152, 173; uninhibited, Zionist, 152, 180; violent dialogue, 95, 106–9, 213–14, 221, 223, 238; warfare as integral to lordship, 88; Zionist as racialized, 132. *See also* expulsion; four-dimensional violence

violent dialogue, 95, 106–9, 221, 223, 238; within self, 213–14

Walcott, Rinaldo, 273n2
Wall. *See* Separation/Annexation Wall
Walsh, Catherine E., 10
warrior class, 73, 87–88, 129, 290n48
West Bank, 3–4, 108; "Judea and Samaria," 168; limited sovereignty, 221. *See also* Separation/Annexation Wall
Westphalian nation-state, 17, 40, 44, 46, 72, 284n80
wholeness, 160–62
Wolfe, Patrick, 63, 83, 86, 173, 283n73, 289n33, 292–93n68, 300n70;

elimination, logic of, 91, 93–94, 293n71; Indigenous-settler distinction necessary for, 125–26; on return, 298n28

women's movement, Palestinian, 223–25, 239, 241, 248–55; colonial modernity challenged by, 255; four main committees, 249; obstacles faced by, 253; togetherness, practice of, 249–50

Ze'evi, Rehevam, 303n8
Zertal, Idith, 169, 170–72, 305n33, 306–7n43
Zionism/Zionist ideology, 38, 54, 274n20, 298–99n38, 303n8; abandonment in, 125, 138–39; "absolutist discourse" of, 133–36; arch-Zionists, 168–69; "cleansing" of the Arab Jew/Jew Arab of Arabness, 133–34, 135–36; and colonial modernity, 117, 133, 152, 179–80; cultural, 236; de-Zionization, 232–33, 261, 268; different viewpoints within, 146, 213; Eurocolonial discourse embraced by, 300n70; failure to deal with Jewish Question, 145; foundational myth of, 129–30; Greater Land of Israel ideology, 129, 156, 163, 166–68, 173–74, 304n22; hatred of Jewish Jews and Palestinians, 146; homogeneity, imposition of, 122–23; Israeli survivors of, 232; "liberal," 166–68; master ethnos/race, separation of, 29, 138–39; and non-Zionist

Jewish life, 117, 147–48, 175, 178; racialization of Indigenous-settler distinction, 117, 129–39; racism permanent in ideology of, 138; "reformed," 117, 128; "return," discourse of, 129, 136, 148, 164, 267, 298n28; theological and political entwinement, 172–73; zero-sum perspective, 124–25, 189; Zionist settler colonial nationalism, 117, 129–39. *See also* Indigenous-settler distinction; Israel

Žižek, Slavoj, 182

zoē (qualified life), 99–100

Zreik, Raef, 124–25, 297n17

Printed and bound by CPI Group (UK) Ltd, Croydon, CR0 4YY

31/07/2025

14712032-0003